D0077025

Voices of Jacob, Hands of Esau

Jews in American Life and Thought

Stephen J. Whitfield

ARCHON BOOKS

1984

LUTHER NORTHWESTERN
SEMINARY LIBRARY
2375 Como Avenue
St. Paul, MN 55108

E 184
.J5W5

© 1984 Stephen J. Whitfield.
First published 1984 as an Archon Book,
an imprint of The Shoe String Press, Inc.,
Hamden, Connecticut 06514
All rights reserved
Printed in the United States of America

The paper in this book meets the guidelines for
permanence and durability of the
Committee on Production Guidelines
for Book Longevity of the
Council on Library Resources.

Library of Congress Cataloging in Publication Data

Whitfield, Stephen J., 1942-
 Voices of Jacob, hands of Esau.

 Includes bibliographical references and index.
 1. Jews—United States—Intellectual life—Addresses,
essays, lectures. 2. United States—Civilization—Jewish
influences—Addresses, essays, lectures. 3. Jews—Southern
States—Addresses, essays, lectures. 4. United States—
Ethnic relations—Addresses, essays, lectures.
5. Southern States—Ethnic relations—Addresses, essays,
lectures. I. Title.
E184.J5W5 1984   973'.04924   83-25720
ISBN 0-208-02007-1

This book is dedicated to

Alexander and Rosa Ioffe,
Grigory and Natalia Rosenstein,
Yevgenny and Rimma Yakir
and their children

78-72-0-1-0

Contents

Part IV   The Jew as Southerner

Acknowledgments

I am grateful for permission to republish or draw upon articles that appeared in the following journals and anthologies:

Judaism (Fall 1979) for Chapter 1
Jewish Social Studies (Winter 1980) for Chapter 2
Congress Monthly (February 1981) for Chapter 3
American Jewish History (December 1980) for Chapter 4
Judaism (Spring 1983) for Chapter 5
Judaism (Spring 1980) for Chapter 6
Midstream (February 1978) for Chapter 7
Sarah Blacher Cohen, ed., *From Hester Street to Holly-wood* (Indiana University Press) for Chapter 8
Moment (March-April 1981) for Chapter 9
Moment (October 1981) for Chapter 10
American Jewish History (September 1982) for Chapter 11
Nathan M. Kaganoff and Melvin I. Urofsky, eds., *Turn to the South* (University Press of Virginia) for Chapter 12
American Jewish History (March 1982) for Chapter 13
Marc Lee Raphael, ed., *Approaches to Judaism in Modern Times* (Scholars Press) for Chapter 14
Reconstructionist (June 1981) for Conclusion

In shaping the views that characterize this book, many persons have through their conversations and their writings earned my gratitude. These individuals are so numerous that I must regretfully preserve their anonymity. Donald Altschiller, Lewis Feuer and Richard King all made me feel that this project might have merit, and Jim Thorpe brought it to life. But special thanks are due Janice Friedman and Shirley Meymaris for typing it, and David Starr provided crucial editorial assistance.

S.J.W.

Introduction

One Friday evening in Boston, I was invited with others to share a Sabbath meal with a youngish couple active in their synagogue and in Jewish communal affairs. Everyone took pleasure in the weekly renewal of such observances as the benediction over the candles, the prayers over bread and wine, the singing of *zemirot*. Some of the guests washed their hands. The occasion was aglow with sincerity and authenticity. But one feature would have puzzled the ancestors of those who had gathered to welcome "the Sabbath bride." Before the rituals, our hosts had thoughtfully provided everyone with marijuana.

No student of the American Jewish condition can appreciate it fully without some sense of irony, and this book has been composed out of a certain wonder at the paradox of so ancient and fragile a people replenishing itelf in the social flux of the United States. Whatever the transformations in the society outside, the spirit within somehow manages to persist and even thrive. To stress the conservation of tradition is to minimize the historical effects of assimilation, and communal survival is a prospect that some spokesmen for Orthodoxy and some representatives of Israel have doubted can be accomplished in the Diaspora. Yet to ignore the resilience of the Jewish people in finding itself—in rolling with the punch in hard times, in summoning reasons to remain distinctive in good times—is to fudge one of the clearest conclusions to be drawn from the historical record. Any student of modern Jewry therefore must be ambivalent. The erosion of a cohesive minority under the impact of secularization and civil freedom should be noted, and yet it is also striking how tenacious many Jews have been in keeping at least the husk of faith and the sense of peoplehood. Indeed, as religious observance has waned, many Jews have become even more committed to an ethnic self-definition.

The doubleness of vision that the study of American Jewry requires is, of course, one feature of the larger pattern of Diaspora life. For if the Jews have their own "Jewish problem," a split within their own collective soul between assimilationist impulses and ancestral allegiances, its biblical roots can be suggested in chapter 27 of Genesis, in which Jacob deceives his father and deprives his twin brother of his birthright. Jacob, the future patriarch who was to be known as Israel, can be said to represent—in all his troubling failings—the spirit of Judaism itself; and his voice was the manifestation of that spirit. Esau was the hunter whose hands suggest force and physical strength; and he became the ancestor of the Edomites and, the rabbis believed, even of the Romans, that is, Gentiles. But Esau never ceased to be the brother of Jacob, whose own descendants must come to terms with the power that the heirs of Esau can project and even with the allure of their ways. The biblical struggle over a birthright symbolically foreshadows the dual legacy of the modern Jew.

The tension between a minority culture and majority pressure is stamped upon this book as well. Because my parents—refugees from Nazi brutality—raised me in a Southern community whose neighborhoods and schools were overwhelmingly Protestant, I could hardly be unaware of the pervasive influence of the Gentile ways. Nor could I be unconscious of their appeal. But in such communities and elsewhere, the voice of Jacob could not be entirely stilled; and several generations of Jewish life in the United States have resulted in institutions that in some respects are flourishing as never before. Three such signs of vitality—Brandeis University, the American Jewish Historical Society, and *Moment* magazine—I have been privileged to observe at close quarters; and I have absorbed their impact. Such decisive experiences undoubtedly have colored the chapters that follow. All, or nearly all, of them reflect this general sense of doubleness, the author's conviction that American Jews may barely resemble their ancestors even while remaining different from their contemporaries.

Such a claim requires specific focus and evidence. This book does not pretend to be comprehensive; pertinent subjects, such as the fate of religion and the state of Israel, largely are ignored. But if the history of the Jews has not yet merged into the history of everyone else in America, that is also true of America itself, whose eccentric history has included the offering of sanctuary and hope to the Jewish people. That is why this book begins with Europe and especially with the effort of American Jews to fathom the depths of twentieth-century political absolutism. So debased was the human estate under the impact of totalitarianism and particularly the Holocaust that the effort to comprehend it cannot be entirely successful, but the opening section of the book describes that intellectual attempt. The most original and searing account of the modern version of tyranny was provided by Hannah Arendt, whose work is briefly analyzed here, since it has been more fully treated elsewhere.[1] The sinister light cast by the history of Nazism and Stalinism puts into special relief the radically different fate of those Jews who were fortunate enough to find refuge in the United States.

How historians have sought to identify the distinctiveness of the American Jewish experience, and how the Jews themselves have formulated a political response to American society, are discussed in the next section of the book. The relatively tolerant and egalitarian conditions of that society caused the legacy of radicalism—an intelligible response to European injustices—to flicker without entirely dying. Yet despite the unparalleled prosperity that Jews generally have enjoyed with other Americans since the Second World War, the Jews themselves have remained liberals. Such stubbornness deserves emphasis and explanation. For their political style remains one of the oddest ingredients in Jewish life, and their reluctance to make a dramatic shift to the right has been the despair of Republicans, an enigma to historical materialists, and perhaps even an insult to common sense.

Those who immigrated here came from societies that tended to be closed, traditional, ascriptive, in which high culture itself often was an enclave of aristocrats by breeding if not by birth. The children and grandchildren of such immigrants were remarkably quick to perceive the possibilities and opportunities inherent in mass culture. Perhaps more so than any other ethnic group, the Jews have been beguiled by the representation of reality and the formation of fantasy in the popular arts. The Jews invented not only ethical monotheism but also, to a considerable degree, Hollywood; and with 3 percent of the general population, they generate 80 percent of America's professional comedians. Their impact upon journalism—one of the few occupations specifically granted constitutional sanction—also has been considerable. Yet such explosions of talent as the Jews have demonstrated in popular culture generally have been neglected by scholars. The third section of the book therefore is devoted to this theme, which has obvious pertinence to the tension between assimilation and particularism.

That conflict has been felt acutely in the region that relatively few Jews have penetrated, in part because of the South's reputation for racial bigotry and for cultural homogeneity. Southern Jews therefore are worth studying not because they are exotic but because there the hand of Esau has perhaps been most powerful and effective, the voice of Jacob barely audible. Yet here too the record is mixed, elusive, fascinating. Even as Jewish life now seems to be seeping out of the small towns of the region, Sunbelt communities like Atlanta and Houston and the burgeoning state of Florida report vital signs, though not necessarily those that the inhabitants of the *shtetl* would have found familiar.

Like virtually every other book about contemporary American Jewry, this one takes for granted the validity of Jewish life and the importance of its preservation. But unlike many other accounts of the Jewish condition, this volume is not animated by anxiety, or fear, or a mood of crisis. These are not autopsy notes. Certainly the memory of the horrible destruction of European Jewry during the Second World War demands both mourning and vigilance, but it need not produce exaggeration of anti-Semitic feeling in the United States. The institutional structure of discrimination has almost entirely collapsed, and those citizens who would wish the Jews ill are marginal and impotent. Anyone concerned with the destiny of American Jewry therefore should be attentive to Jewish self-expression, and should examine how the benign challenges of the larger society have been confronted. Some Jews have chosen to impersonate Esau, to walk in the ways of the Gentiles. But it remains a source of surprise and wonder how many others have sought to locate the sources of their identity in certain enduring values stemming from irrevocable facts of birth. The voices that many modern Jews have heard often have been faint and ambiguous, but they have outlasted the force of temporal power. That is why the tone of this book is, ultimately, so hopeful.

One example comes from the career of the *New Yorker* artist, Saul Steinberg, who had emigrated from Rumania to study architecture in Italy in the 1930s. In 1940 he received his diploma, awarded in the name of King Victor Emmanuel, who was then (thanks to Mussolini's aggressive wars) the official ruler of Albania and of Ethiopia as well. The diploma listed Steinberg as being "*di razza Ebraica*" (of the Jewish race). "It was some kind of safeguard for the future," Steinberg has recalled, "meaning that although I was a *dottore* I could be boycotted from practicing, since I am a Jew. The beauty for me is that this diploma was given by the King; but he is no longer King of Italy. He is no more King of Albania. He is not even the Emperor of Ethiopia. And I am no architect. The only thing that remains is *razza Ebraica!*"[2]

The diploma tells much about the might of kings. This book is intended to suggest some meanings which, even in America, may be indelible in the *razza Ebraica*.

Part I

In the Shadow of Europe

1

American Jewish Intellectuals

and Totalitarianism

A variant of the tyranny known to the ancients, totalitarianism is distinctive to the twentieth century. It has antecedents, but no equivalent in the extent of its power for the devastation of civilized life, in the scope of its domination over all forms of human enterprise, and in the annals of cruelty. "As a source of sorrow and suffering to the human race," George Kennan observed in 1953, "this phenomenon has overshadowed every other source of human woe in our times; for it has demeaned humanity in its own sight, attacked man's confidence in himself, made him realize that he can be his own most terrible and dangerous enemy." The diplomat-historian added that "although we Americans have not been directly affected by it, to many of our countrymen it has come to appear as the greatest of all our American problems—to some of them, I fear, as the only one."[1]

This chapter attempts to record the impact of totalitarianism upon some of Kennan's countrymen who were peculiarly affected by it. They were intellectuals, and therefore were beguiled by the dream of Marxian socialism more than other Americans; many were haunted by the Stalinist violation of that dream. They were Jews, and therefore had to come to intimate and immediate terms with the paranoically thorough war conducted against the "non-Aryans" of Nazi-occupied Europe. But they were also independent thinkers, adhering to no consensus, bereft of any common institutional loyalties, rarely subscribing to the faith of their ancestors. What they shared, and why they are worthy of scrutiny, is that, just as they were especially sensitive to the threat of nazism and Stalinism, so too they exercised a significant influence on American intellectual life.[2] It should be added that intellectuals and Jews were hardly alone in absorbing the shock of totalitarianism, and, even among them, figures as conspicuous as Morris Raphael Cohen and his pupil, Paul Goodman, seemed to regard this modern tyranny as quite peripheral to their concerns. But because the seamless web of the past has to be cut somewhere, it may not be unwarranted to focus scholarly attention on a group that was especially articulate in its opposition to totalitarianism.

Because Jews were disproportionately members of Marxist parties and because they were the victims of Nazi racial hatred, American Jewish intellectuals generally showed little interest in Italian fascism, though it was the matrix of the term itself. Three years after seizing power, Mussolini described *"la nostra feroce volontà totalitaria"* (our fierce totalitarian will) and considered the term an apt label for the Italian political system (*lo stato totalitario*). He and the philosopher Giovanni Gentile made the word part of their official expositions of fascist doctrine; and Gentile introduced the word to Americans in an article in 1928. The efforts of some Nazis to translate *lo stato totalitario* made little headway because of the primacy of race over state in the movement's ideology, and Hitler himself rarely used the term. In the Russian language "totalitarian" is pejorative, applied only to fascist states and never to the Soviet regime or to the ruling Communist party.[3] Yet nazism and Stalinism were so distinctive and unprecedented in their subjugation of large masses, so persistent and grandiose in their ideological claims, and so incomparably ruthless in their use of terror and torture, that they alone—and not the fascist movements in Italy and elsewhere—can properly be considered totalitarian.[4]

However varied the responses to this phenomenon in the social sciences, in philosophy and religion, and in intellectual journalism, it is still possible to discern the outer limits of Jewish sensibility and belief. Despite the absence of communal authority, despite the independence of Jewish intellectuals, some contours to their reaction to totalitarianism can be traced. Perhaps not many would have shared the judgment of Harold Rosenberg that it would be "intellectually degrading and morally degenerate" to show "commiseration for the Nazis as 'human beings.' ... To defend the human status of Elite Corpsmen, whose 'heroism' consisted of purging themselves of all traces of human feeling . . . represents a decadent application of the Christian principle of turning the other cheek." But no Jewish intellectual, however sympathetic to pacifism, asserted, as the Reverend A. J. Muste did in 1940, that "if I can't love Hitler, I can't love at all." Whatever their reservations about the trial of Adolf Eichmann in Jerusalem in 1961, it did not occur to Jewish writers to reach for comparisons with the trial of Jesus, though the theologian William Stringfellow conceded the following differences: "Eichmann's condemnation does not save a single man from bondage and service to death, while the condemnation of the other defendant set men free from death and from the power of death in their own sin. In both trials, Israel has been confounded in her longing for righteousness."[5]

In the same year that Muste hoped to be able to love Hitler (and still love the rest of humanity), the neo-Thomist philosopher Mortimer Adler felt so troubled by empiricism and skepticism in the academy that he announced: "We have more to fear from our professors than from Hitler." It is doubtful that many Jews shared Adler's suspicion that the Nazis, like the Babylonians and Assyrians, might even be a divine instrument for chastising the Jews and cleansing a civilization. Five years later such professors would have been able to point out, for example, that the million Jewish children whom the Nazis starved to death and murdered were too young to have followed Adler's argument against empiricism and skepticism. Nor were there any echoes in Jewish thought of the optimism expressed by the Catholic metaphysician Pierre Teilhard de Chardin, with regard to the Nazi experiments at Dachau, that "man, to become fully man, must have tried everything to the end." He added that, "monstrous as it is, is not modern totalitarianism really the distortion of something magnificent, and thus quite near to the truth? . . . The great human machine . . . must work—by producing a superabundance of mind."[6]

Another contrast can be established with one who clearly rejected the totalitarian model, like B. F. Skinner. But the psychologist did so merely because of its "aversive consequences," which he classified along with "a gambling enterprise, uncontrolled piecework wages, the sale of harmful drugs, or undue personal influence." Noam Chomsky commented that Skinner's system of values—the disdain for freedom, the insensitivity to the higher mental faculties, the refusal to render judgment on cultural survival—is quite compatible with the totalitarian ethos. "It would be improper to conclude," Chomsky warned, "that Skinner is advocating concentration camps and totalitarian rule (though he also offers no objection)." Nor would many Jews, no matter how antagonistic to communism, have agreed with W. Averell Harriman's view in 1945 that "Hitler's greatest crime was that his actions had resulted in opening the gates of Eastern Europe to Asia."[7] These statements may help to define the boundaries of even the pluralism of the intellectual enterprise among American Jews.

The immigrants who thereby were spared the fate that befell European Jewry were responsible for some of the first studies of totalitarianism. Without using the word itself, Hans Kohn's "Communist and Fascist Dictatorship: A Comparative Study" was one of the earliest essays to identify the distinctiveness of contemporary tyranny. For Kohn, a Smith College historian who had attended the same Prague Gymnasium as Franz Kafka, "the two types of dictatorship are entirely opposite as regards their aims and their philosophy of life. They are similar (and different from all other forms of dictatorship) in claiming absoluteness for their philosophy and in their effort to indoctrinate the masses." The first scholar to make the comparative study of totalitarian dictatorships the subject of a book was another émigré, Sigmund Neumann, who taught political science at Wesleyan University. *Permanent Revolution: The Total State in a World at War* stressed the unique dynamism and militancy of such regimes, but the author's focus was insufficiently discriminating. While placing "special emphasis upon the Fascist autocracies," Neumann did not neglect to discuss the Soviet regime, but, oddly enough, the First World War was labeled "totalitarian" and static authoritarian governments such as Francisco Franco's also were analyzed in such terms.[8]

The next wave of studies was written mostly by refugees from Germany and Austria: Erich Fromm's *Escape from Freedom* (1941); Bruno Bettelheim's *The Informed Heart: Autonomy in a Mass Age* (1960), which drew upon a couple of striking wartime articles; and the series of *Studies in Prejudice* sponsored by the American Jewish Committee, the most famous of which was T. W. Adorno et al., *The Authoritarian Personality* (1950). Whereas Franklin D. Roosevelt had promised "freedom from fear," these studies underscored "the fear of freedom" (the British title of Fromm's book). Generally better known than the earlier efforts in comparative political analysis, these books were brilliantly extended "remarks on the psychological appeal of totalitarianism." To a considerable degree, their subject was what one of the authors of this school, Erik H. Erikson, called "totalism"—a susceptibility to "doctrines offering a total immersion in a synthetic identity (extreme nationalism, racism, or class consciousness) and a collective condemnation of a totally stereotyped enemy of the new identity." These writers therefore limned the disintegration of stable identity, the loss of "wholeness," the common feelings of helplessness and loneliness, the vulnerability to unanticipated economic and social pressures, and "various forms of rigidity and of avoidance of ambiguity." For all their insight into the despair and fanaticism that enabled vast crimes to be committed with such conscienceless indifference, these works tended to make totalitarianism synonymous with nazism (and, more rarely, with fascism); and thus the value of the concept for comparative purposes was severely reduced.[9]

Though Franz Neumann was also to shift his attention from institutional analysis to the problem of anxiety in politics, his *Behemoth: The Structure and Practice of National Socialism* was perhaps the most formidable of the efforts of refugee intellectuals in traditional politics and economics. A Marxist labor lawyer deprived of his German citizenship soon after Hitler took office, Neumann converted himself into a political scientist in England and then in America, where he helped reconstruct Frankfurt's Institute for Social Research, became the chief expert on Germany within the wartime Office of Strategic Services, directed initial research at the Nuremburg war-crimes tribunals, and taught political science at Columbia University. While acknowledging the supremacy of the leader, the movement and the race over the state in Nazi ideology, Neumann was not adverse to calling Germany a "totalitarian state." But his emphasis on cartelization and other trends associated with capitalism caused Neumann to neglect other kinds of structural similarities with the Soviet Union.[10]

Several explanations may be offered for this focus on Germany's "totalitarian monopoly capitalism" and the avoidance of systematic study of the Russian experience. *Behemoth* and the studies in social psychology were composed in the shadow of the Second

World War, when the immediate and lethal threat was posed by the German enemy rather than the Soviet ally. Neumann, the former legal adviser to the Social Democratic Party of the Weimar Republic, was understandably more attuned to the dangers emanating from the right rather than the left. Nazi barbarism and nihilism, which subverted culture itself, appeared more repellent to the intellectuals than Stalinism, which did not defiantly repudiate rationalism and which was sometimes buttressed with classic texts of social analysis. Jewish origin alone probably cannot account for the virtual identification of totalitarianism with nazism, for roughly the same analysis could be found in contemporary works such as Bronislaw Malinowski's *Freedom and Civilization* (1944) and Ludwig von Mises's *Omnipotent Government* (1944). Yet non-Jewish refugee scholars tended to pay closer attention to the Soviet dictatorship. As the reputation of leftist scholars like Neumann went into eclipse during the Cold War, prominence was accorded Joseph Schumpeter's mordant envoi to enterprise, *Capitalism, Socialism and Democracy* (1942); Friedrich von Hayek's *The Road to Serfdom* (1944), which became a best seller on the strength of its anti-New Deal aura; and Carl Friedrich and Zbigniew's Brzezinski's standard text, *Totalitarian Dictatorship and Autocracy* (1956), which suffers from the unconvincing inclusion of Italian fascism.

But the supreme effort among the refugee intellectuals to record the political, psychological and moral meaning of the totalitarian experience, and indeed the paradigmatic formulation of the parallel between nazism and Stalinism, was Hannah Arendt's *The Origins of Totalitarianism*. Its analytical power was recognized by virtually all reviewers; two later assessments can be taken as representative. "Her thinking," Alfred Kazin observed, "has a moral grandeur suitable to the terror of her subject." And in his memoir of New York's intellectual community, Irving Howe recalled: "To recognize that we were living after one of the greatest and least explicable catastrophes of human history, and one for which we could not claim to have adequately prepared ourselves either as intellectuals or as human beings, brought a new rush of feelings." Arendt's book, Howe continued, made a "strong impact, mostly because it offered a coherent theory, or at least a coherent picture of the concentration camp universe. We could no longer escape the conviction that, blessing or curse, Jewishness was an integral part of our life."[11]

Admittedly, Arendt's reputation among scholars of modern European and especially Jewish history was hardly as secure as among intellectuals generally, and she herself revised some of her early views. She also had a penchant for uncovering the most paradoxical and often implausible explanations for the behavior of totalitarian movements and regimes. In retrospect, as the worst tensions of the Cold War subsided, the parallel between nazism and Stalinism appeared to some critics as strained, the documentation from the Soviet experience dubious and manifestly thin.[12] Nevertheless her book was undeniably a contribution to the understanding of what its British title identified as "the burden of our time," and *samizdat* and other dissident literature from the Soviet Union in the 1960s and 1970s has by no means invalidated Arendt's speculative accomplishment.

To take only one example, she had argued that anti-utilitarianism was characteristic of both systems. The Nazi violation of rationality, common sense and even the imperatives of military survival need no elaboration, which is why Albert Camus in *The Rebel* distinguished between the Nazis' "irrational terror" and the Bolsheviks' "rational terror." Yet in a nation that supposedly was laying the economic foundations for socialism, the Stalinist regime hired more guards and watchmen—not even counting NKVD militia—than miners and railwaymen combined. By 1938 one Russian citizen in twenty had been arrested, mostly for phantom crimes and according to arbitrary categories of enemies of the state. Evgenia Ginzburg has recalled that another prisoner told her: "As a Tartar, it was simpler to make me a bourgeois nationalist. Actually they did put me down as a Trotskyist first, but Rud sent the file back, saying they'd *exceeded the quota* for Trotskyists but were *short* on nationalists, though they'd taken all the Tartar writers they could think of." The construction of the White Sea–Baltic Canal cost the lives of an estimated one hundred thousand slave laborers; but when Aleksandr Solzhenitsyn visited the canal in 1966, it was virtually deserted, too shallow to be used.[13] In denying the justification of any economic rationale, Arendt may have exaggerated the irrationality of totalitarianism and discounted the prevalence of stupidity and incompetence in human affairs. But she demonstrated a remarkable gift, to borrow the lapidary phrase of Henry James, for "the imagination of disaster."[14]

Thereafter the definition of totalitarianism was focused increasingly on the Soviet Union. Arendt had applied the concept only to the period of Stalin's rule, when Bolshevism was most complete in its scope and most cruel in its methods. Other analysts were less discriminating, such as Bertram D. Wolfe, a former leader of the American Communist opposition whose mind in 1940 "was more on Trotsky in 1917 than on Hitler in Paris." In 1961 Wolfe insisted that "the Soviet state has existed longer, is more total, the power of Stalin and his successors more absolute, the purges bloodier and more sweeping and more continuous, the concentration camps larger . . . than anything Mussolini dreamed of or Hitler introduced. Only in his crematoria did Hitler's imagination exceed the deeds of Stalin." There were only five passing references to nazism in Wolfe's study of *Communist Totalitarianism*; and in denying that he could "deduce much from a comparison with other modern totalitarianisms," the author was revealing that the idea had become for him a pejorative word, that the function of the term was not so much analytical as polemical.[15]

By the 1950s it was apparent to all but the slowest learners on the Left that the Bolshevik revolution had not accelerated the leap from the "realm of necessity" into the "realm of freedom" but instead into a different and more extensive form of domination. The state had not withered away, nor had a classless society emerged. For many intellectuals the assumptions of socialism had to be either discarded or revised, and no one was better equipped for that task than Sidney Hook. Like Wolfe a product of the milieu of City College, Hook had studied Marxism in Berlin and Moscow before engaging in communist organizing activities in the early 1930s, when, at New York University, he was also the lone American Marxist enjoying a regular faculty appointment. But Hook had defined as his project the blending of dialectics with native pragmatism; he became an implacable foe of Stalinism during the Great Purges, branding as "totalitarian liberals" those Westerners who combined domestic dissidence with apologetics for Soviet tyranny.[16]

After the Second World War and the passing of his mentor, John Dewey, Hook's stature was confirmed as the last exoteric American philosopher, a logician still addressing complex questions of social and foreign policy. Though he had once called the Roman Catholic Church "the oldest and greatest totalitarian movement in history," he called totalitarian those societies in which "there is an absolute and interlocking monopoly of power—economic, juridical, military, educational, and political—in the hands of a minority party which countenances no legal opposition and is not removable by the processes of freely given consent." By that definition not the church but the Soviet Union was the most fully realized totalitarian order, and for Hook the consequences were inescapable: "Whoever believed that Nazi expansionism constituted a threat to the survival of democratic institutions must conclude by the same logic and the same type of evidence that Soviet Communism represents today an even greater threat to our survival, because the potential opposition to totalitarianism is now much weaker in consequence of World War II."[17]

Arendt had thought of totalitarianism in terms of nazism, and her imaginative projections into the logic of the Soviet system had been based on her understanding of the Third Reich. For Hook the "ideal type" had become Stalinism, which required the dedicated opposition of democrats even if it also indirectly benefited capitalism. By the early 1950s the shadow of totalitarianism helped account for the waning of radical energies, and adherence to democratic socialism seemed to mean a commitment to democracy at the expense of socialism. The specific positions Hook adopted became increasingly consistent, in result if not in premises, with those of conservatives, who tried to tighten their own case by positing an austere either/or for the modern political economy. For example, Milton Friedman of the University of Chicago argued that "there are only two ways of co-ordinating the economic activities of millions. One is central direction involving the use of coercion—the technique of the army and of the modern totalitarian state. The other is voluntary co-operation of individuals, the technique of the market place."[18]

The economic competition that conservatives valued had its analogue in the liberal advocacy of pluralism. Hans Morgenthau, also of the University of Chicago, warned that "there is only a small step from the destruction of the freedom of competition—that is, imperfect democracy—to the destruction of competition itself—that is, totalitarianism." That imperfect democracy had to be defended, which even Franz Neumann argued; and his own Marxism became so attenuated that, far from advocating a dictatorship of the proletariat to establish a classless society, he praised a heterogeneous society, "in which religions, classes, parties, groups confront each other. There can be no principle of adjustment other than that of competition." Such emphasis on the value of pluralism, heightened by the fear of totalitarianism, suggested an important shift in the liberal mind, which earlier had not shrunk from the enlargement of state power. In 1941, for example, Max Lerner was not uncomfortable about writing that "a democratic dynamism will involve the use of many means which we are asked to call 'totalitarian' and thus to surrender to the dictators." But "planning, military might, executive power, an administrative elite are as compatible with democracy as with totalitarianism."[19] Such statism hardly disappeared from the liberal agenda in the postwar period, but it was put on the defensive in an atmosphere fraught with the threat of a total state in the East; and it was more reassuring for Americans to define their country in terms of its autonomous factions, its voluntary associations, its bustling interest groups and veto groups.[20]

Pluralism was seen as offering special protection to minorities from the dangers of mass politics, as a form of life insurance against the fanaticism that might erupt under conditions of widespread anomie and alienation. William Kornhauser, a Berkeley sociologist, claimed that the "common property of a mass (rather than class) base helps to explain the similarity between fascism and communism, namely their totalitarianism." A less academic version of antipopulism animated Walter Lippmann's last important book, *The Public Philosophy*; its antagonism to majority rule looks overheated unless understood in the context of the rise of totalitarianism—"the supreme political heresy of our time." Lippmann considered totalitarianism a perversion of democracy itself, for it was a "modern form of despotism which ... springs directly from the people." This accusation of "heresy" was quite deliberate, for the "full-fledged totalitarians, Lenin, Hitler, Stalin" made God "their enemy, not because they did not believe in the Deity, but because they themselves were assuming His functions and claiming His prerogatives." The religious tincture here was rather uncommon, even if Lippmann clearly had in mind a civic creed rather than individual piety; nor was his solution to the problem of unchecked majorities widely shared. After acknowledging the assistance of Mortimer Adler, Lippmann called for the restoration of political authority in accordance with the doctrines of natural law.[21]

Although the conservative school of Leo Strauss flourished in pockets of the academy beginning in the 1950s, the appeal for a public philosophy failed to resonate in a society so imbued with relativism and pragmatism. Many intellectuals nevertheless shared Lippmann's fear of the totalitarians' "terrible doctrine that utopia must be brought about by an indefinitely prolonged process of unlimited revolution which would exterminate all opposition, actual and potential." The passions that once activated the political enterprise fell under suspicion, as the best was deemed not only as the enemy of the good but also as the occasional ally of the worst. In a set of essays dedicated to Hook, Daniel Bell carved the epitaph for the utopianism of the previous decades, the period blasted by "worldwide economic depression and sharp class struggles; the rise of fascism and racial imperialism in a country that had stood at an advanced stage of human culture; the tragic self-immolation of a revolutionary generation that had proclaimed the finer ideals of man; destructive war of a breadth and scale hitherto unknown; the bureaucratized murder of millions in concentration camps and death chambers."[22]

Bell not only chronicled but also pleaded for "an end to chiliastic hopes, to millenarianism, to apocalyptic thinking—and to ideology." Hostility to messianism, preference for incremental reform, advocacy of compromise and civility—these were the values of other sociologists as well, such as Seymour Martin Lipset, Edward Shils, Lewis Feuer, David Riesman. Richard Hofstadter's critiques of populism and of "the radical right" in the 1950s provided historical amplification of these concerns. The same message came in bottles from Jews abroad, from the Englishman Isaiah Berlin in his *Four Essays on Liberty* (1969), from the Frenchman Raymond Aron in *The Opium of the Intellectuals* (1957), from the Israeli J. L. Talmon in *The Origins of Totalitarian Democracy* (1960). The exhaustion of radical activism, Bell concluded, drew upon the realization that "there are other, more debasing forms of degradation and dehumanization—the systems of totalitarianism—than economic exploitation."[23]

Such conclusions came to be so widely shared in American

society that they lost some of their original force and meaning. For it had been the radical intellectuals associated with *Partisan Review*, its longtime editor, Philip Rahv, recalled, who had been "the first to discern the totalitarian essence of the Soviet myth. Since then, however, that minority political grouping has lost its bearings, continuing to denounce the evils of Communism with deadly sameness and in apparent obliviousness of the fact that . . . anti-Stalinism has virtually become the official creed of our entire society."[24] So prevalent was that creed that, when one of the Communists imprisoned under the Smith Act struck up a friendship with a member of Murder, Inc., the gangster's sister was horrified: "My God, Bob, you'll get into trouble." It became fashionable to distinguish the comity of American politics from the dogmatism and fanaticism endemic in totalitarian movements. It was tempting to contrast the Jefferson who assured Americans in his first inaugural address that "We are all republicans—we are all federalists" with the Lenin who took responsibility for the red terror of the secret police by remarking, "We are all Chekists."[25]

Not all Jewish intellectuals invited themselves to the national celebration, however; and the persistence of the idea of totalitarianism, especially in the 1960s, paradoxically helped to reinvigorate the tradition of dissidence and estrangement.

Among radical critics, the term, while not as favored as among conservatives and liberals, took two forms, the more idiosyncratic of which, characteristically enough, was adopted by Norman Mailer. Inoculated against the rationalism generally cherished by Jewish intellectuals, Mailer exalted the spontaneity of instinct and was bewitched by the therapeutic potential of individual violence. He was appalled by whatever deadened the senses, and virtually everything that deadened the senses he called totalitarian. "Every time one sees a bad television show," the novelist warned, "one is watching the nation get ready for the day when a Hitler will come. . . . It is meretricious art and so sickens people a little further. Whenever people get collectively sick, the remedy becomes progressively more violent and hideous. An insidious, insipid sickness demands a violent far-reaching purgative." America was permeated with "totalitarian architecture, totalitarian superhighways, totalitarian smog, totalitarian food (yes, frozen), totalitarian communications." In 1968 Mailer reminded his readers that "for years he had been writing about the nature of totalitarianism, its need to render populations apathetic, its instrument—the destruction of mood.... Totalitarianism was a deodorant to nature." Thus the antiseptic atmosphere of the Apollo 11 moon landing, "Aquarius" wondered, might be "a potential chariot of Satan, the unique and grand avenue for the new totalitarian."[26]

While apparently slapping a single pejorative term on whatever offended him, Mailer was in fact rattling the bars of the iron cage of bureaucratic rationality. He was especially struck by the sterile language of officials and technicians, which he called "totalitarianese, which is to say technologese, which is to say any language which succeeds in stripping itself of any moral content." Yet oddly enough Mailer's own use of the term was insouciant to the point of recklessness. To call the feminist critic Kate Millett "pure Left totalitarian" because of the arid dogmatism he ascribed to her *Sexual Politics*, or to call James Baldwin "totalitarian" for having accused Mailer of ignorance of Negro life, was hardly a model of scrupulousness and sensitivity in the use of language.[27]

The radicals' other deployment of the term was often on a more theoretical level, to blur the distinction between the regimes of Hitler and Stalin and the democratic societies of the West. Totalitarianism thus became an extreme version of the conformity exacted by the "tyranny of the majority"; and the coercive and full terror that Arendt, for example, considered integral to totalitarian rule was stripped from the new definition. In *One-Dimensional Man* Herbert Marcuse labeled as totalitarian "not only a terroristic political co-ordination of society, but also a non-terroristic economic-technical coordination which operates through the manipulation of needs by vested interests." He added: "Not only a specific form of government or party rule makes for totalitarianism, but also a specific system of production and distribution which may well be compatible with a 'pluralism' of parties, newspapers, 'countervailing powers,' etc."[28] Such a definition rendered the United States as "totalitarian" as the Nazi Germany from which Marcuse had fled three decades earlier, though interestingly enough the Brandeis University philosopher did not apply the term in his scholarly study of *Soviet Marxism* (1958).

Like Mailer, Marcuse associated the idea with the Western commitment to technology, expressed particular dismay over the infection of language itself, and condemned the repression of instincts as vigorously as liberals had denounced the oppression of peoples under Soviet and Nazi domination. In failing to follow the path of his best friend, Franz Neumann, toward liberal democracy, Marcuse helped to rob a concept of its historical precision and analytical pertinence—and even of its moral sting. As the Nestor of the New Left in the late 1960s, Marcuse influenced younger radicals; it is not coincidental that one of his former students rendered the following historical judgment: "American democratic capitalism became the most complete and effective form of totalitarianism. Opposition caved in, the Cold War began. Soon monopoly capitalism extended itself everywhere."[29]

In the 1960s even less radical criticism managed to domesticate the idea—or at least the memory—of totalitarianism. In recording the "progressive dehumanization" that reduced housewives to infantilization and to feelings of unfulfillment and emptiness, Betty Friedan did not shrink from calling the American home, rather oxymoronically, a "comfortable concentration camp." Admittedly housewives were not "on their way to the gas chamber," but they were trapped in roles that depersonalized them. "The women who 'adjust' as housewives, who grow up wanting to be 'just a housewife,' " Friedan warned, "are in as much danger as the millions who walked to their own death in the concentration camps—and the millions more who refused to believe that the concentration camps existed." Drawing exclusively upon Bettelheim's *The Informed Heart*, her book *The Feminine Mystique* found the cult of domesticity analogous to "the destruction of self-respect" in the concentration camps. Like the inmates of Dachau and Buchenwald, American women "learned to 'adjust' to their biological role. They have become dependent, passive, childlike; they have given up their adult frame of reference to live at the lower human level of food and things.... They are suffering a slow death of mind and spirit."[30]

In such analyses palpable injustices were inflated at the cost of debasing and demeaning the martyrdom that millions had suffered under totalitarianism. But this passage in *The Feminine Mystique*, in its very straining for a historical parallel, suggested that the deformities and pains of American life may have their own particular manifestations, that our social antagonisms and private dissatisfactions may be best understood as enmeshed in the very syndrome of values Americans cherish. In the demand for equality and opportunity, Tocqueville had over a century earlier seen the harbinger of a "species of oppression . . . unlike anything that ever before existed in the world." Groping unsuccessfully for a name for such despotism, he preferred instead to describe it: "minute, regular, provident and mild." The government would keep citizens "in perpetual childhood.... It provides for their security, foresees and supplies their necessities, facilitates their pleasures [and] manages their principal concerns.... Thus it every day renders the exercise of the free agency of man less useful and less frequent."[31] Here already was recognized the threat that the "fear of freedom" posed for a mass society; here already was envisioned the possibility of "a non-terroristic economic-technical coordination which operates through the manipulation of needs by vested interests."

But it was hardly necessary, in seeking to accommodate the understanding of totalitarianism to the American experience, to corrupt the vocabulary of human catastrophe or to trivialize the horrifying enigma of the Holocaust. Drawing upon the reports of some of the survivors of the Nazi camps, the historian Stanley Elkins speculated brilliantly on the process by which the African personality might have been transformed into the docile, submissive, infantile stereotype known as Sambo. Elkins did not claim that the Southern antebellum plantation was an early version of the concentration camp, or that they were equivalent. Instead he suggested that, just as infantilization had occurred rapidly among the middle-class Jews committed to the concentration camp universe, similar psychological mechanisms might have been at work from the Middle Passage to the slave pens to the plantations. *Slavery*, quite apart from the pyrotechnic historiographical debate it generated, is an especially telling example of how recent European political history affected meditations on human character and conduct.[32]

Submissiveness was also the object of a series of ingenious experiments conducted by the Yale psychologist Stanley Milgram. These experiments were conceived as an extension of the studies of his teacher, Solomon Asch, who tested the willingness of subjects to dismiss their accurate sense impressions for the sake of conformity to group pressure. The Asch study was cited in the 1953 conference of the American Academy of Arts and Sciences as evidence of totalitarian potential in the United States, but Milgram recalled "trying to think of a way to make Asch's conformity experiment more humanly significant. Just how far *would* a person go under the experimenter's orders? It was an incandescent moment, the fusion of a general idea on obedience with a specific technical procedure." Highly publicized, televised and criticized, the Milgram experiments gauged the willingness of human beings to inflict pain on presumably harmless strangers. Depending on the variations in the experimental paradigm, about half of those tested imposed the maximal "electric shocks" (despite warnings of danger and severity). No one walked out of the experimental room in protest.[33]

Milgram himself quite explicitly and frequently noted the totalitarian precedents for his experimental results, citing *The Authoritarian Personality* and the writings of Arendt and Fromm as "part of the *zeitgeist* in which social scientists grow up." Though he did not dispute the aptness of labeling his work "the Eichmann experiment," Milgram refused to confine its implications to the Third Reich: "To focus only on the Nazis, however despicable their deeds . . . is to miss the point entirely. For the studies are principally concerned with the ordinary and routine destruction carried out by everyday people following orders." The psychologist felt obliged to "conclude that Arendt's conception of the *banality of evil* comes closer to the truth than one might dare imagine."[34]

Daniel Bell, among others, disputed Milgram's understanding of the implications of the experiment, which showed only that "a helpless individual, where there is no possibility for independent inquiry, will accept the word of someone he feels is more technically competent in the matter. . . . To make the comparison Mr. Milgram makes, is, 'at best,' to repeat some liberal banalities ('we can all' be guilty), and at worst to be a libel on ordinary human beings." Bell therefore was unpersuaded by Milgram's claim that American concentration camps could be staffed with ease.[35] But such criticism was less than devastating, since the history of totalitarian rule showed the possibility of blocking any "recourse to independent judgment" when a regime monopolizes the instruments of propaganda and terror. Those who refused to inflict death in the concentration camp universe risked severe penalties. Those who refused to inflict presumably dangerous shocks in New Haven and Bridgeport risked no penalties, yet only about half the subjects refused to transmit the highest voltage. Rather than bristling at such "libel on ordinary human beings," Bell might have pondered the historical and experimental record of how many such persons acted.

Milgram's work raised to a new level of sophistication and reverberation the problem of "obedience to authority" that is posed so inescapably for the student of totalitarianism. For the historian of recent American attitudes, it would be tempting to contrast Milgram's orientation with the conclusion to an enormously popular novel of the 1950s, Herman Wouk's *The Caine Mutiny*. After having destroyed Captain Queeg on the witness stand during the court-martial of the mutineers, the attorney Barney Greenwald turns on his clients by asserting that authority must be obeyed even if mad or wrong. With drunken crudeness (but surely with authorial endorsement), Greenwald proclaimed the necessity of allied victory in World War II by any means necessary: "When all hell was breaking loose and the Germans started running out of soap and figured, well it's time to come over and melt down old Mrs. Greenwald . . . who was keeping Mama out of the soap dish? Captain Queeg." The historical inaccuracy of this view of German conduct (converting human flesh to soap is one atrocity the Nazis did not commit) is less salient here than the illustration of the authoritarian temper in the struggle against totalitarianism.[36]

But with the unprecedented use of techniques of civil disobedience in the 1960s, the problem of acceptance of authority appeared in a new guise, and on this subject no consensus emerged among writers of Jewish origin. Hook for example warned that "civil disobedience is at best a danger to democracy" and therefore might in fact encourage the forces of totalitarianism. Arendt by contrast welcomed civil disobedience and sought to secure its place within the American legal and political system. Justice Abe Fortas was of two minds. His pamphlet against civil disobedience opened with the following hypothesis: "If I had lived in Germany in Hitler's days, I hope I would have refused to wear an armband, to *Heil Hitler*, to submit to genocide. This I hope, although Hitler's edicts were law until allied weapons buried the Third Reich." Fortas seemed unaware that the choice of actively supporting the German government was not open to Jews anyway, but no matter: democracy, he argued, required respect for the law, which itself was subject to change. As an instance of change, Justice Felix Frankfurter had in two Supreme Court opinions (the first for the majority) denied the right of schoolchildren to refuse to salute the flag for religious reasons, acknowledging the force of majority rule. A generation later Justice Fortas himself affirmed the right of schoolchildren to wear black armbands to protest the Vietnam War and insisted that "in our system, state-operated schools may not be enclaves of totalitarianism."[37]

Although the unprecedented nature of modern domination had not elicited a common response to the problem of obedience to authority, American Jewish intellectuals did tend to emerge from the era of totalitarianism with a burnished realism and a sober appreciation for the advantages of power. The central themes of Yiddish literature, two of its disseminators wrote, had been "the virtue of powerlessness, the power of helplessness, the company of the dispossessed, the sanctity of the insulted and injured." But the Second World War did much to overcome the Jewish objection to martiality and militance, and many Jewish intellectuals, while acknowledging that power can corrupt, came to see little virtue in powerlessness and many dangers in helplessness. Probably none would have followed to its logical end Barney Greenwald's defense of Captain Queeg, and many did not share Hook's conclusion that hostility to communism had to be as uncompromising as the struggle against nazism. But Harold Rosenberg had demanded the assumption of "the burden of revenge" and reprisal, and Michael Walzer also accepted the necessity of dirty hands. Since "Nazism was an ultimate threat to everything decent in our lives," Walzer justified in retrospect the bombardment of German cities, choosing to "wager this determinate evil [of killing civilians] against that immeasurable evil." The defeat of the Third Reich could have been considered so urgent that he "dared to say that there will be no future . . . for civilization and its rules unless I accept the burden of criminality."[38]

Bruno Bettelheim insisted that, contrary to the message of a film such as Lina Wertmuller's *Seven Beauties*, concentration camp survival "has little to do with what the prisoner does or does not do. For the overwhelming majority of victims, survival depends on being set free either by the powers who rule the camps or—what is more reliable and desirable—by outside forces that destroy the concentration-camp world by defeating those who rule it." The Chicago psychoanalyst, himself a survivor of Dachau and Buchenwald, added that "even Solzhenitsyn, who demonstrated . . . the most remarkable ability to survive under unspeakably horrible conditions ... would not have survived if he had not been set free by those who rule the Gulag Archipelago." In his analysis of wartime Jewish resistance, Oscar Handlin also concluded that "the Nazi state could be destroyed only by a still greater and still stronger accumulation of power. There must be something in this experience from which a world still dominated by power can learn."[39]

But here too the lessons varied. Having been born in the ashes of the Holocaust, the state of Israel from the beginning made dependence on military force central to its policies. A quite piquant defense of this dependence was offered by the Canadian novelist Mordecai Richler, who noticed a British political cartoon in 1970 that showed an aged Egyptian at the mercy of approaching Israeli bombers: "Who is the Jew, the caption asked. Well now, if these *are* the alternatives, I'd rather we had the bombers and they made do with the sticks this time out, if only because it offers some assurance that, should they be required, there would now be planes to spare to destroy the railway heads leading into the extermination camps." Upon relinquishing his responsibilities as secretary of state, Henry Kissinger claimed to have had "no higher aim than to repay in some small measure my debt to this country, which saved me from totalitarianism." Yet of the ironies associated with his role in "a world still dominated by power," perhaps none is more striking than his advice to President Gerald Ford that, consistent with the policy of detente, the White House should not receive the Nobel Prize-winning Russian novelist who was probably the world's most famous survivor of totalitarianism.[40]

Besides such gritty paradoxes of realism and of respect for power, a further generalization may be offered: many intellectuals expressed an enhanced appreciation of the precariousness and preciousness of survival itself. Pitted against the boasts of the "fierce totalitarian will," Jewish writers often enunciated hope for the triumph and resilience of decency over the circumstances of gratuitous cruelty and suffering. Such concern for the value of survival, such a refusal to concede to death its dominion, can be shown readily. Even at the height of the Cold War, David Riesman's "Observations on the Limits of Totalitarian Power" noted "how hard it is permanently to destroy most people psychologically. Once the terror is removed, they appear to snap back, ravaged as in any illness, but capable of extraordinary recuperative efforts." In anticipating in 1957 an end to the terror in the Soviet Union, in detecting a "tendency toward 'normalization,' " Daniel Bell cast early doubt on the future applicability of the concept of totalitarianism itself. The belief in resilience permeated the writings of the Yale psychiatrist Robert Jay Lifton, who studied the *hibakusha*—the survivors of the bombing of Hiroshima—and who testified that "being a Jew . . . has a great deal to do with my concerns with dislocations and survivals."[41] The journalist Dorothy Rabinowitz portrayed the fate of a few of the Holocaust survivors who immigrated to America; they have their fictional analogues in the protagonists of Edward Lewis Wallant's *The Pawnbroker* (1961), Saul Bellow's *Mr. Sammler's Planet* (1970), and Isaac Bashevis Singer's *Enemies, A Love Story* (1972). There was also the work, not easily classifiable or assimilable, of Elie Wiesel who, after his memoir *Night* (1958), generally chose to write "around" rather than "about" the direct experience of the Holocaust. Those days and nights, he said, "cannot be described . . . cannot be communicated." Wiesel's comparatively early interest in "the Jews of silence," still half hidden in the shadow of Soviet totalitarianism, was another manifestation of an imperative to bear witness to the burden of our time.[42]

For some, survival was indeed possible because there was an outside world offering the chance of refuge, and even the responsibility of bearing witness made sense only if others needed to be warned of the character of totalitarianism. That is why it can be important to study American efforts to understand the phenomenon, and why one of the earliest reports from a survivor of the Soviet labor camps was entitled *Tell the West* (1948). Its author, Jerzy Gliksman, lived to participate in the major American scholarly conference on totalitarianism in the postwar era, in Boston in 1953.[43] His more famous half brother did not: as a leader of the Polish-Jewish Bund, Victor Alter fled upon the Nazi invasion of Poland to avoid being killed as a Jew; in fleeing to Russia, he was murdered as a social democrat instead, a representative of all the souls trapped and doomed under totalitarianism. Yet as that era recedes deeper into the past, as the survivors themselves disappear, the meaning of that historical experience is likely to shift. The concept of totalitarianism, because it is circumscribed by time, is subject to fluctuation; the word itself may lose much of its emotional resonance, even if it remains in our dictionaries.

For Jewish intellectuals the meaning of that experience evoked no unifying pattern of responses, suggested no common framework of analyses, offered few applicable "lessons" and perhaps even fewer consolations. It remained in important ways elusive, though no segment of American society was better equipped to fathom the unfathomable. For Jewish intellectuals had generally been immersed in Freud, whose *Civilization and Its Discontents* had constituted an early warning system against the aggressions lurking so close to the surface of rationality and social order. These thinkers were quick to grasp the relevance of Kafka, whose "In the Penal Colony" and *The Trial* helped make *k* the most ominous letter in the alphabet of anxiety. But the sisters of both Freud and Kafka perished in the Holocaust, for which no explanation was finally satisfactory. Already in 1948 the critic Isaac Rosenfeld, having read so many of the accounts of the Holocaust, realized that "by now we know all there is to know. But it hasn't helped; we still don't understand. . . . There is no response great enough to equal the facts that provoke it."[44] That is still so.

2

The Holocaust in the

American Jewish Mind

The United States has been no exception to the generalization once offered, with pardonable exaggeration, by Harold Rosenberg: "For two thousand years the main energies of Jewish communities in various parts of the world have gone into the mass production of intellectuals." During the peak of Eastern European Jewish migration, at the turn of the century, the term "intellectual" was by coincidence imported into the American language from France, where it had characterized the defenders (often Jewish) of Captain Dreyfus. Since then many American Jews have placed such a high value upon thought, have risen to so conspicuous a place in the learned professions, that sometimes it has appeared as though the modern intellect has been, like the violin, a disproportionately Jewish instrument. The passionate commitment to ideas, as well as volubility and tenacity in pursuit of abstractions, have been so commonly attributed to modern Jews that Khrushchev's description of them cannot be dismissed as atypical: "They are all individualists and all intellectuals. They want to talk about everything, they want to discuss everything, they want to debate everything—and they come to totally different conclusions!"[1]

Until the Holocaust. The murder of six million people staggered belief; its magnitude and incomprehensibility resisted efforts at description. Here, for example, is a representative statement addressed in 1948 to an audience of literary intellectuals: "The simple eye of the camera shows us, at Belsen and Buchenwald, horrors that quite surpass Swift's powers, a vision of life turned back to its corrupted elements which is more disgusting than any that Shakespeare could contrive. . . ." Thus Lionel Trilling confessed a share in the failure to articulate a commensurate response, since "before what we now know the mind stops; the great psychological fact of our time which we all observe with baffled wonder and shame is that there is no possible way of responding to Belsen and Buchenwald. The activity of mind fails before the incommunicability of man's suffering."[2]

This loss of the power of thought has barely been rectified in the decades since Trilling's admission. The simple unblinking eye of the camera has remained more forceful than speech, which ceased to be an essential instrument for the representation of reality. No words in our vocabulary have regained their integrity in rendering human experience intelligible when we are confronted with such torment, such depravity, such desolation. For the survivors no retribution is imaginable, no revenge adequate. For American Jews from that moment until the present, no full understanding is possible, no judgment quite satisfactory.

The historian of such attitudes is therefore confronted with a nearly insoluble task. Trained to interpret public and private documents, to locate explicit cultural positions, to translate in retrospect assorted means of direct communication, the historian here finds mostly muffled responses, fragmentary statements, stifled cries. In dealing with the impact of the Holocaust, the American historian for once has to learn how to decode near silence, how to draw meaning from the extinction of feeling. In evaluating one consequence of the Holocaust, in ascertainng how and where the shocks of this calamity have been registered, in handling evidence that is elusive and impressionistic, no scholar can pretend to offer a conclusive or systematic treatment of this topic. Nevertheless the subject of the impact of the Holocaust on American Jewish intellectuals merits attention.[3]

It was noted in the previous chapter that the New York intellectuals described by Irving Howe "were living after one of the greatest and least explicable catastrophes of human history." Yet they could not be said to "have adequately prepared ourselves either as intellectuals or as human beings" for the horror of genocide, of total evil. The feelings of guilt and remorse thus aroused were therefore "mostly unarticulated," rarely permitted to come to the surface. Nevertheless it is striking how rarely the memory of the Holocaust elicited direct concern and contemplation, apart from Yiddish writers such as Jacob Glatstein and Chaim Grade. In essays on the subject of American Jewish identity published a decade apart by two of the most versatile and alert of American intellectuals, neither Harold Rosenberg nor Daniel Bell made more than a passing reference to the disaster. Neither indicated that it had irrevocably affected his own or anyone else's Jewishness, that it had permanently come to haunt their lives.[4]

The significance of this omission is more noticeable when we focus on the thinker most responsible for making identity the central issue in the lives of individuals. Since Erik H. Erikson is rarely if ever discussed within the ambit of Jewish life, it may be especially useful to do so here, and to remind ourselves more generally of the phenomenon of "the non-Jewish Jew" reticent about his ethnic origins.[5] Of the large number of intellectuals who have constructed often elaborate and ingenious escape routes from their own past, Erikson ought to be deemed a paradigmatic figure. As an immigrant, he has incorporated the experience of every white American or his ancestor. As an American, he is a strikingly self-made man so intent on establishing his own identity that he used as his surname not his stepfather's but one he had chosen and bestowed upon himself. In "making a name for himself," he became his own father, thus embodying the values Tocqueville found so characteristic of America: "Among democratic nations . . . the woof of time is every instant broken and the track of generations effaced. . . . Democracy makes every man forget his ancestors . . . [and] throws him back forever upon himself alone." Raised as a Jew in Europe by his mother and stepfather, Erikson has only the most marginal of relationships to Jewish life in the United States; this problematic and ambiguous connection with his own origins further suggests how representative of a certain kind of American Jewish intellectual he is.[6]

Even when writing about the tangled roots of Hitler's childhood and about the fanaticism of the totalitarian mind, Erikson has managed to skirt a direct confrontation with the Holocaust. Even when writing about the European refugees of the 1930s, he has been evasive, noting only that "migration means cruel survival in identity terms . . . for the very cataclysms in which millions perish open up new forms of identity to the survivors."[7] It may be no accident that his own notions of the life cycle and the eight ages of man make little if any allowance for the impact of catastrophes upon individual consciousness, for the possibility that sensibility may be altered under the weight of such historical disasters as the Holocaust.

It may be valuable to examine more closely the major subjects of Erikson's own scholarly concern, the relatively young. In 1944 some of the most promising and accomplished American writers of Jewish origin participated in a symposium in the *Contemporary Jewish Record*. They included Trilling, Clement Greenberg, Isaac Rosenfeld, Muriel Rukeyser and Delmore Schwartz. The symposium was nominally on the topic of literature, but the participants also were asked to address the question of whether the awareness of the young American writer "as artist and citizen [has] been modified or changed by the revival of anti-Semitism as a powerful force in the political history of our time." It was a year after the revolt and destruction of the Warsaw ghetto; and yet they expressed no sense of urgency, no sense of obligation as writers or as Jews to incorporate the experiences of persecution and mass murder in their depiction of human actuality. The only exception was Albert Halper, the memorialist of *Union Square*, who acknowledged that "Hitler has made me different." Halper added that "the cries of five million expiring Jews outside my window ... beg me to tell of them, to speak for them." Not even Halper, however, took the occasion to affirm a genuine affiliation with the American Jewish community. All the symposiasts' windows were shut, so that they were unable to hear (in Trilling's phrase) "a single voice [from that community] with the note of authority—of philosophical, or poetic, or even of rhetorical, let alone of religious, authority."[8]

A generation later *Commentary* conducted a larger symposium on the topic of "Jewishness and the Younger Intellectuals," and the pattern persisted. In his introduction Norman Podhoretz listed the forces that might have led to some revision of Jewish self-definition since the Second World War: the eclipse of radicalism, the invigoration of religion, the emergence of Israel, the end of anti-Semitism in the public culture of the United States, and the phenomenon of "making it" into the highest realms of the economy, society and culture. Though not asked to do so by *Commentary*, only two of the thirty-one symposiasts stressed the imprint of the Holocaust on their lives. The novelist Barbara Probst Solomon struck a common note in acknowledging her disaffection from the main currents of minority life, yet she recalled that she most felt like a Jew "the day I saw a deserted concentration camp." The sociologist Elihu Katz observed among other Jews "the agony, and the guilt, of bearing witness to the destruction of European Jewry" and, as for himself, claimed to "feel strongly about remembering the Nazis. I do not see how to do this without institutionalizing personal and communal rituals of remembrance." These were fugitive thoughts, and there were a few others less decisively expressed. One of the questions posed by *Commentary* dealt with attitudes toward Israel, but few of the responses related its value as sovereign refuge to the antecedent horror of nazism. One contributor put a peculiar twist on the motif of guilt by asserting that "the Jewish tradition ultimately bears some responsibility for Nazism, for the latter is Old Testament racism stood on its head."[9]

While the few contributors who made fleeting references to the Holocaust were among those most hostile to organized Jewry, it might be argued that both the 1944 and 1961 symposia were biased in their sampling in favor of universalists and against believing Jews, whose cognizance of the extinction of an entire culture and its members might be closer to the surface. But such a possibility is not borne out by the testimony of the actual adherents of Judaism. Will Herberg's existentialist *Judaism and Modern Man* (1951) opened with the statement that "horrors which only yesterday we all believed had been banished once and for all from human society . . . have come back in the most virulent form."[10] But no further mention of the Holocaust was made after the introductory observation; nor, in his role as sociologist in *Protestant-Catholic-Jew* (1955), did Herberg discern any influence of those events on the religious expression of midcentury American Jewry. Such horrors apparently did not direct Jews toward the restoration of faith. But less conventional thinkers and writers than Herberg were equally unable to pursue the implications of the Holocaust, a subject almost completely avoided in *Judaism* magazine's 1961 symposium entitled "My Jewish Affirmation." The twenty-one contributors were the wise sons' counterattack against *Commentary*'s wicked sons earlier that year. The participants included Robert Alter, Arthur A. Cohen and Michael Wyschogrod, who later would break their silence.

Further proof that the theologians were as baffled and stunned by the moral import of the annihilation camps as everyone else came in 1966, when *Commentary* sponsored its symposium on the condition of Jewish belief. Seymour Siegel asserted that "first and foremost, Jewish thought must try to fathom the meaning of the European holocaust. . . . For all Jews (and non-Jews as well) it remains the most agonizing question of our age." Yet it seemed a question that religious thinkers were helpless to answer, and a question that few seemed willing even to pose. Richard Rubenstein was therefore "amazed at the silence of contemporary Jewish theologians on this most crucial and agonizing of all Jewish issues. . . . To see any purpose in the death camps, the traditional believer is forced to regard the most demonic, anti-human explosion in all history as a meaningful expression of God's purposes. The idea is simply too obscene for me to accept." Rubenstein predicted that "the full impact of Auschwitz has yet to be felt in Jewish theology or Jewish life. Great religious revolutions have their own periods of gestation." He added that "no religious community can endure so hideous a wound without vast inner disorders."[11]

Two decades later no such disorders can be said to have wracked the American Jewish world, but otherwise Rubenstein's speculation has been at least partially confirmed. Some theologians have tried to come to grips with the implications of the establishment of an earthly hell, of suffering beyond measure and devastation without purpose, of death without the traditional transfiguration of martyrdom for faith. Appreciation for the salience of the writings of Emil Fackenheim, Eliezer Berkovitz, Irving Greenberg, Rubenstein and others should not go unrecorded.[12] Such thinkers have helped enlarge our terrible understanding of a universe in which, as Spinoza remarked, those who love God ought not to expect God's love in return.

Nevertheless it is easy to form the impression that Christian thought is no less painfully seeking to confront this dreadful intervention of the demonic in history. For Christians the Holocaust has had consequences in challenging the postulates of faith and problematic conduct. Among martyrs to Nazi cruelty, Dietrich Bonhoeffer may have had at least as great an effect on Christian thought as Leo Baeck has exerted on Judaism. The devastating indictment of the papacy of Pius XII in *The Deputy* should not obscure the fact that a German Protestant, Rolf Hochhuth, made the Holocaust into a Christian problem more forcefully than the

Holocaust has been connected to the Judaic tradition. Indeed one proof of the power of Hochhuth's drama is that, before the New York production, an American religious organization warned of the threat to "harmonious interfaith relations." To which the drama critic Robert Brustein replied: "If such a cause is contingent on the suppression of truth, then we are better off without it."[13]

That a play like *The Deputy* was written in Europe is not surprising, because very few Amerians have dared to tackle so awesome and auspicious a subject. Until William Styron, no major American novelist has allowed himself to be drawn into this vortex, although—to confine the discussion to the Jews—Saul Bellow (in *Mr. Sammler's Planet*), Isaac Bashevis Singer (in *Enemies: A Love Story*) and Edward Lewis Wallant (in *The Pawnbroker*) have effectively placed protagonists who survive the Holocaust into American settings. Others, even the most ambitious, such as Norman Mailer, have sensed where to stop, have known what the limits are, have grasped that Auschwitz, although historical actuality, is unimaginable and defies ready translation into artistic images. Even a historian like Lucy Dawidowicz devoted only a few brief passages in *The War Against the Jews* to the nature of the annihilation camps. What Eugene Ionesco once said of the universe is even more applicable to the *univers concentrationnaire*—"a desert of dying shadows." Although Lawrence Langer's survey, *The Holocaust and the Literary Imagination*, makes no pretense to completeness in its analysis of the representation of atrocity, it is noteworthy that only one work written by a native American author is studied (Anthony Hecht's poem, "More Light! More Light!").[14]

Since the novel normally requires mimesis of some kind and drama requires the re-creation of characters and setting, poetry may be the literary art least likely to falsify the experience of extreme torment. In any event the most arresting work by a serious American writer is a poem. The lines from Sylvia Plath's "Daddy" are no doubt familiar: "An engine, an engine / Chuffing me off like a Jew. / A Jew to Dachau, Auschwitz, Belsen. / I begin to talk like a Jew. / I think I may well be a Jew." She was not, of course, and yet her gift for identifying the artifacts of atrocity ("A cake of soap, / A wedding ring, / A gold filling") led George Steiner to call "Daddy" "one of the very few poems I know of in any language to come near the last horror. It achieves the classic act of generalization, translating a private, intolerable hurt into a code of plain statement." Yet can a private hurt, however intolerable, legitimately be contrived to bear the freight of emotion associated with the Holocaust? Does poetic license permit personal tribulations in normal life, which led to Plath's own suicide by gas, to be compared to an experience as radically alien as genocide? Irving Howe has answered quite rightly in the negative, arguing that no one born in Wellesley, educated at Smith, living in placid England, has any reason to describe her skin (as Plath did in "Lady Lazarus") as "bright as a Nazi lampshade / . . . My face a featureless, fine / Jew linen." Her emotional intensity is simply out of moral and aesthetic control; and a sensibility that sought death (for which she felt "a call") offered, through a gratuitous act of empathy, an insult to those whose prayer for the gift of life was unanswered.[15]

This particular episode in contemporary cultural history marked an important break in the pattern of unarticulated feelings, in ending the paralysis of blunt speech. Such a break probably was inevitable, since even the argument for maintaining silence had to be made as eloquently as possible, and numbness could not permanently suppress the need to communicate shock, pain, and rage. Nonetheless, merely because the event no longer is regarded as unspeakable, not every writer can earn the authority that requires us to listen. Even if Plath was the wrong kind of artist to interject herself among the passive mourners, the Holocaust could not forever be blocked from consciousness in our everyday world, as though the screams of the victims were without resonance.

Especially since the 1967 war, and once more in the aftermath of the 1973 war, when Jewish fate again seemed to hang in the balance, the need to talk around—if not always about—the Holocaust has more frequently and ineluctably asserted itself. The complications and uncertainties of politics may have made private remembrance more feasible, and the treachery and corruptibility of language may have made silence preferable. But in the last decade or so, the impulse to come to terms with the destruction of Jewish life in Europe has become explicit. Despite the decisive Israeli victories in war, anxieties about Jewish survival inevitably percolated through the Diaspora. In the United States, the renewed interest in ethnicity made particularism respectable. Even earlier, the Eichmann trial, and the cognate uproar in Jewish intellectual circles provoked by Hannah Arendt's report of it, should also be mentioned (see chapter 4), as well as the need to explain the Jewish fate to one's children.[16]

Increasingly, it seems, the radical extremity of the Holocaust has been absorbed partly in our own sense of normality, incorporated into an accepting sense of the recent past. For intellectuals and everyone else, the absolute evil of a generation ago has been kept distant for the sake of sanity, and yet immediacy also has been necessitated by the obligations of mourning. In the last decade, whether on television or in symposia, whether in college courses on the Holocaust or in the curricula of public schools, ordinary discourse has been expected to bear paradoxes that cannot be resolved, antinomies that cannot easily be accommodated to the American condition, which Benjamin Franklin once described without irony as a "happy mediocrity." A nation once noteworthy for its innocence, proud of its immunity from the complicity of history, increasingly is asked to recall and comprehend the ideological murder of a million children. Those who were there and are still alive cannot be expected to relive their most unbearable years for the sake of those who are unlikely to understand. Nevertheless, survivors, bystanders, and their descendants all will be torn between the need to make the Holocaust intelligible, which risks trivialization, and the recognition of the incomprehensibility of the Holocaust, which risks oblivion.

Now that the balance is veering toward explicitness rather than muteness, a reminder may be useful that the shock of the Holocaust was there all along in the dark fantasies and subterranean fears of many of our most reflective writers. Perhaps the historian of the American mind must learn to be more resourceful and subtle in piercing the silence that long enveloped the subject. Perhaps we need a second look, for example, even at those magazine symposia, which in this respect had seemed such forums for innocence. In his 1944 contribution to the *Contemporary Jewish Record*, Alfred Kazin had briefly mentioned "fascist cutthroats" but made no other allusion to the mass murders then being committed. Yet his recent memoir dates a year earlier the beginning "of the nightmare that would bring everything else into question, that will haunt me to my last breath." *New York Jew* records the critic's "private history of the world," in which he "took down every morsel of fact and rumor relating to the murder of my people." From that moment the lineup was an essential part of Kazin's mental world: "I could imagine my father and mother, my sister and myself, our original tenement family of 'small Jews,' all too clearly—fuel for the flames, dying by a single flame that burned us all up at once."[17] From the 1944 symposium it could not have been guessed how constant has been the pressure of the Holocaust, how forcefully it has exerted itself on the memory and imagination of one of our most influential critics.

In the 1961 *Commentary* symposium, Robert Jay Lifton, an American-born psychiatrist best known for his studies of the psyches of Asians, mentioned nazism in passing. Nevertheless, a decade later, in the introduction to a book dedicated to Erikson, Lifton claimed that "being a Jew is very much part" of the equipment he brings to his professional interests, "and has a great deal to do with my concerns with dislocations and survivals, and with man in history in general. My writing about Hiroshima is affected, and I hope informed, by my relationship as a Jew to the Nazi persecutions—and my comparison of the two holocausts [Nazi and nuclear] becomes an imperative personal task as well as a logical intellectual one." It may be dubious to bracket together Hiroshima and Treblinka because of "the unmanageable dimensions of technological violence, the absurd or disconnected deaths, and . . . a particularly intense form of creative guilt." Nevertheless it is honorable to acknowledge that intellectual preoccupations have been permanently scarred by the extermination of one's fellow Jews.[18]

In the 1961 *Judaism* symposium, Michael Wyschogrod shared in the general silence. Since then he has emerged as a cogent critic of Emil Fackenheim's famous "eleventh commandment" to preserve Jewish identity in order to deprive Hitler of a posthumous victory. Wyschogrod has argued that "if I remain a Jew basically to frustrate Hitler's design, I place Hitler's evil design at the heart of Jewish faith. It does not belong there. . . . The holocaust cannot be made to yield a new lease of life for Judaism." It would be just as misplaced, however, if this desolation of our community were removed from Judaic thought, since the most severe questions about God's justice and mercy cannot be suppressed whenever the Holocaust is meditated upon. They are questions that, in the wake of this historical calamity, must be addressed. Otherwise theology would be doomed to charges of evasiveness and irrelevance. Nevertheless, Wyschogrod's position, which is shared by others, in no way can be interpreted as a sign of the muffled impact of the Nazi horror, which he escaped as a child in 1939. No one who minimized its meaning could have written: "Rarely does a week go by that I do not read or reread a book about the holocaust. The subject rarely leaves my consciousness. I believe it is the key to understanding me, should anyone be interested.... My personality may be explainable on quite other grounds than the holocaust. But I do not believe so."[19]

Since any exploration of this topic must not be restricted to those affiliated with organized Jewry, it would be appropriate to insist that the influence of the Holocaust can be detected well outside the precincts of institutional and even personal affirmation. Mailer, for example, has been a conspicuously non-Jewish Jew who, at one time at least, masqueraded as a "white Negro." In his 1957 essay of that title, he attempted to explain some of the character transformations emerging from the underside of American society. In championing these altered identities, Mailer noted "the psychic havoc of the concentration camps and the atom bomb upon the unconscious mind of almost everyone alive in these years.... We have been forced to live with the suppressed knowledge that the smallest facets of our personality or the most minor projection of our ideas ... could mean ... that we might still be doomed to die as a cipher in some vast statistical operation in which our teeth would be counted, and our hair would be saved, but our death itself would be unknown, unhonored, and unremarked." Few American Jewish intellectuals offered an equally hospitable welcome to the death-defying hipster, which only proves the aptness of Khrushchev's complaint that Jews come to "totally different conclusions." But the historian of the impact of the camps on American Jewry will have to look in places as wayward and personal as Mailer's essay.[20]

A final example suggests the dimensions of the subject. For Trilling's earlier notation on the power of photographs to show absolute and unprecedented evil has a suitable analogue in a meditation on the silent art by another, younger American disconnected from normative Jewish life. For the Holocaust even seeps into Susan Sontag's *On Photography.* "One's first encounter with the photographic inventory of ultimate horror is a kind of revelation," she has written. "For me, it was photographs of Bergen-Belsen and Dachau which I came across by chance in a bookstore in Santa Monica in July 1945. Nothing I have seen—in photography or in real life—ever cut me as sharply, deeply, instantaneously. Indeed, it seems plausible for me to divide my life into two parts ... I was twelve," Sontag has recalled. "They were only photographs—of an event I had scarcely heard of and could do nothing to affect, of suffering I could hardly imagine and could do nothing to relieve. When I looked at those photographs, something broke. Some limit had been reached, and not only that of horror; I felt irrevocably grieved, wounded, but a part of my feeling started to tighten; something went dead; something is still crying."[21]

3

Anti-Semitism and the Problem of Evil:

The Case of Hannah Arendt

More than two decades ago Israeli agents captured Adolf Eichmann in Argentina. His trial opened in Jerusalem in April 1961, lasted fourteen weeks, and resulted in his conviction for "crimes against the Jewish people, crimes against humanity, war crimes and membership in criminal associations." After an unsuccessful appeal, the former lieutenant colonel of the SS was hanged in May 1962.

Although the capture and trial of Eichmann aroused legal controversy, it is doubtful whether any other court of law, anywhere else, could justifiably have reached any other verdict on his guilt. The fact that Eichmann had directed the transportation of the Jews of Nazi-occupied Europe to their deaths was not in dispute. What remains as puzzling and elusive as ever is the nature of the human being who performed such a task with such incontrovertible diligence. Twenty years after Eichmann appeared inside a glass booth before the civilized world, his motives and his character have defied fully satisfactory explanation.

The most striking and celebrated account was provided, not by the prosecution, but by the *New Yorker* magazine reporter who covered the trial, Hannah Arendt. In her book on the subject, *Eichmann in Jerusalem: A Report on the Banality of Evil*, she formulated a disturbing image—original in its thesis, modern in its implications, bold in its definition of criminality. For Arendt argued that the defendant simply had been unaware of his own wickedness. He neither had killed anyone personally, nor had he ordered anyone to be killed. He was neither a pervert nor a sadist. Because his character was so devoid of force, even of demonic force, Eichmann seemed to her "terribly and terrifyingly normal." Arendt later recalled being astonished "by a manifest shallowness in the doer which made it impossible to trace the incontestible evil of his deeds to any deeper level of roots or motives."[1] Eichmann was the sort of mass murderer for whom annihilation was not fiendish and not monstrous. It was instead impersonal and abstract—a matter of following rules, obeying orders, arranging schedules with the utmost meticulousness and dedication.

The observer from the *New Yorker* resisted the temptation to define Eichmann as the culmination of millenia of bigotry. It is true that his superiors had claimed that their own anti-Semitism was racial and "scientific" rather than religious and emotional. Yet the ex-lieutenant colonel himself seemed to hate neither by reflection nor by instinct. He lacked the obsessive wrath that might attach itself to an "idea." He told his Israeli captors that he felt no hatred for the Jews, and Arendt believed him, finding in him no "firm ideological convictions," and no compulsive malignancy. Though Eichmann prided himself on being an "idealist," he really believed in nothing. Though the consequences of his actions were horrible, he exhibited no emotional connection with them. There was no idea Eichmann would have been willing to die for—certainly not the myth of the master race; he lived only for the enhancement of his own career. "Except for an extraordinary diligence in looking out for his personal advancement," Arendt concluded, "he had no motives at all."[2]

Gershom Scholem was the first to point out that this interpretation differed markedly from Arendt's earlier exploration of modern tyranny, *The Origins of Totalitarianism* (1951).[3] In that book Arendt had insisted that the absolute had erupted in the politics of the Third Reich and of the Soviet Union. Under Hitler and Stalin, everything had become morally permissible and humanly possible. Hell, which previously had been only imagined, had been established on earth—and this condition she had termed "radical evil." Yet in observing Eichmann in Jerusalem, in studying the awful trajectory of his career, Arendt realized that evil also could be banal. The defendant's wickedness had lacked depth or deliberateness: "Eichmann never realized what he was doing." His career had demonstrated not fanaticism but thoughtlessness, not diabolism but shallowness, not anti-Semitic fury but an eerie indifference.

Though Scholem himself dismissed her subtitle, "the banality of evil," as a "catchword" rather than "the product of profound analysis," Arendt had coined a phrase that has become an inescapable part of the language of modern intellectual life.[4] She denied intending the phrase to constitute a philosophical doctrine or thesis, but nevertheless there is an elusiveness and ambiguity to the term that she might have remedied. Arendt did not mean that banality is itself evil, nor did she assert that evil is always banal. (Whereas Eichmann held a series of conventional jobs in Argentina—managing a farm, working for a citrus business and at an automobile plant—Josef Mengele, the mephitic doctor at Auschwitz, is reportedly alive in Paraguay, having been actively engaged in the extermination of Indians.) Though Arendt was struck by Eichmann's apparent normality, she never claimed that everyone has his propensities, that anyone could have done what he did.

Eichmann therefore represented something unprecedented, something peculiarly dangerous. His thoughtlessness and distance from reality helped wreak more devastation than had his motives been malign, because he served dutifully as a bureaucrat in a modern state. Having risen to a position of responsibility within the Reich Security Head Office (R.S.H.A.), Eichmann felt guided by his sense of official responsibility. His conscience would have bothered him only if he had *not* obeyed orders, and when those orders required the deportation of Jews, such a bureaucrat could not have imagined any alternative to subordination. That is why one of the most perceptive sentences in Arendt's book is her claim that "evil in the Third Reich had lost the quality by which most people recognize it—the quality of temptation."[5] That is also why the allegations of the defendant's personal feelings toward the Jews, upon which the prosecution placed such emphasis, seem not entirely on target.

At the end of the nineteenth century, Nietzsche's descent into madness was punctuated by his wish: "I am just having all anti-Semites shot."[6] In the twentieth century the effort to have all the Jews murdered did not affect the murderers' sanity, for within a totalitarian system it was possible to kill without hatred or any other emotion, without a sense of guilt, without remorse. Eichmann was of course judged legally sane and fully competent to stand trial, and this phenomenon disturbed other commentators. It occured to Elie Wiesel, who also noticed the defendant's utter banality, that "if he were sane, I should choose madness. It was he or I.... We could not inhabit the same universe."[7] The monk Thomas Merton, in reflecting on the puzzle of Eichmann's personality, also surmised that the sane may be "the most dangerous," for they may be immune to what traditionally has passed for the demands of private conscience.[8]

Such reactions were understandable, even though it is dubious to define the problem as the perils of sanity. That is not a quality of which modern life boasts an excess. Eichmann's short-circuited sense of moral responsibility was so unnerving, so staggering to contemplate, that it was tempting to find refuge in the villainy depicted by the prosecuting attorney, Gideon Hausner, who "knew Eichmann to be a cunning, flint-hearted plotter, with a demonic personality which certainly was completely indifferent to the suffering he inflicted ... and which reveled in the exercise of power." Eichmann, the prosecutor added, "was possessed of a dangerous, perverted personality."[9]

Several psychologists concurred. The results of the Szondi test, which is designed to locate antisocial impulses in criminals and which the prisoner had taken ten times, were sent to Szondi himself, who told the Israelis: "You have on your hands a most dangerous person." The psychologist claimed to have tested more than six thousand criminals in twenty-four years, and this particular subject, whose identity presumably had not been disclosed, Szondi considered the most remarkable. An American political scientist, Michael Selzer, sent Eichmann's drawings to six other psychologists as part of the Bender-Gestalt and the House-Person-Tree tests. The scientists were told only the subject's sex, age, and the attribute of his having been famous. Five of the psychologists' responses emphasized his violent personality, obsessive-compulsive nature, and paranoia, and were not—according to Selzer—"particularly surprised to learn that his name was Adolf Eichmann."[10] (The sixth psychologist, undoubtedly no liberal, had figured out the subject to be much like Adlai Stevenson.)

There may have been a reason why those five psychologists were not "particularly surprised" when Eichmann's identity was revealed. As Thomas Litwack, a psychologist at John Jay College, pointed out, the diagnosticians could have assumed, since the test was presented to them by a political scientist, that an important political figure was being evaluated. It would also have been a fair assumption that the subject had suffered a terrible breakdown or committed atrocities, for "why else would he have been subjected to psychological tests?" It would have been more impressive had the psychologists "picked Eichmann's drawings out of a random sample of drawings as being done by someone particularly violent or psychopathic."[11] This particular diagnostic skill Selzer's participants had not been asked to demonstrate. There is something much too pat about the audacity of the conclusions that Szondi and the other psychologists are reported to have reached. Anyone as hideously violent as the subject was supposed to have been should have appeared in the criminal courts of Austria or Weimar Germany. Yet far from having exhibited such dangerously antisocial tendencies, Eichmann was an entirely law-abiding citizen and stable family man. But even if his emotional life had been as violent as the evaluations suggested, the tests could in no way establish a link between such aggressiveness and the virulence of the anti-Semitism that the prosecutor and others attributed to him.

The brutality of the interior life sometimes claimed for Eichmann resembles less that of the typical party functionary than of the especially violent criminal. Here a comparison might be drawn to the two main characters in Truman Capote's "nonfiction novel," *In Cold Blood*. One of them told Capote he had not intended to harm a Kansas farmer, Herbert Clutter, and his family. The killer remembered Clutter as "a very nice gentleman. I thought so right up to the moment I cut his throat."[12] Between such multiple murderers and Eichmann, some parallel perhaps can be traced in terms of the absence of any human connection, any remorse, any emotional weight to be attached to their crimes. They were frighteningly estranged from the rest of the human race. The differences, however, are also striking—even apart from the fact that the criminals in *In Cold Blood* wanted to disguise their own identities and cover their tracks, whereas totalitarian executioners seek to obliterate all trace of their victims. For Eichmann could not be plausibly regarded as a psychopathic criminal writ large, given an SS uniform and some railroad schedules and allowed to gratify his lust for blood. Had the Weimar Republic not collapsed, the lethal impulses supposedly detected in the House-Person-Tree Test almost certainly would have been suppressed. Unlike other kinds of political criminals (Macbeth, for example), Eichmann never plotted to murder any of his superiors. He thus fit successfully into a totalitarian universe noteworthy for its absence of coups d'etat. Such propriety and self-control may have been admirably devised to shield him from the awareness of his own wickedness.

In the Third Reich distance could be achieved between the executioners and their victims, between the oral command and the implementation of the Final Solution. Eichmann was a new kind of criminal, not because he could not restrain his violent impulses, but because he operated within a political system dedicated to genocide. His character and his crimes showed how magnified was the problem that Freud posed earlier: "The state has forbidden to the individual the practice of wrong-doing, not because the state desires to abolish wrong-doing, but because the state desires to monopolize it."[13] Yet in an important sense, Freud's own *Civilization and Its Discontents* did not anticipate the specific threat that totalitarianism engendered. His book stressed the irrational aggressiveness pressing so near the fragile membranes of organized society, the subterranean fury that might at any moment burst through the surface of civility. Yet the Nazi extinction policy could be so thorough and so effective in part because its agents were not rampaging cossacks but clerks scrupulous in their obedience to regulations. The "scientific" racism of the Third Reich, of which Eichmann was an instrument, proved to be far more lethal than base passions could ever have been.

This sinister aspect of normality is not hypothetically confined to totalitarian rule in Europe in the 1930s and 1940s. It would be foolish to assume that anyone would have organized the transportation of Jews to their deaths, as Eichmann did. Nevertheless, a willingness to commit abhorrent acts under cover of authority is unlikely to be limited to the fraction of the populace that is psychopathic. That was the point of the psychological experiments supervised by Stanley Milgram, in which "scientists" ordered unwitting subjects to administer shocks to ostensible participants in a learning test. Drawn from the ranks of ordinary people, almost two-thirds of the subjects were willing to inflict upon slow "learners" shocks of maximum voltage, which were supposed to be highly painful and very dangerous.

Although controversy still simmers from Milgram's interpretation of his results, he was justified in concluding that "Arendt's conception of the banality of evil comes closer to the truth than one might dare imagine. The ordinary person who shocked the victim did so out of a sense of obligation—a conception of his duties as a subject—and not from any peculiarly aggressive tendencies."[14] Those who pressed the maximum voltage felt no particular antagonism toward their victims, just as Eichmann was neither sadist nor ideologue, just as SS men became camp guards only because—for one reason or another—they were unfit for military service. Milgram applied the concept of the banality of evil more indiscriminately than Arendt would have allowed for. But his ingenious experiment suggested an empirical validation for her "catchword," and indicated how morally unlimited might be acts sanctioned by authority.

Eichmann in Jerusalem was so constructed that, in arguing that such turpitude was novel and therefore misunderstood, the author sometimes appeared to be taking the side of the defendant. In order to penetrate the void of Eichmann's personality, Arendt accepted at many strategic points his own interpretation of his conduct and motives, his own memory as well as his admissions of forgetfulness. While it is impossible to exaggerate the crimes of the Nazi regime, it is conceivable that the prosecution might have overstated the particular foulness of Eichmann's own character. Therefore, an attempt to rectify the balance in the interest of truth would necessarily make the defendant look a little better. The evidence did not always support her interpretation; Eichmann's zeal to annihilate all Hungarian Jews, for example, exceeded his actual orders. But by projecting herself into the circumstances of his life, Arendt—herself a refugee from barbarism—in no way excused his crimes or absolved him from the charge of genocide.

Though Eichmann thus was depicted as less diabolical than in the prosecutor's interpretation, the man in the glass booth became repulsive in a new way. By observing him so carefully and imaginatively, Arendt extended our knowledge of the nature of evil. Murder itself is of course ancient. It occurred as early as Genesis 4, when Cain, jealous about divine disrespect for his own offerings, "rose up against Abel his brother, and slew him." In history or in literature, few murders thereafter have been depicted as being as motiveless as Eichmann's criminality, as effective and as shallow. Evil in Milton and Goethe is demonic and represented with implacable intensity, and in Melville's Billy Budd, the jealous Claggart is gripped by an innate depravity. Unlike Shakespeare's Richard III, the former traveling salesman for the Socony Vacuum Company expressed no intention "to prove the villain." The poet Robert Lowell therefore commented, after reading *Eichmann in Jerusalem*, that he could not "think of a more terrifying character in either biography or fiction or one conceived in quite this manner."[15]

To affirm the originality of Arendt's portrait is not the same thing as accrediting her historical accuracy. Although no other explanation of his character has evoked such interest, its very cohesiveness and completeness suggest the probability of overstatement. Human history and human motive are too treacherous for any single analysis to encompass. But unless Arendt was entirely wrong, there is a sobering lesson to be drawn from her book. She refused to depict Eichmann as only the latest embodiment of the hatred that has scarred the history of the Jews. She suggested that anti-Semitism cannot adequately account for his criminality, that it was bureaucracy as well as ideology that made him dangerous. Little more than a generation ago, neither a dutiful conscience nor official conscientiousness was an obstacle to mass murder. On the contrary, such virtues facilitated genocide, making the recognition of evil more problematic than had been suspected previously. That means that a lethal destructiveness, which once befell the Jews of Europe with such finality, still must be considered a threat—to everyone.

Part II

In the Light of America

4

The Challenge of American

Jewish History

Almost two centuries after the first Sephardim arrived in North America, Henry Wadsworth Longfellow visited Newport, where the first synagogue had been erected but where the Jewish community no longer flourished. After walking through the cemetery, he was inspired to write the following lines: "How strange it seems! These Hebrews in their graves ... / But ah! What once had been shall be no more! / The groaning earth in travail and in pain / Brings forth its races, but does not restore, / And the dead nations never rise again."[1] What is also strange here is the poet's assurance. For however finite and futile the human struggle on earth may be, however abbreviated the span of even the longest civilizations has been, however difficult it is to wrest any sort of victory from the treachery of oblivion, nothing in the lines Longfellow wrote in 1852 would enhance his reputation as a prophet. Yet the assumption is an ancient one that the Jews would disappear as a distinctive people, and how such predictions have been confounded remains the largest puzzle of Jewish history.

The amazement that such religious and national continuity evokes also has been an impetus to scholarly inquiry, for the question of survival lurks beneath the specific research, the genealogies, the monographs that are so much of the texture of Jewish historiography. It is a question that lingers because it is so resistant to a satisfactory solution. Most students of the American Jewish heritage probably have been intrigued or haunted by the issue of how such a people endured. What has animated so many of the investigations these scholars have pursued may well be awe. For the Jews have sometimes succumbed to historical change, but how they have adapted to and prevailed over such pressures is bound to inspire curiosity. The ablest of their chroniclers have understood that history need not be a mortuary science but is in fact a book of life. Its annals may not allay anxiety or provide consolation for anyone. But only by knowing what we have been, historians insist, are we likely to realize what we are.

Of the ways in which the Jews have been historically depicted, two are noteworthy; if either paradigm seems unduly simplified or exaggerated, that may be because the two versions of the past are unsuitable models for a sophisticated historiography. One interpretation might be summarized as profiles in courage; the other might be called profiles in *tsuris*. The first has reflected an understandable effort by the spokesmen of an often beleaguered minority to be presented in the most favorable light, and cannot easily be distinguished from apologetics. It has consisted largely of the contributions Jews have made to host societies, whose standards and values our ancestors are alleged to have exemplified. The cast of characters has been primarily confined to the "first families," who in Eastern Europe were known as the *sheyneh layt*. This paradigm undoubtedly survives in the kinds of books many Jews once cherished as children, for it satisfies the thirst in the young to be touched by the superlative; the ages of heroism that began with Moses and Judah Maccabee have been updated to end with Jonas Salk and Mark Spitz. Yet for all its charm, such a reading of the past has been abandoned among serious scholars, for it cannot accommodate the individual complexities and moral shadings that history discloses for those who are open to its nuances.

The other paradigm is a common interpretation of the experience of the Diaspora. It was concisely stated by Ludwik Bernsztajn vel Niemirowski, who became Sir Lewis Namier. A Zionist activist, Namier once explained why he elected to devote himself to British parliamentary politics in the eighteenth century: "There is no Jewish history; there is only a Jewish martyrology."[2] Evidence enough can be marshaled in support of such a generalization. But since the sense of terrible adversity is so ingrained in the spirit of the Jewish people, the contours of this paradigm need not be elaborately traced. Its applicability is not obvious, however. One need not admire all the ingredients of the American dream, or even assert that its promise largely has been fulfilled, in order to acknowledge that martyrology has not reverberated in the Jewish memory or experience in the United States. An interpretation that stresses persecution, in a nation that has known no pogroms, is unlikely to be convincing. A paradigm that is written in terms of martyrdom, when no American Jew has been seriously impeded in his or her faith, does not address itself to the Jewish condition in America.

The kind of historical writing that is needed can neither confine itself to the re-creation of heroes and heroines, nor devote itself to lamenting the legacy of anti-Semitism. Nor should institutions such as the American Jewish Historical Society merely be service stations for those eager to disentangle their roots or to determine when their forebears arrived, however decent such impulses are. As the practice of history has shifted from how ancestors are to be praised to how problems are to be defined, the primary aim ought to be simply to tell the truth. Bravado aside, that goal is central to the historian's enterprise. The truth, which is the effort to make a representation correspond with its object, takes a daily beating in the marketplace of ideas, and is notoriously elusive; yet it is the scholar's job to establish it. Its pursuit is not made any easier in a society that—as Frances FitzGerald's recent analysis of history textbooks in secondary schools reveals—sometimes defines the truth as whatever will be widely accepted and believed. Nor is the task rendered any easier if Jewish historians yield to the natural impulse to stress what will help in the defense of minority rights, what will vindicate the Jews' own high opinion of themselves. To resist such psychological as well as social pressures calls for special gifts of poise, balance and judiciousness; it might mean working especially hard on the night shift in interpreting the unattractive facets of communal life.

The complexities of understanding and writing about this past are reminiscent of the legal controversy that ensued in Israel concerning eligibility under the Law of Return, when one member of the Knesset said that anyone crazy enough to consider himself a Jew is a Jew. For one of the nicest things about being a Jewish historian is that no certification is necessary; he or she does not have to be a professional. Far more than any other social science, history is accessible; neither its methods nor its idiom prevent amateurs from satisfying the highest standards that those with professional training have formulated. Though amateur standing as such probably confers no advantages, it has never been a disqualification for writing a competent and even elegant history. This is especially true in American Jewish historiography, in which the number of professionally trained persons always has been quite small. The work of research and dissemination often has been done by those who do other things for a living or at least were educated to do so.

Many of those untrained as historians or archivists or scholars of any sort have found a special fascination in local history. The back issues of, say, the *American Jewish Historical Quarterly* and *American Jewish Archives* emphasize the study of particular Jews in particular places—the families they belonged to and married into, the synagogues and lodges and federations they organized and headed, the neighbors they knew, the stores and businesses they established, the monuments to individual initiative and group solidarity they left behind. In some measure their world, while it cannot be recovered, at least will not be lost, thanks to the labors of those who have dedicated themselves to local history. But however valuable such research has been, much of it is not really history but a prerequisite to it. Antiquarianism cannot be a surrogate for history because the significance of episodes and events must be accounted for. Scholarship requires generalizations that have explanatory power, and it is speculative reach and the systematic impulse that amateurs usually tend to repress. Thus local history can only be intellectually satisfying when it is redeemed by the sense of a relation to larger patterns, within which urban and regional variations can be identified and understood. Unless the community records and the family diaries are pierced with questions, unless the task of the historian is seen as problematic rather than simply preservationist, the promise of local history may evaporate.

The demography of American Jewry, at least in the twentieth century, has complicated matters. With slightly less than half of all American Jews still living in Greater New York, the inclination is natural to generalize about American Jewry by reference—often covert and unconscious—to ethnic and religious life in one city. Today the second-largest concentration of Jews in the world is not in Tel Aviv, however, but in Los Angeles. And even though it is a common tendency to think of the South as a WASPs' nest (with fewer than 1 percent of the population below the Mason-Dixon line identifiable as Jews), there are enough Jews there now to have made the Southern Confederacy, had the Union armies lost, the fourth-largest Jewish community in the world. Generalizations about American Jewry may be skewed or misleading if researchers of these and other communities lack the capaciousness of spirit and precision of method to gain a hearing.

The grand possibilities of local history, perhaps only in recent years, have become apparent. Only two examples can be mentioned here. One needs no introduction, since for thirty-three weeks in 1976 it was a best seller, and won a National Book Award as well. It was, incidentally, written by someone formally untrained in history. Its range and ambition, its poignant blend of sentiment and critical refinement, its evocative power and richness of insight should not disguise the fact that, generically, *World of Our Fathers* is local history. Irving Howe's volume demonstrates that an extravagance of spirit is by no means incommensurate with the study of a particular community. And while only New York, among the cities where Jews settled, could justify such an expenditure of intellectual energy or could activate the unwinding of so thick a spool of rhetoric, it also ought to be noted that there is an elegiac aspect to Howe's achievement. It is not simply that the author chanted *kaddish* for the concentrated proletarian *Yiddishkeit* that flourished for only a couple of generations, or that no such community—poised so delicately between its Old World heritage and its New World aspirations—could last. The way in which Howe told that story is also significant, for he synthesized our knowledge of his subject without radically enlarging or amplifying it. The tableaux that comprise *World of Our Fathers* are familiar; the assaults upon our ignorance lie only in the details. It is a book that sustains with an implacable beauty, and brings to a lapidary conclusion a conventional way of writing about communal experience.

The newer form of social history is perhaps most effectively shown in Steven Hertzberg's book about Atlanta after the Civil War, *Strangers Within the Gate City*. Its author is not even an academic, though he is professionally trained; indeed, no amateur is likely to have exploited the computer so adroitly. The book's tables and charts, its advanced methods of sampling and quantification in the use of city directories and censuses are rendered with an exactness that has hitherto largely eluded the students of such communities. Hertzberg has not been afraid to violate what some historians regard as an eleventh commandment ("thou shalt not commit sociology"); therefore we know much about the occupational status, the upward mobility, the residential patterns and generational fluctuations of Atlanta Jewry, and of how it differed from Gentile neighbors.

Here too there are perhaps no major surprises. But what makes *Strangers Within the Gate City* a model of its kind of urban history is the closeness with which the author has followed the Atlantans into their homes and houses of worship, into their places of business and into the voting booth. He has observed some of their interactions with other whites and with blacks. As with Oscar Handlin's pioneering study of the Irish, *Boston's Immigrants* (1941), one feels that, in some satisfying sense, the author has come to know the people he has subjected to investigation. Handlin's dissertation had been subtitled "a study in acculturation," reflecting an interest in how ethnic groups successfully adapted to the general contours of American society. (The Irish captured city hall shortly after 1880, when Handlin's account stops.) Yet Hertzberg's dissertation is as much a saga of perseverance as a testament to acculturation, and since it ends with the lynching of Leo Frank, *Strangers Within the Gate City* may seem to suggest a more chastened view of the American dream. The book subtly alters our perception of the most shameful anti-Semitic incident in American history, however, by placing it within the context of the experience of Atlanta Jewry. For other white Atlantans were hardly inhospitable to Jewish settlers, and the city was by no means parsimonious in the opportunities it afforded. The frame-up and murder of Frank were truly an aberration; and a year after the lynching, another Jew was elected president of the city's Chamber of Commerce.[3]

Hertzberg's is the kind of social history that students of Jewish communities increasingly are expected to write, and he at least has avoided the temptation to seek safety in numbers. Given the shagginess with which historical records are often kept, given the authority that our society invests in precision of measurement, it is all too easy to find explanation and legitimacy in the deceptive certainty of numbers, at the expense of human meaning and value. Other branches of American historiography already have suffered from such overconfidence, and perhaps Jewish historians should need no special warning. In the 1920s, when President Lawrence

Lowell attempted to restrict Jewish admission to Harvard, he claimed that 50 percent of all the students caught stealing books from Widener Library the previous year had been Jews. When a distinguished alumnus then asked Lowell exactly how many undergraduates had in fact been caught, the president replied, "Two."[4] While such deliberate manipulation of evidence may be rare, skepticism remains one of the habits we cannot afford to suspend. Scholars who once were able to embellish weak arguments with Latin phrases may now seek refuge in multiple regression. Though "softer" data can be abused too, the apparent conclusiveness and finality of figures impose a special sensitivity. Wherever possible, therefore, numerical results need to be weighed against and corroborated with traditional historical evidence.

Apart from "cliometrics" or quantitative history, the most noteworthy of the methods that are helping to reshape our sense of the American Jewish past is oral history. Until fairly recently its use largely was confined to the reminiscences of the famous and the important—often those who, for whatever reason, chose not to write memoirs and autobiographies. The interviewers who practice oral history not only have refined their techniques but also have broadened their scope, so that historians now are no longer content to round up the usual suspects. Historical writing now does not unduly chronicle the impact of elites; it embraces everybody. The tape recorder makes available what otherwise would be unknown or neglected. It permits the silent ones to speak, all those mute inglorious Miltons and Jakes and Ethels; and that is a marvelous fulfillment of the democratic promise. Yet there is a paradox here. While future historians—and their readers—will be obliged to become able to think quantitatively, the definition of the craft has been widened to incorporate those who, for all practical purposes, had been insufficiently literate. Sophistication of technique has come to coincide with egalitarianism in the use of sources.

There are also dangers of overconfidence in the reliance on oral history as well. Perhaps no facet of what historians do—short of finding a cache of Lincoln letters—can be more exhilarating than interviewing citizens in their anecdotage. In listening to their stories, many of which may even be true, the enthralled oral historian may allow powers of discrimination to atrophy, may forget the necessity to distill other kinds of evidence. And the results of such interviews

still must be evaluated and embedded within a framework of interpretation, which alone can attach significance and resonance to the
particular and the concrete.

Such methods nevertheless are confirming as well as altering
our comprehension of what it has meant to be Jewish in America.
For example, upward mobility, or "making it," long has intrigued
those who have probed that meaning; and the enormous popularity
of *Our Crowd* (1967), written by a novelist-turned-historian, Stephen Birmingham, suggests how widely that interest has been shared.
The hunger for success has been so emphatic in American Jewish
life that when the son of Sol Chaikin, the president of the International Ladies Garment Workers Union, became a dress manu-
facturer himself, no shame apparently befell the family, though
Chaikin *père* presumably has devoted his life to struggling against
such employers. Adherence to the American ideal of success can be
explored in several ways. Eli Evans, another gifted amateur, relied
heavily on oral history for his "personal history" of Southern Jewry,
The Provincials, a tale that concludes on a bittersweet note. "The
drama of Jews in the South," Evans has written, "revolves around
the fathers who built their businesses for the sons who didn't want
them."[5] It is unlikely that the effects on such families could be
calibrated without the practice of interviewing possible survivors of
such house-to-house fighting.

In recent years historians more often have resorted to the digital
computer to chart the generational patterns of occupational advance
and retreat. What have been especially illuminating are comparisons
with other immigrants. The capital that the early generations of
Irish managed to accumulate tended to go into housing rather than
into schooling, which is what the Jews saved for; and the insistence
that Italian children go to work as early as possible apparently served
as an impediment to that group's upward mobility. One of the most
famous monographs in recent American Jewish historiography,
Thomas Kessner's *The Golden Door* (1977), ratifies with statistics
what has long been observed. The reasons for spectacular Jewish
achievement are not agreed upon, however; and since cultural values
surely raised the trajectory of Jewish mobility, numerical formulations can go only so far. Social historians have generally endorsed,
or at least have been uncritical of, the ascent from rags to respectability, if not to riches. Yet with roughly equal consistency, novelists

and dramatists of Jewish origin have been almost painfully aware of the price of success. In plays from Clifford Odets's *Golden Boy* to Arthur Miller's *Death of a Salesman* and *The Price* to Dick Goldberg's *Family Business*, in novels from Abraham Cahan's *The Rise of David Levinsky* to Nathanael West's *A Cool Million*, Budd Schulberg's *What Makes Sammy Run?*, Mordecai Richler's *The Apprenticeship of Duddy Kravitz*, and down to Joseph Heller's *Good as Gold*, the American dream of material success is seen as tarnished with disastrous moral and social consequences. The larger the bank account and the longer the résumé, the more doomed the soul. This discrepancy between literary sources and sociological formulations can hardly be resolved here, but it should be added that someone whose reading would be confined only to American Jewish social history would be barely aware that such disquietude exists. Moreover, the consistency of the historical evidence means that a particular urban environment has not been important, suggesting a certain explanatory limitation to social history.

No scholar engaged in such social history, in the interplay of family and generations, in the definition of status and the pursuit of self-fulfillment, can be unaffected by women's history. Of all the forces that are impinging upon the reorientation of American Jewish historiography, heightened curiosity about women offers the greatest promise of a radical reinterpretation of our past, of special annexations of historical insight. Nowhere is the necessity of breadth of interest more apparent. The point need not be belabored that the vast bulk of historical writing has been about men, almost entirely in their public activities. As a result, an important dimension of the past—including the American Jewish past—has been overshadowed. The democratic impulse that animates oral history is especially pertinent here, since women have so sporadically and uncommonly entered the public arena on which so much historical research has centered. History should include her story too, and it is by now a commonplace of criticism that the world of our fathers had mothers in it too.

In the scholarly restitution that is now occurring, in the more synoptic vision that women's history invites everyone to share, it is possible that the historian of Jewish women has an easier assignment than the historian of other ethnic groups. For Jewish women have sometimes transcended the limitations that have ordinarily characterized the female condition, the cult of domesticity and the ethos of submissiveness. Not all of the Jewish past is private and inconspicuous. Before Purim several years ago, a placard was posted in the student center at Brandeis University by a feminist organization seeking to expand its membership. The sign announced: "Esther liberated her people—but did she also liberate herself?" While no answer was provided, Jewish women have not been entirely absent from the public scene, even though none has enjoyed Esther's opportunity to affect so decisively the destiny of a people. Other examples could nevertheless be cited. The first famous case in the history of psychoanalysis, "Anna O.," was in fact Bertha Pappenheim, who not only freed herself (with her therapist's help) from her own private anguish; she also became an early feminist and the founder of the first German Jewish women's social work organization. And a clever feminist poster of several years ago might be recalled, a photographic blowup of the former Golda Meyerson of Milwaukee, later of the Knesset. Its caption—"But can she type?"—sabotaged not only the myth of male supremacy but also conveyed the impact upon Jewish life such women have exerted. Hadassah, for instance, is the largest volunteer women's organization in the United States, period.[6]

Nor have Jewish women been inconspicuous outside organized Jewish life, although more of a scholarly effort should be made to incorporate them within an interpretation of the American Jewish experience. More directly as exploited workers than as Jewish women, some acted with resplendent valor in the first third of the century in defense of the rights of labor. In the early twentieth century, probably no one in public life displayed a more impressive gallantry and integrity than Emma Goldman. In the careers of several social workers, politicians, pacifists, and attorneys, allegiance to the ideals of social justice has been readily observable.

Women's history is likely to make its most innovative impact, however, in the private sphere; the lives that have been led in introspection, or as daughters, sisters, wives, and mothers, need to be comprehended. The vicissitudes of private life, of family relationships, and of the struggle for female independence in the last couple of decades could to some degree be charted in the writings of three Jewish women from the Midwest. As the author of *The*

Feminine Mystique (1963) and its sequels and as a founder of the National Organization for Women, Betty Goldstein Friedan of Peoria has done as much as anyone to alter the cultural and social climate within which women think of themselves and which affect their relations with men. Yet changes in the last twenty years also could be measured in the advice columns of the twin daughters of Abraham and Rebecca Friedman of Sioux City, Iowa, who as "Dear Abby" Van Buren and as Ann Landers have exerted an influence on the mores of Middle America as great as was the impact of the *bintel brief* on the promised city. The special contribution of women's history may be to achieve a more effective integration of the private and the public. A revised historiography therefore would rectify the present imbalance by indicating how, in studying the experience of American Jewry, the private realm has helped to shape public discourse even as larger institutions and forces have affected the Jewish family and personality.

The field least susceptible to these changes is political history, in which traditional approaches—if not conclusions—have sufficed. Virtually all historical analysts have broadly confirmed the popular stereotype about the leftist predisposition of Jews. While most American Jews never became radicals or even underwent political disenchantment with the American dream, a high proportion of American radicals have been Jews. One of the many moving passages in Whittaker Chambers's autobiography is his recollection of his first Communist Party meeting in 1925, in which the mother of the pamphleteer Benjamin Gitlow wailed: "Cumreds!" she pleaded, "the potato crop has failed in Ireland and thousands of peasants are starving to death. Cumreds! What are we doing to help the starving workers and peasants of Ireland?" To Chambers, "Mother" Gitlow "was Communism in action. That short, squat, belligerent woman, pleading in a thick Yiddish accent for food for hungry Irish peasants, personified the brotherhood of all the wretched of the earth."[7] It was a vision that seared some Jews everywhere. In an era in which the wages of workers were so pitifully low, the attraction of socialism, communism and anarchism was understandable. But even after Jews advanced into the middle class and often into its upper reaches, a leftist sympathy for the downtrodden—usually in the form of liberalism—persisted. The relationship between Jewishness and leftism did not, however, become subject to full historical inquiry until 1979, and even the author of *Jews and the Left*, Arthur Liebman, is not a historian but a sociologist.

If the field of diplomatic history remains a lively one, it is in part because of a book published in 1968, *While Six Million Died*, by a television journalist, Arthur D. Morse. His book pierced through the nimbus of sanctity that had surrounded the reputation of Franklin D. Roosevelt and ignited much scholarly research into American policy toward Nazi Germany, toward the refugees seeking to escape its terror, and perhaps even toward the policies of Roosevelt's successors toward the state of Israel. Academic historians such as David Wyman, Henry Feingold and Saul Friedman reached such similar conclusions about Roosevelt's indifference toward the refugees that his administration's reputation for humanitarianism has not recovered, and it is not foreseeable how it could be entirely salvaged.[8] Another result of the recent work in diplomatic history has been to raise sobering questions about the caliber of communal leadership. If social historians have felt free to trace the patterns by which private wealth has been accumulated, even at the risk of reinforcing stereotypes about the Jews, then political historians have allowed themselves fewer inhibitions than in the past in examining the nature of Jewish leadership. They have wondered whether, while catastrophe was enveloping the communities of Europe, the spokesmen for American Jewry could not have been more vertebrate and responsive, and whether a unified policy could not have been more efficiently formulated.

That such historical issues are so salient is, in itself, a kind of tribute to the tolerance Jews generally have experienced in America. The controversies that erupt in Jewish public life, the demands that Jewish leaders have made on elected officials, usually have been associated with the defense of foreign brethren precisely because American anti-Semitism has been so temperate. Even Longfellow, in "The Jewish Cemetery at Newport," wrote indignantly of the "merciless and blind" "burst of Christian hate" that brought such agony and death upon Jews elsewhere in the Diaspora. In this respect comparisons are important—not an abstract ideal of human fraternity. The historical malevolence of American society toward blacks and Indians need not be underscored, for members of minorities have observed too often that the Statue of Liberty has had

her back to them. Moreover, compared with other industrial societies, our country has been off the chart in the extent of its individual and mob violence; according to American folk wisdom, "a
Smith & Wesson beats four aces." Yet violence against Jews has
been remarkably rare in American history. Anti-Semitism here has
been mild or muted, and its relative absence is what needs to be
noted. For the historian as detective, it is the dog that did not bark.

Of course, there has been social discrimination. Eddie Jacobson, for example, had served with Captain Harry Truman in the
First World War and then became his partner in an unprofitable
haberdashery in Kansas City. Yet Jacobson's widow later recalled
that "the Trumans never had us at their house. [Bess Truman's
family,] the Wallaces[,] were aristocracy in these parts; and under
the circumstances the Trumans couldn't afford to have Jews at their
house." Such remarks (extracted by an oral historian) are unsettling
in the light of modern European experience, for there the process
that began when emancipated Jews were considered unfit to enter
the salons ended with the political decision that all Jews were unfit
to inhabit the earth. Yet Truman, who could not entertain Jews in
his living room in Missouri, met with Jacobson in the White House
during a desperate moment in the diplomatic struggle over the U.N.
partition plan in the spring of 1948. And Jacobson, concocting a
farfetched historical parallel between Andrew Jackson and Chaim
Weizmann, managed to persuade the reluctant president to meet
with the Zionist leader—thus accelerating the drive toward state-
hood and recognition.[9] It was one of those bizarre and unpredictable
episodes that punctuate the history of nations, and which may make
its students wonder about the suitability of the computer to aid
them in their work.

Which gets us to the most curious omission in the writing of
American Jewish history. I refer to a field of research that until
1982 was almost never reflected in the pages of *American Jewish
History*. It is an area that has been unjustly ignored and to which
scholarly attention should be drawn. It is a splendid source of evidence and historical material, and its subject matter is entirely compatible with the effort to make history accessible to the nonacademic
and nonprofessional community. It is usually termed popular culture, or the popular arts, but what it really means is the study of
how the Jews have been represented to themselves, and to others.

Consider, for instance, the case of Israel Zangwill's play *The Melting-Pot*, which was first staged in 1908. At its opening night in Washington, D.C., President Theodore Roosevelt shouted from his box, "That's a great play, Mr. Zangwill!" For many years thereafter, in many cities in the United States and also in London, enthusiastic audiences agreed. It entered school textbooks and, because of it, a phrase graced the American language. It is in part a love story, in which the persistence of Old World antagonism keeps apart a Russian-born Jew named David Quixano and a Russian-born Christian named Vera Revendal. (Her father, a czarist colonel, had murdered David's relatives in the Kishinev pogrom of 1903.) Togetherness triumphs at the end, after David's spectacular new symphony on the American dream has just been performed. The sun sets on the Statue of Liberty in the background and, before the curtain slowly falls, the lovers exult in their predictions that the diverse peoples and races that have immigrated to America will "all unite to build the Republic of Man and the Kingdom of God."

Such sentiments ricocheted with such impact because they reinforced the expectations of earlier Americans, not only Zangwill's contemporaries. In the first secular meditation upon American identity, the French farmer Hector St. John de Crèvecoeur described the new man, the American, as an amalgamation of several Caucasian nationalities. Oddly enough, almost three-quarters of the white immigrants and their descendants living in America in 1782 had come from Britain. But Crèvecoeur found himself in relatively heterogeneous New York and therefore might be forgiven for his error, since he communicated an openness to pluralism that was to become magnified in later centuries. Ralph Waldo Emerson almost coined the phrase "melting pot" himself; and it is fitting that the first Jew he ever met was Emma Lazarus, whose poem welcoming the oppressed is of course at the base of the statue in the backdrop of Zangwill's play. The dramatist himself is a study in ambiguities. A celebrant of the New World and of its possibilities of brotherhood, he was born and died in England. He seemed to be a militant assimilationist, forsaking Judaism and marrying a Christian and forbidding the circumcision of their eldest son. Yet he was also a Zionist with an unflagging sense of allegiance to the Jewish people. He nevertheless concluded that Palestine itself need not be the national home for oppressed Jews; British East Africa, he thought for a while, would do. The extraordinary tensions Zangwill embodied were reflected in *The Melting-Pot* itself, and scholars like Neil Larry Shumsky and Arthur Mann recently have attempted to sort out those tensions and to explain the ambivalence that riddles the play. For the piece itself does not in fact make a forthright case for assimilation, and can support the view that ethnic loyalties and traditions are worth honoring and preserving.[10]

If Zangwill and his play seem confused, the impact of *The Melting-Pot* may be explained by the amorphousness of the society that accepted its message so eagerly. Although the United States, unlike most Western nations, was created on the basis of explicit principles embodied in documents, Americans themselves have tended to be casual about dogmas and ideologies; therefore, hatreds sometimes have a way of sputtering out. In a society in which factions of the Ku Klux Klan now admit Catholics as members, in which the Black Muslims now accept whites (formerly "blue-eyed devils") into their sect, in which the leader of the Nazis who sought to march in Skokie, Illinois, is himself the son of a Jew who had spent several months in Dachau, one can doubt whether the bigots take their doctrines as seriously as they take their press releases. The formlessness, the openness, the latitudinarianism of American life have ensured a setting in which almost anything is possible.

Here ascription has counted for little, and ancestry could be concealed or forgotten. Writing in 1783 to his relatives, Haym Solomon warned them: "Your *yichus* is worth very little here."[11] In America a Jew could do virtually anything, be almost anyone. Judah Touro could help erect the Bunker Hill Monument, and the Levy family could restore Monticello, and Emma Lazarus could define the meaning of "the Mother of Exiles." National sanctums have not been off limits to Jews, nor has Christianity itself. If Stephen Schwartz could write a popular musical (*Godspell*) based on the Gospel according to St. Matthew, if Leonard Bernstein could compose *Mass*, if Irving Berlin could not only dream of a "White Christmas" but march in the "Easter Parade," no wonder Irving Berlin also could ask so happily that "God Bless America." In twentieth-century fiction the supremely American character changes his name from James Gatz; being isolate, mysterious, rich, and something of an outlaw, he springs from "his Platonic conception of himself." Today Jay Gatsby's mythic equivalent may be, like his creator, a

Minnesotan, Bob Dylan (born Robert Zimmerman), whose identity has been even more protean—folk song populist, remotest of rock stars, phantom of the Opry, anything. Adjusting his yarmulke at the Western Wall one year, then claiming to have found Jesus, Dylan never has broken stride, for he seems to know instinctively that here it is possible to be a white Negro, a non-Jewish Jew, a Jew for Jesus, even an observant Jew. Or take the case of Allen Ginsberg. "Buddhist Jewish pantheist" is how he once described his own religious convictions; and the poet himself—the son of a Communist whom he lovingly memorialized in "Kaddish," the smiling subject of a popular "underground" poster of the 1960s in his Uncle Sam hat and suit—has come to embody many of the paradoxes of American Jewish identity. Ginsberg's life has even strangely reproduced art, for his most permanent and publicized relationship has been with Peter Orlovsky, the son of a White Russian cavalry officer, thus mirroring the theme of *The Melting-Pot* itself.[12] *Oib men lebt lang genug, vet men alles derleben* (if you live long enough, you'll live to see everything).

Scholarly papers should continue to examine the rabbinic experience, the cantorial experience, the evolution of synagogues and denominations, the character of worship. Yet it is also helpful to remember that a decisive minority of American Jews never has affiliated with congregations, and it is reliably reported that many of those who have joined congregations are not pious. Many Jews have been more committed to supporting religious liberty than to using it. For better or for worse, the story of the American Jew is also the story of how Max Aronson of Little Rock became Gilbert M. Anderson and finally Bronco Billy, the first of the cowboy movie stars. It is also the story of how new standards of female eroticism were established when Theodosia Goodman, the daughter of a Cincinnati tailor, became Theda Bara, which is an anagram of "Arab death."[13] It is also the saga of how Jules Garfinkle became John Garfield and how Bernie Schwartz became Tony Curtis and how Michael Goldbogen became Mike Todd. The historian of Israeli identity cannot ignore the process by which the son of Itzhak and Sara Persky of Poland transformed himself into a minister of defense and parliamentarian named Shimon Peres. But the career of Peres's cousin Betty Persky should also be deciphered; she transformed herself into Lauren Bacall. More recently the story should include

Barbra Streisand, showing that a nose with deviations isn't such a crime against the nation, and concluding that for herself as well cartilage is fate. It is also the story of why George Segal and Dustin Hoffman and Art Garfunkel kept their names as well.

This would make a fascinating study in acculturation and ethnic persistence, in which visions of ourselves became an inextricable part of the movies, the most distinctively twentieth-century art. Through those ribbons of dreams we Americans have confronted ourselves more fully than in any other medium, and thus we have presented ourselves to a curious and often captivated world. Sometimes the Jewish presence could be discerned on the screen; and while the lineage could be traced from *The Jazz Singer* to Alvy Singer (the lover of Annie Hall), that did not happen frequently. It has been far more common for the Jews of Hollywood to imagine what the Gentile world has wanted to see of itself. The implications have been perhaps best expressed by John Updike's eponymous Henry Bech, a novelist whose "own writing had sought to reach out from the ghetto of his heart toward the wider expanses across the Hudson; the artistic triumph of American Jewry lay, he thought, not in the novels of the fifties but in the movies of the thirties, those gargantuan, crass contraptions whereby Jewish brains projected Gentile stars upon a Gentile nation and out of their own immigrant joy gave a formless land dreams and even a kind of conscience . . . To Bech, it was one of history's great love stories, the mutually profitable romance between Jewish Hollywood and bohunk America, conducted almost entirely in the dark, a tapping of fervent messages through the wall of the San Gabriel Range; and his favorite Jewish writer was the one [Daniel Fuchs] who had turned his back on his three beautiful Brooklyn novels and went into the desert to write scripts for Doris Day . . . "[14]

This transaction in the dark has had its equivalents in other popular arts as well. Zangwill's David Quixano believed that the new American he envisioned would be, in his words, a "superman." It was left for two other New Yorkers, Joe Shuster and Jerome Siegel, to invent Superman (1938-   ) himself. He was urban, unlike other kinds of folk heroes such as the Yankee, the frontiersman, or the lumberjack; and, according to Leslie Fiedler, he was an idealized version of the goy. A certain phase in the history of popular culture culminated with the poster after the Six-Day War in 1967, showing a Hasid emerging from a telephone booth. Underneath the traditional garb was worn a jersey with the letter *shin* on it, proving that he was not merely a walker in the city. But since the dawn of the century, after a rabbi's son named Ehrich Weiss made himself into Houdini, truly a name to conjure with, the scourge of spiritualists as well as the victor over every physical obstacle, it has been tempting for us to speculate that Superman was really Jewish all along. How the artifacts of popular culture are converted into the facts of scholarly argument has been the province of only a few literary critics and sociologists, but more historians should interest themselves in this subject as well.[15]

Even when some Jews grew up to become writers and intellectuals, the pervasiveness of the common life and its legends and myths could not be escaped entirely. For Jewish writers arrived in the higher strata of culture a couple of generations after their equivalents had become conspicuous in mass entertainment, and therefore to write about Jews or about America meant coming to terms with vaudeville and Broadway and radio, and with the borscht belt. (You don't have to be Jewish to be funny, but today 80 percent of all professional comedians are from an ethnic group that is less than 3 percent of the general population.) The serious Jewish writer staking out a claim in the imagination of America therefore is the legatee not only of the working-class radicalism of the ghetto but of the vulgar Marxism of Groucho and his brothers, a kinsman not only of Kafka's Joseph K. but of the Catskills' Danny Kaye as well. Before there was a Richard Tucker, there was a Sophie Tucker. Even the vaudeville team of Weber and Fields affected the formulation of an urban aesthetic in which the photographer Alfred Stieglitz pioneered.[16]

When scholarly space and time are short, it may be necessary to think in terms of metaphor rather than measurement, in terms of symbols rather than statistics. The black experience in modern America, the ordeal of Afro-American identity, could be told in shorthand through the career of Ray Charles. Born in abysmal Georgian poverty, blinded by an illness at the age of six, orphaned at the age of fifteen, Charles stayed in school long enough to learn Braille before he became a musician. An invisible man for whom the outside world also was hidden, he became a narcotics addict at the age of sixteen, and was locked into a life of private pain, social segregation, and grinding poverty to which his bent blue notes provided the only clue. Awful as his life was, Charles refused to surrender. When he wanted to leave the Deep South, he asked someone to place his finger on a map at the farthest spot away that was still within the borders of the United States—for he was still an American, a native son. The spot was Seattle (where his career really began).[17]

The popular arts can illuminate what it has meant to be Jewish as well. Michael Igor Peschkowsky was born in Berlin in 1931, a year after Ray Charles. His father was a physician who had fled from Russia after the Bolshevik Revolution, and his grandmother had provided Richard Strauss with the libretto for his opera *Salome*. His grandfather had been Gustav Landauer, a theoretician who sought to combine socialism with anarchism, and a leader of the Bavarian Communist government in Munich (1918–19), whom White Guard reactionaries assassinated. Michael Igor Peschkowsky came to the United States in 1939, a seven-year-old who knew only two English sentences: "I do not speak English" and "Please do not kiss me." He later became a pre-med student at the University of Chicago, intending to become a psychiatrist, before he switched to the theater. As Mike Nichols, he has displayed a deftness of comic observation, a satiric bite, an urbanity, and a quickness that many Jews claim to find familiar.[18]

Whereas Ray Charles's music, with its plangent blend of rhythm and blues and its twang of country and western, can only have originated in the United States, many Jewish artists and entertainers have drawn—at least implicitly—from more cosmopolitan sources. The Jews are an integral part of the nation of immigrants—so much so that, late in the Eisenhower era, when the first exchange of classical musicians between the United States and the Soviet Union was arranged, Isaac Stern explained what it entailed: "They send us their Jews from Odessa, and we send them *our* Jews from Odessa." The American pattern therefore corresponds with certain aspects of Jewish history elsewhere in the Diaspora, but it has a distinctiveness and a fascination all its own; scholars must catch the American accent in which the nation's Jews have narrated their lives. That story is not entirely one of triumph and survival, and it is touched with poignancy. But the regret that Yiddish is almost entirely lost may be cushioned by the reminder that Philo, who wrote only in

Greek, and Maimonides, whose *Guide to the Perplexed* was in Arabic, did not know Yiddish either. They were not thereby prevented from enriching the life of the Jewish people, and perhaps Americans can find some comfort in that. For the Zionist, it is painful that so few have made *aliyah*. Yet in an era in which about 350,000 Israelis (half of whom are *sabras*) currently prefer to reside in this country,[19] Jews who try to fathom their experience here have no reason to be defensive.

However, there is every reason to be serious about the historian's task. Either the past can be infused with dramatic meaning and enlivened with a sense of the grandeur and mysterious destiny of the Jewish people, or we might as well call it sleep. For it is possible to imagine more congenial responsibilities than studying American Jewry. It would probably be more pleasant, say, to write a restaurant column for a daily newspaper in San Francisco; and the suspicion lingers that it is probably more lucrative to pursue other callings, like repairing faucets. The larger society is more concerned about whether our pipes hold any water than whether our theories do. But that priority need not rob the vocation of the American Jewish historian of all honor. Just as the unexamined life is not worth living, so too the unexamined past diminishes the conditions of life. The Jewish patrimony therefore must be faced not only with amazement at its signs of continuity and plenitude, but also with breadth of curiosity and fidelity to the ideals of critical scholarship. For a heritage that one refuses to squander might even mean a future that will not be forfeited.

5

The Legacy of Radicalism

Any exploration of the radical roots of American Jews necessarily begins with an appeal to the historical record, perhaps at the moment when modern European society eroded the walls of the ghetto. For the sake of convenience, that moment can be dated as 1743, when the rationalist philosopher Moses Mendelssohn entered Berlin at the Jews' Gate. The guards' log book fails to emphasize the auspiciousness of the episode, noting only that "today there passed through . . . [the gate] six oxen, seven pigs, one Jew."[1] Since then the civil societies of the West have had to define the place of a peculiar minority in their midst, and individuals beginning with Mendelssohn have been required to choose between the particular and the universal, between religion and secularism, between ethnic and tribal loyalties and national and cosmopolitan allegiances. Some civil orders, most importantly the United States, never bothered to distinguish Jews from other religious groups or to endow ethnicity with corporate status; and many of their brethren, especially in Eastern Europe, emerged slowly if at all from their ethnic enclaves. But after many centuries of exile as outcasts, the Jews were on occasion to become a searing political problem, and were themselves to be confronted with unprecedented political choices and opportunities.

The historical meaning of the radical option, and the evidence that can be elicited to document and amplify it, are large enough to make compression a painful necessity. One form of excision is the omission of the lives of the ordinary, since most historians operate on the star system. This chapter is in that tradition. But adequate generalization about the radical proclivities of the nation's Jews ultimately must draw on the experience of the unexceptional, who need not be neglected. And indeed, in such memoirs as Robert Warshow's portrait of his father, "An Old Man Gone" (1951), in such novels as E. L. Doctorow's *The Book of Daniel* (1971), in such oral histories as Vivian Gornick's *Romance of American Communism* (1977), and in such journalistic re-creations as "Susie," who went from Berkeley's AEPhi House to antiwar activism and radical feminism in Sara Davidson's *Loose Change*, such figures happily have escaped the doom of oblivion.

But any specific treatment of the relationship of the Jews to radicalism can begin plausibly with Karl Marx, whose version of socialism was to define it in every inhabited continent for more than a century. Although he died only a century ago, probably no other individual—apart from the founders of the great religions, millennia ago—exerts so decisive an influence on the planet. And it is also one of the many ironies that colors this topic that the Jewish people often have been stigmatized for begetting him, even though Marx was baptized a Lutheran and matured without the benefit of any Judaic learning. He was nevertheless the descendant, on both his father's and mother's sides of the family, of many generations of rabbis, including the famed Meir Katzenellenbogen of sixteenth-century Padua. Heinrich Marx was baptized shortly before his son's birth in 1818, and six years later Karl formally became a Christian.

In later years he felt free to stoop to bigotry, often compounding it, as in his description of Ferdinand Lassalle, the founder of German social democracy and his rival, as a "Jewish nigger." But Marx also attempted, on one occasion, to render his anti-Semitic views in abstract form. In a tract entitled *Zur Judenfrage*, he defined the Jews solely as an economic entity whose "worldly god" was money. Writing in 1844, Marx condemned the Jews for assuming (under duress) the exclusive status of capitalists, and he urged their disappearance in the wake of proletarian revolution. Yet in the U.S.S.R., in the first nation to undergo a successful proletarian revolution and to profess to be guided by Marx's doctrines, the most prized consumer item was invented and still is sold by Jewish capitalists—the Levi Strauss family of California. More pertinent, however, to any account of the ordeal of Jewish radicalism has been Marx's vision of a world without Jews, for his patrimony was a dream of universal human solidarity, undivided by class or race or religion or ethnicity or nationality. By precept and example he encouraged the sense that the Jews should renounce not only their commercialism but also their particularism—and could go first toward such a utopia. This was the invitation that was to attract the generations of Jews who were to succeed Marx in honoring the socialist impulse.

By the age of twenty-three, Marx already had been hailed as "the greatest, perhaps the only, genuine philosopher now alive, who will soon ... attract the eyes of all Germany."[2] The prescient and perceptive author of these remarks was Moses Hess, who made Bakunin and Engels into communists too. Hess was also the first important socialist to attempt to reconcile his radicalism with his Jewish identity; his book *Rome and Jerusalem* (1862) was an early Zionist classic. Certainly others besides Hess believed that Jewish allegiances did not have to be jettisoned for the sake of a classless society, and indeed accepted John Calvin's description of utopia as "a foolish fantasy the Jews had"[3]—although Calvin's value judgment was reversed. The persistence of the Labor Zionist movement, now virtually a century old, has testified to the appeal of blending socialist ideals with a commitment to the land of Israel, and in the kibbutzim such an amalgamation was made operational. The impact of the bund on the Eastern European masses need not be chronicled here. But it should be noted that it did not die from within. This valiant organization was among the victims of totalitarianism, symbolized by the fate of its two Polish tribunes, Viktor Alter and Henryk Ehrlich, who fled from the German invaders in 1939, only to be executed as independent socialists in Moscow.

These were among the efforts to reduce the friction between socialism and particularism. But it was more common, at least among the leaders and theoreticians of the left, to submerge Jewish identity in a generalized movement to emancipate the working class and to enlighten humanity. In the writings of some radicals, such displacement is easy to discern, as the burdens of parochialism are abandoned for the sake of wider fraternal feelings. When the fifteen-year-old Lassalle writes, "Oh, when I yield to my childish dreams, it has always been my favorite idea to see myself, sword in hand, leading the Jews to make them independent," it is easy to trace his substitution, as a revolutionist, of the proletariat for "the chosen people"—the title of Harold Laski's first, unpublished book. Written at the age of nineteen by the future chairman of the British Labour Party, the manuscript depicts the Jew as always desiring, "because he has been so separated from his fellow-men, to declare himself one of them . . ."⁴ Judaism itself, which promised a Messiah to redeem not only its own adherents but also all humanity, seemed to ratify such a transcendence of alienation.

A few radical Jews went to remarkable lengths to distance themselves from whatever smacked of the plight of the pariah. Rosa Luxemburg threw herself so energetically into the shaping of three Communist parties—in Russia, Poland and Germany—that she wrote in exasperation to a correspondent in 1917: "Why do you come to me with your special Jewish sorrows? I cannot find a special corner in my heart for the ghetto. I feel at home in the entire world."⁵ But the world did not reciprocate, and Luxemburg's compassion and concern went unrequited. Not only did she lose the struggle within bolshevism to defend some measure of democratic process, she also was among the first to be murdered by the German fascists who eventually left no Jew alive in her own village of Zamosc, one of the countless Jewish communities that neither socialism nor cosmopolitanism had managed to save from destruction. An extreme of another dimension was achieved by the French socialist Simone Weil, author of a poignant account of French factory life, *La condition ouvrière* (1937). In contrast to the Jewish historical record of a facility for survival, Weil exalted self-sacrifice, and once proclaimed: "Whenever I think of the crucifixion . . . I commit the sin of envy."⁶

Throughout Western Europe many Jews were seeking earthly forms of salvation; and they often rose to prominence in radical movements, perhaps spurred by whatever echoes they heard of prophetic demands or of messianic cries. No historian of German socialism can ignore the legacy of Eduard Bernstein, champion of revisionism and gradualism; he anticipated much of the course of socialism in Western Europe itself. Intellectuals such as Kurt Eisner and Gustav Landauer became activists, and their efforts to establish Soviet republics after the First World War were crushed brutally. The neo-Marxism of the Frankfurt School for Social Research has become the lingua franca of much intellectual discourse; the school's major and minor figures were, almost without exception, Jewish by birth. After Jean Jaurès himself, the dominant figure in twentieth-century French socialism was Léon Blum, a Third Republic prime minister who, for all the keenness of his intelligence and the grace of his personality, could neither control the forces of aggression in Spain and Germany nor undermine defeatism at home. The acknowledged leader of the French student revolt of 1968 was Daniel Cohn-Bendit, and it should not have come as a surprise that one of the four Communists inserted into Mitterand's Socialist cabinet is a Jew, Charles Fiterman, the Polish-born minister of transportation.

But the immediate antecedents of Jewish radicalism in the United States were located in Russia, where Marxism attracted the inhabitants of the Pale of Settlement in a way that the earlier populism of the Narodniki never could. As Professor Arthur Liebman has explained, Marxist "emphasis on cities and workers as opposed to rural areas and peasants struck a responsive chord in young men whose roots had been cut off from the soil ... [Marxism] also did not attribute near mystical appeal to sections of the Russian population or their particular institutions," since the ideology claimed to be scientific and rational.[7] But its aura of idealism also seemed to resound from at least part of the enduring heritage of the Jewish people, and the result was a disproportionate contribution to the leadership of the Marxist factions in Russia. Early Bolsheviks such as Pavel Axelrod, Menshevik heroes such as Julius Martov, Theodor Dan, and Raphael Abramovitch, and Bolshevik leaders such as Lev Kamenev, Grigory Zinoviev, Karl Radek and Mikhail Borodin—the Comintern's representative in China—can only be mentioned here.

But especially striking was the role of Lev Davidovich Bronstein, who adopted his jailer's name of Trotsky and, already at the age of twenty-five, was a demiurge of the revolution of 1905. Joining the Bolsheviks two months before the October revolution of 1917, Trotsky undoubtedly was the most talented Jew ever to enlist in the modern socialist movement. The chairman of the American Red Cross Commission to Russia, Colonel Raymond Robins, called him "a four-kind son-of-a-bitch, but the greatest Jew since Jesus Christ."[8] That was puffery. But the force of Trotsky's personality, the brilliance of his mind and the sweep of his eloquence were quite overwhelming; even Lenin proposed that he head the revolutionary government. Instead, with no military experience, Trotsky created the Red Army. There is no reason to romanticize him, however, for he was trapped inside the dogmas of Marxism, respecting no truth outside the party and no right of democratic opposition anywhere. His own principles compelled him to surrender the moral and intellectual weapons needed to resist tyranny. Imperious in victory, Trotsky was also ennobled in defeat, mostly using his formidable powers of language to assuage the bitterness of exile and to rally some of the opponents of Stalin, a tyrant who feared Hitler less than he feared the heresiarch of bolshevism. In a strange way, the final years as an outcast drove Trotsky closer to the fate of the Jewish people, from whom he had long estranged himself. Exiled in 1929, he posted early warnings against the dangers of Nazi barbarism, as he was hounded from Turkey to France to Norway to Mexico, where a GPU agent drove an ice axe into Trotsky's skull and later was fittingly awarded the regalia of the Order of Hero of the Soviet Union. A few years before the assassination, however, Trotsky had evinced a previously undetected sympathy for Zionism; speaking for a few hours in Mexico with a socialist labor Zionist from Palestine, he did not rule out the possibility of seeking refuge there. Had Trotsky managed to escape the GPU and live another eight years, he would have been eligible under the Law of Return.[9]

Ever since the Bolsheviks seized power from the Kerensky government, many Jews harbored the optimistic sense that the obscurantism and desolation of the Romanov autocracy had been extinguished, that anti-Semitism and other forms of prejudice had been destroyed, that an egalitarian society might be established. The internationalist proclamations of the Bolsheviks, who believed that the revolution could be preserved in Russia only if extended elsewhere, were even more appealing for Jews. The leader of the Hungarian Communists, who briefly seized power in 1923, was Bela Kun, that is, Cohen. Two years later, when the Communist Party held its founding congress in Cuba, a Yiddish interpreter had to be summoned for the *sección hebrea*, which was ignorant of Spanish, the language of the island's workers and peasants. Even today there is a cemetery in Montevideo, Uruguay, which, oddly enough, represents the triumph of sectarianism over universalism: it is for Jewish Communists. No wonder then that, when Arthur Koestler wrote his valedictory to Stalinist political morality, *Darkness at Noon*

(1941), he did not even notice that the novel's protagonist, Nikolai Salmanovich Rubashov, was a Jew.[10] So deeply had some segments of Jewish life been infected with bolshevism that some leftist Kibbutzim canceled Purim festivities in 1953 because the celebrations would have interfered with the Israelis' mourning of the death of Joseph Stalin.

Jewish families begat revolutionary or revisionist socialists almost everywhere. Chaim Weizmann's brother, Shemuel, was one; and Gershom Scholem's brother, Werner, represented the Communists in the parliament of the Weimar Republic. Even Albert Einstein considered himself a socialist. And despite its own unfriendliness to radical ideologies, the United States did not until the 1920s impose limitations on immigrant Jews, who were often susceptible to such politics. Landing on its shores were many fleeing from czarist oppression who, through their manifestos and pamphlets, were in effect countersigning the call for revolution that Marx had issued earlier.

But the first Marxist firebrand in the United States was Daniel De Leon, whose origins Samuel Gompers once ascribed to "a Venezuelan family of Spanish and Dutch Jewish descent with a strain of colored blood. That makes him a first-class son of a bitch." Gompers, himself an immigrant Jew from London, got some of De Leon's background wrong, including the canine ancestry, probably because De Leon's Socialist Labor Party kept trying to undermine the American Federation of Labor. But it is plausible, as his most recent biographer has argued, that De Leon renounced his own Jewish identity for the sake of shaping a future that would belong to the oppressed of all races and nationalities. Having been raised in the Sephardic community of Curaçao, he wanted the Jew to be submerged into a larger American type and thus advocated amalgamation. De Leon propelled himself so ferociously from his own distinctive origins that he urged his coreligionists to celebrate the American holiday of Christmas.[11]

But most radical Jews opted not for the Socialist Labor Party, whose fortunes were virtually identical with De Leon's own career, but for the Socialist Party of America, formed in 1901. Its most frequent candidates for president were authentic sons of the Middle Border, such as Eugene V. Debs, a former member of the Indiana state legislature, and Norman Thomas, who had been Warren Harding's paperboy in Marion, Ohio. But the party's financial support came largely from such trade unions as the International Ladies Garment Workers, the Amalgamated Clothing Workers, the Furriers and Millinery Workers. By the First World War, the most widely circulated Socialist paper in the country was in Yiddish— the *Jewish Daily Forward*. Its editor, Abraham Cahan, had been so convinced that socialism was the natural political faith of the immigrant that, in his novel about a lonely capitalist, *The Rise of David Levinsky* (1917), the protagonist avows only incidental adherence to free enterprise: "Had I chanced to hear a socialist speech, I might have become an ardent follower of Karl Marx."[12] That is precisely what Jurgis Rudkus, the Lithuanian immigrant employee of the Chicago abbatoirs, does in Upton Sinclair's *The Jungle* (1906), and the propagandist who converts the protagonist into a socialist is a Polish Jew. The party's leading theoretician, Morris Hillquit, had in fact been born in Latvia, where his first language had been German, his second Russian. Only after he picked up English in New York did he proceed to learn Yiddish so that he could inspire the Eastern European masses of the East Side. A reliable campaigner, an attorney who specialized in unpopular causes and clients, and a fluent pamphleteer, Hillquit was the triple threat of American socialism. *La pasionaria* of the Corn Belt, Kate Richards O'Hare, nevertheless charged that Hillquit "never knew that the Hudson River was not the west boundary of the United States."[13] The charge was unfair, if only because Victor Berger, a part-Jewish immigrant from Austria, represented a Milwaukee district in the U.S. Congress. The only other member of the Socialist Party to be elected to the House of Representatives was Meyer London of the old East Side.

But probably the most impressive Jewish radical of that era was not a socialist but an anarchist. Emma Goldman was a kinetic orator and polemicist, a labor organizer, a believer in both the necessity of individual freedom and the nobility of collective action, a scathing foe of capitalism and militarism, a champion of birth control and other women's rights, and a popularizer of avant-garde European culture. American parents therefore tried sometimes to frighten their children by warning them that, unless they behaved, Emma Goldman would get them. Instead the federal government got her, along with her anarchist comrade, Alexander Berkman.

Primarily at the instigation of the head of the General Intelligence Division, J. Edgar Hoover, then only twenty-four, Goldman was deported back to the Russia from which she had fled thirty-three years earlier. Goldman lacked any specific feelings of solidarity with the Jewish people, but it was a tribute to the integrity of her beliefs that she became as hostile to bolshevism in Russia as she had been to czarism earlier.

But in the 1920s at least, Soviet Russia commanded the sympathy and support of many Jewish radicals. In that period the Communist Party published nine daily newspapers, of which the one with the largest circulation, the *Freiheit*, was in Yiddish. It outsold the English-language *Daily Worker*.[14] After the defeat of the Russian reactionaries and their White Armies, after the nightmare of the pogroms in the Ukraine, communism seemed to offer the assurance that Jews would suffer no social discrimination in a movement that appealed to their humanitarianism, to their tendency to favor rationality, to their habit of disputing about the interpretation of revered texts, and to their personal ambitions as well. American Communist Party membership probably did not exceed 15 percent of Jewish origins in the 1920s, but the proportion in its leadership was much higher. And even after the first generation—Benjamin Gitlow, Jay Lovestone, William Weinstone, Bertram Wolfe, Max Shachtman—could no longer worship a god that failed, Jews continued to dominate the party. Almost half of the Communist leaders indicted under the Smith Act were Jews, as was the editor of the *Daily Worker* in the 1950s, John Gates. Most of Hollywood's "Unfriendly Ten" were not only Communists but also Jews (although, as the director Billy Wilder quipped, "two of them were talented; the rest were just unfriendly"). Early in the 1960s, when a Maoist faction, the Progressive Labor Party, split from the Communist Party, most of its leaders were of Jewish birth.

By then, however, radicalism in the United States was widely presumed to be as dead as chivalry. The dream of a humane socialism barely had survived its perversion in the Soviet Union and its satellites, with their forced famines, their mass purges and mock trials, their executions, the alliance with nazism from 1939 to 1941, and the devastation of human life and spirit in the arctic wastes of the Gulag Archipelago. When Nikita Khrushchev revealed to the twentieth party congress in 1956 that Stalin had been something of a despot, even the slow learners in the American subsidiary of the movement got the message; Khrushchev's own brutal suppression of the Hungarian workers' revolution later that year dashed remaining hopes. Moreover, American capitalism had survived the awful crisis of the Great Depression, and after the Second World War, Marxist predictions of economic collapse were falsified by an era of unprecedented, astonishing prosperity. The political repression labeled McCarthyism, although it extended wider than the writ of the junior senator from Wisconsin, finished off many of the remaining ambitions of American communism.

Radicalism waned among Jews for special reasons, as the immigrants from Eastern Europe and their children ascended more quickly into the middle class and upper middle class than almost any other ethnic group. Their income matched that of the most respectable Protestants, such as the Episcopalians and the Congregationalists. Only the husk of the working-class world of the second generation remained, although many of its survivors were socialists still—some of them very still. The dramatic regulation of the economy the New Deal wrought had helped fulfill old ideals and had tempered the worst excesses of the sweatshops and the buccaneer capitalism of the past. Both the *Jewish Daily Forward* and the leadership of the garment workers unions backed Roosevelt rather than Norman Thomas for president in 1936, and thereafter the bulk of the Jewish voters remained firmly within the liberal wing of the Democratic Party. Although Communists such as Julius and Ethel Rosenberg conventionally dismissed charges of Soviet anti-Semitism as "slander," evidence could not be ignored that the U.S.S.R., which had supported Arab rioters aginst Jews in Palestine in 1929, which had concluded a pact with the Third Reich a decade later, was systematically eradicating Jewish culture as well as religion within its borders, often by murdering the creators and custodians of Jewish institutions. American public life by contrast was eliminating not Jews but, instead, anti-Semitism itself. The sense of estrangement born of exile largely dissipated.

But the 1960s provided a twist to the plot, a surprise ending to this parable of reconciliation with America. In the civil rights movement, the anti-poverty campaign, the demands of students, the rebirth of feminism, and above all the opposition to military intervention in Vietnam, radicalism once again erupted, and Jews were again disproportionately represented and were conspicuous as leaders. Most of the white freedom riders in the South and most of the white participants in integrationist activity in Mississippi were Jews.[15] When the Students for a Democratic Society needed a site for the group's 1965 convention, one of its leaders, Richard Rothstein, rejected New York. "The Midwest," he argued in a memo, "is ... the only place where a more sociologically representative (you know what that means) and geographically representative conference can take place."[16] A university dean of admissions denying the existence of a quota on Jews could not have put it more circumspectly.

The next year more than half the delegates to the national SDS convention were Jewish. When psychologist Kenneth Keniston interviewed a representative sample of the activists engaged in the Vietnam summer in 1967, five out of the fourteen *Young Radicals* portrayed in his book were of Jewish background, which is about ten times the Jewish percentage of the general population. The most famous of the student rebellions of the 1960s was the first—the free speech movement at Berkeley in 1964. The eleven members of its steering committee included Bettina Aptheker (the daughter of Communist Party historian and editor Herbert Aptheker), Art Goldberg, Suzanne Goldberg, Michael Rossman, Stephen Weissman, and Jack Weinberg (who put into circulation the phrase, "You can't trust anybody over thirty").[17] That summer, near Meridian, Mississippi, the corpses of three civil rights workers were discovered. For the crime of having tried to persuade black citizens to register to vote, a local black named James Chaney had been beaten so viciously that the physician who performed the autopsy compared the disfigurement to high-speed auto accidents. The other two victims were Michael Schwerner of Brooklyn and Andrew Goodman of Queens.

Judaism itself played a role in the civil rights movement. Some rabbis marched in demonstrations with their Christian colleagues. There is also the little-known case of Charles McDew, a black from Ohio who attended Orangeburg's segregated South Carolina State College. During Religious Emphasis Week, McDew asked visiting Protestant ministers whether he would be allowed to worship in their churches. They told him no. When a rabbi invited him to his synagogue, McDew became sufficiently intrigued that he converted to Judaism. The news of the first sit-in in Greensboro, North Carolina, spurred him to head a local sit-in movement, and McDew claimed to have been inspired by Hillel's definition of ethical action: "If I am not for myself, then who is for me? If I am for myself alone, then what am I? If not now, when?" McDew learned other Jewish expressions as well. Thrown into "the hole" of the East Baton Rouge jail, where he was tortured and lost thirteen pounds during his ordeal, he became the favorite display of right-wing groups touring the jail to stare at the "nigger communist." When two high school girls on such a tour whispered to him, "Say something Communist," McDew replied in Yiddish with a vulgar anatomical allusion. He became the second chairman of the Student Nonviolent Coordinating Committee.[18]

Professor Lewis Feuer has pointed out that, insofar as there has been continuity in the American student movement in the twentieth century, Jews are responsible for it. Because of the high proportion of Jewish students attending Columbia University in the 1960s, it is unsurprising that the activists of 1968, such as Mark Rudd, were primarily Jews. It is more interesting to observe that the elders over thirty whom the New Left least distrusted were writers like Paul Goodman, an anarchist who was a product both of Hebrew school in his childhood and of City College in his youth; Herbert Marcuse, an alumnus of the Frankfurt School who was teaching at Brandeis University; and Noam Chomsky, the MIT linguist whose academic subspecialty was Hebrew grammar and who had been in the left Zionist youth movement. The journalist whom the New Left most widely admired was Isidore Feinstein, himself a college dropout. Under the nom de plume of I. F. Stone, he blended once a week—then every other week—the pamphleteering of outrage and excoriation with close readings of official documents. The "think tank" of the New Left was the Institute for Policy Studies, whose key figures included Gar Alperovitz, Richard Barnett, Marcus Raskin and Arthur Waskow. Even the foreign film that won perhaps the biggest following among the sixties radicals, *The Battle of Algiers*, had been done by a Jew, Gillo Pontecorvo, whose brother, the Italian nuclear physicist Bruno Pontecorvo, had defected to the Soviet Union at the zenith of the cold war.

The most enduring of the protest movements to flourish in the 1960s, however, was the women's drive for equality. Its main thrust, epitomized by Betty Goldstein Friedan herself, had been liberal. But several of the most radical feminists, such as Susan Brownmiller, Shulamith Firestone and Naomi Weisstein, have been of Jewish birth. Far less resilient has been the Youth International Party, or Yippies, created by Abbie Hoffman and Jerry Rubin, with an assist from the editor of *The Realist*, Paul Krassner. Such lists could be extended. But an appropriate conclusion was drawn by President Richard Nixon. He was not much of a student of the constitutional limitations on executive power, but he was a good sociologist in advising his daughter, Tricia, not to attend a museum opening because "the arts—they're Jews, they're left-wingers—in other words, stay away." And on the White House tape released in September 1981, the president and H. R. Haldeman have just learned of the indictments of eight radicals accused of crossing state lines to riot at the 1968 Democratic National Convention in Chicago. Nixon wonders aloud whether all the indicted conspirators are Jews, or whether (as he later correctly surmises) only about half are.[19]

And yet a demurrer must be registered. Among the few Americans who have been radicals, a disproportionate number have been Jews—and yet few Jews have been radicals. Ever since Moses Mendelssohn crossed over into Berlin and inaugurated the Jewish entry into the civil order of the East, some of his coreligionists have been conservative, many have been apolitical, most have been liberal. Therefore to analyze the association of American Jewry with radicalism is to study a phenomenon that is pertinent to the heritage of dissent but which is marginal to American Jewish life.

Nevertheless, few Jews have been violinists, or theoretical physicists, or comedians, or psychoanalysts. Yet no one curious about the destiny of this ancient people would maintain that their contributions to these modern professions are irrelevant to the development and to the social significance of such fields. Neither the historian nor the social scientist is obliged to scrutinize only majorities, and so long as it is recalled how few Jews ever have been involved in radical protest, the theories that have been formulated to account for such commitment deserve consideration.

One theory, originally devised to explain liberalism among American Jews, has been stretched to include radical proclivities as well. Perhaps most fully developed in Lawrence Fuchs's *Political Behavior of American Jews*, the emphasis is on the religious imperatives of *tikun olam* and on the prophetic insistence on social justice. Fuchs and others have speculated that the Judaic tradition has stimulated the concern for justice in this world rather than for mercy in the world to come, has validated the life of the mind as well as moderate pleasures of the flesh. A love of learning may have released spiritual yearnings and idealistic expectations that have directed some Jews to radicalism. Moreover, an immunity to asceticism may have enhanced the demand to accelerate earthly happiness, which is threatened by economic misery and political oppression.[20]

Such a thesis is not without its flaws. Those who are most pious and best-informed about normative Judaism are rarely radical at all, and often are not even liberal. Jews who are the most radical are often the most ignorant of their religion, including the concept of *tikun olam*. They could indeed have recited all that they knew about sacred doctrine while standing on one foot. But since the transmission of values is often elusive and difficult to specify and corroborate, this theory cannot be entirely dismissed. Generations of emancipation, assimilation and acculturation have not yet extinguished a distinctive and often cohesive sense of peoplehood, and the centrality of religious ideas to that definition of Jewish culture cannot be evaded. Louis D. Brandeis, for example, grew up in a home without religious instruction, and he did not attend any synagogue. Nevertheless, when a White Houe visitor once remarked to Woodrow Wilson what a pity it was that a man as great as Brandeis should be a Jew, the president replied that Brandeis would not have been so great a man were he *not* a Jew. The heritage of the Jewish people sometimes can work in mysterious yet recognizable ways; and if the Brandeis brief was a liberal response to exploitation and the *Bintel Brief* was a social response to cultural tension and uncertainty, then radicalism ought to be located on the same continuum of "justice hunger" (Meyer Liben's phrase).

The Judaic tradition is also tenacious enough to withstand tendentious readings as well as sentimentality and idealization. In the posturings of their "death house" letters, for instance, Julius and Ethel Rosenberg invoked the appropriate antecedents for their own politics. "At Hebrew school," Julius Rosenberg wrote, "I absorbed quite naturally the culture of my people, their struggle for freedom from slavery in Egypt." Hanukkah meant "the victory of our forefathers in a struggle for freedom from oppression and tyranny. [It] is a firm part of our heritage and buttresses our will to win our own freedom."[21] Such efforts to update one important feature of the Jewish past were repeated in the Haggadah of the "freedom seder" that Arthur Waskow, the son of an immigrant socialist tailor, published in 1969. His people, the Haggadah reads in part, "must stop collaborating. Jewish businessmen must stop buying grapes from farmers who exploit their hired laborers; Jewish organizations must not lend money to banks that oppress Black people; Jewish political leaders must not serve the military-industrial complex."[22] The persistence and pervasiveness of such explicit sympathy for the disadvantaged warranted Clarence Darrow's advice to other defense attorneys to value Jews as jurors.[23]

The bookishness of much of the modern radical sensibility also may be connected to an equivalent intellectual seriousness in Judaism. Ever since Marx set the example by spending his days in the British Museum reading room, from its 9 A.M. opening till its 7 P.M. closing, revolutionary leaders have tended to be the products of libraries rather than slums. Although an anti-intellectual strain has surfaced in radical movements, exalting laborers and peasants who work with their hands, that tendency has existed in part because so many Jews have joined and led these causes. Early in the 1930s, still the only Marxist professor in an American university was Sidney Hook, a comrade in the American Workers Party; and in the 1950s, the only Marxist economist teaching in a major American university was Paul Baran, a former member of Germany's Young Communist League.[24] Others like them may have immersed themselves in such movements out of what they had gleaned from a religious tradition that has expected the world to accommodate the desire to end hunger and pain, suffering and indignity. These days, when a materialist or economic interpretation of history is unfashionable, social scientists reach for their word processors when they hear the word "culture." And Professor Fuchs's theory has the advantage of incorporating into the historical development of Jewish culture itself the radicalism to which many Jews have subscribed.

Another explanation that has been articulated for such dissidence has been status deprivation. Thus anti-Semitism and the disabilities it has commonly entailed have driven Jews to try to surmount discrimination through political and social change. The political sociologist Robert Michels argued in 1915 that "the legal emancipation of the Jews has not ... been followed by their social and moral emancipation." He added that "everywhere in the Jewish race there continues to prevail an ancient and justified spirit of rebellion against the wrongs from which it suffers; and this sentiment, idealist in its origin, animating the members of an impassioned race, becames ... transformed into a revolutionary impulse towards a grandly conceived improvement of the world."[25] Certainly in the writings of Lassalle and others, this transformation can be discerned. Otherwise Michels's argument, like some others that have crossed the Atlantic, lacks visible means of support. For the intensity of bigotry cannot be historically correlated to the eagerness of Jews to seek systematic alternatives to the status quo. Those who have been most talented or wealthy or ambitious did not necessarily turn left when they were turned down or turned away. Since most Jews did not yield to the radical impulse, this theory does not differentiate between liberalism and more drastic responses to exclusivity; it does not explain why other Jews in the Diaspora turned to Zionism, for example.

But if broadened, the theory of status deprivation can be salvaged, by reversing the dictum of Charles Péguy that what begins in mystique ends in *politique*. The Hebrews had been designated a kingdom of priests, a holy people. They had created one of the world's most ancient civilizations. Their low demographic profile had not prevented them from engendering the two most successful religions to advance universalist claims, Christianity and Islam. They had challenged some of the most powerful empires of the ancient world—Egypt, Assyria, Persia, Rome. And yet their descendants were pressing pants, driving milk wagons, peddling trinkets. They were deprived of sovereignty in a land of their own, deprived of the right of collective self-defense against their enemies, deprived of common laws, deprived even of a common vernacular. The wealthy few were accused of subverting the established social order; the impoverished masses were suspected of hoarding wealth, gained through guile and deceit. Such conditions and such accusations, burdened with an additional charge of deicide that was leveled against an entire people, could be appreciated only by those with a taste for the absurd. The discrepancy between an exalted religious and historical status and a low civic and economic state, and between their own ethical sensitivities and the cruelty their neighbors often exhibited, might not only elicit a sense of resigned irony. Such anomalies might also heighten recognition of the injustices that have scarred the human enterprise, might also trigger the need to remedy gross unfairness through devotion to revolution. Estranged from many of the customs and pieties of Western society, the Jews could call into question its claims of reason and honor.

Thus broadened, the thesis of status deprivation helps to explain the theoretical and practical leadership Jews often provided the radical movements they joined. So grandiose a destiny as a chosen people, so central a role in the moral universe, it may be speculated, might have had the effect of instilling the pride and sanctioning the ambition that leadership requires. The damaged self-esteem that, according to some psychologists and sociologists, impairs the success of certain American minorities and women seems not to have hampered the Jews, whom Charles de Gaulle after the Six-Day War called *"un peuple d'élite, sûr de lui-même et dominateur"* (an elite people, sure of itself and dominating). Immigrants familiar with the Bible could be heartened by the story of Joseph, who overcame hardship in Egypt; because of his industriousness and superior talents and his adaptability to a foreign land, Joseph became the first of the great Jewish interpreters of dreams. Especially in America, limits on the ambitions of Jewish immigrants could never be imposed or even defined. The philosopher William Barrett recalls being so impressed by the young academic Henry Kissinger that he predicted Kissinger one day would rise to become a dean.[26]

Confidence of success does not account for a flair for spearheading leftist movements, but then neither does poverty nor hardship explain the allure of socialism. But for all the horrors of the sweatshops, the pitifully low wages, the dangers manifested in such tragedies as the Triangle Shirtwaist fire, the relentless and tedious routine, the seasonal precariousness of the jobs themselves, other American workers had it even worse. And yet the sharecroppers, the migrant workers, the cotton pickers, the miners were even less likely than garment workers to conclude that socialism was the solution to their plight. It was customary for Negroes to aver that it was tough enough being black without also being Red. During the administration of Andrew Jackson, thousands of Cherokees were driven along a "trail of tears" into exile in the West. Yet despite their bitter ordeal and the deaths that ensued, the Cherokees' political profile has not resembled the Jews'. Other areas of the country were as wracked by poverty as the metropolitan centers where the Jews congregated; occasionally, as in the Southwest, socialism promised to be a remedy. But generally neither the party nor the ideology inspired any allegiance in the United States, for reasons that make the appeal to Jews all the more intriguing.

Even Adam and Eve were dissatisfied with Paradise, or at least with an aspect of its ecological policy, and America was certainly east of Eden and less than ideal. Nevertheless, to analyze such a society and then to transform it politically became one of the toughest assignments in the dialectical history of class struggles. But let me take a few practice shots at an explanation. Low as living standards were a century ago, they were higher than Europe's. To the dismay of Daniel De Leon, bread-and-butter trade unionism often seemed to work and to provide benefits, which is why Gompers abandoned the socialism of his European youth. Ever since the Jacksonian era, most white adult males had been granted suffrage, so that political reform within the system was imaginable. The tradition of the two-party system was also tenacious enough to retard the formation of effective third parties, partly because of the larcenous behavior of the Democrats and Republicans toward the clever ideas of their rivals, who were quadrennially left hanging there, twisting slowly in the wind.

Other reasons for the failure of socialism go beyond institutional arrangements. The nation was honeycombed with racial, ethnic, sectional, and religious antagonism, but there was strikingly little class consciousness. When Lenin read a newspaper account of a labor dispute in London, during which the bobbies played soccer with the strikers, he fumed that no revolution in England was foreseeable. Yet class consciousness in Britain was even better developed than in the United States, where ethnic identity often has overpowered the sense of membership in the proletariat and the feeling of solidarity with the dispossessed. The force of ethnicity can be measured even in those documents that ostensibly report poverty and economic injustice. In Jacob Riis's How the Other Half Lives (1890), the cultural diversity of the New York slums is more piquant than the deprivation the immigrants and their children share. In Upton Sinclair's The Jungle the pathos of immigrant adaptation is more credibly conveyed than any metamorphosis toward socialism.

In the early plays of Clifford Odets, the wounds that his working-class Jews inflict upon one another seem to cut deeper than any hurt that the capitalist economy has caused them. Even in a movie such as Martin Ritt's *Norma Rae* (1979), the friendship between the New York labor organizer and the Southern woman who is his Galatea is more interesting than the all-purpose strike-fund-support film the director may well have intended.

Nor could the socialist ideology, with its faith in working-class solidarity, get far upstream against the national stress on individual mobility and achievement. The radical offer to escort everyone to utopia together had to compete with the highly personal optimism and individual ambitions that American life contrived to foster. Contrasted with the demanding task of transforming an entire political economy, it appeared easy to transform one's self, to be whatever one wanted to be, to be unencumbered by the boundaries of ancestry and birth, to pick out the green light at the end of the dock that so many Americans anxiously were seeking. It appeared more plausible to rise *from* one's class rather than *with* it; therefore even the underprivileged took the socialist platform—to apply Max Beerbohm's phrase—"with a stalactite of salt."

In understanding the Jewish radical as a serial character in modern American history, a final possibility has to be explored. It may be the most intriguing theory of all, because it ricochets so sharply within the framework of the Jewish condition itself. It addresses the mystery of how the world of our fathers and mothers can be perpetuated, for it is the problem of *toledot*, of generations. The fear that there will be terminal Jews, that the present or the next generation will be the last, has been a persistent cause for alarm in Jewish history. Simon Rawidowicz's famous essay on "The Ever-Dying People" is ironic testimony to this fear, which was intensified for the immigrants who came to a reputedly godless land. In the original film version of *The Jazz Singer* (1927), still the most compelling treatment of a Jewish milieu that Hollywood has rendered, the four generations of cantors that distinguish the Rabinowitz family will not be extended, as Jack Robin pursues a career on Broadway. A classic of the Yiddish theater repertoire was Jacob Gordin's *The Jewish King Lear*, which provided Jacob Adler with one of his most celebrated roles. So effective was the actor in conveying a father's torment that, according to his own daughter's recollections, a member of the audience once rose from his seat, raced down the aisle and yelled: "To hell with your stingy daughter, Yankl! She has a stone, not a heart. . . . Come, Yankl, may she choke, that rotten daughter of yours."[27] The danger that parental values will not be firmly transmitted haunts Sholom Aleichem's Tevye as well, and is replicated in *Fiddler on the Roof*.

Whether the family constellation sheds any light on the connection between American Jewry and radicalism remains open to dispute. Some, such as the psychologist Kenneth Keniston and the journalist Midge Decter, have noticed the continuity between the liberal values of the parents and the radical commitments of their children. The sociologist Seymour Martin Lipset has concurred, stressing that the liberal politics of Jews, whose income lifts them into the upper strata, have produced "a schizophrenic existence."[28] Others, such as Professor Lewis Feuer, have monitored "the conflict of generations," the break that signifies a political expression of Oedipal opposition. The evidence is mixed. The recent arrest of Weather Underground member Kathy Boudin has underscored the support given her by her mother and father, a prominent civil liberties attorney who has represented Communist clients. E. L. Doctorow's novel, *The Book of Daniel*, deftly portrays two generations of radicals, from the Stalinism of the Isaacsons to the New Left ideology of Daniel who, with his apolitical sister, Susan, is raised by the Lewins, liberals who live in tony Brookline, Massachusetts, and are devoted to civil liberties. The authority of the novel is hardly diminished by the fact that Michael and Robert Meeropol, the sons of Julius and Ethel Rosenberg, were involved in the New Left themselves. Others, however, seem not to have absorbed their political values at the dinner table. Trotsky's father was a landowner without sympathy for the left. Mark Rudd's father pursued a military career before selling real estate, and Abbie Hoffman's was, if anything, a conservative and a Republican.

And yet the complexity of the Jewish tradition, in which the quest for justice has prevailed even after affluence, may be said to confirm the radicalism even of children whose fidelity to that tradition was inadvertent. That may be why the Jews managed to sustain a tolerance for radicalism—if not necessarily a dedication to it—longer than anyone else. Such tolerance—and the strength of family loyalty it implied—may be why, even after growing up with little contact with poverty and discrimination, Jewish youths joined the New Left in disproportionate numbers. However vaguely, they still felt a little like strangers in the land of Egypt. And their parents, whatever their reservations, usually did not repudiate their revolutionary sons or daughters. As Marxists the members of the Frankfurt School sought to dry up the sources of their parents'—and their own—security. Yet politics did not provoke disinheritance. Only when Max Horkheimer married his father's secretary, for instance, did temporary estrangement result. As Professor Martin Jay has commented, "It was apparently much harder for his parents to get used to the idea that Horkheimer was marrying a gentile than that he was becoming revolutionary." The break was sharper in the home of Gershom Scholem's father, who broke off relations with another son, Werner, not when he joined the German Communist Party, but when he married outside the faith (to which the father did not subscribe anyway).[29]

Abbie Hoffman's recent autobiography, *Soon to be a Major Motion Picture*, not only is an estimable record of cultural revolution, American style. With great vividness, Hoffman's book also taps some of the intricacies of feeling coursing through the Jewish family. His own special knack, he writes, was "to make outrage contagious," and he did so with increasing defiance of the middle-class conventions of gentility in which he was raised. Depicting his Worcester synagogue as "about as religiously stimulating as a Ramada Inn," Hoffman claims to have extracted from Jewish history a certification of rebellion against authority, plus "a cluster of stereotypes." Education at Brandeis University he credits with having introduced him to a sense of himself and to an appropriate stance against the world, and Marcuse was one of his favorite teachers. The autobiography insists that the past was never repudiated as he moved toward Yippiedom. Nor did Hoffman *père* reject him, despite a comment to an interviewer about what "a bright student" Abbie was: "He could have been somebody, a doctor or a professor—now we have to read the papers to see which jail he's in." The son asserts that his father "never (to use a gentile expression) disowned me," however.

With its emphatic Jewishness, *Soon to be a Major Motion Picture* also makes apparent how weakly political fashions can withstand certain feelings associated with home and family. When his political activities had been most publicized, Hoffman had defined himself primarily as a kid, championing the youth culture against capitalist co-optation and political repression, and seeking to influence what he termed Woodstock Nation. Placed on the witness stand during the Chicago conspiracy trial, he was asked to identify himself; and the exchange went as follows:

A. My name is Abbie. I am an orphan of America....
Q. Where do you reside?
A. I live in Woodstock Nation.
Q. Will you tell the court and the jury where it is.
A. Yes. It is a nation of alienated young people. We carry it around with us as a state of mind in the same way the Sioux Indians carried the Sioux nation around with them. It is a nation dedicated to cooperation versus competition....[30]

Later asked his occupation, Hoffman replied that he was "a cultural revolutionary. Well, I am really a defendant ... full time."[31] Here, it might be noted, is a curious parallel with Alexander Ginzburg, Soviet dissident, whose nationality a judge once asked him to specify (the famous "fifth point" on a Soviet internal passport). Ginzburg replied: "Prisoner." Yet in order to defy Soviet anti-Semitism and to associate himself with the Jewish tradition of resistance to tyranny, Ginzburg substituted his mother's for his father's name.[32]

By 1981 Hoffman appears to have forsaken the cult of youthfulness that really had little to do with radicalism and which was closer to Ponce de Leon than to Daniel De Leon. It may be possible to live a long while like a kid, but it makes little sense to die as one. Or so Hoffman may have concluded. He therefore acknowledges, rather poignantly, that he "came into this world acutely aware of being Jewish and [I] am sure I'll go out that way."[33]

That seems to be the lesson that others have learned as well. For all the difficulties that Jews have felt in attempting to define and perpetuate a distinctive culture, it has outlasted all the political surrogates that some radicals have struggled to find for it. Morris Raphael Cohen, who taught philosophy to many young socialists at City College, once remarked that "no change of ideology—no matter how radical—can make a man cease to be the son of his parents." That is why some have come to realize that they were Jews before they were socialists, and may still be affected by that fact long after the enthusiasms of their youthful days are past. When Philip Rahv, the long-time editor of *Partisan Review* and virtually the prototype of the deracinated Jewish radical intellectual, died in 1973, a large part of his estate was left to the state of Israel—which he sometimes wished he had settled in, or so he told a friend.[34] Even Howard Fast, once the representative middle-brow novelist of the Communist Party, once blacklisted and jailed (and perhaps better known as having been the father-in-law of Erica Jong), is writing multivolume sagas of several generations of an ethnic family. Writers once took pride in being radicals, citing the Latin etymological origin *radix*, meaning "root", and they liked to announce that they intended to go to the root of things. Now, while roots still matter, the meaning has altered; writers allude to their ethnic consciousness, defining who they are according to what and where their ancestors have been.

The change suggests a certain abiding quality, as well as the recognition that the radical experience is often a story of disenchantment, of emancipation from false hopes and false messiahs, from simplicities and certitudes. Much remains to be learned not only *about* radicalism but also *from* the entire theory and practice of democratic dissent; few would wish the yearning for justice to be smothered in a shroud of complacency and selfishness. As long as the political process is subject to the pluralistic demands of interest groups, and as long as the skies over Washington are black with the Lear jets of lobbyists defending business interests, those without voices or power need to be championed.

But many radicals who sought to transpose essentially religious feelings into political engagement were unaware of inserting into politics the most corrupting elements of faith as well—dogma and superstition. Some radicals were slow to realize that even idealism, for all its attractiveness, is a quality that ought to be judged not merely by its intensity, but by its consequences, by its scope, and by its compatibility with the sense of discrimination and proportion. Citizens whose formative years were spent in the grip of socialism should be credited with realizing the pertinence of politics in altering reality, often for the benefit of those who care nothing for civic issues. But many problems defy political remedy, for we bear deeper wounds that not even time itself can heal and which have proven to be the fate of our species. The maturation that some Jews found in and beyond radicalism therefore dictates a conclusion expressed most economically by William Blake, who asked: "What is the price of experience? Do men buy it for a song, or wisdom for a dance in the street? No, it is bought with the price of all that a man hath."

6

The Persistence of Liberalism

The United States never has been immune to the bacillus of anti-Semitism that is so inescapably a part of the history of Europe, and artifacts of American bigotry can be conjured up readily, available as evidence of the betrayal of the egalitarian dream. Such an indictment might be highlighted by a presentation of a copy of General Grant's Order Number 11, intending to make the Department of Tennessee *Judenrein* in twenty-four hours; the guest register at Saratoga's Grand Union Hotel, which Joseph Seligman and other "Israelites" were not permitted to sign; assorted "Gentiles Only" signs and advertisements; a restricted real estate covenant; a sample issue of the *Dearborn Independent*; the noose from which dangled the mutilated body of Leo Frank; some sheets replete with the insignia of the Ku Klux Klan. The exhibits and the examples could be multiplied.

But though we cannot, in Lincoln's phrase, escape history, we can misread it, and can, by narrowness of perspective, distort its meaning. We can acknowledge the pathology of prejudice in which American institutions have been implicated, but we are not thereby obliged to exaggerate that legacy. Lincoln himself rescinded Grant's order three weeks later, and, after a longer interval, Henry Ford professed to be shocked and ashamed to discover anti-Semitism in the editorials appearing in his name. Jews built their own resorts in the Adirondacks and elsewhere, and formed their own defense organizations that have helped drive open discrimination underground and often into oblivion. In 1948, the Supreme Court ruled that restrictive covenants could not be enforced.[1] The lynching of

Leo Frank is notorious because it is horrifying and because it is virtually unique; it typified no pogroms. And when Thomas Dixon's novel, *The Clansman*, was transformed into *The Birth of a Nation*, the most celebrated of all silent motion pictures, he explained that the film's title referred to the Aryan nation. Yet, rather than despising Jews, Dixon admired them as "the greatest race of people God has ever created." And when, during the Depression, the novelist was forced to sell the North Carolina estate that had been purchased with his share of the film's profits, the new Jewish owner converted the land into a retreat for the B'nai B'rith Youth Organization and for human relations conclaves.[2] Although God had promised Abraham that his "seed shall possess the gate of his enemies" (Gen. 22:17), the bill of sale of even a racist such as Dixon cannot be cited as proof.

More than a dozen years ago the standard reference work, the *American Jewish Year Book*, dropped its separate entry on anti-Semitism—thus perhaps confirming George Washington's electrifying promise to Jewish congregations almost two centuries earlier. The new government, the president had vowed, would give "to bigotry no sanction, to persecution no assistance,"[3] and nowhere else in the Diaspora has that promise come so tantalizingly close to fulfillment. Nowhere else has the public culture been so receptive to Jewish interests and rights, to both the hunger for acceptance and the impulse to remain different. For example, political parties specifically advocating the oppression or expulsion of Jews are absent from the annals of American elections, although movements with such programs erupted in the German and Austrian empires in the late nineteenth century. In central Europe, a political party with "Christian" in its name was announcing that it was against the Jews. Thus, when the last regent of Hungary was introduced to a visiting secretary of the YMCA, he expressed pleasure at meeting the American representative of what Admiral Horthy called "such an important anti-Semitic organization."[4] Something of the contrasting actuality of American life is suggested by an incident reported by one of my colleagues. His young son once noticed the neon-lit sign atop the YMCA building in Boston and proclaimed that the initials stood for the word yarmulke.

Already half a century ago, the sociologist Robert Park recommended that the study of American Jewish history and culture be required in the general curriculum of all high schools, since such an inquiry promised fuller understanding of representative American lives.[5] Jews became acculturated so rapidly, absorbing national values as though by osmosis, that, in the twentieth century in particular, the ancient danger of persecution has been displaced by the different problem of identity. Fears of the Gentiles have given way largely to anxieties about assimilation. Having found a liberal atmosphere and a competitive economy congenial, American Jews have risen strikingly from poverty and obscurity. No immigrant group distanced itself more quickly from the proletarian world of its own antecedents, and almost no other religious group has coagulated so completely in the middle class. In 1890, New York's "Jewtown" had been a choice example of how "the other half" lived; by 1963, its surviving remnant was only glancingly included in the destitute one-fourth to one-fifth comprising "the other America."[6] For already during the Great Depression, when one-third of the population was still "ill-housed, ill-clad, ill-nourished," some Jews were trying prominently to break the cycle of poverty through the drafting and implementation of laws and government programs. Tocqueville's description of the bar as the American equivalent of an aristocracy is relevant, even if the estimate that one of every five lawyers is Jewish is too high.[7] His perception into the largely "commercial passions" of the Americans further suggests how representative the Jews are, for, in locating their primary occupations—and often preoccupations—since their arrival here, business has been decisive. At least on the surface, then, Jews may be, as Robert Park suggested, like other Americans, only more so.

The pattern of advance—from *shtetl* to steerage to slum to suburb—became so common, and faith in reward for hard work and individual achievement so tenacious, that the traditional sense of transience and homelessness largely has subsided. In a recent interview, an Orthodox woman in Boston recalled that her brother and all his friends, when growing up, obeyed the Halakic requirement to keep the head covered at all times—by wearing baseball caps.[8] Earlier in the century, hyphenated Americans often sought to efface the hyphen and, at least until recently, were more anxious to demonstrate how snugly they fit into this society than how they might improve or enrich it.

But, despite appearances of homogenization, ancestral allegiances have not become extinct, and ethnic differences have not been bleached out. Almost two decades ago, an article in *Look* magazine entitled "The Vanishing American Jew" reverberated in some apprehensive precincts,[9] for the vital signs of group survival seemed to be flickering and the eclipse of endogamy seemed to signal the end game for Jewry. Since then, intermarriage rates have continued to soar (while, in addition, the birth rate has skidded). Nevertheless, the Jew has not yet vanished (as *Look* has), and neither ethnicity nor religion can be considered moribund in American life generally. The official pretense of complete Americanization could, in the past, be maintained for regular three-year intervals, until each election year, when the realities of traditional loyalties were enforced on attentive political candidates. That pretense has itself faded with the realization of how slowly assimilation has occurred. And even if the direction is clear, the velocity of change has been overestimated. For Jews, along with other minorities since the mid-sixties, have experienced a process that began in self-defense and then invited self-discovery. The mandatory 3-I tours of American politicians—to Ireland, Italy, and Israel—are almost ás much a staple of campaigning as are the prayers of three clergymen—Protestant, Catholic, and Jewish—that are required to sanctify civic ceremonies.

Although they are courted and counted as much as larger ethnic groups, even their own Bible notes how small a people the ancient Hebrews were, and, in the world today, the total number of Jews is equal to the statistical error in the latest Chinese census.[10] Less than 3 percent of the American population, they cannot seek safety in numbers. Nor do they have the clout that can be derived from the efficiency of central organization. Within the various American Jewish communities, no way yet has been found to impose political or ideological conformity or to ensure the implementation of the policies of their spokesmen. No wisps of white smoke ever signal who their leaders are. Unlike Jews in other countries, they have no chief rabbi, although Irving Howe's history recounts the remedy offered by an immigrant from Moscow who arrived in New York in 1893. Hayim Vidrowitz had a sign placed on his door, giving his name and designating as his title, "Chief Rabbi of America." When asked by whose authority Vidrowitz had assumed that responsibility, the rabbi replied, perhaps rather sheepishly: "The sign painter's."[11]

Decentralization of authority and the proliferation of parallel organizations also mean that, contrary to some right-wing fantasies, it is quite impossible to devise a conspiracy among members of this highly talkative group (some of whom don't speak to one another). No Jewish politician ever has been identified as supremely qualified to articulate its interests. In fact, Jews long have been somewhat underrepresented among elected officials, perhaps for fear of arousing dormant prejudice. Abe Lincoln could get away with being ambitious, but Abe Ribicoff might always be accused of being "pushy." Beginning with antebellum Senators Judah P. Benjamin of Louisiana and David Levy Yulee of Florida, many Jews have represented states or districts in which the number of their coreligionists has been too negligible to raise specters of "bloc voting." In 1939, when President Roosevelt nominated Felix Frankfurter to the Supreme Court, several influential Jews, including the publisher of the *New York Times*, attempted to scuttle the appointment on the ground that it would heighten anti-Semitism.[12] Old Diaspora habits die hard, even in America.

Yet, despite handicaps of demography, community organization and anxieties entangled in ancient memories, the Jews have exerted a certain influence on American life and, especially, since the New Deal, on politics.

Why is this so? The recognition that candidates and officials have accorded to them is a result, in part, of the calibrations of the federal system, for "who gets what" is dependent on where they live. In one survey a couple of decades ago, Jews expressed a preference to live in neighborhoods that are about 50 percent Jewish; and while it can be assumed that this percentage is not an ideal for most Gentiles, Jews have exhibited what *Fortune* magazine once called a "notorious" tendency to "agglomerate."[13] Almost a decade ago, Harvard College was considering a change in its policies, and a dean of admissions suggested that, in order to achieve greater diversity in the student body, recruitment should get outside "the doughnuts around the big cities." To which a Jewish faculty member promptly replied, "Those aren't doughnuts; those are bagels."[14] Not by design, the Electoral College gives a certain form of minority preference, and those whose homes comprise the doughnuts and bagels of the great cities in the most populous states have a magnified influence in the winner-take-all system of presidential elections. The equality promised in the Declaration of Independence is, in fact, modulated by zip codes. While the Jewish presence in the biggest American city long has been conspicuous, it is less known that the second largest concentration of Jews in the world is not in Tel Aviv but in Los Angeles. Jews also vote more than other groups, casting 4 percent of the ballots. That extra 1 percent beyond their proportion of the general population may seem miniscule, but it means three-fourths of a million votes,[15] in a system so delicately balanced that 55 percent of the vote in a presidential election is considered a landslide.

Nor should the historical contributions of Jewish intellectuals be minimized, since they have helped to locate the proper place of minorities in a democracy and to formulate the rules under which natives and newcomers alike have played. In societies emphasizing ascription as much as achievement, it was possible through conversion (Disraeli), wealth (Bleichröder), assimilation (Dreyfus before the affair), talent, and luck (all of the above) to *beat* the system. But in reflecting on the implications of democracy, in therefore stigmatizing the entrenchment of privilege, some Jews were able to *change* the system.

Here is a predilection as recognizable and special as a signature. Perhaps the first theorist of the secular and democratic state founded on the ideal of civil liberty was Spinoza, whose arguments were formulated not long after other Sephardic Jews were first landing in New Amsterdam. The poet who hailed America as the "mother of exiles," and whose sonnet welcoming the oppressed is at the base of the Statue of Liberty, was Emma Lazarus. The playwright of *The Melting-Pot*, which envisaged the transfiguration of European hatreds into new loyalties, was Israel Zangwill. The anthropologist who inaugurated the liberal environmentalist interpretation of race, observing adaptation and plasticity in the attributes of former Europeans and their descendants, was Franz Boas. The historian who wished to record the particular tale of these immigrants, and then realized that "the immigrants *were* American history," is Oscar Handlin.[16] The literary critic who interpreted the central tradition of American fiction as the transcendence of bigotry through an interracial buddy system is Leslie Fiedler. The theologian whose grasp of the implications of religious pluralism was perhaps most resonant was Will Herberg. The philosopher who coined the phrase "cultural pluralism," out of the conviction that the diverse heritages of the new Americans should neither be fudged nor forgotten, was a rabbi's son, Horace Kallen. Among the first constitutional lawyers, specializing in arguments before the Supreme Court in defense of the rights of minorities and the underprivileged, was Louis Marshall, the spiritual ancestor of Jack Greenberg of the NAACP's Legal Defense Fund and of Ruth Bader Ginsburg of the women's movement. Marshall was also the most persistent advocate at Versailles of the insertion of legal clauses in the constitutions of the newly created states after World War I, designed to protect national minorities. The refugee lawyer who invented the word *genocide* to describe the ineffable fate of the Jews in Nazi-occupied Europe was Raphael Lemkin, who deserves to be more widely known also for his efforts to brand the destruction of any people or race as a crime in international law. The native-born attorney who helped formulate the United Nations' Universal Declaration of Human Rights was Joseph Proskauer. Among the first authors to use *ethnicity* in our contemporary sense is Erik Homburger Erikson,[17] although the Oxford English Dictionary gives credit to the sociologist David Riesman, a former law clerk to Justice Brandeis, who himself affirmed the compatibility of the ethos of individualism with the persistence of ethnic loyalty. "The new nationalism adopted by America," Brandeis announced in a Fourth of July speech in 1915, "proclaims that each race or people, like each individual, has the right and duty to develop, and only through such differentiated development will high civilization be attained."[18]

The less precarious status and political security of Jews in the United States may be a result, in part, of their having thought about the ramifications of democratic pluralism for a long time. No wonder, then, that the black novelist Ralph Ellison has regarded his native land as "freer politically and richer culturally because there are Jewish Americans to bring it the benefit of their special forms of dissent ... and their gift for ideas which are based upon the uniqueness of their experience."[19]

This commitment to the perpetuation and accommodation of differences—in *e pluribus unum*—is itself an expression of Jewish distinctiveness. Beneath at least some of those baseball caps, special attitudes are crystallizing before going into general circulation. Many Jews have manifested an orientation toward civil society that does not mirror the patterns of others. These differences may be marginal, but are, nevertheless, discernible—just as the American atmosphere has altered the idiom of Jewishness, tempering the authenticity of the connection to tradition. Their lives may be kosher-style rather than kosher. But however uncertainly and ambivalently, they are custodians of a tradition that stretches back sinuously into the deepest and most mysterious past. Their history is not yet identical with everyone else's. Several years ago the Nobel Prize-winning Israeli author, S. Y. Agnon, asked Saul Bellow whether his novels had been translated into Hebrew. When the American replied in the affirmative, the Israeli writer is reported to have exclaimed, "Good. Then you are safe."[20] Since more than two hundred times as many people in the world can speak English as know Hebrew, Agnon's assurance of the continuity of the Jewish people may be awesome in its audacity. But the *kaddish*, the prayer for the dead, extols God without even mentioning death; and the festival of Hanukkah is designed to commemorate the miracle of a cruse of oil that burned for eight days instead of one. A communal capacity to survive long has defied historical plausibility, and this will to prevail against all odds continues to animate many Jews.

But Agnon's remark also suggests that the Jews can bring the dimension of time to a nation oriented instead to the triumph over space, a nation whose span of generations easily could be tucked into a few of those biblical begats. The American political heritage is so brief that one of its most lustrous figures, Justice Oliver Wendell Holmes, Jr., could know both John Quincy Adams and Alger Hiss; and the ahistorical secularism of Jefferson's characteristic remark, "The earth belongs always to the living generation,"[22] could be contrasted with the expansive awe of Ps. 24:1: "The earth is the Lord's . . . the world, and they that dwell therein." Jefferson spoke *for* America, which is why those also conscious of dead generations sometimes have had to speak *to* America.

The diachronic sense does not, in itself, humanize; one common school teacher in Linz, Austria, Dr. Leopold Poetsch, was responsible for teaching history to both Adolf Hitler and Adolf Eichmann.[23] But a sense of the past, if enlarged with empathy, can offer a deeper perception of human possibility and dignity and, even in American politics, the Jews belong to the party not only of memory but of hope. What the critic Elizabeth Hardwick discerned in their fiction—"a spirit of international rationalism . . . a broader, old libertarian, humane . . . tradition"[24]—is also applicable to their political life. Harkening back to the rock of ages, they also feel at home in the age of reform. The Jews have characteristically wished to make idealism operational, to extend the conventional boundaries and amend the codes of popular sovereignty. Other minorities have engaged in politics primarily to defend traditional lifestyles or to advance economic demands, and they generally have been satisfied, not when elected officials have seen the light, but when they have felt the heat. That is the law of thermodynamics under which representative government in America ordinarily has worked, and the Jews have not been entirely unfamiliar with its effects. But they also have been devoted to principles whose connection to economic self-interest may be considered paradoxical, for their votes do not correspond to their bank accounts, or to their business and home addresses.

Instead, Jews often have pumped visions of social justice into a polity that long has been condemned or celebrated for its evasion of ideology. American candidates ordinarily know that a platform is designed to stand on, not to run on; the quintessential electoral slogan, "Tippecanoe and Tyler Too!" might be contrasted with "Liberty, Equality, Fraternity," or even Lenin's "Peace, Land, Bread." American politicians have long ignored dogmas as deals are struck; ideals are left to others. In the nineteenth century and well into our own, only well-bred Protestants showed any inclination to apply ethical abstractions to the processes of government. As genteel civic reformers, they enunciated principles of fair play while they battled corruption in morality plays that often closed after one act. By the midtwentieth century, however, the Jews have become perhaps the most conspicuous players for political stakes that apparently are more high-minded than self-interest.

The Jews might have been expected to show greater appreciation for the postfeudal system that has encouraged the commercial passions and stimulated the accumulation of private wealth. They have shown their gratitude by welcoming the welfare state. Shortly after the Second World War, adherents of eight religious groups were asked whether they favored "guaranteed economic security." Agreement with this position meant repudiation of laissez-faire capitalism. The Catholics, who had the highest percentage of believers below the middle class, were first by a slight margin. The Jews, with the smallest proportion of their members engaged in manual labor, were second.[25] A decade later another questionnaire revealed that "*middle*-class Jews were more likely to express the view that the government is doing too little [to regulate the economy] than were *working*-class members of either the white Protestant or Catholic groups."[26] Those who have had to meet payrolls have, therefore, shown the least resentment toward welfare rolls. In the early 1970s, in their support for welfare for the poor and for national medical programs, Jews were even more progressive than they were two decades earlier, and still quite divergent from other whites.[27] Not entirely persuaded by American traditions of self-reliance, many Jews realize that no one wears bootstraps any more. Pecuniary motives do not explain this willingness to revise classical capitalism with policies nourished by heavier taxation of the more comfortable classes. Such attitudes, however, may show the influence of the ideals of social justice,[28] as though, despite the advantages of bourgeois life, many Jews remain experts in estrangement, unable to ignore the Passover reminder of having been slaves in Egypt.

More agreeable than other groups to governmental policies intended to improve the well-being of the dispossessed, the Jews also exhibit distinctive spending patterns of their own. For all their dedication to what still is called—perhaps quaintly—the Protestant ethic, they seem unwilling to lay up treasure upon earth and, according to one sociologist, "spend more on the 'good life' for themselves and their families than do Protestants at the same income level."[29] Accountants know whether a country club is Jewish or Gentile by comparing the food bills with the liquor bills,[30] and in many cities Jews also are ravenous in their consumption and subsidization of cultural activities. No longer need one take too literally the etymology of "philanthropy" to acknowledge the extraordinary willingness of Jews to part with their wealth in private charity, especially for causes in their own particular community and for Israel. In 1972, for example, more than half a billion dollars was raised through the United Jewish Appeal, local federations and Israel bonds, while the Red Cross was raising $132 million from all Americans, including Jews.[31] This generosity also embraces politics. In a conversation once with Ben Bradlee, President Kennedy bitterly remarked that his wife's stepfather had given only $500 in the 1960 campaign and added, hyperbolically, the "the only people who really gave during political campaigns now were Jews."[32] His assistant, who served as liaison with Jewish contributors, could not recall that any of them asked for something in exchange for picking up the tab, and a former aide to Senator Edmund Muskie has called them "the most altruistic givers in the country."[33]

The most favored causes and candidates have been overwhelmingly liberal. The Jews may be naturally conservative, as Disraeli suspected;[34] if so, in twentieth-century America at least, they have been remarkably slow to discover their own interests. They have tended to support the government when it attacks social and economic privilege, and have found incomprehensible Lord Melbourne's definition of the entire purpose of government: the prevention of crime and the preservation of contracts. Yet the Jews generally have not allowed statism to calcify into a dogma, and have not participated in the campaigns of conservative moralists to proscribe certain forms of personal conduct. Such activists, often from other religious groups, who oppose freer access to abortion, birth control, divorce, pornography, gambling, and alcoholic beverages, rarely have found enthusiastic allies among the Jews, whose own ethical tradition promotes acceptance of the natural world and repudiates asceticism.[35] Poverty and lifelong celibacy never were Jewish ideals, and although temperance was expected, the pleasures of this world were not stigmatized. Conservative moralism is, therefore, alien to most Jews who, in this respect, would deny a major role to government.

Liberalism was also manifested in hostility to McCarthyism, even though the repertoire of its eponymous leader never included overt anti-Semitism;[36] no group has shown itself more committed to the principles articulated in the Bill of Rights. Here again the relation to ethnic interest is not obvious. The First Amendment could be read more selectively than many Jews have done, since it protects not only all worshipers but, also, political extremists such as Klansmen, bundists, fascists, white supremacists and Nazis. The hemorrhage of Jewish members from the American Civil Liberties Union, after it agreed to defend the right of Nazis to march in Skokie, suggests that freedom of assembly can be construed—and opposed—in blatantly ethnic terms. Before the Skokie controversy, Jews comprised an estimated 40 percent of the ACLU's membership;[37] even afterward it remains much higher than the fraction of Jews in the general population would warrant.

This disproportionate dedication to the strategic freedoms may not always correspond to the particular rights of Jews, but it is quite consistent with a general adherence to liberalism unmatched by other groups. Examining the political attitudes of residents of Detroit, Gerhard Lenski discovered that black Protestants were liberal on questions of the welfare state and civil rights, but not with regard to international affairs and civil liberties. White Protestants were hostile to racial integration and to government intervention in the economy. Catholics also opposed civil rights, and were moderate—but not liberal—on questions of freedom of speech, foreign aid, and governmental regulation of the economy. Only the Jews were classifiable as liberal in all categories, especially when civil rights were at issue.[38] In a society that is considerably less than an antechamber to utopia, such consistent views are not, in my opinion, disgraceful—merely, compared with Gentile attitudes, eccentric.

An interpretation of the Jews' role in politics that stresses self-interest or economic motivation does not do them justice, and the movement in support of Soviet Jewish emigration is an example. The arrival of refugees in the United States, whose allure eventually outstripped that of Israel, has not enhanced the social status of Jews who have lived here for generations. Immigration is unrelated to the economic welfare of American Jews, except insofar as they have been obliged to tax themselves somewhat more heavily to provide social services for immigrants. In contrast to the importance of Israel, the cause of Soviet Jewry has been only marginally connected to the strengthening of religious and cultural institutions and the perpetuation of Jewish identity in America. Support for brethren in Russia has created friction with the only nation posing a military threat to American security. Nor has support for the free emigration of Soviet Jews been merely a coefficient of historical resentment against communism. One explanation remains: idealism.

Their political impulses often have been tinged with utopianism, and the radical disposition of Jews has been noticed—and feared—far more than their natural conservatism. Centuries of persecution in Europe denied them much expectation of a stake in society, and the French revolutionary extension of entitlements marked a caesura in Jewish history, a disintegration of ghetto walls, an end to political isolation. But genuine equality, which is asymptotic anyway, still was cruelly denied; and deprivation and exploitation in America helped inspire working-class radicalism, especially in the first third of the twentieth century.[39] Among the once-flourishing American socialist newspapers, the daily with the highest circulation was in Yiddish, the *Forward*. The views that it expressed represented a combustible product of centuries of victimization and discrimination, combined with messianic expectations and imperatives. Those values—often in distorted form—showed up virtually everywhere that Western Jews could be located: in the Pale and in Palestine, in North America and in Cuba. It may be more than a curiosity that Mark Zborowsky, the coauthor of a standard book on *shtetl* culture, *Life Is With People*, was Trotsky's secretary in exile—while spying for the NKVD.[40] In America after the Second World War, revolutionaries have been more often spawned in libraries than in slums (one precedent is Marx himself); and it is revealing that one contributor to a 1961 *Commentary* symposium took for granted the fact that most of the campus dissidents he had known were Jews.[41] While many such radicals have been born into Jewish families, only a minority of Jews have been radicals—and many of them did not remain so. The belief that America was different from the continent was expressed sharply by the immigrant Jew who dominated the labor movement for a third of a century. A trade unionist here, Samuel Gompers claimed that he "would be a Socialist in Germany and in Russia a nihilist."[42]

A touching but little-known description of the process of moderation can be found in a 1903 essay by Voltairine de Cleyre who, after a convent education and a conversion to anarchism, decided to tutor the immigrant poor in Philadelphia. In the dozen years that she "lived and worked with foreign Jews," she wrote: "I have taught over a thousand, and found them as a rule, the brightest, the most persistent and sacrificing students, and in youth dreamers of social ideals ... I myself have seen such genuine heroism in the cause of education practiced by girls and boys, and even by men and women with families, as would pass the limits of belief to the ordinary mind." Yet despite "cold, starvation, self-isolation ... [and] exhaustion of body even to emaciation," most of de Cleyre's students somehow managed "to visit the various clubs and societies where radical thought is discussed, and sooner or later ally themselves either with the Socialist Section, the Liberal Leagues, the Single Tax Clubs, or the Anarchist Groups." Yet the teacher could not hide her discouragement, for the newcomers' attitudes toward society were not directed to transforming it so much as toward making it: "As the years pass and the gradual filtration and absorption of American commercial life goes on, my students become successful professionals ... and the old teacher must turn for comradeship to the new youth...."[43]

This eulogy for immigrant radicalism did not also mean the death of cosmopolitan and humanitarian ideals. That was a funeral that succeeding generations of Jews somehow missed, as their responses to questionnaires and to candidates demonstrated. A larger fraction of Jews than in any other religious group consider themselves to be independents rather than partisan loyalists.[44] But beginning with their massive support for Al Smith in 1928, they have agglomerated notoriously in the liberal wing of the Democratic Party. Their fervor for the New Deal was so intense that a Republican judge quipped: "The Jews have three *velten* [worlds]: *di velt* [this world], *yene velt* [the next], and Roosevelt."[45] Diverse interest groups and minorities joined the coalition that was forged in the 1930s, but none exceeded the Jews in adhesiveness to the reforms promised in that rendezvous with destiny. In 1960, the proportion of Jews voting for Kennedy was greater than the proportion of Catholics and equal to the percentage of blacks. In 1964, relatively more Jews voted against Goldwater, the most explicitly conservative candidate in memory, than did any other group of whites, regardless of income. In 1968, the percentage of the Jewish vote for Hubert Humphrey was closest to that of the poor racial minorities, such as the Puerto Ricans and the Chicanos. In the polling booth, Jews found the candidacy of George Wallace, the heresiarch of the most conservative bloc in the Roosevelt coalition, as repugnant as blacks did.[46]

Because of the contrast in candidates, the 1972 election is especially illustrative. The incumbent organized perhaps the least subtle appeal to white ethnic groups in recent times, against an opponent who was perceived, among other things, as a bit "soft" on Israel.

Yet, despite much speculation that conservatism was gaining adherents among Jews (which was partly true), despite predictions that their heritage of liberalism was about to be jettisoned, and despite Senator McGovern's opéra bouffe blunder in New York's Garment District when he ordered milk with his chopped chicken liver, he got a higher percentage of Jewish votes than, say, Adlai Stevenson did in 1956. President Nixon attracted the support of three-fourths of all residents of high socioeconomic areas and won a majority of all groups of white ethnics—except for Jews, who cast two out of every three of their votes for the liberal, Democratic candidate.[47] In fact, if the rest of the country had voted the way the Jews did, George McGovern would have been elected president with the most impressive landslide in history. Four years later, Jimmy Carter, the more liberal candidate, got 71 percent of the Jewish vote, a far greater mandate than he got from his fellow Southern whites. The full historical significance of the 1980 election is not yet certain, but for the first time since the impact of Al Smith Jews did not cast the majority of their votes for the Democratic candidate. While Ronald Reagan was decisively defeating the incumbent, he lost to Carter among Jews by about five percentage points (44 percent to 39 percent). The liberal Republican John Anderson, running as an independent, got about 15 percent of the Jewish vote. In local races, such as the U.S. Senate race in New York, ardent liberals such as Elizabeth Holtzman got three times as many Jewish votes as conservative candidates such as Alfonse D'Amato, who in fact defeated her. This record of unwavering liberalism and plebeian voting patterns may be familiar; that should not detract from its importance.

In recognizing the continuity of this voting pattern, and in specifying the ingredients of middle-class achievement, of some sympathy for the downtrodden, of fidelity to civil rights and civil liberties and philanthropy, I am reminded of Lev Kopelev's memoir of Soviet Russia, *To Be Preserved Forever*. As the Red Army advanced into Germany in 1945, its soldiers perpetrated many crimes of rape and murder, looting and pillage. Although he was a Jew well aware of the Nazi policy of genocide as well as a loyal Communist pained by the destruction of his homeland, Major Kopelev protested the vengeful behavior of the rampaging Soviet soldiers. He had believed in "the Socialist morality of our army," but, for calling attention to the dishonor,

Kopelev was forced to spend nine years in Soviet prisons for what his interrogator labeled "bourgeois humanism."[48]

No other phrase is as precise or as evocative in summing up the Jewish style in American politics as well. No other phrase more aptly describes the Jewish struggle to imagine a society in which the right to be equal is secured, without threatening the freedom to be different. Because Jews are primarily middle class, their transcription of prophetic standards of righteousness necessarily has been incomplete, inexact and unsatisfactory. Because they are influenced by humanism, too, they do offer reassurance that the thirst for justice has not yet been slaked and that complacency has not utterly triumphed among them. Since these are generalizations, exceptions must also be granted: There are plenty of illiberal Jews, bigoted Jews, philistine Jews, even *Realpolitiking* rabbis. The relative absence—or dormancy—of anti-Semitism, combined with secure location above the poverty level for the majority of Jews, enlarges the danger that an individualist ethos and smugness may outstrip awareness of the plight of others. But, on the whole, their ballots and their beliefs reflect a desire to make the good life more compatible with an open society; and if "bourgeois humanism" ever were declared a crime in the United States, many more Jews also could be found guilty.

Part III

The Jew in Mass Culture

7

The Enchantment of Comedy

Consider the difficulty if all the American Jews who have contributed to our precious fund of humor were to be named under the condition in which Passover celebrants sing the stanzas about a young goat, an only kid (*Had Gadya*), that is, without pausing for breath. Here, for example, is a partial list, from A to Z, from Alan Arkin and Woody Allen to Zeppo Marx and Zero Mostel: Jack Benny, Henny Youngman, Sheldon Leonard, Jack E. Leonard, Elaine May, Danny Kaye, Mike Nichols, Don Rickles, Ed Wynn, Eddie Cantor, George Jessel, George S. Kaufman, Shecky Greene, Ben Blue, Phil Silvers, Harry Golden, Rube Goldberg (who also appears in the Random House unabridged dictionary as a noun), Dan Greenburg, David Steinberg, Saul Steinberg, George Burns, David Frye, David Levine, Sam Levene, Sam Levenson, Joseph Levitch (now Jerry Lewis), Jules Feiffer, Jan Murray, Murray Schisgal, Neil Simon, Soupy Sales, Goldie Hawn, Dick Shawn, Mort Sahl, Morey Amsterdam, Joey Adams, Joan Rivers, Lenny Bruce, Bruce Jay Friedman, Bud Yorkin, Jack Carter, Jackie Mason, Joseph Heller, Joey Bishop, Alan King, Norman Lear, Bert Lahr, Louise Lasser, Fran Lebowitz, Tom Lehrer, the Stanley Kubrick who directed *Dr. Strangelove*, the Marilyn Monroe who starred in *Some Like It Hot* (she counts because she had converted to Judaism three years earlier, after two hours of religious instruction),[1] Art Buchwald, Herblock (really Herbert Block), William Gaines and Al Feldstein of *Mad* magazine, Montagu Glass, Marvin Kitman, Wallace Markfield, Marshall Efron, Mel Brooks, Albert Brooks, Red Buttons, Al Capp, Gabriel Kaplan, Robert Klein, Allan Sherman, Shelley Berman, Fanny Brice, Barbra Streisand, Dorothy Rothschild Parker, Milton Berle, S. J. Perelman, Carl Reiner, Gene Wilder, Billy Wilder, Sid Caesar, Abe Burrows, Abbie Hoffman, Buddy Hackett, Belle Barth, Ralph Bakshi, Rabbi Baruch Korff (Watergate's Gimpel the Fool, the man of perfect faith), Arthur Kober, Victor Borge, Philip Roth, Walter Matthau, Rodney Dangerfield (né Jack Cohen), Myron Cohen—and there are undoubtedly others too humorous to mention, but enough. Even if this list wasn't swollen to include the names of Minnie Marx's only kids, Leonard (Chico), Adolph (Harpo), Julius (Groucho), Milton (Gummo) and the aforementioned Herbert (Zeppo), plus all those generally anonymous backstage gag writers——dayenu. Enough already.

Therefore we may need reminding how few of the most conspicuous achievements of American humor have come from the 3 percent of the population in the twentieth century that has been Jewish. No Jew—or anyone else, for that matter—has equaled the best comic fiction of Mark Twain, who could be at once hilarious, profound, resonant, and marvelously sane. Some of the stories of Ring Lardner and James Thurber have become permanent adornments of American letters. The political commentary of "Mr. Dooley" (Finley Peter Dunne) has not been surpassed, unless by Russell Baker of the New York Times. No student of film can possibly ignore Chaplin, Keaton (Buster, not Diane), or Fields. No historian of American humor can deprive Robert Benchley and Will Rogers and Bob Hope of the honor they deserve. Attention should also be paid to the criticism of H. L. Mencken and to the fiction of Vladimir Nabokov. It is significant that Constance Rourke's classic American Humor: A Study of the National Character, with its focus on the nineteenth century, includes only one paragraph on Jews—and that is in conjunction with dialect jokes.

W. H. Auden once was asked his definition of a minor poet; he replied that if you place two poems by the same author side by side and can't tell which poem was written earlier, that is a minor poet. By that peculiar test, almost all the comic folk listed at the top qualify as minor. Their work rarely moves beyond the single entendre or suggests growth into more complex possibilities; it remains, in other words, about as adult as the short-sheeting that is the soul of wit in summer camps. (At the moment is the additional factor, George Burns has observed, that, with the death of the vaudeville circuits, "there's no place to be lousy anymore"—except in the 96 percent of American homes that have television sets.)[2] Nevertheless, American Jewish humor at its best—which will be suggested by the examples to follow rather than by explicit critical judgments—is so unlousy that it comes within striking distance of satisfying Nietzsche's plea for art, which we need in order not to perish of truth.

A final warning to be issued is one that students of humor seem to consider virtually obligatory: he who can, does; he who cannot, explains the joke. The analyst of comedy is inevitably typecast as the straight man, playing Dr. Spielvogel to Alexander Portnoy, that self-described character in a Jewish joke. It is widely known how tedious the standard theoretical works on humor are. Even Freud's *Wit and Its Relation to the Unconscious* has earned, I think unfairly, a reputation as perhaps the dullest book he ever wrote, with the exception of *Three Contributions to the Theory of Sex* (both of which, it so happens, were published in 1905).

Everyone knows how deadly it is to attempt to explain a joke, for to analyze humor is to vivisect, to kill a living thing in the very act of examining it. Although there is a Jewish joke that a peasant laughs three times (once when he hears a joke, once when it is explained to him, and once when he understands it), the systematic understanding of the sources and meaning of humor has eluded every scholar's grasp. No one has been able to generalize successfully about what is funny, or what makes it funny, or what makes some funny things last. Saul Steinberg once said that "trying to define humor is one of the definitions of humor." It is tempting simply to assert that the essence of comedy may be ultimately indecipherable and unfathomable, and leave it at that.

But someone still has to try to straighten out the place after the hysterics have had their hour on the couch and the anarchists their night at the opera; the method of my approach to madness differs from the primarily literary analysis that American Jewish humor usually has elicited.[3] In its focus on the social implications of the subject, this chapter is intended to manifest greater interest in what makes Sammy run than in what makes Saul Bellow. For humor—both expressed and appreciated—is central to the subculture of American Jewry, the kind of badge Jews pride themselves on wearing, an acknowledged sign that certifies membership in a community. At the moment, humor is a way, in a relatively tolerant society, of keeping up the resistance level to what many Jews fear, which is less the loss of faith than the loss of identity. Many can live more easily with atheism than with utter assimilation, and since we moderns play for lower stakes than salvation, humor has become more suitable than in the past. It is one of the dominant threads of memory and group consciousness, a style that disarmingly proclaims that "we" are still different from "them."

For humor is *cosa nostra, unser shtick*, our thing. It percolates through the associations of Jews, helping to sustain not only individual energies but collective resources as well. It helps to define one group's place in the amorphous and anxious society that is America. Russell Baker once observed that, unlike himself, Art Buchwald *looks* like a humorist. Baker did not mention that Buchwald also happens to look Jewish, and those two attributes have by now become blurred. While once assessing her peers, Phyllis Diller called Jackie Mason "very funny. Just to hear him talk makes me laugh. He wouldn't have to say anything funny—that very thick Russian-Jewish accent just makes me fall down."[4] When salted with Yiddish, wise-cracks seem to have the added preservative of folk wisdom, and like so many stereotypes, the Gentile impression of Jews as jesters has more than a tincture of truth. For even among nonprofessionals within the Jewish community, the comedian's impulse to work the room can be irresistible. For example, in his memoir of the most subtle American historian since Henry Adams, Alfred Kazin recalled his first meeting with Richard Hofstadter: "Of course he was telling jokes, doing the impersonations that would regularly send his friends to the floor. . . . Then and afterward, for thirty-four years, he could reduce me to more helpless laughter than any professional jokesmith in American life."[5] Hofstadter!

Newsweek reported that a Grossinger's *tummeler* emeritus, Mel Brooks, is enough of a friend of a CUNY literature professor named Joseph Heller for the latter to assure us that the private rather than public Brooks is the more funny and intelligent. Philip Roth, self-styled disciple of Henny Youngman as well as a National Book Award winner for fiction, admired Lenny Bruce's work and can be—on the page or in person—as funny as Bruce, who was after all a professional nightclub comedian.[6]

Consider the implications. Think of the likelihood of friendship between, say, Thomas Wolfe and W. C. Fields, or between James Baldwin and Richard Pryor. Nor is it likely that William Styron has ever felt himself in competition with Johnny Carson, or Truman Capote with Red Skelton, that they ever have thought they just might be better than pros who had emerged from the crucible of the Catskills. It therefore seems appropriate that the first major American novelist who was also a Jew, Nathanael West, had for a brother-in-law a Marx Brothers scenarist. It seems appropriate that the only play written by today's most respected American novelist (and he's also a Jew) has for a protagonist a Jewish professional comic.

Saul Bellow's play, *The Last Analysis*, prefigured the rise of the Jewish comic as a less peripheral, a more representative, figure within American popular culture. *Lenny*, for example, has been inescapable—the Broadway play and the Hollywood movie both seemed to argue that because Bruce was rough he must have been a diamond. Mordecai Richler's disclaimer that Bruce "didn't die for *my* sins" is a useful clue that, however malicious the prosecutions may have been, he was the sort of person who would have self-destructed in Sodom and Gomorrah. Nevertheless Bruce's influence on other comedians has been important, the interest in his career enormous. Several other works of fiction and drama have made a Jewish comic the central character, such as Wallace Markfield's *You Could Live If They Let You*, in which a put-down artist named Jules Farber is trapped inside his own hysterically unpleasant identity. Irvin Faust's *A Star in the Family* chronicles the career of Bart Goldwine, who never made it to the Palladium. The French novelist Romain Gary's *Dance of Genghis Cohn* deals with the dybbuk of a nightclub comedian killed in a Nazi extermination camp who haunts his German tormentor—a mixture of slapstick and horror that has become something of a specialty of the house of Israel. Of Neil Simon's major plays, the least funny is *The Sunshine Boys*, the odd couple redivivus as two aged comedians. "You're a funny man, Al," Willie tells his ex-partner, who replies: "You know what your trouble was, Willie? You always took the jokes too seriously. They were just jokes. We did comedy on the stage for forty-three years, I don't think you enjoyed it once." "If I was there to enjoy it," Willie responds, "I would buy a ticket."[7]

It is Willie who is closer to Judaic tradition, in which the enjoyment of life is hardly the first commandment. Gen. 21:6 reports that in her old age Sarah gave birth, an idea she found so amusing that her son was named Isaac ("he shall laugh"). But laughter is an uncommon response both in and to the Bible, whose figures are not memorable for their levity. The Greeks at least made Thalia, the muse of comedy, one of the three Graces; and Homer permitted his gods to laugh. Even the Purim spiel, the farcical recycling of the Book of Esther in which the town wag—the "Purim rabbi"— did parodistic send-ups of sermons and rabbinic responsa, dates from the Middle Ages. And it was the *shtetl* that institutionalized the *badkhen*, the emcee at weddings, the remote ancestor of the so-called Toastmaster General of the United States, George Jessel, and of the roastmasters of the Friars Club. Here is the job description of the *badkhen*: "To be a master of his art, he must command rapid transitions between extremes as well as concentrated bursts of melancholy or of joy. At its highest, his performance combines the skills of actor, poet, composer, singer, commentator. The *badkhen* may merely be some local wit, drafted for the occasion. A really great one, however, is known far and wide and is constantly in demand. His solemn speeches sound vibrant notes of duty or of grief. His ditties may enter into the realms of folk song. His jesting may be simple and 'folksy' or may draw on a wide range of learning— satirizing and parodying the flights of *pilpul* and drily deflating scholarship with free use of puns, homonyms, and innuendo."[8]

But Jewish humor as we recognize it today can barely be traced much earlier than the eighteenth century. It was sparked by the friction of emancipation, by the fateful encounter with Christian neighbors of the Jews emerging from the ghettos of the West and the *shtetlach* of the East. Since telling a joke is an oral art, historical records yield few gems that can be dated with certainty. But in written form, Jewish wit can be found little earlier than Heinrich Heine, who, along with Ludwig Boerne, is credited with the invention of the German feuilleton, the casual humorous monologue in which a few Jews have excelled down through the Viennese café wits to Perelman and Allen. Heine helped transmit to Jews who came after him the pertinence of irony, the prism of double and multiple meanings simultaneously held and accepted. It is the natural response of a people poised between two worlds: one, the matrix of ghetto and *shtetl*, to which they can no longer return; the other, the civil society of the West, in which they could not be fully at ease.

In the United States, at least since the third wave of immigration beginning in the late nineteenth century, that note of irony could be heard, with all the ambivalence and ambiguity, all the tension and estrangement, all the posturing and self-consciousness, all the desire to go native and the fear of letting go, all the sense of inferiority and sense of the ridiculous that marginality in American life implies. (It is arguable whether Simmel or Veblen should be credited with refining the concept of marginality, but whoever it was deserved the rest of the afternoon off.) Although Jews have been sufficiently within American culture to adhere to and understand its ideals as if by osmosis, complete social acceptance has been denied or at least dubious. To the banker Otto Kahn has been attributed the definition of a kike as "a Jewish gentleman who has just left the room." Although anti-Semitism in America has been relatively mild, its Jews have had reason to deem their fate poignant and odd and thus requiring the palliative of laughter. "I have always been far more pleased by my good fortune in being born a Jew than my critics may begin to imagine," Philip Roth has written. "It's a complicated, interesting, morally demanding, and very singular experience, and I like that."[9]

However singular that experience may be, the precise ways in which "we" are still different from "them" are so hard to pin down that Lenny Bruce may have committed the fallacy of misplaced concreteness in one of his most famous routines: "I'm Jewish. Count Basie's Jewish. Ray Charles is Jewish. Eddie Cantor's goyish. B'nai B'rith is goyish; Hadassah, Jewish. Marine Corps—heavy goyim, dangerous. Koolaid is goyish. . . . Evaporated milk is goyish even if the Jews invented it. Spam is goyish and rye bread is Jewish. . . . As you know, white bread is very goyish. Fruit salad is Jewish. Lime jello is goyish. Lime soda is *very* goyish. . . . Black cherry soda's very Jewish," etc. etc.[10] In Walter Bernstein's script for *The Front*, Woody Allen's Gentile girl friend reminisces that, when she was growing up, the worst sin in her family was to raise one's voice.

Woody Allen responds that, in *his* family, the worst sin was to buy retail. However sly such redistributions of cultural categories, what is also very Jewish is the marginal man's fascination with difference, with mapping out the boundaries of Jew and Gentile on their common ground in America. The autobiographical walker in the city, Alfred Kazin, could see from his Brownsville neighborhood the lights of Manhattan, the borough that symbolized making it in America, which was so far away that "even the I.R.T. got tired by the time it came to us, and ran up into the open for a breath of air before it got locked into its terminus."[11] Out of that ghetto and others like it came kids who had practiced one-liners and whole monologues the way other kids in other ghettos had practiced hook shots and lay-ups, with comedy providing a form of handling the need for the security of an ancient and consoling identity as well as the hunger for conformity and normality.

Humor thus served as an opiate of the Jewish masses, a painkiller for the incongruities of an exilic past so terrible at its worst that it was daring to hope for a Messiah competent enough to redeem it, a past so strained with the extreme compensations of messianism and idealism that on Sukkoth the pious Jews of Europe prayed for rain for the crops of Palestine even though neither the crops nor the Jewish settlements of Palestine were in existence. Against such exorbitant demands placed on common sense, a humor could develop that might deflate the absolutism of the purely interior life, a humor that might engage the paradox of both the absurdity of such dreams and their necessity for Jewish survival. The distinctiveness of Jewish humor, Robert Alter has argued, is this need to set the limits of the ordinary and the mundane on the pretensions of the mythic and the apocalyptic, the need to reduce the extravagance of idealism to the proportions of the familiar.[12] A proverb such as "If you want to forget all your troubles, put on a shoe that's too tight" not only softens a cardinal fact of Jewish history, which is suffering, but has its reverberations in the New World as well. Much of the hilarity of Mel Brooks' two-thousand-year-old man is a result of the effect of an endearingly accented *zeyda* who domesticates historical romance and punctures the transcendence of legend (Shakespeare is denigrated for his sloppy penmanship, Napoleon is remembered as "short, right?") The most predictable structure of a Woody Allen witticism is the juxtaposition of the lofty and the immediate, getting at least a smile out of the wish that even the Almighty might be housebroken: his parents' values were "God and carpeting."

The savoring of such juxtapositions and paradoxes comes naturally to a people that is both vilified and chosen, a people whose place in society is so bizarre, so problematic, so defined by others as well as themselves. There may be little point in being Jewish without this awareness of ambiguity, this sense of how bittersweet life is, this recognition of how apt is the symbolism of the Hillel sandwich that mixes *haroset* and *moror* on Passover the way the *badkhen* mixed and manipulated the emotions at weddings. The psychic imperative to "swallow pain with a smile," as Langston Hughes said of black Americans, may explain the high saline content of Jewish humor, that unanatomical proximity of funny bones to tear ducts. Even among our comics, Judaic law does not prohibit grave images. When *Esquire* put Woody Allen on its cover, it boasted: "We did it! We finally did it! We got Woody Allen to laugh!" Picture others as disparate as Myron Cohen and George S. Kaufman and Shelley Berman and Ed Wynn and Bert Lahr: they are so melancholy, so unlike the expectations we might have of jolly clowns. They don't even bother to laugh on the *outside*, and though we are assured of the value of laughing when it hurts, many Jewish comics are almost unsettling in their own apparent failure to achieve catharsis through comedy.

The bleakness may be the result of an especially troubled encounter with the limitations of the human condition itself. At its most acute, Jewish humor is a *comédie noire* based on the desperate knowledge that, after all the pain we will have inflicted upon one another, we will each be led away from the cell, one by one, into the darkness. Laughter is thus the response to a cosmic punch line, to the paradox of love and death, to the odd necessity of having to live together and having to die alone. (Pardon the shorthand.) Comedy suggests a certain dignity in being able to exit laughing, and it is the imprisonment of mortality that especially perturbs some of these humorists. John Yossarian, an Assyrian-American in the novel *Catch-22* (but a Jew in Heller's earlier manuscript version), wants to "live forever or die in the attempt." Brooks, the creator of the rapidly aging 2,013-year-old man, has proclaimed his desire for "immortality in my lifetime." "Why are our days numbered,"

Woody Allen asks, "instead of, say, lettered?" And as Boris Dim-
itrovich Grushenko in *Love and Death*, he realizes that "everyone
has to go sometime. I have to go at 6 A.M. It was supposed to be
5 A.M., but I have a good lawyer." The fear of dying is the theme
of Dorothy Parker's resigned "Résumé": "Razors pain you; / Rivers are damp; / Acids stain you; / And drugs cause cramp. / Guns
aren't lawful; / Nooses give; / Gas smells awful; / You might as
well live."[13] One of the curiosities of literary history is that Parker
has gotten classified as a humorist, as an artificer of light verse.

Although Franz Kafka managed to escape categorization as a
humorist, it is said that he laughed till the tears came to his eyes as
he read his mordant tales aloud to his friends. In describing Kafka's
attitude toward the universe, Albert Camus was reminded of the
joke of the man seen fishing in a bathtub. "Anything biting?" a
friend asks. "Of course not, dummy"—goes the reply—"can't you
see this is a bathtub?"[14] Inhospitable though the universe is, incom-
mensurable though life is, most of us cannot play long enough,
knowing that the only game in town is fixed. And humor is the
impulse, before we are taken away by the *malekh-hamoves*, to fling
a custard pie in the face of ultimate defeat.

But there is a special animus to Jewish humor, for some of the
descendants of those who had to wear yellow badges on their sleeves
grew up even in America with chips on their shoulders. Humor,
or more precisely wit, has been not only a shield against the outside
world but also a weapon against the goyim, a way of getting even.
It too is one of the needle trades. Perelman once told an interviewer
that he sprinkled Yiddish words in his feuilletons "for their invective
content. There are nineteen words in Yiddish that convey gradations
of disparagement from a mild, fluttery helplessness to a state of
downright, irreconcilable brutishness." Markfield has observed that
"Yiddish, in the hands of a Jack E. Leonard or a Buddy Hackett,
is like a wet towel in the hands of a locker-room bully; it cuts, slices
. . . shames, undermines, puts down."[15] I can only add that the
incorporation of its vocabulary has helped give our American prose
a whiplash sting. It is no accident that the stand-up comic's greatest
boast, after his or her act is done, is to offer backstage postmortems
such as "I killed them out there" and "I knocked them dead." Not
only when aggressive drunks have to be controlled is there an air
of menace around some comedians, especially Jewish comedians,

who sometimes seem ready to unlatch the door in the back of the brain and let some of the scorpions out. "I don't want to make just another movie," Brooks has insisted. "I want to make trouble. I want to say in comic terms, '*J'accuse.*' "[16] And even though he himself need not be taken too seriously on this point, gall is indivisible from the style of the likes of Don Rickles and David Levine, for beneath the waves of mirth, an undertow of anger almost threatens to pull us under. Not for nothing does Freud's book define wit so heavily in terms of hostility and aggressiveness and, significantly, so many of his examples are Jewish jokes.

Nor is cruelty rarely far below the surface in comedy; the ridicule of foibles is often close to the contempt for flaws. Sometimes the criticism is what ethologists study as intraspecific aggression— the humorist attacking the perpetrators and victims of "humor," as in the Duke and Dauphin chapters of *The Adventures of Huckleberry Finn*, or in Lardner's "Haircut," or in Bruce's Palladium routine. It is hard to miss the broader streak of misanthropy not only in Clemens and Lardner but also in Fields and certainly in the famous humor of the American Southwest. "The stories the Westerners laughed at were sickeningly violent, as exaggeratedly cruel as the tall talk was blasphemous," Professor Kenneth Lynn has written. "Their characteristic hero was some king of brutes, some champion brawler . . . [or] prodigious drinker. . . . What counted was his savage heart." However distant Mike Fink may appear from Eustace Tilly, a memoir of the *New Yorker* suggests that its most gifted humorist fit this pattern: "It was in Thurber's nature to wish to inflict pain," and he apparently was unhappy unless he could get his friends to squabble.[17] Laughter is an acceptable way to disguise the derision we may privately feel for the hapless victim toward whom we are supposed to display compassion.

In offering us a compromise between the pity that conscience requires and the smug relief of having avoided the fate of the luckless, American Jewish humor also skirts the edge of nastiness. In *The Day of the Locust*, West wrote that "it is hard to laugh at the need for beauty and romance. . . . But it is easy to sigh." Yet his two major novels, populated with grotesques, usually are considered early veins of black humor, at which it is not easy to sigh. Roth's *The Great American Novel* includes a squad from an insane asylum that takes the field against the fabled Ruppert Mundys, as well as a couple of midgets (one of whom is hailed as "a credit to his size") and a one-armed outfielder whose handicap enables a batter to score an inside-the-mouth home run. *Love and Death* shows a convention of village idiots. Brooks is especially pleased with the scene in *Young Frankenstein* in which a blind monk clumsily plays host to the monster. And although Brooks reacted vehemently to the charge that in *Blazing Saddles* Mongo's name is an abbreviation of mongoloid, it strains credulity that the director would not have assumed that audiences would make that association. A wall thus has been breached that the psychiatrist Theodor Reik noticed had been erected around Jewish humor in Europe: "Mockery at a crippled condition, physical affliction and ugliness as well as old age, with its many complaints, is amazingly rare as a subject of Jewish witticisms."[18] The dangers of the coarsening of sensibility, especially in our century, cannot be dismissed; there was a need for walls against sadism and ugliness.

But even if Dr. Reik's claim cannot be substantiated fully for American brands of Jewish humor, the relative absence of cruelty toward the helpless and the handicapped may be credited not only to the recalcitrance of humane values but also to a shift in targets, to displacement. Hostility takes the form, as Dr. Reik and many others have noticed, of masochism, of the self-deprecation that—as an Israeli amazon informs Portnoy in the "Alex in Wonderland" section of the novel—may be the essence of Diaspora humor. Again it is Heine, the first of those Enlightenment Jews to recognize that life is—or at least should be—a tale told by an ironist, who gets there first: "I cannot relate my own griefs without the thing becoming comic."[19] It is not so much that Jews see themselves as victims but that the victimization is rendered ludicrous and thus bearable in the very act of shrill insistence. Playing sorrows fortissimo may drown out the silence of God.

Neil Simon once distinguished between "writing Gentile" (for example, *Barefoot in the Park*) and "writing Jewish" (for example, *The Odd Couple*), by which he meant more than inflections and phrasing: Jewish is more than black cherry soda and rye bread; it is "martyrdom, and self-pity, and 'everything terrible happens to me.' " For Portnoy, whose confession ends with a primal scream, for the Peter Tarnopol of *My Life as a Man*, for Gene Wilder's Leo Bloom in *The Producers* and his young Dr. Frankenstein, for the

Alan Arkin characters in *Little Murders* and *Hearts of the West*, among others, the title of Freud's first major book is applicable: studies in hysteria. (In the film version of *The Seven-Percent Solution*, Freud was played by Arkin.) When one adds Albert Goldman's description of Joe Ancis, reputedly the funniest man in Brooklyn, the ur-Lenny Bruce ("From a block away you can feel the waves coming off this guy. An aura, a sonic boom of hysteria, his face is coming in like the head of a rocket"),[20] one conclusion to be drawn is that the stoic ideal is goyish, having a tantrum is Jewish.

Perhaps the best recent example is Simon's own Mel Edison, the frantic forty-seven-year-old prisoner of Second Avenue, the wisecracking victim of urban civilization and its discontents. He hears everything. The heat is oppressive, tropical. The toilet doesn't stop flushing. He gets indigestion from a health-food restaurant ("I haven't had a real piece of bread in thirty years. . . . If I knew what was going to happen, I would have saved some rolls when I was a kid"). The garbage outside is piled up so high that Edison predicts their fourteenth-floor apartment will soon be on the second floor. Not even the cactus plant is surviving. After six years of therapy, his psychiatrist had died, and when his wife, Edna, suggests treatment with another, he replies: "And start all over from the beginning? . . .It'll cost me another $23,000 just to fill *this* doctor in with information I already gave the dead one." When Edna also proposes that they move to the countryside or out West, Mel counters: "And what do I do for a living: Become a middle-aged cowboy? Maybe they'll put me in charge of rounding up the elderly cattle." When his wife refuses to be spoken to "like I'm insane," he replies: "I'm halfway there, you might as well catch up." Their apartment is robbed. Laid off, wandering the city in search of employment, Mel reports to his wife that he "played two innings of softball yesterday . . . With a day camp for fourteen-year-olds. . . . Harvey, the right fielder, had to go for a violin lesson, so I played the last two innings." Alas, he cannot claim to have saved the day: "I struck out, dropped two fly balls and lost the game. . . . They wanted to kill me. . . . I know I can make the team, I just have to get my timing back. If I don't find a job maybe I'll go back to camp this summer." His wife encourages him: "It would take me two minutes to sew in your name tapes . . . "[21]

From Jack Benny, who was (according to Fred Allen) "the first comedian in radio to realize that you could get big laughs by ridiculing yourself instead of your stooges," to Rodney Dangerfield, whose insignia is the plaintive "I don't get no respect," the Jewish comic has bent the self-definition of martyrdom to his own purposes. There are undoubtedly biographical explanations here, in that several comedians seem to have found their vocation already as children too puny to use their fists against bullies and chose to live by their wits instead. Such traumas were then transmuted, as in Perelman's shuddering recollection of a grammar school "fiend incarnate, a hulking evil-faced youth related on both sides of his family to Torquemada and dedicated to making my life insupportable. . . . Too wispy to stand up to my oppressor, I took refuge in a subdued blubbering, which soon abraded the teacher's nerves and earned me the reputation of being refractory. . . . " As a child Woody Allen once won two weeks at an interfaith camp, "where I was sadistically beaten by boys of every race, creed, and color."[22] As an adult, in *Play It Again, Sam*, he pleads with a mugger: "Don't shoot...I'm a bleeder." Even in the scene in which Portnoy acknowledges the self-deprecatory quality of Jewish humor, he is both sexually frustrated and physically overpowered by the six-foot kibbutznik, Naomi.

But Jewish jokes go well beyond this emphasis on helplessness, this delineation of the boundaries of circumstance. So completely are faults, vices, embarrassments, shames lingered over that it is not easy to decide whether such humor was created by Jews or by anti-Semitic Gentiles. When the fingerprints can be incontrovertibly identified, as in *Portnoy's Complaint*, Marie Syrkin could make not only the apparently obligatory accusations of self-hatred against Roth but also could note parallels between the analysand's revelations and Nazi images of Jews as defilers of Gentile maidens. (Roth still counted his blessings: "Had she not been constrained by limitations of space, Syrkin might eventually have had me in the dock with the entire roster of Nuremberg defendants.")[23] But the novelist was only culminating and indeed synthesizing an important and psychologically healthy tradition, which accepts some of the very accusations of anti-Semites, turns those crimes inside out, and thus blunts the impact and absorbs the shock of bigotry. Marginal men and women thus nervously discharge their own anxieties by giggling

at them and thereby hope to escape their spell. You think that's
bad? the Jew tells the anti-Semite. Can you top this? . . . Markfield's
Jules Farber wags his finger at a group of matrons and spits out:
"Remember, never be ashamed that you're Jewish; it's enough that
I'm ashamed that you're Jewish."[24] Jews not only kid their own
ostensible group characteristics but also, paradoxically, attack some
brethren for not being Jewish *enough*—hence the in-group popularity of jokes about Reform Jews. With the patent decline of anti-
Semitism since the end of the Second World War, Jews have become
comfortable enough to realize—as the success of musicals such as
Funny Girl and its star attests—that a nose with deviations *isn't*
such a crime against the nation. The humorist can be less effectively
stigmatized as an informer to the goyim, who can now hear in-
jokes on talk shows and read them in best sellers, which is after all
where the gripes of Roth are stored.

The animus remains. In a way, Jews are out to shame the goyim
by insisting upon a shared humanity, by emphasizing aspects of
human nature that polite Gentile society has chosen to minimize or
ignore. American Jewish humor is fueled with vitriol and concocted
to wash away protocol. If genteel society condemns the "dirty
Jews," then the accused will sometimes perversely admit to the
charge, indeed affirm a certain kind of faith—I stink, therefore I
am—as a way of asserting the commonness of the dust from which
all of us have sprung and to which even the genteel will return. The
lines were more easily drawn in the late nineteenth century, when
Edmund Clarence Stedman complained that the word "sewer" appeared three times in *A Connecticut Yankee in King Arthur's Court*;
when Richard Watson Gilder protected the readers of *Century* magazine from such offensive expressions as "We was always naked,"
"Dern yer skin!" and "I was in a sweat" in the serialized version
of *The Adventures of Huckleberry Finn*; when Louisa May Alcott
got Huck removed from the Concord library. Good taste in that
sense has been unable to sustain itself in the twentieth century,
particularly after the acceptance of *Ulysses*. (Judge Woolsey's famous 1933 decision also disclosed an interesting clue into puritan
culture when he termed the effect of the novel "somewhat emetic"
rather than "aphrodisiac"—which made it all right.) In the past
couple of decades, the difficulty of drawing a line has become almost
insuperable. When an appeals court temporarily overturned the con-

viction of Captain Howard Levy, the dermatologist who had refused to train Green Berets, for conduct unbecoming an officer and a gentleman, the court acknowledged its failure to find a commonly accepted definition of what a gentleman is.

But for most of Western history, it has been understood that, whatever else a gentleman is, he could not be of the Hebraic persuasion. Jews not bound by their own religious scruples thus have been free to explore those areas beyond the rim of good taste, free to press their noses—their less-than-classic profiles—against the glass of form. No wonder then that in recent years so many of those associated with blue language—Mailer, Roth, Allen Ginsberg, "Dirty Lenny"—have been Jews, as have been their attorneys, as is Gershon Legman, who is the leading scholar of pornography, the Aristotle of the dirty joke, the Linnaeus of the limerick, the author of a veritable Syntopicon of *shmutz*. Indeed Freud himself cited several Jewish jokes about the lack of fastidiousness, the indifference to the codes of proper behavior by which Jews recognized their own differentiation from Gentiles. Among Einstein's favorite non-scientific reading during his final years at Princeton was Emily Post's manual of etiquette, passages of which caused him to cackle with delight.[25] (The fact that the rules governing the conduct of ladies and gentlemen must have seemed to Einstein about as exotic as the winter ceremonial of the Kwakiutl is another bewildering example of why it is so difficult to classify humor.) Groucho Marx once wrote to the sleazy gutter rag *Confidential* as follows: "If you continue to publish slanderous pieces about me, I shall feel compelled to cancel my subscription." Even S. J. Perelman, whose literary persona was least shabby genteel, eventually repatriated himself from England because he had found "too much couth" there. Another Marx Brothers associate, Herman Mankiewicz, once attended an elegant dinner party, drank too much during dinner, and then vomited on the table. The emetic effect caused a hushed silence, which Mankiewicz himself broke by assuring the host: "It's all right. . . . The white wine came up with the fish."[26] Given this sort of heightened self-consciousness about propriety, it should not be surprising that the first movie not so much *in* bad taste as *about* bad taste, *The Producers* (with its play-within-a-film of a Nazi musical on Broadway), should be by that Flatbush fabulist, Mel Brooks.

One of the ways to puncture the pretensions of the Gentiles is to make them Marranos, secret Jews, as in all the jokes whose punchlines reveal that certified goyim such as Santa Claus, Richard Nixon, Billy Graham, and the pope break out into Yiddish. There are Jewish-accented Indians in *Cat Ballou* and *Blazing Saddles*, Jewish-accented robots in *Sleeper*, a Jewish-accented black cabbie in *Bye Bye Braverman*. Sherlock Holmes has become Shlock Holmes, and James Bond has become Israel Bond, agent oi-oi-seven, thus broadening Bernard Malamud's parody of the most familiar of all syllogisms: all men are mortal.... Instead, all men are Jews—because all men suffer. But when Gentiles insist on their gentility, the characteristic response is to make Shylock a straight man and ask, hath not a goy organs? Jewish humor has more than its share of crudeness and lewdness—human equalizers when social barriers are raised and tradesmen and peddlers forced to enter from the rear. William James, hearing Freud deliver his 1909 lectures at Clark University, called him "a dirty fellow." What movie critics call "lusty" in foreign films, Billy Wilder once caustically lamented, they call "dirty" in his films.[27] When Woody Allen's psychiatrist asked him in *Take the Money and Run* if he considered sex dirty, he replied, "Yes. If you do it right." Ring Lardner's campaign against the suggestive lyrics heard on the radio might be contrasted with Zero Mostel's nitty-gritty recording of *Songs My Mother Never Taught Me* or with a few real Jewish mothers, the red hot mommas such as Sophie Tucker, Belle Barth, and Totie Fields. They all illustrate the warning issued by Rabbi Akiba that "jesting and levity lead a person to lewdness."

Had Lenny Bruce been better educated, had he read for instance Denis de Rougement's *Love in the Western World* (a study of how, between the eleventh and twelfth centuries, the French invented love—that is, the romantic version, the idealization of passion), he might have added to his list that love is goyish, sex is Jewish. Whether Alex Portnoy (who wanted to "put the id back in Yid") or the compulsive, aging adolescents in *Carnal Knowledge*, whether the leering and aggressive opportunist that was Groucho's screen personality or many of the figures Woody Allen has played, all are essentially prisoners of sex with a remarkably high recidivism rate. In much of American Jewish humor, love is folly and an illusion. Except for some artificial sweeteners added to the endings, Billy

Wilder's best comedies have all the romantic sentimentality of a police blotter. The conclusion to Dorothy Parker's "Unfortunate Coincidence" is not similarly marred: "By the time you swear you're his, / Shivering and sighing, / And he vows his passion is / Infinite, undying— / Lady, make a note of this: / One of you is lying."[28] They are as far removed from the romantic ideal as the domestic pieties of a Sam Levenson are from Sophie Portnoy, whose parental love is perceived as disguised aggression, a will to power that threatens autonomous manhood with infantile dependency. Even when other Jews—in Hollywood, on Broadway, in the radio and television studios—have sold dreams of redemptive love, much of the aim of American Jewish humor has been to illumine the disparity between fantasy and actuality, to cross the chasm between ideal and real by walking upon a banana peel.

Yet such humor is dependent on those public dreams and official pieties for its own ironic effects. Take, as only one minor example, the post-World War II consoling myth of the "good German." The notion was briefly mocked in *One, Two, Three* by director-scriptwriter Billy Wilder (whose mother perished at Auschwitz), and more directly and savagely in Richler's novel *Cocksure*, in which a British gentleman after the war "had collected case histories and compiled a book, elegantly produced if necessarily slender, about all the charitable little acts done by Germans to Jews during the Nazi era. Here a simple but goodhearted sergeant offering spoonfuls of marmalade to Jewish children before they were led off to the gas chambers, somewhere else a fabled general refusing to drink with Eichmann or a professor quoting Heine right to a Nazi's face."[29] But generally a direct encounter with the Holocaust has been avoided; even Brooks did not mention the almost ineffable in *The Producers*, as though even bad taste has its limits—at least so far. Perhaps because one "good German" was not associated with the war against the Jews, Werner Von Braun was a favorite target. He was satirized in the Tom Lehrer ditty about the "widows and cripples in old London town / Who owe their large pensions to Werner Von Braun," the "big hero" who "learned to count backward to zero."[30] He was also lampooned as Dr. Strangelove (admittedly with elements of Herman Kahn and Henry Kissinger thrown in as well). And when Hollywood produced a film about the cosmetic aspects of the rocket engineer's career entitled *I Aim for the Stars*, Mort Sahl offered a subtitle: *But I Hit London.*

So much for one myth anyway. Since reality is so elusive and so amorphous, since a ubiquitous substitute has been found in what are called the mass media, American Jewish humor has relied heavily on those filters of "experience" and has played upon the meretriciousness of popular culture even as it partakes of it. In the nineteenth century, Hawthorne and Henry James fired their famous salvos against American society as too thin to bear the weight of serious, intricate, complex fiction. But in the twentieth century, Philip Roth has argued that American social reality, refracted through the prisms of publicity and celebrity, has become too rich for novelists to keep up with, that the facts of national life are too wildly improbable and irrational to sustain the standard methods of verisimilitude. Indeed we now know that almost anything can happen on television, including murder and the confession of murder, and we are braced to expect almost any affront to dignity, any insult to the intelligence, any violation of integrity, any banality, any assault on privacy. We should not be astonished if Indira Gandhi shows up as a special guest on Merv Griffin's show seated next to a crooner, a starlet, and a guru, or if Jean-Paul Sartre and Simone de Beauvoir had appeared on *The Dating Game*. The media may have become *the* great American subject, and humorists have tried so hard to keep up that parody is almost synonymous with American Jewish humor itself.

For example, *Mad* magazine mimics comics, movies, advertisements. Much of *Your Show of Shows* consisted of TV takeoffs on movies, while *The Groove Tube* was a movie send-up of television. Like Allen, Perelman specialized in parody for the *New Yorker*, and even Perelman's autobiographical pieces were often accounts of silly movies (*Cloudland Revisited*). Unlike Russell Baker, who is an essayist on the psychopathology of everyday life and of politics, Art Buchwald characteristically imagines dialogue in which politicos lampoon themselves. Most of Brooks's films have been parodies, as were most of Allen's early films. The best section of Alan Lelchuk's *American Mischief*, the killing of Norman Mailer, parodies the killing of Clare Quilty in Nabokov's *Lolita*. Malamud's *The Natural* is not only a satire on baseball but a parody of *The*

Waste Land. Among Portnoy's zaniest impulses is the magnification of his shame into newspaper headlines, to see how his crimes would look in the media.

It may be an important limitation that, in darting so naturally from the unconscious to commerce and from the id to the ad, some comics have so little to draw upon except their own sometimes recondite knowledge and memory of movies, comic books, sports, radio shows, and other forms of popular culture. Many humorists are too heavily dependent not on the direct observation of social incongruities and human folly but on the ways in which they have already been treated, however inadvertently, in the media; and that world is simply not textured enough to be consistently and maturely exploited. The risks of vacuity and preciousness should not be minimized; it is dreary to contemplate the endless recycling of the popular arts.

But what salvages the best of American Jewish humor is often the continuation of Heine's achievement in shaping language itself for comic purposes. The Jews are not the only people to claim to have talked to God but are perhaps the only people to have talked *back* to God, to have attempted to bargain and negotiate. Soon after Freud devised the method that was soon nicknamed "the talking cure," the Catholic intellectual Charles Péguy succinctly presented the case for Jewish verbal resourcefulness: The Catholic has been reading for two generations; the Protestant for three centuries; the Jew has always read. One might add that the Jew has long been talking about, arguing about what he has read, in contrast to the customary image of the saint in Christian mythology as mute or possessing a speech defect. The sufferer in modern Jewish lore undergoes, like Bellow's Philip Bummidge, Roth's Portnoy and Tarnapol, Erica Jong's Isadora Wing, the talking cure. The polar opposite of the Christian saint who is struck dumb is the Jew who *shpritzes*, the perpetuator of an oral tradition (Scheherazade should have been Jewish). "Interior monologue, free association, stream of consciousness—these are the fancy words for the *shpritz*," Albert Goldman writes. "Out . . . in the Bensonhurst-Boro Park Delta of Jewish humor, the Basin Street of Jewish jazz . . . Lenny [Bruce] first learned to be funny . . . funny being equivalent to vital, strong, honest, and soulful. Funny guys were the guys who told the truth. Guys with an original point of view, a private language, a sound.

The Jewish equivalent of the black jazzman. A hero." What dazzled Dick Gregory about Bruce was that "here's a man [who] can do three hours on any subject."[31]

In the pantheon of immortal silent film comedians there are no Jews, who have historically been more comfortable within the world of sound rather than gesture, of idea rather than image. There are exceptions: the drawings of Saul Steinberg and the caricatures of David Levine (although, to strengthen the generalization, the cartoons of Herblock and Feiffer depend on the cleverness of captions and dialogues), the pregnant silences in the skits of Jack Benny (and in the plays of that British merchant of menace, Harold Pinter), the sublime grace of Harpo Marx and the silly mugging of Jerry Lewis. And yet even the most physical of the Jewish clowns of the 1950s, Sid Caesar, was a master of mimicry of fake foreign languages. Even he required scripts from what ought to be considered the Groton of gag writers—for Brooks, Simon, and Allen all rendered unto Caesar the things that were Caesar's before they established celebrated careers of their own.

At its most authentic, Jewish humor demonstrates a sensitivity to language as the vehicle of truth, has helped verbalize anxieties, has contributed its desperanto to the articulation of the modern mood. Jews have dominated comedy record albums if not silent films ("hear O Israel" to Nichols and May, to Berman, to Allan Sherman, to Sahl, to Brooks and Reiner, to David Frye). They also have altered the form of professional joking, as Wallace Markfield has remarked, from "the old-style Bob Hope-type monologue, with its heavy reliance upon a swift sputter of gags plucked from card indices, then updated and localized. It is involuted, curvilinear, ironic, more parable than patter. A Jackie Mason, for example, will start from a basic absurdity . . . [and] work around, over, and along it like a good Talmudist."[32]

The pious Jew who explicates the mysteries of the word is not too distant a relative of the comedian who encounters life through the exercise of intelligence, even when it is intelligence itself that is being kidded. Consider the following joke supposedly explaining the "secret of telegraphy," of which Immanuel Olsvanger has found three versions. The Arabic version asks us to "imagine a huge dog having its head in Beirut and its tail in Damascus. Pull the dog's tail in Damascus and the bark will be heard in Beirut." Here is the

Russian version: *First Russian:* "Imagine a horse, its head in Moscow and its tail in Tula. Pinch the horse's nose in Moscow and it will wag its tail in Tula. And so it is with telegraphy." *Second Russian:* "Yes, but how do they telegraph from Tula to Moscow?" (Something may be getting lost in translation.) And now the Jewish version: *First Jew:* "Imagine, instead of a wire, a dog, whose head is in Kovno and whose tail is in Vilna. Pull the tail in Vilna and the bark will be heard in Kovno." *Second Jew:* "But how does wireless telegraphy work?" *First Jew:* "The very same way, but without the dog."[33]

Although the Jewish version renders the explanation of telegraphy as futile as ignorance of it, the very mockery of the circularity of reasoning pays a certain tribute to the need to make the universe a little less perplexing. Perhaps that is why Philip Roth felt himself in competition with Lenny Bruce, or why Joseph Heller feels at home with Mel Brooks, or why Woody Allen is the thinking man's comedian despite his own limited formal education (he was expelled from one college for "cheating—it was a rather delicate situation because it was with the dean's wife").

Much of Allen's humor is based on an exaggeration of the word, an excess of ratiocination. He is too clever for his own good; he's the kind who would've been a stowaway on the *Titanic*. He thinks too much: he couldn't marry one woman because she was an atheist, and he's an agnostic, and they could not agree "what religion *not* to raise the children up in." Woody Allen is a survivor of the village of Chelm, where the responses to life are theoretically plausible and practically ridiculous—intellectuality gone berserk, as the unexamined premise moves inexorably if unpredictably toward its bizarrely inappropriate conclusion. Kidnapped as a child, Allen was freed when FBI agents surrounded the house and, since they had failed to bring along tear gas cannisters, instead "put on the death scene from *Camille*. Tear-stricken, my abductors gave themselves up." Sentenced to a chain gang, several of the prisoners escaped even though they were "chained together at the ankles, getting past the guards posing as an immense charm bracelet." Several years later Allen was hired briefly by an advertising agency to prove that it would employ minority groups. Placed at the front desk, Allen "tried desperately to look Jewish," even reading his "memos from right to left. But I was eventually fired for taking off too many Jewish holidays."[34] In such routines the spaciousness of the interior life of the Jew is simply further inflated with laughing gas; it is not punctured from outside but exploded from within.

But from late nineteenth-century Russia comes a story that best shows the compatibility of the comic spirit with the imperative of rationality:

When Jews could not travel outside the Pale of Settlement without official permission, an aged scholar from Odessa finally was able, after months of negotiation, to be allowed to travel to Moscow. After one train stop, a young man got on and sat down opposite him. The old scholar looked at him, and the following interior monologue took place: "He doesn't look like a peasant, and if he isn't a peasant, he probably comes from this district. If he comes from this district, he must be Jewish because this is a Jewish district. But if he is Jewish, so where could he be going? I'm the only one in the district who has permission to travel to Moscow. To what village would he not need permission to travel? Oh, just outside Moscow there's a little village of Mozhaisk, and to Mozhaisk you don't need permission. But whom could he be visiting in Mozhaisk? There are only two Jewish families in the whole of Mozhaisk, the Linskys and the Greenbaums. I know the Linskys are a terrible family, so he must be visiting the Greenbaums. But who would undertake a trip at this time of the year unless he were a close personal relative? The Greenbaums have only daughters, so perhaps he's a son-in-law. But if he's a son-in-law, which daughter did he marry? Esther married that nice young lawyer from Budapest. What was his name? Alexander Cohen. Whom did Sarah marry? Sarah married that no-goodnik, that salesman from Zhadomir. It must be Esther. So if he married Esther, his name is Alexander Cohen and he comes from Budapest. Oh, the terrible anti-Semitism they have there now. He probably changed his name from Cohen. So what's the Hungarian equivalent of Cohen? Kovacs. But if he's a man who changed his name from Cohen to Kovacs, he's a man who shows a basic insecurity in life. However, to change his name because of anti-Semitism, a man would need status. So what kind of status could he have? A doctor's degree from the university." At this point the old scholar got up, tapped the young man on the shoulder and asked "Dr. Alexander Kovacs?" "Why, yes," the young man replied, "but how did you know?" "Oh," said the old scholar, "it stands to reason."[35]

Comedy is perhaps born from the failure of the world to conform to the standards of reason, born from the need to expose the *senselessness* of violence, of malice, of ignorance. Joseph Heller, the ribald demystifier of the insane logic of modern warfare, claims that he was not even "aware that *Catch-22* was a *funny* book until I heard someone laugh while reading it." In it the psychiatrist, Major Sanderson, tells Yossarian what is wrong with him in a way that also implicates the most serious humorists: "You've been unable to adjust to the idea of war.... You have a morbid aversion to dying.... You have deep-seated survival anxieties. And you don't like bigots, bullies, snobs or hypocrites."[36] And since the hope for peace and justice is generally violated with such impunity, at the root of commedy is likely to be intense pain, some wound which makes it easier than might be expected for comedians, for example, to play tragic or dramatic roles on stage and screen. The scar tissue shows.

Woody Allen has not been alone in speculating that "it's some kind of privation or suffering not necessarily economic that turns someone into a comedian."[37] It is therefore not inappropriate to conclude with a passage about privation. It is from Kafka, of course, to whom several humorists have paid their own sorts of homage. For if our days were to be lettered instead of numbered, K. would do nicely as the unit of the alphabet that best adumbrates the terror of our age. In *The Producers* Mostel reads aloud the opening line of "Metamorphosis"—only to dismiss it as too absurd. Kafka's surname was the one word Bruce uttered after one of his arrests. Roth has recalled that "the only time Lenny Bruce and I ever met and talked was in his lawyer's office, when it occurred to me that he was just about ripe for the role of Joseph K. He looked gaunt and driven, still determined but also on the wane, and he wasn't interested in being funny—all he could talk about and think about was his 'case.' "[38]

The famous passage that follows is the epigraph to Roth's most lyrical and moving story and can be, I think, interpreted as a paradigm of the humorist's situation, the outsider's appeal to and resentment of our recognition and our sympathies. Once a famous attraction, now a circus sideshow freak ignored by the public, the hunger artist is about to be removed by an overseer who is also unimpressed by such extraordinary but limited feats. " 'I always wanted you to admire my fasting,' said the hunger artist. 'We do admire it,' said the overseer affably. 'But you shouldn't admire it,' said the hunger artist. 'Well then we don't admire it,' said the overseer, 'but why shouldn't we admire it?' 'Because I have to fast, I can't help it ... Because,' said the hunger artist, lifting his head a little and speaking, with his lips pursed, as if for a kiss, right into the overseer's ear, so that no syllable might be lost, 'because I couldn't find the food I liked. If I had found it, believe me, I should have made no fuss and stuffed myself like you or anyone else.' Those were his last words, but in his dimming eyes remained the firm though no longer proud persuasion that he was still continuing to fast."[39]

8

The Comedy of Disenchantment:

The Case of Jules Feiffer

The intense involvement of Jews in the mass production not just of ready-to-wear apparel and cosmetics but also of laughter should not obliterate critical distinctions. In the creation of comedy, those whose work is marked by freshness of style and resonance of vision are uncommon. The authentically talented are, as in all the arts, rare. Jules Feiffer therefore deserves to be judged a singular figure. Few creative figures approach him in the exactness of his view of life, in the virtuosity of his art and in the consistently high standards his work has attained. He is not quite a comic strip creator, although his syndicated cartoons look more or less like comic strips. Although he is politically savvy, he is not a political cartoonist like Herblock. Although our national leaders are instantly recognizable in his work, he is not, like David Levine, a caricaturist. His cartoons probably constitute "the primary stylistic inspiration" of *Doonesbury*, and they have influenced others.[1] Feiffer's one animated cartoon, *Munro*, won an Academy Award in 1961.

He is more than a pictorial artist, and is indeed even more than a triple threat. For Feiffer is also a novelist, a movie scenarist, and above all a dramatist who, according to John Lahr's prediction, "has all the assets to become one of American theater's major craftsmen." For more than three decades, many Americans have been heard to call themselves and one another Feiffer characters; he has given us images of ourselves. In transferring such arresting figures from page to stage, Jules Feiffer has become "one of those artists who compel life to conform to their visions."[2]

A few comic artists have gained greater prominence and influence, especially as performers in films. Almost no one else has exhibited Feiffer's versatility, though perhaps his only counterpart is James Thurber, an exquisite and often haunting fabulist for the *New Yorker*. It is no disparagement of Thurber's stature to note that, of his two plays, one was with a collaborator and the other adapted from his own work. And when another *New Yorker* cartoonist complained to Harold Ross, "Why do you reject drawings of mine, and print stuff by that fifth-rate artist Thurber?" the editor promptly corrected him: "Third-rate."[3] Satire was largely outside of Thurber's range, but it has been Feiffer's specialty, and if he is to be categorized at all, it may as well be with the nightclub and cabaret artists who emerged from the underground by the end of the 1950s. Speaking at the 1964 obscenity trial of one of them as a defense witness, Feiffer paid tribute not only to Lenny Bruce but also to Mort Sahl and Mike Nichols and Elaine May, who "came along at a time in America when they were desperately needed.... They were making human and political commentaries that could not be published in this country." The satire that had been flourishing by 1964, including *Catch-22* and *Dr. Strangelove*, "has grown out of the atmosphere ... in these little clubs."[4]

The confrontation with that cabaret world invigorated Feiffer's own sense of artistic promise and possibility, and stimulated him to graft a second career onto his first. As cartoonist and dramatist, he has sought to press the language and logic of his characters so far that both the shock of recognition and the release of laughter are effected. Since both expressions of his satiric impulse are still in midpassage, it is not necessary to make inflated claims for his comic importance. He can, however, already be identified as a representative figure in the history of Jewish-American drama and in the social context of the popular arts.

For Feiffer's work is an example of the dissolution of minority culture and the absorption of ethnic creativity within the mass culture of American society. In less than two generations, the artistic power and appeal of *Yiddishkeit* had largely expired, with a suddenness that lent special nobility to the gesture of a Nobel Prize to Isaac Bashevis Singer. "What does it mean to be a poet of an abandoned culture?" Singer's compatriot Jacob Glatstein once wondered. "It means that I have to be aware of Auden but Auden need never have heard of me."[5] What the immigrants had created and sustained was abandoned by most of their children and grandchildren, who were often raised on the dreck of radio serials, comic books, Saturday matinees, Tin Pan Alley songs, and sports lore. For many talented and ambitious Jews of the second and third generation, the claims of a minority culture held little or no interest compared with the lure of the popular arts. The generalization holds as much for New York and other metropolitan areas as for smaller places such as Hibbing, Minnesota, the hometown of Bob Dylan (whom Auden, as late as 1965, professed not to have heard of either).

It is noteworthy that the first significant American novelist of Jewish origin, Nathanael West, described his *Miss Lonelyhearts* (1931) as "a novel in the form of a comic strip."[6] But West was ahead of his time in teasing serious purpose out of mass culture. It was perhaps not until the 1950s that the lines blurred that once separated the vulgate arts from what had been considered their opposite. (Here was one symbolic meaning to the 1956 marriage of Marilyn Monroe to Arthur Miller; with his horn-rimmed glasses and pipe, his Jewish liberalism and pleas for moral responsibility, Miller seemed to personify the idea of the highbrow.) In that decade several Jews who rose to prominence had been nourished—heavily if not exclusively—on the aesthetic equivalent of junk food, which was then made the butt of mockery.

For example, those Feiffer had praised—Bruce, Sahl, Nichols and May—plus Woody Allen a little later, turned the material of popular culture into parody and often into a kind of social criticism. Others shifted back and forth, like Philip Roth, who claimed to admire not only the ouevre of Henry James but also the one-liners of Henny Youngman, or like Leonard Bernstein, who composed symphonies and an opera and had also worked in Tin Pan Alley under the pseudonym of Lennie Amber. Milton Babbitt, perhaps the most cerebral of serious contemporary composers, was once a prolific writer of pop songs. Another giant of American composition, Aaron Copland, the Brooklyn-born student of Nadia Boulanger, also wrote movie scores. When Copland told Groucho Marx of his consequent "split personality," the comedian replied: "It's okay, as long as you split it with Mr. Goldwyn." An even wider split has distinguished Erich Segal, who lectured on Roman comedy at Yale while coauthoring the script for the Beatles' animated *Yellow Submarine*. André Previn also has moved easily between symphonic orchestra conducting and show business composition. Mordecai Richler's grandfather had translated the *Zohar* into modern Hebrew, but he himself wrote novels about pushy Canadians bereft of Judaic learning; one of them observes that his generation learned of mortality when Lou Gehrig was benched, and learned of evil from the Wicked Witch in *The Wizard of Oz*. Wallace Markfield's first novel followed a gang of four New York intellectuals who remember everything about radio shows and comic strips. One of these characters will be giving a course in the fall on popular culture "From Little Nemo to L'il Abner."[7] Long before 1968, when French radical students led by Daniel Cohn-Bendit were repeating slogans such as "*Je suis marxiste, tendance Groucho*," American Jews had fashioned dissidence out of dross. That alchemy is what makes Feiffer's career so emblematic.

His parents had immigrated from Poland when both were teenagers. He was born in 1929 and spent most of his life, until the age of 22, in the east Bronx. The economic system was not at its most benign, and it was not difficult to discover that "nice guys finish last: landlords, first." Feiffer "observed, registered things, but commented as little as possible." It was, in other words, an intellectual's childhood. He was unathletic ("one of my great desires to grow up was that, as I understood it, adults did not have to take gym") and bored by school, except for art classes. He loved comic books—especially Will Eisner's *The Spirit* and Milton Caniff's *Terry and the Pirates*—for theirs was "a believable world on the comic page. What was important to me from the beginning was telling a story and creating characters." Just shy of credits for NYU, Feiffer went to work for Eisner, himself a Jew, and attended the Pratt Institute of Art. After two dreadful years in the Army (1951-53), he returned to New York and entered psychoanalysis. In 1956 he showed up with a batch of cartoons at the office of *The Village Voice*, which Dan Wolf, Ed Fancher, and Norman Mailer had founded a year earlier. It was virtually an epiphany. A mere three years after Feiffer came up out of nowhere, Stephen Becker's standard *Comic Art in America* was already willing to crown Jules an innovative figure in the history of graphic humor.[8]

By then the vivisector of Greenwich Village had become syndicated, even in the London *Observer*. Leslie Fiedler, before he admitted his own fascination with pulp comics, reported from Mon-

tana that "everyone digs Jules Feiffer." Indeed his cartoons won
the admiration of Flannery O'Connor, a Catholic Southerner, and
the British critic Kenneth Tynan, who praised Feiffer as a "profoundly funny" artist who had wrought "a minor revolution . . .
in the art of drawing for newspapers."[9]

Although an *Art News* critic considered Feiffer "surely one of
the best artists we have," his place in the pantheon is not incontrovertible.[10] Here a comparison may be instructive. Feiffer is not
alone in his appreciation of Saul Steinberg, who has referred to
himself as "a writer who draws." But that description is far more
applicable to Feiffer himself, a man who illustrates his ideas. Steinberg's ideas, by contrast, are fully incorporated in the drawings
themselves.[11] Feiffer's faces generally undergo very minute changes
of expression; his art calibrates only slight shifts of gesture and
emotion. He gets his effects less as a draftsman than as a dramatist.
Through their spoken and private idiom and their rituals of self-
deception, his characters betray themselves and indicate the meaning
of their own identities. It is as though the comic-strip characters
on which he grew up had been rendered vulnerable to the psy-
chologizing of others, although the armor of their own self-delusion
is rarely pierced. *Feiffer's Marriage Manual* (1967), for example, is
truly adult entertainment, the sophisticate's *Blondie*; indeed in one
series the husband turns into Dagwood Bumstead. In *Feiffer's Album* a woman whom Superman saves from a mugging evaluates
with such devastating effect his compulsive derring-do, his exhi-
bitionism, and his flair for prancing about in "skin-tight, effeminate
leotards" that Superman suffers an anxiety attack, his omnicom-
petence diminishing and Krafft-Ebing.[12] Feiffer's characters are, as
the title of another collection partly labels them, explainers—to each
other but mostly to themselves. They are not, to be precise, con-
versationalists, since they tend to talk past rather than to one another.

Tynan therefore recognized the primacy of Feiffer's ear—"an
odd tribute to pay to a cartoonist." Others too stressed the acuteness
of Feiffer's dialogue, although one of his readers, Vladimir Nabokov, voiced a minority opinion: "Too many words."[13] (Given the
compressed force of Feiffer's language when he needs it and the
fidelity with which he has recorded the loopiness of the vernacular,
the novelist's objection is unconvincing, especially since the narrator
of *Lolita* asserts that for the pain of existence there is only "the

melancholy and very local palliative of articulate art.")[14] As the apolitical concern with "interpersonal relations" in the 1950s yielded to the open conflicts and rage of the 1960s, Feiffer's art increasingly embraced the duplicity of official speech and the rhetorical camouflage of reality. In a decade in which "pacification" did not mean peace and racism required code works, Feiffer became increasingly devoted to exposing the corruption of language. He claims to have been the first cartoonist to oppose the American intervention in Vietnam (1963). As his opposition to the Johnson administration deepened, the *New York Post*, for example, shifted his cartoons from the editorial page to the comic section, and then dropped him entirely. Feiffer found Johnson "a glorious subject" for caricature; eventually so many other cartoonists were drawing and quartering the president that Feiffer gleefully announced that "these are the best times since Boss Tweed."[15] He also published a savage series of cartoons about Johnson's successor, and showed as much animus toward Nixon antagonistes as Herblock achieved. But by then Feiffer's satiric instincts could no longer be confined to about half a dozen panels in a weekly cartoon.

For he had been lured down the enchanted aisles of the American theater. As a cartoonist limning the daffiness of contemporary life, Feiffer had observed a symmetry of approach in the skits of Nichols and May—and he was hooked. His first play, the one-act *Crawling Arnold*, was suitably included in a revue that Nichols himself staged in 1961. Nichols also directed a Feiffer skit, "Passionella," in *The Apple Tree* on Broadway in 1966. Feiffer also wrote the original screenplay for Nichols's *Carnal Knowledge* (1971); Kenneth Tynan had staged another exploration of sexual relations, "Dick and Jane," in *Oh! Calcutta!* two years earlier. Alan Arkin, one of the improvisors who had worked with Nichols and May in The Second City, directed Feiffer's first full-length play, *Little Murders* (1967), as well as the film version, which Feiffer adapted. The play won the Obie (for best off-Broadway work), the Outer Circle Drama Critics Award, and the London critics' prize for best foreign play. Arkin also directed *The White House Murder Case* in 1970. Feiffer has conceived four other works for the stage: *God Bless* (1968), which bombed in New Haven and London: *Knock Knock* (1976), which ended up on Broadway to critical enthusiasm; *Hold Me* (1977), a revue; and, most recently, *Grownups* (1981).

It was inevitable that his plays would be accused of resembling cartoons, and that he would be dismissed in some precincts as not fundamentally a writer for the theater at all. It is hard to resist the suspicion that his dramaturgical credentials would not have been questioned had he spent formative years in sailors' dives and before the mast. Such criticism of his plays nevertheless must be confronted. To Feiffer himself it has meant only "that there's a continuity [with the cartoons], that I write like me."[16] His plea of nolo contendere means, in effect, that Feiffer writes like no one else. In some instances the continuity has been deliberate. An early cartoon strip about fallout shelters and rioting at the United Nations was expanded into *Crawling Arnold*, and the revue *Hold Me* also was transferred in part from strips to skits. Such transitions are so feasible because Feiffer conceives his cartoons in such dramatic terms, and he has claimed to enjoy the challenge of working within the limitations imposed in each medium—whether of space or time. His targets have seemed similar, and the characters in his cartoons long have been on the verge of going to pieces before he put them *in* pieces for audiences to laugh at so anxiously.

On both page and stage, Feiffer is a miniaturist, relying on economy of means for his effects. He writes about a very limited number of characters in a landscape devoid of detail. There is little upholstery, or incorporation of a wider world. Only the psychological states are thick with implication, as the characters try desperately to convey impulses they themselves may not understand and to pick up the signals of others. Since there is nothing monumental or ambitious about his plays, they are not obliged to be brilliant but, as was once said of early Hemingway, "merely perfect." Though Feiffer's lines have the snap of comic authority, he is not notably original in theme or technique; his debts to the antinaturalism and the antic terror of the theater of the absurd are obvious. He has left large assertions about the human estate to other playwrights, however. Instead Feiffer has been satisfied to comment on subtle changes in the atmospherics of American life. With the weird exception of Joan of Arc and her voices (in *Knock Knock*), all of the characters in his plays have been contemporary Americans.

The scale of his work, which emerges naturally from his experience as a cartoonist, has rendered his dramatic enterprises especially suitable for small or cabaret theaters. That is also why there is something unsatisfactory about his two movies. The grisly humor of *Little Murders* depends on the claustrophobia and paranoia packed within the walls of the Newquist family's apartment. For little is gained by moving the camera into the streets, where the menace is somewhat abated when the imagination of the audience has less work of its own to do. The apparent clarity and precision of the cinema's powers of observation diminish the terror by distorting the pressure of the violence inflicted on the beleaguered New Yorkers. The problem with *Carnal Knowledge* is somewhat different. Despite the standard length of the film and its frequent close-ups, the characters are so one-dimensional and reductive that they lack credibility and verisimilitude. The two male characters are more illustrations of an idea (like depersonalization) than recognizable types who assume a life of their own independent of the thesis they are supposed to embody. Jonathan and Sandy are conceived so exclusively in terms of their sexual attitudes that the camera is restrained from showing anything else in their lives—neither money nor politics (as Mort Sahl pointed out), nor work nor family feeling nor sports. The film's characters, Pauline Kael complained, lack "even eroticism, even simple warmth"; she even defended the acting honor of Candice Bergen, who was "given scenes of emotional stress that are probably unplayable (since they don't make sense)."[17] At such close range and with such relentless immediacy, the camera simply demands more than Feiffer's characterizations managed to provide.

Within the limitations he has imposed on himself, he has chosen to record the ruling obsessions and fashions of his time. Having noted the ambiguity of the triumph of "psychological man" in the 1950s, he depicted the political and social turmoil of the 1960s from an independently radical perspective and then, in the 1970s, reflected the receding importance of public conflict. By working within the groove of history in order to comment upon it, Feiffer can pass muster as well as anyone as a modern instance. Nevertheless, for all his sensitivity to the zeitgeist, a corrosively skeptical temperament has kept him disenthralled, detached, and nonpartisan. His plays have little to affirm and usually no message to communicate. If they are united by a common theme, it is a familiar one: Truth must be distinguished from fantasy, rationalization, mendacity, and delusion. Buried within the mockery of modern conventions, the deflation of language, the surreal leaps of logic, and the quick stabs of wit is a warning about the treachery of social reality—and, perhaps, an invitation as old as the Delphic injunction.

Crawling Arnold documents the transition from the age of private anxieties to the political preoccupations of the 1960s. Its cast of characters includes Barry and Grace Enterprise, who descend into the family fallout shelter and cower before authority as much as they fear the bomb itself; Millie, the maid who spends part of her time denouncing "white imperialism" before the U.N.; and Miss Sympathy, a social worker who whispers to Millie her support of "the aspirations of your people." But the central character, the Enterprises' 35-year-old son, Arnold, engages in apolitical protest: He regresses.[18] Like the protagonist of Joseph Heller's Something Happened (1974), who announced, "When I grow up I want to be a little boy," Arnold has chosen to repudiate the responsibilities of adulthood. Growing up in Crawling Arnold means acceptance of the normality of atomic terror, submission to irrational authority, conformity to the pieties of middle-class liberalism, the suppression of natural emotions in favor of the banalities of social convention, and commitment to the stability of the nuclear family (the pun is unavoidable). The imperatives of satire therefore have stacked the deck in favor of Arnold, whose withdrawal represents a deeper kind of sanity (although not necessarily of wisdom).

Arnold's parents cannot accommodate themselves to his apparent perversity and irrationality, although their own grasp of reality is far from perfect. What the reality consists of, beneath the surface of "togetherness" and submissiveness, makes Crawling Arnold the farcical analogue of Freud's Civilization and its Discontents. For Arnold has smashed the sound system that will announce that the civil defense drill is over, and he is about to extract sexual favors from Miss Sympathy, who reveals to him that he falls "into my spectrum of attractiveness." The play thus hints at the aggressive and libidinal forces lurking in the subterranean recesses of society. Since the play is a farce, no genuine evil is evoked or analyzed. Arnold describes his own destructiveness as "naughty" behavior; his conflict with social convention is snap, crackle, and pop, not Sturm und Drang. The protagonist's escapism may be viewed as a wacky extension of Feiffer's own experience of maturation. Having worked in the comic book "shlock houses" of Manhattan during

World War II, he came to realize that his bosses, "who had been in charge of our childhood fastasies, had become archetypes of the grownups who made us need to have fantasies in the first place."[19]

Disenchantment has deepened with his next—and still best—play, *Little Murders*. Staged in 1968, it was written against the backdrop of violence that is likely to be long associated with the 1960s. Within a five-year period, the assassinated had included a president and his brother, civil rights leaders Medgar Evers and Martin Luther King, and Malcolm X (murdered during National Brotherhood Week). The national murder rate doubled between 1963 and 1971. Had the rate remained constant, anyone born and remaining in a major American city would be more likely to meet an untimely end than an American soldier facing combat in the Second World War. However, violence was no urban monopoly. In 1967, one year after Truman Capote had published his account of the extinction of a Kansas family, Charles Whitman climbed to the top of a tower at the University of Texas and murdered fourteen people. Whitman, whom his psychiatrist had labeled "an all-American boy," also was a product of the age of anxiety: Besides his several guns and snack food, he brought with him to the tower a spray deodorant.[20]

The extravagance and grotesquerie of American violence threatened to outstrip the most gallant efforts of black humorists to imagine something more nightmarish. Feiffer's response was to chart the decomposition of the bourgeois family amid relentless beatings and random snipings on city streets. The Newquists are "an Andy Hardy family" that has already lost one son to an unknown assassin before act 1. The father tries to get through each day "in planned segments"—mornings without getting shot, afternoons without a knife in the ribs, a return home without finding the apartment burglarized or the rest of his family slain. At the end of the day, he can report to the other Newquists, "It's murder out there." His wife is batty and dim-witted, his remaining son a simpering absentee from the family constellation. The daughter, Patty, is described by Feiffer as "an all-American girl, Doris Day of ten years ago." Through strength of will she hopes to prevail over the madness and mayhem around her. Although her previous boyfriends were homosexuals, she finally latches onto Alfred Chamberlain, a self-proclaimed "apathist." With his paralyzed energies, Alfred is the stock Feiffer cartoon figure of the 1950s, suddenly dropped into the turmoil of the 1960s. He responds to his weekly sidewalk beatings by daydreaming through them. After their wedding Patty is killed by a bullet through the Newquists' window. As the play ends, the surviving members of the family, including Alfred, are inspired to pick up the gun themselves, and take turns shooting at pedestrians outside.[21]

The surreal dimensions of *Little Murders* are ghoulish extensions of the apprehensions of the audience. Feiffer has heightened such fears by punctuating his play with the introduction of characters whose lapsed authority testifies to the utter helplessness of the middle class. A magistrate, Judge Stern, garrulously reminisces about the immigrants' pursuit of the American Dream; but such earnest expectations of improvement, which are undermined daily by the evidence of urban anarchy, turn Alfred off entirely. (Alfred's intimacy with his own father is so minimal that he never called him Dad, or any other name: "The occasion never came up.")[22] The minister who marries Alfred and Patty, Rev. Dupas of the First Existential Church, is no spiritual leader at all but a hip, mindless defender of every form of behavior and belief. He embodies the anomie and moral inadequacy of institutions that once compelled allegiance, and the monologue he delivers—with its short-circuiting of sense and its flights of self-delusion—happens to be the funniest episode in the play. Finally there is Lieutenant Practice, a police officer who manically concludes that all the violence must reflect a vast conspiracy to extinguish authority. Paranoids can have enemies too, and the policeman (played by Alan Arkin in the film) is shot down by the surviving Newquist child as an arbitrary act of vengeance for Patty's death.[23] Rev. Dupas already has been slain, and there is every anticipation that the slaughter will continue. Contemporary fears thus have been pushed almost to their logical limits, with the playwright combining merriment and dread in equally effective doses.

The White House Murder Case was staged a year before the publication of the Pentagon Papers. Both document the discrepancy between the official explanation and the actual justification, between the public pronouncement and the private motive. In Feiffer's play, the war in Vietnam is history; the United States is fighting guerrillas in Brazil. Instead of Charlie, the enemy is Chico. The Pentagon's Operation Total Win has failed. When American counterinsurgency forces are accidentally killed by their own illegal nerve gas, the administration of President Hale decides that "the American people must be told the truth." That means it will lie, and blame the Brazilians themselves for the American deaths. The president's wife, a peacenik opposed to her husband's policies, threatens to leak the actual facts to the *New York Times*, whereupon she is stabbed to death with a sign pleading, "Make Love Not War." Eventually the assassin confesses: it is the postmaster general, a political operator concerned about the forthcoming election. That fact also cannot be revealed, so her death is blamed on food poisoning.[24]

Although part of the action takes place in Brazil, *The White House Murder Case* is not, strictly speaking, an antiwar play. Feiffer's real subject is duplicity—the political definition of truth as whatever is most useful and convenient, whatever "works." That definition undermines the very basis of classical democratic theory, which requires a citizenry enlightened enough to judge the policies of its elected representatives. Yet in less than two centuries of the presidency, what had begun with Washington, who supposedly could not tell a lie, had come down to Nixon, who apparently could not tell the truth. But Feiffer's play made no attempt to account for this mendacity or to present the causes and consequences of widespread and willful deceit. Evelyn Hale decries the insertion of advertising values into democratic politics, but this clue is undeveloped and unrelated to the possible vulnerability of the political process to manipulation and deception.[25] Instead the play shrinks the motives of politicians to the crassest sort of self-interest, cloaked in lies. Henry Adams once wrote of President Monroe that his character "was transparent; no one could mistake his motives, except by supposing them to be complex."[26] That, however, is the theatrical problem with Feiffer's comedy, at least once the melodramatic shock of Mrs. Hale's impalement is assimilated. All the characters are replicates of Adams's image of Monroe, which means that they are too reductive, too lacking in nuance, too illustrative of a single insight to sustain dramatic interest.

The cynicism and moral outrage that found artistic expression in *The White House Murder Case* found complete legal protection as well. Feiffer had helped to demonstrate that by 1970 freedom of political criticism was almost entirely complete. "For the first time in almost twenty-five hundred years," Robert Brustein concluded, "it is possible to satirize the highest leaders of government on the stage without fear of physical harm or legal retribution." But the very indulgence of audiences and of authorities robbed satire of much of its sting. A typically clever Feiffer cartoon had shown President Johnson including a bigot in his special commission designed to promote consensus. "The White House requested [the honor of owning] the original," the cartoonist recalled. "Talk about effectiveness." Under such conditions the possibilities of saying no in thunder or in jest were rapidly becoming exhausted. "Everybody knew everything anyway," Feiffer added. "Everybody knew how bad it was. You couldn't disturb or shock or create new discontent because there was so much old discontent that still hadn't been absorbed."[27]

Instead of silence, instead of repeating himself, he chose to explore sexual politics. It is sometimes hard to recall that in *The Naked and the Dead* (1948), Norman Mailer could not record fully the profanity of infantrymen, or that ten years later congressional interest had been aroused by Al Capp's fondness for the number 69 in the home addresses and license plates in *L'il Abner*.[28] By the end of the 1960s, however, words could be used on stage and in print with a freedom perhaps never before imagined. "Obscenity" itself, which literally referred to what could not be put on stage, lost its meaning almost entirely. Feiffer, who had testified in Lenny Bruce's trial in 1964, participated in this enlargement of expression as well. In 1971 the manager of a movie theater in Albany, Georgia, was convicted under a state obscenity statute for showing *Carnal Knowledge*. Two years later the Supreme Court, after viewing the film, overturned the conviction. Speaking for the majority, Justice William Rehnquist held in part that the depiction of nudity was not in itself grounds for nullifying the guarantees of the First and Fourteenth amendments. Nor did the film exhibit "the actors' genitals, lewd or otherwise," and the depiction of sexual conduct was not "patently offensive." Censorship alone is hardly an index of artistic merit (because her ouevre "incites to incest," South Africa banned the fiction of Jacqueline Susann, for example).[29] But the court's decision in *Jenkins* v. *Georgia* made it less likely that artistic issues would be confused with police powers.

There are indeed cinematic problems with *Carnal Knowledge*,

arising largely from the obsessiveness enforced on Sandy and especially Jonathan. They are prisoners of sex, spending much of their
life sentence in what amounts to solitary confinement, because of
a failure to integrate sexuality with the rest of experience. In the
summation of the philosopher Ernest Becker, both the sensualist
(played by Jack Nicholson) and the romantic (played by Art Garfunkel) are "pitifully immersed in the blind groping of the human
condition." The cruelty and hollowness of their attitudes toward
women have resulted in disillusionment and emptiness, but the bleak
moral of the film—its implacable seriousness—was lost on feminist
critics in particular, who accused Feiffer and Nichols of sharing the
very attitudes that *Carnal Knowledge* seemed to mock. "No contemporary film," Joan Mellen claimed, "offers as vicious a portrait
of female sexuality. . . . All the women in this film are shallow, crass
or stupid." She added that Feiffer's and Nichols' "tone and the
absence from their film of women at least as articulate as the men
amounts to a smug assent, a silent endorsement." Although Molly
Haskell found "one intelligent-romantic woman of that film, Candice Bergen, [she] cannot be envisioned beyond the moment she
outlives her romantic usefulness to the men, and so disappears from
the movie." The Ann-Margret character "is presented as a harridan
so that Nicholson can emerge with more dignity and sympathy than
he deserves. We get an image that purports to indict the men,"
Haskell concluded, "but that insidiously defends them, not least
through the satisfaction they take in degrading the women."[30]

What these criticisms miss is that Feiffer, as a satirist, hardly
exempts women from the humanity he habitually indicts. The mis-
ogyny of the characters makes them quite unsympathetic, and should
not obscure the misanthropy of their creator, since no affirmative
images of humanity are projected onto the screen. *Carnal Knowledge* comprises the fullest statement Feiffer has presented about the
sexual comedy of self-deception and disenchantment, a subject he
has treated in the entire course of his career as a cartoonist as well.
The opening bull session between Jonathan and Sandy, on whether
it is better to love or be loved (a dialogue as old as Plato's *Phaedrus*),
is the echo of countless panels depicting the uncertainties and am-
bivalences linked with desire. In transferring such cartoons to the
screen, Feiffer and Nichols failed to produce an unqualified artistic

success. But they touched an important contemporary nerve whose conscientious objection to the ongoing war between the sexes still reverberates.

After *Carnal Knowledge* the author apparently realized that his pessimism was at wit's end. He professed to be "worn out by evangelizing," with rounding up the usual suspects. The point was "to start working out ways of living a life." His writing had always vibrated with intelligence, but not with whatever consolations and satisfactions the world might surrender. So Feiffer's next play marked a new phase—it not quite from alienation to accommodation, then at least toward allowing room for fantasy rather than requiring reason of human beings. James Thurber once drew a famous cartoon of a seal above a bed, with the wife finishing the argument with her husband: "All right, have it your way—you heard a seal bark!" *Knock Knock* is the dramatic equivalent of the seal in the bedroom. As with the screenplay for Nichols, the primary characters are two men. But its subject, as Feiffer once explained, is "the absolute collapse of logic . . . how two particular people deal with the irrationality of order and, finally, the collapse of order."[31]

The two people are Abe, a former broker, and Cohn, an unemployed musician, who have been living in a cabin in the woods. Abe is willing to grant some powers to the imagination; Cohn trusts only his senses. Havoc enters their lives with the arrival of Joan of Arc, who is seeking a sort of Noah's ark that soon will ascend to heaven. It is she who offers the only glimmer of affirmation in a Feiffer play that is not meant to be risible. Joan tells Abe and Cohn that they "should be self-sufficient, but not alienated, not despairing, not sneering, not cynical, not clinical, not dead unless you are dead, and even then make the most of it."[32] Her plea for the avoidance of extremes is as bromidic as Judge Stern's paean to the American Dream in *Little Murders*, but this time some credence is to be granted amid the absurdity. There is mugging in *Knock Knock*, but it is the vaudeville version, not what happens on mean streets. *Knock Knock*, which reaped the best reviews of Feiffer's theatrical career, is more silly than slashing, and its humor is rather pointless, indeed deliberately childish. During the run of a musical in which she was appearing, Mary Martin once commented: "I told Lady Bird [Johnson]—she came to see us—that I wanted the president to see *I Do, I Do* because it's not against anything."[33] That is precisely the trouble with Feiffer's recent play. It in fact knocks nothing, and therefore amounts to an abandonment of the playwright's distinctive resources.

In praising the play, *Time's* reviewer located it within the context of Jewish humor— "skeptical, self-deprecating, fatalistic and with an underlying sadness that suggests that all the mirth is a self-protective mask hiding imminent lamentation."[34] Those terms may stretch *Knock Knock* a little beyond recognition, but it would be hard to deny that there is a Jewish dimension to Feiffer's interpretation of life. There is admittedly little in his topics or his langauge that betrays ethnic consciousness. Given the satiric possibilities inherent in North American Jewish life, which Roth, Richler, Markfield, Heller, and others have exploited with fiendish delight, it is noteworthy that Feiffer usually has avoided this topic. There are occasional characters, such as Abe and Cohn and Judge Stern, and occasional Yiddish words (such as *schlepp*) that have entered the American idiom. The cartoons occasionally have included Jewish mothers, smothering with love and aggression, as well as a figure named Bernard Mergendeiler, the sort of victim who might be called a schlemiel if that term had not replaced Christ-figure as the most overused term in the critical lexicon. But otherwise there is little that is explicit for the student of Jewish American expression to identify.

The only exception is *Grownups*, a three-act play that Feiffer first wrote in 1974. After revisions, it opened at the American Repertory Theatre at Harvard in 1981, and later that year on Broadway. Like the entirety of Kafka's fiction, the word "Jew" does not appear in it. But the useful term *schlepp* does, although none of the characters betrays any sign of ethnic involvement or religious observance. All the characters are members of one family—the parents, sister, wife, and daughter of a *New York Times* reporter named Jake—and all are manifestly Jewish. All these relatives make demands on Jake that he finds exorbitant. All his problems stem from his failure to function like an autonomous adult when he is within the bosom of his family, which, according to one estimate, is about a 42D. When Jake's sister, Marilyn, who shares his frustration and helplessness, gets the inspired notion of killing their parents, he dismisses the proposal as "a short-range solution." Set in Marilyn's New Rochelle kitchen and in Jake's Manhattan apartment, *Grown-*

ups shifts rather jerkily from tense satire of suburban banality to the acrid atmosphere of generational and marital warfare; the play lacks the formal resolution of its antecedents in the Jewish domestic dramas of the 1930s and 1940s. But *Grownups* not only offers welcome flashes of comic insight but also a remorseless flair for picking at the scabs of familial resentment and indignities that is compelling in its urgency and even its savagery.

To assert that Feiffer lacks the ethnic involvement of, say, Odets or even Neil Simon is not to dismiss the pertinence of Jewishness entirely. Feiffer's life—from the east Bronx to the *Village Voice* and the theater—has been spent primarily in settings and institutions in which the presence of other Jews has been noticeable. Already by 1930 a popular history textbook was informing public school children that the Jews were "conspicuously successful in the various forms of theatrical enterprise."[35] The creators of the first of the great comic book heroes, Superman, were, like the three founders of the *Voice* itself, Jews. They were among those who shaped the institutions and values within which an artist like Feiffer has operated, and they must have exerted some influence on his vision of the Americans who populate his cartoons and plays. True, it is possible to exaggerate the importance of locale to an author's development. (Kipling wrote *Kim* in Vermont, of all places, which is also where Solzhenitsyn completed *The Gulag Archipelago*.) But it would be impossible to divorce Feiffer's stance and style from his lifelong residence in New York, from the pungent wit, nervous energy, open anxieties, quickness, and rancor that so many other New Yorkers have defined as sophistication. The city's inhabitants have accepted the thrusts of psychoanalysis more easily than the Viennese or Middle Americans have, and this appropriation of the Freudian vocabulary in daily life also is reflected in Feiffer's work. The ambience that he has absorbed has been largely devoid of deliberate incorporation of Jewish culture and themes, and is entirely secular in orientation. Nevertheless the flavor and spirit of that ambience has been heavily and unmistakably Jewish, as though amplifying the jocular definition of an assimilationist as one who only associates with Jews who refuse to associate with Jews.

The artistic and commercial energies of New York Jews have been largely without politically radical implications. Those who have gravitated toward the theater and other popular arts rarely sought fundamental changes in the social order. But those writers and artists who have been the most dissident, daring, and satiric have come disproportionately from one ethnic group. What Nixon once told H. R. Haldeman about the arts—"they're Jews, they're left wing—in other words, stay away"—is rather more sound as sociology than as advice. For the existence of Jewish conservatives—and philistines—does not negate the fact that, wherever attacks have been mounted against elites and established values, Jews are likely to be found.

One episode, while hardly conclusive, may be suggestive. During the 1969 Chicago conspiracy trial, Judge Julius Hoffman continued to dine at the Standard Club, which well-heeled and successful Jews had established. One day his luncheon calm was violated when myrmidons of the counterculture decided to eat at the Standard Club too. They included defendants Jerry Rubin and Abbie Hoffman; radical organizer Saul Alinsky; publisher Jason Epstein, who was writing a book hostile to the judge's conduct of the trial; Norman Mailer; and Jules Feiffer, who had attended the Democratic Party convention the previous year as a Eugene McCarthy delegate. Judge Hoffman rearranged his seat to avoid seeing them. The connection between Jewish background and political and cultural rebelliousness may be as close as handcuffs.[36] From the status of outsiders, from the distancing of marginality, many Jews indeed have developed a combative stance toward the rest of society, even after allegiance to Judaism itself has evaporated. "To the degree that there is anti-Semitism in the world, I acknowledge being Jewish," David Levine has proclaimed. "In the same sense, when cartooning is ridiculed, I confess to being a cartoonist."[37] Feiffer's actual relationship to his ethnic origins may not be much more positive than that, but his satiric animus, his leftist perspective, his urban irony and his psychoanalytic spirit help give his work a Jewish component in the sense that a Jew is most likely to have created it.

Whether that work is of enduring significance is, of course, another question. Satire, in George S. Kaufman's bon mot, "is what closes Saturday night"; and posterity rarely revises such quick and devastating judgments. The targets of satire may suffer from familiarity, given the constancy of human affairs; its humor may leave audiences wondering whether it seemed funny at the time. Feiffer may have realized these dangers and may be trying to get beyond satire. Yet to do so may be too subversive of his own talent, which has been to serve as a touchstone of the fashions and follies of his time. It is true that his plays tend to be subjugated to a thesis, which may limit their appeal even as delusiveness, political chicanery and sexual stereotyping persist. It is true that Feiffer's capacity for breathing the semblance of life into his characters is undeveloped, but if that were the test of mature art, Damon Runyon would be hailed as a better writer than Samuel Beckett. It is also true that Feiffer's range is restricted, for he cannot find quite as much dignity and value in life as others have managed to avow. As the narrator of his novel *Ackroyd* puts it, "I see like a cop; I see prejudicially; I collect evidence; what can't be included as evidence is not seen; doesn't exist."[38] What Feiffer has seen, however, has been reported with gem-cutting precision, and the requirement to be uplifting too ought to be branded as demeaning and antagonistic to the imperatives of art, Feiffer's included.

It might also be recalled that what helps make life bearable is the exposition of its incongruities in comic modes. Few of Feiffer's contemporaries have been as unerring and as unsparing in the representation of folly. Few have shown such clarity in the perforation of the confusions, the rationalizations, the deceptions behind which we hide. Few contemporary artists have drawn healthier laughter from pumping irony into the solitude and sadness that may be intrinsic to life. Such claims are not always susceptible to proof, although social scientists reportedly have devised a measurement for enjoyment, broken down into units known as benthams. By enlisting both the cartoon and the drama in the case against humanity, a college dropout from the Bronx has generated more benthams than we had any right to expect.

9

All That Jazz

Consider the treatment of American Catholicism in fiction or film, and it probably will confront the question of authority. Consider the depiction of American Jewry, and the issue of assimilation probably will be faced or sidestepped. Pick up a classic American novel, and you often will be reading about males in nomadic isolation: Natty Bumppo, Captain Ahab, Huck Finn, Jay Gatsby. But to imagine Jews in American literature is to see them as members of families rather than as men without women. They inevitably are entangled—for better or for worse—with their parents, and probably with their spouses and children.

Hence the recurrent impulse in the mass arts to resurrect *The Jazz Singer*. The recent movie, which opened in 1980, left generally unfavorable reviews in its wake, undoubtedly sank some of its investors' wildest hopes, and left art on the rocks. But it cannot be judged entirely according to the conventions of film criticism. It belongs instead to the realm of myth, where it shapes collective fantasies and insinuates itself in the memory. A myth does not have to be truthful to be believable, but what is peculiar about the recent version is its dogged fidelity to the present condition of American Jewry. That is why *The Jazz Singer* has run aground artistically. It permits its dramatic tension to loosen precisely because it reflects the social reality that thoughtful students of Jewry ought to ponder.

There have been six earlier versions of this parable of ambition in conflict with tradition. In 1917 an appearance by Al Jolson in Champaign, Illinois, so inspired an undergraduate named Samson Raphaelson that he wrote a short story entitled "The Day of Atonement." In it Jakie Rabinowitz, a Lower East Side boy descended from nine generations of cantors, transforms himself into Jack Robin, the greatest "mammy singer" in vaudeville. He also falls in love with a dancer named Amy Prentiss and is disowned. Then, on the night he is to open on Broadway, Robin is asked to replace his dying father in the chanting of *Kol Nidre* in the Hester Street *shul*. Abandoning the opportunity to launch an exceptionally promising theatrical career, Robin shows himself to be a loyal son and a good Jew after all. The worshipers are enthralled by "the golden notes of this young singer of ragtime as he rendered '*Kol Nidre*' with a high, broken sobbing which, they insisted critically, surpassed his father's in his best days." Applying himself to the "grief-laden notes with a lyric passion that was distinctly his own," Jack Robin attracts such notice that Broadway stardom is implicitly assured after all.[1]

Everybody's Magazine published "The Day of Atonement" in 1922, and Jolson, himself the immigrant son of a cantor and then widely regarded as the big enchilada of popular entertainment, heard in it so many echoes of his own career that he wanted to star in the dramatization of the tale. Raphaelson therefore adapted it for the stage—and instead it featured George Jessel, who thus was given his first break as a dramatic actor. The play might have enjoyed a remarkable run on Broadway had Jessel not made a Hollywood commitment; when Warner Brothers snapped up the film rights for *The Jazz Singer* (for $50,000), it was assumed that the comedian would re-create his stage role.

After that, accounts vary. But it appears that Jessel and Warner Brothers engaged in a dispute over money, and the studio made two decisions that lifted its property from shmaltz into legend. One was to replace Jessel with Jolson, upon whom Jack Robin had been modeled anyway. The other decision was to utilize a new Vitaphone sound-on-disc process. On August 6, 1927, a Warner's theater in New York presented eight shorts, from the overture to *Tannhaüser* to a recitation by John Barrymore, in Vitaphone, and the results were encouraging. Despite the formidable cost of re-equipping its movie houses for Vitaphone, Warner Brothers decided to shoot Jolson's six songs with sound, including "*Kol Nidre*," "Blue Skies," and "Mammy"—the last two being Jolson standards. But the irrepressible star also interpolated some spoken words of his own in the musical sequences, and his confident promise that "You ain't heard nothin' yet!" became an uncannily accurate inauguration of the sound era. Nevertheless historians are obliged to classify *The Jazz Singer* as a silent film in which the songs and a few lines of dialogue are recorded on disc; the first truly complete sound film was Warner Brothers' *The Lights of New York* (1928).[2]

But when *The Jazz Singer* opened on October 6, 1927, pop iconography was instantly created; the blackface balladeer down on one knee crying for his Mammy elicited not only tears but also mimicry across the continent. Walt Disney quickly did a cartoon parody, with Mickey Mouse as *The Jazz Fool*; Henry Ford, who disliked the new syncopated rhythms, blamed the craze on the Jews. No wonder. Though minstrelsy had been born as early as 1842, such routines had become by the early twentieth century a vehicle for Jewish entry into mass entertainment. Not only old black Jolson but Eddie Cantor and George Burns specialized in the application of burnt cork, and Sophie Tucker had been billed as a "Coon Shouter." George Gershwin, another cantor's son, and Irving Berlin, with his "Alexander's Ragtime Band," performed equivalent roles as composers. The Jew had become a soul brother because no other persona seemed so congenial. The emotions to be conveyed were too deep and complicated to be directly expressed. Black and blue, the Jewish entertainers could communicate with ambiguity the pathos of the oppressed yearning to breathe free. Four years after the premiere of the film, the literary scholar Constance Rourke stressed in *American Humor* that being Negro was one of the three great fabrications of national character in the popular consciousness, one of the three most available ways of defining one's self on native grounds. For a Jewish vaudevillian to pretend to be a Yankee or a frontiersman—Rourke's other choices—was a more difficult process of drawing up citizenship papers, a less resonant strategy for infiltrating the national imagination.

Even as it chronicled the rise of a blackface entertainer, *The Jazz Singer* became just about the closest look that Hollywood ever took at the distinctive atmosphere of American Jewish life. Never again was a major studio to reveal so intimately the ferocious impulse that propelled so many Jews into the dominant culture. The movie business itself was primarily a Jewish invention. But the scrap dealers peddling their celluloid fantasies were too anxious or too shrewd to draw attention to their own origins. They generally covered their

tracks. But for once the Jews tackled the myth of themselves, refusing to disguise the intensity of the ambitions simmering in the
ghetto, the hunger for recognition that gnawed at its residents, or
the hurt that the desire for affirmation sometimes inflicted.

Exuding the kind of authority and razzle-dazzle that glows in
the dark, Jolson embodied all the compressed and crude force that
was seeping out of the ghetto. Anticipating the burst of energy that
would raise his "co-religionists" into the most upwardly mobile of
all American minorities, prefiguring the impact that would make
itself conspicuously felt in so many enterprises and endeavors—
from criminality to Nobel Prizes, Jolson was telling the rest of the
nation that he wanted it all and wanted it fast and that he had
whatever was needed to get it. Jolson was, arguably, the first American superstar; what he asserted, at twenty-four frames per second,
was that ultimately only talent counts. That intangible commodity
still may be more valuable than anything available on the spot market
in Rotterdam.

Yet the 1927 film was far from a masterpiece, and only Jolson
himself triumphed over its egregious sentimentality. Alan Crosland,
who directed The Jazz Singer, is not remembered today. Nor is
Alfred A. Cohn, who adapted the play for the screen, having specialized in Irish-Jewish romances such as The Cohens and the Kellys.
Warner Oland, who played Jack Robin's father, Cantor Rabinowitz, is better known for his later role of Charlie Chan. Raphaelson
himself apparently hated the film, protesting that it fudged the character development essential to the original story and play. He later
wrote some distinguished film scripts, especially for director Ernst
Lubitsch. He also tutored creative writing at the University of Illinois (one of his students was Hugh M. Hefner), and reportedly
was involved in the nascent Israeli movie industry.[3]

But neither Jolson nor others could let go of so evocative a melodrama. In 1936 he starred in a radio version in New York, and in
1947 in another one. Jessel tried several times to revive the play (no
extra credit for guessing his proposed lead), but without success.
Then in 1952 Warner Brothers updated The Jazz Singer, making
Danny Thomas (who is of Lebanese extraction) a Korean War vet-
eran who returns home to a suburban Philadelphia congregation.
Again Jack Robin must choose between following in his father's
footsteps and becoming a popular singer. The script required him

to fall in love with Peggy Lee, but studio executives were persuaded by a resourceful rabbi that the subject of intermarriage did not belong in so uplifting a film. Peggy Lee's character therefore was made into a Jew by inserting a line about not having attended a seder since she left home.

The effect of this slight alteration either on the maturation of cinematic art or on the intermarriage rates cannot easily be ascertained, but the remake, as Robert L. Carringer has noted, did register the vicissitudes of American Jewish life since the 1920s. Warner Oland's Cantor Rabinowitz had been narrow-minded, intolerant, and unsympathetic. But at least he had represented a commitment to a vibrant religious tradition, however inapposite to Jack Robin's nature. By contrast Danny Thomas's father (played by Eduard Franz) urges his son to perpetuate the cantorial vocation primarily because they had lived so long in the same house (not God's, presumably), and because they had graduated from the "same university."

Moreover, when the 1952 cantor is on his deathbed, he undergoes a sudden change of heart, recognizes the merit of his fellow alumnus's show business career, and asks his son to forgive *him*. Then the cantor makes a miraculous recovery and joins his wife in the audience to cheer on their son the crooner. The vocation to which the 1927 *chazzan* had consecrated his life has become in 1952 something irrelevant to the cantor himself. Equally revealing is another contrast. In a comic episode in the 1927 version, Jack Robin and too many others present Cantor Rabinowitz with prayer shawls for his sixtieth birthday. In the remake Danny Thomas's character instead presents a gift to his mother for her birthday; rather than a *tallit*, it is a three-quarter-length mink coat.[4]

NBC wreaked further damage on the authenticity—such as it was—of the original fable when it was telecast in 1959. Eduard Franz again played the cantor, Molly Picon was his wife, and Anna Maria Alberghetti was the Gentile inamorata of Jack Robin, this time played by a somewhat subdued Jerry Lewis. It is no secret that television has been subject to lapses of taste, but there has scarcely been a more striking instance than when Jerry Lewis sang *"Kol Nidre,"* the most hallowed declaration in Jewish liturgy, in blackface.[5]

This brings us to the most recent effort to revitalize so tenacious a myth. The 1927 version was compelling largely because Jolson did not pretend to be playing Jack Robin; he knew he was playing himself. Having transformed himself from Asa Yoelson of Srednik, Lithuania, Jolson belted out the ballads that had already made him famous on stage, knowing that such music was what movie audiences wanted to hear. Even "Folks, you ain't heard nothin' yet!" had been uttered nine years earlier, during a benefit at the Metropolitan Opera House, when Jolson had followed Enrico Caruso's rendition of "Vesti la Giubba" and thus established the supreme example of chutzpah. (Caruso was amused.)[6] By shooting the finale in Jolson's personal palace, the Shuberts' Winter Garden Theatre, the makers of the 1927 film were deftly blurring the distinction between the actor and his role, the man and his mask.

Neil Diamond is the first solo performer to play the Winter Garden since Jolson in 1937, but there most resemblances end. Despite the difference of two generations, however, certain paradigmatic ingredients in Diamond's career can be highlighted. His father was in dry goods. He attended the same Brooklyn high school and sang in the same chorus as Barbra Streisand. He went to NYU but dropped out before graduating—like Woody Allen, another Brooklynite who went from writing to performing his own material. Diamond's professional career began as a Tin Pan Alley song plugger (the score for *Fiddler on the Roof* was written in the next cubicle). By 1967 he had already tied Frank Sinatra as *Cash Box*'s top male vocalist. Every one of his albums had gone either gold ($1 million in sales) or platinum (one million albums sold); almost 50 million of his records have been purchased in less than two decades. Few of these albums seem to have been sold to critics, however, who have largely ignored him. For example, Diamond is mentioned only twice, briefly, in the authoritative *Rolling Stone Illustrated History of Rock and Roll*. But he is a dominant figure in an industry that has become more economically powerful than the movie business itself. That is why, without ever having acted before, Diamond received an unprecedented $4 million contract to star in another remake—more money than Warner Brothers realized on the original film.[7] It is difficult to contemplate Diamond's career except in terms of megabucks. But since there would be an inevitable and inescapable sound track album anyway, casting him in the latest version of *The Jazz Singer* was not, in principle, mistaken.

In principle. In practice, however, he revealed no flair for acting. As Jess Robin, the assistant cantor in an Eldridge Street synagogue where his father (Laurence Olivier) serves as well, Diamond was bland and inert and had trouble maintaining eye contact with anyone. Although his baritone was effective and his saturnine presence not unpleasant, he released no sense of creative vitality, conveying none of the passion that might have hurtled such a character from lower Manhattan to Los Angeles. Diamond's songs also have been forgettable, as well as dissociated from the character of an Orthodox Jew. Unlike Jolson, who put across other men's material, Diamond had to pretend to be a composer too. It is almost impossible to realize cinematically the interior life of a creative artist, but Diamond compounded the problem with ballads unrelated to the religious enclave in which Jess Robin is supposed to have emerged. The songs reflect instead the milieu of commercial music, such as the Brill Building that hatched Neil Diamond himself.

But the flaws of the 1980 version go deeper, even deeper than the listless direction or the colorless script, which is also vulnerable to Raphaelson's complaint about undeveloped characterizations. The adaptation is credited to Stephen Foreman, whose own earlier script was submitted to another studio, which sagely abandoned the project as "too Jewish." In fact the problems go so deep they actually become interesting, because what has happened to the myth is that it has been subverted by history. The social reality of contemporary Jewry no longer makes credible a tale so fraught with the tension between communal sanctions and self-fulfillment, between tradition and ambition. The latest *Jazz Singer* cannot be accommodated to aesthetic criteria, not merely because of the clumsiness of the moviemakers, but primarily because the vagaries of the Jewish condition have sabotaged the very forms and textures that made the protagonist's dilemma so poignant. The ambience of immigrant *Yiddishkeit* that had pervaded the cantor's life and had given it dignity has vanished, along with the power of the community to shame those who were alienated from it.

So significant a loss has not escaped the attention of the 1980 moviemakers (including Diamond, whose contract gave him total script approval as well). Their effort to adjust the fable to that loss can be understood as fragments of a mirror that Hollywood has held up to contemporary American Jewry. The most recent adaptation of the myth comprises the meaning of the film itself, justifying an analysis of its message.

Perhaps the most noticeable change in the story is the omission of the mother. Before Freudian theory could extend its influence and could generate its own anxieties, the capacity of the Jewish mother to express and to elicit love seemed quite as awesome as any of the primordial forces that other cultures hoped to appease. The mammy singers knew their customers. Sophie Tucker could always bring down a house of Jews by recalling "My Yiddishe Mama," and Jessel had starred in a silent film entitled *Mamma's Boy*. In his novel *Ragtime* (1975), E. L. Doctorow observed that a *rebbetzin*'s son, Harry Houdini, was "destined to be, with Al Jolson, the last of the great shameless mother lovers."[8] The tear-drenched tenderness between Sara Rabinowitz and her errant son could be depicted, in that unsophisticated era, as overwhelming, and *The Jazz Singer* milked so much pathos that Tevye the dairyman could have gotten rich. Even the 1952 remake retains the central role of the mother (played by the exquisite Mildred Dunnock, fresh from her triumph as Mrs. Willy Loman in *Death of a Salesman*). But by 1980 it had become impossible for mass culture to invent a Jewish mother except as a stereotype. She has become a stock figure, a target of derision. Stick her in a comic monologue or a play, and the laughs are guaranteed. Put her in a melodrama, and the giggles may unhinge the desired effect. Give her an affectionate relationship with her son, and the laughs will get even louder.

The script for the 1980 film solves this problem by killing off the cantor's wife with a terrorist's bullet before the plot begins. At 39 Neil Diamond may be a little old to be nursing an Oedipus complex anyway. Instead he is given the wife Al Jolson never had: her name is Rivka—the name of the cantor's wife in the original short story. Now the father and the wife assume the weight of an unbroken Jewish past and must make the appeal to Diamond's ancestral loyalties. Sir Laurence Olivier, whose descent from the bard to *The Betsy* has been painful enough already, thus has become the chief source of sentimentality, which is emotion in excess of the circumstances that provoke it. He is obliged to do all the weeping that Eugenie Besserer did in 1927.

The cantor's personality thus is rendered softer and more humane than was the first Rabinowitz's. But the consequence is also a certain decline in stature; he is bereft of what the Romans called *gravitas*. The authority of the Judaic tradition, the stringency of its moral imperatives, and especially the sublime quality of its sacred music are diminished because the *chazzan* is now less remote. The first *Jazz Singer* put the celebrated Cantor Yossele Rosenblatt in the film, but not once in the new version does Olivier "chant" alone. Never is he shown transfigured by the haunting music he presumably is capable of conjuring into being.

Rivka, played by the Israeli-born Catlin Adams, is likewise inadequate to the task of making the Judaic heritage vital and adhesive. Content to teach Hebrew school, she lacks drive; for all her sweetness, she is a young fogy. Rivka therefore is mismatched against Molly Bell, the character who was called Amy Prentiss in the short story and Mary Dale in the 1927 film. Molly is a Los Angeles recording agent who becomes Jess Robin's manager, lover, and eventually the mother of his son. She is granted almost all the witty lines, understands Jess's needs, and is prettier than Rivka too. In 1927 Mary Dale had been a blond Anglo-Saxon. But the gap has narrowed in 1980 because Molly is an ethnic herself. She has shortened her own name to Bell, speaks in what resembles a New York accent, and can make terms such as *shiksa* and *schmuck* trip from her tongue. As Molly, Lucie Arnaz gives the only high-voltage performance in the movie.

The current script vastly enlarges the romantic element in the plot, even as it minimizes the threat posed to the tribalism depicted in the original film. Raphaelson's short story had been published in the year that Anne Nichols's perennial *Abie's Irish Rose* opened on Broadway, and both communicated the hope that exogamy might erase the antagonisms that long cursed the Jewish people. This was the faith that had informed other works as well, such as Zangwill's *The Melting-Pot* and D. W. Griffith's film, *The Romance of a Jewess* (both 1908). In that era American Jews were no more tempted by the marriage altar than by the baptismal font, but the purveyors of popular art showed an advanced interest in testing out the national promise of equality and the dream of success. Here too the lives of the entertainers often anticipated later trends, with Jolson marrying Gentiles such as the dancer Ruby Keeler. (As with Jess Robin, Diamond's own first wife was Jewish but not his second, whose family is reputed to have arrived on the Mayflower.) The notion that love might obliterate racial and ethnic barriers has been a theme that Jewish popular artists often have tapped; nothing else raised more clearly the possibility of Jewish absorption into the larger society.

Since intermarriage now may be about as statistically likely to befall Jews as divorce, both phenomena are introduced in the 1980 remake. Whereas the Mary Dale of 1927 had asked the mammy singer to renounce his heritage for the sake of show business, Molly Bell demonstrates how baseless the ancient Jewish anxieties about intermarriage really are. Endowed with sensitivity and empathy, she is attentive to the religious traditions that her lover and husband seems willing to forsake. Although she commits that gaffe of preparing a ham dinner for Jess, she also lights the Shabbat candles, her head covered. And when his father cannot sing on Yom Kippur, it is she who insists that Jess go to the Eldridge Street synagogue in his place to declare all the vows. The startling lesson to be drawn here is that the Judaic legacy is important—if it matters to a Gentile. It is an outsider who thus sanctifies the meaning of the world of our fathers.

The new film must somehow defend the integrity of that world in order to establish the dramatic tension required to animate the plot. But the defense is weaker than the earlier incarnations of the fable had offered. The original story and play had ended with the return to Hester Street, as Jack Robin answers the call of "something in the blood." The 1927 film let the tension go slack with an epilogue consisting of Jolson doing "Mammy" at the Winter Garden. The hero therefore wins everything—his mother's heart by showing such fidelity to his roots, his girlfriend's heart by returning to the limelight, and America's heart by so dynamic and emotional a performance in *shul* and on stage. Warner Brothers was therefore false to life, which rarely contrives to present those sentenced to it with compatible goals. But at least the 1927 *Jazz Singer* made the basic choices seem consequential and the victories touching; at least it acknowledged the grip that religion exercised over many Jews. Because Cantor Rabinowitz appeared to embody an unrelenting devotion even as he lay dying, his son could not fail to be moved, and could sing thereafter with a win-one-for-the-Gipper frenzy.

Such religious fervor rarely complicates the lives of most of today's Jews, and the latest *Jazz Singer* reflects this secularization. Unlike the 1927 *chazzan*, who had died shortly before the Yom Kippur service, Olivier is only suffering from high blood pressure.

Neil Diamond sacrifices nothing by singing *"Kol Nidre,"* because the television special he has been rehearsing will be beamed after the Day of Atonement anyway. Had the protagonist been asked to sacrifice his career, he surely would have refused. And since the show is telecast after the High Holidays, the cantor can be in the audience, sitting next to Molly, when Jess Robin performs while wearing a sort of sequined *tallit.* Thus the central dilemma of the original version is drained of meaning and significance.[9]

Nor does the movie formulate a convincing justification for the cantor's earlier objections to a commercial music career. The new version does not put in context his desire to keep the Judaic world as hermetically sealed as possible. In one of the most amazing non sequiturs in the American cinema, Olivier mentions the Holocaust as a reason for Diamond not to visit a Los Angeles recording studio. What eventually reconciles father and son is not a fuller appreciation of the vocation each man has chosen, but the simple fact that Oliver has become a grandfather. It is family ties that bind, not shared values—with the old cantor rather than his son making the compromise that reunites the family. Diamond affects no deeper understanding of the religious calling, and parenthood does not seem to implicate him more completely in the fate of the Jewish people. Instead Olivier, gleefully and proudly clapping among Diamond's fans, shows that he's not a fanatic or an oddball after all. *The Jazz Singer* is therefore a parable of modernization, a sign of the eclipse of the sacred. In making so meager a case for piety, the film partakes of the atmosphere that most Jews breathe.

Jewish neighborhoods bear little resemblance to the Hester Street of the 1920s. The Orthodox enclave on Eldridge Street is therefore unrepresentative, and the relationship of the synagogue to the urban drabness enveloping it is never probed. The filmmakers have taken the evidence of skidding Jewish birth rates so seriously that the aged rabbi serves a congregation composed primarily of the geriatric; Jess and Rivka seem to have no friends their own age. His best friend is black, which betrays the movie into incorporating a blackface scene in an otherwise all-Negro nightclub that must have made enlightened filmgoers cringe. There are no black-Jewish tensions; and there is no mention of Israel, a nation of whose existence the characters in this movie are unaware.

But at least *The Jazz Singer* is honest about the values it is asking its audiences to accept. The only way the fifth commandment is going to be obeyed is if the father honors the youthful quest for self-satisfaction. For the film endorses the American ideal of individualism and celebrates the openness of a country where, as Tocqueville commented in the 1830s, "the track of generations is effaced." Beaming its message directly at the youth market, the movie offers the promise that in America parents will not—cannot—impede the climb to the top. Unlike some other show business sagas, *The Jazz Singer* spares us a demonstration of how terrible success is, how corrupting everything can be when you are rich and glamorous and can touch the stars. Compared with the excitement of Jess Robin's new career, as waves of adulation float over him wherever he strums his guitar, who *would* rather remain anchored in grimy Eldridge Street? Even without the creative fulfillment and popular acclaim Jess Robin enjoys at the end, most American Jews abandoned such dispiriting neighborhoods long ago.

In minimizing the pertinence of religious and ethnic differences, *The Jazz Singer* projects an irony of which its makers seem unaware. Al Jolson was the unmistakable product of an immigrant community, and yet his very success—the pride and identification that he fostered—helped to erode that community. By proving that they could make it in America, the popular entertainers and the businessmen behind them made the distinctive subculture of the immigrants seem parochial, stunted, and doomed. Mass entertainment was partly responsible for unifying the nation. But in articulating our common dreams and in permeating much of our experience, it also homogenized our lives and helped to shatter the context of the particular. The effect can be observed, for example, in the Yiddish theater, which Raphaelson, curiously enough, covered for the *New York Times*. From Muni to Matthau, few of the actors who got their start there have preferred to finish there. The allure of mass entertainment, which *The Jazz Singer* exemplifies, has been too powerful for most talented Jews to ignore; when Jolson walks out in blackface, the movie proclaims that "he belongs to the whole world."[10] But in 1980 the fact that Jess Robin is supposed to be a descendant of cantors has nothing to do with his songs, or his creativity, or his soul.

Of course popular culture should not be expected to give us a complete metaphysical examination, although the 1980 version of

The Jazz Singer fails because it is solemn without being serious. As metaphor it nevertheless still exerts an almost subliminal force, and can still arouse feelings usually buried beneath consciousness. By inviting Jews in particular to reconsider the world they have lost, it is a tale that can even transcend its particular re-presentations.

10

In the Big Inning

Virtually the first sustained piece of American Jewish fiction is Abraham Cahan's *Yekl* (1896), and at the outset the conversation turns to baseball. Jake, the protagonist of the novella, is eager to abandon the stigma of being a greenhorn and to become assimilated. He therefore informs another sweatshop worker: "You must know how to *peetch*." But the scholarly Bernstein is indifferent to discussions about "*pitzers* and *catzers*," which provokes Jake to taunt him with what Jake believes to be a decisive put-down: "How hard can you hit?"[1]

Cahan himself was not content with a literary reputation for realistic depiction of the New York ghetto, and as the most influential Jewish journalist of the century, he used the *Forward* to ease the pain of immigrant adaptation to the New World. No wonder then that, as early as 1909, his newpaper published an article on the fundamentals of baseball. Many grandchildren of its readers would become more conscious of what the immigrants had forsaken. When Joan Micklin Silver, the daughter-in-law of the Zionist tribune Abba Hillel Silver, adapted *Yekl* for the screen in 1975, *Hester Street* added a scene in Central Park that showed Jake teaching his son how to hit a baseball. But Silver made it apparent that Jake's poor form would have prevented him from slamming the horsehide very far past the infield.

Ever since Cahan, Jewish novelists have included among their characters not only *rebbes* and revolutionaries, fixers and *fressers*, *allrightniks* and anarchists, vulgarians and violinists, but baseball players as well. Several Jewish novelists have, like even mere "coreligionists," been in the diamond business. Instead of pondering the mysteries of *b'reshit*, these writers have created scenes set "in the big inning." The mansion of American Jewish fiction has room for many memorable and familiar characters, but there are also fielders on the roof; and they too merit at least brief consideration.

Bernard Malamud's first novel was *The Natural* (1952), and it is unique among his books in that no Jew—not even the word—appears in it. *The Natural* must also be regarded as among the most bizarre baseball tales ever written, since it is fashioned from the same medieval legends that provided the mythic pattern for T. S. Eliot's *The Waste Land*. For "the whole history of baseball has the quality of mythology," Malamud has observed; therefore the Holy Grail can become the league pennant, the Fisher King a manager named Pop Fisher, and the knights the name of a New York team. A rookie named Roy Hobbs can assume the responsibility of a heroic quest and can end the dry season with the aid of a magical bat drawn from a tree struck by lightning. But Malamud has understood that the heroism of the Arthurian legends is no longer credible in the modern age. When Hobbs strikes out at the end of the novel, a fan is heard to mutter: "He coulda been a king" (Roy-*roi*, get it?).[2]

The author claims to have been a fan himself "from the time I was a kid and went to Ebbets Field whenever I could," and he drew on actual episodes in the history of the sport in plotting the novel. But the allegorical cargo of the book is so heavy that it threatens to sink respect for the particularities of the game itself. *The Natural* is not naturalistic enough. Endowed with its own distinct rituals, codes, sancta, and traditions, baseball ought to attract on its own the student of manners and morals. The problem with Malamud's tale is that it is not quite baseball that the New York Knights are playing.

Philip Roth solved this problem twenty-one years later in *The Great American Novel*. If the national pastime is myth, then give the athletes names like Gil Gamesh (a Babylonian fireballer who is "the greatest rookie of all time"), John ("Spit") Baal, and Jean-Paul ("Frenchy") Astarte. But make them reek of verisimilitude and individuality; make them real ballplayers. Then put them on the last-place team of a defunct Patriot League, force them to go through the rigors of spring training in Asbury Park, New Jersey, throw them into an exhibition match against a team of lunatics from an asylum, give them a Jewish owner who knows how to let in the waist on their uniforms—and the result is a tour de farce, a true screwball comedy that also emits a Bronx cheer against virtually everything most Americans have deemed sacred. It is superfluous— and irrelevant—to add that only a novelist who also cherishes the game could demonstrate such intimate and intricate knowledge of its lore and lingo. Like all effective satire, *The Great American Novel* cannot entirely disguise a fondness for the targets it so mercilessly assaults.

Contrary to popular belief, Roth's most important organ is his ear, which he has used to record the American idiom with stunning fidelity. His players and sports announcers and newspaper "scribes" sound exactly as they should. No serious student of the written or spoken language can afford to ignore *The Great American Novel*, but it is not a book for the serious; it is for anyone willing to risk being helplessly convulsed with laughter. *The Great American Novel* is nasty and vulgar and wordy and disordered, and it certainly isn't deep. It is an extravaganza of comic inventiveness and inspired zaniness that is exempt from the preoccupation of his other books with the exorbitant demands of mothers and wives and lovers. But careful readers of *Portnoy's Complaint* (1969) may recall that the sole exception to the squalor of the narrator's interior life is the lyrical memory of the boyhood hours spent in center field. Only there did Portnoy enjoy the autonomy and "unruffled nonchalance" that make him wonder why he could not somehow have remained a joyous sandlotter forever.[3]

The grim jokes that aging and mortality represent are deftly recounted in Mark Harris's series of novels about a semiliterate pitcher, Henry Wiggen. *The Southpaw* (1953) traces Wiggen's career from childhood to his rookie year with the World Series-bound New York Mammoths, and shows how he learns to see through the emptiness of the struggle for success at all costs, the dizzying emphasis on fame. Wiggen's wife Holly presumably speaks for the author when she tells the southpaw that statistics "do not show . . . that you growed to manhood over the summer. You will throw no more spitballs for the sake of something so stupid as a ball game. . . . You will never be an island," she adds, "and that is the great victory hardly anybody wins anymore."[4] That victory comes in handy in

Bang the Drum Slowly (1956) with Wiggen's friendship with Bruce Pearson, a third-string catcher dying of Hodgkin's disease. Wiggen insists in his contract with the Mammoths that Pearson not be dropped from the roster unless the pitcher is as well; and together they face the sudden onset of the inevitable.

The last two novels in Harris's tetralogy are less successful or well-known. *A Ticket for a Seamstitch* (1957) limns the national fascination with science, technology, and health, as embodied in a ballplayer named Piney Woods. *It Looked Like for Ever* (1979) juxtaposes the game's promise of renewal (we're back to Malamud's vegetation myth) with the aging of Henry Wiggen. Thirty-nine years old, with nineteen big league seasons behind him, he has lost his fastball. Passed over to become the next manager, Harris's hero is released, and must accept not only his own limitations but also, ultimately, his own mortality.

The New York Mammoths boast a slugging first baseman named Sid Goldman, but it is no secret that Jews in the major leagues have been almost as rare as a double steal. Harris nevertheless was shrewd enough to envision the fictional possibilities of modeling his first-string catcher, Red Traphagen, on Moe Berg, whom Casey Stengel called "the strangest fellah who ever put on a uniform." The son of immigrant Russian Jews who settled in Newark, Berg got a degree in Romance languages from Princeton and a law degree from Columbia; he displayed a flair for science and a command of a dozen languages (including Japanese, Mandarin Chinese, and Sanskrit). Meeting intellectual challenges should have been easy for Berg, but playing catcher for the Dodgers, Red Sox, and other teams must have been a more interesting way to fulfill the dream of a second-generation American. A notoriously weak hitter whose .243 lifetime batting average must have been only slightly higher than his IQ, Berg nevertheless testified to the persistent allure that the game exerted upon even the most scholarly of grown-ups. At the age of seventy, his dying words took the form of the least metaphysical of questions: "How did the Mets do today?"[5]

Berg was also the strangest fellah ever to study phonetics at the Sorbonne (during the off-season), and was unique among Jewish intellectuals in getting up from the sidelines. Isaac Rosenfeld was perhaps the first to grasp the sport's potential for fiction; his 1947 story, "The Misfortunes of the Flapjacks," precedes *The Great*

American Novel in chronicling a team's devastating penchant for defeat. The Flapjacks of the One Eye League can field only eight men when their fourteen-year-old mascot refuses to continue playing shortstop. In one game the team surrenders thirty-eight runs. It loses its supply of bats. It runs out of money. The regular manager is taken away to a mental institution. Finally the Flapjacks are so emaciated from hunger that they lose an exhibition match to a high school squad. Rosenfeld, whose death at thirty-eight was a blow to American letters, managed to capture that sense of victimization that is the schlemiel ticket of the Jewish comedian. But his fable, unlike Roth's novel, is not out for laughs. "The Misfortunes of the Flapjacks" conveys instead a fundamental unfairness in the order of things, a primordial injustice that nothing—neither physical strength nor collective will—can rectify. Even Delmore Schwartz, the laureate of alienation who was nicknamed "the Jewish Franz Kafka," once wondered, "Why don't I feel the same intensity about the writing of poems as I do when I root for the Giants against the Dodgers?"[6]

The vibrancy of the myth of baseball is largely realized in Jerome Charyn's *The Seventh Babe* (1979), whose protagonist, the scion of a Southwestern copper fortune, adopts an identity akin to Babe Ruth's. Narrated in a staccato style, the novel employs the technique perfected in E. L. Doctorow's *Ragtime* of blending fictional figures with historical actors such as Ty Cobb and Kenesaw Mountain Landis. There is also something distinctly modernist (and perhaps Jewish) in Charyn's conception of Babe Ragland, for he is an oddity. He is a left-handed third baseman; he is a misfit on a Red Sox team composed of various outsiders; and he winds up playing in the Negro leagues for a team (the Cincinnati Giants) that is in fact homeless.

The Seventh Babe includes only one Jewish character, Billy Rogovin, a gambler who sets up Ragland for what is interpreted as a bribe, provoking the infielder's expulsion. Like the coarse and sinister Meyer Wolfsheim in *The Great Gatsby*, Rogovin is based on Arnold Rothstein, who is alleged to have fixed the 1919 World Series. So obligatory have such characters become that another gambler, named Scruffy Levinson, contemplates fixing baseball games in *The Sensation* (1975). But Norman Keifetz's novel has a more peculiar theme—a psychological examination of an extremely talented center fielder, Potter Cindy, who exposes himself in front of little girls. (The character was undoubtedly inspired by a professional football player arrested on such charges in the 1960s.) Keifetz's book lacks artistic grace, psychological subtlety or even narrative drive as a sports saga. But in the darkness of its subject, *The Sensation* points to the possibility that the aberrant underside of the game warrants the attention of adult writers and readers.

It is rare for baseball fiction to acknowledge the sadness that is so pervasive an element in human experience, but Eliot Asinof's *Man on Spikes* (1954) does so. The surface of the novel looks familiar: this time the name of the sensational rookie center fielder is Mike Kutner, and he can hit, field, run, and manifest an infectious will to win. But a series of career reversals, including military service in World War II, conspire to keep Kutner in the Class AA and AAA leagues. Confined to the farm system of the Chicago Lions, he is exploited for so long that his chance to play in the majors arrives when Kutner is thirty-five. It is too late. Like Roy Hobbs, he fails to hit in the clutch, although Kutner appreciates through marital love how much more there is to life than baseball. *Man on Spikes* relies little on conventional plotting, and imposes no demands on readers whose technical knowledge of the game may be hazy. Asinof, who played three years in the farm system of the Philadelphia Phillies, assumes that the dugout is as appropriate a setting for human conflict as a New England whaling ship or a Mississippi raft, and so poignant in his account of the indignity of aging that the reader almost accepts this assumption.

Few contemporary novelists are as haunted by the corruption of flesh and spirit as Mordecai Richler, whose satiric thrusts have been so similar to Roth's. As a Canadian, Richler might have been immune to the charm of baseball and could have been expected to stick to hockey and to the mocky opportunists from Montreal who have long been his targets. Yet it is he who once revealed the wry secret that, "like most Jewish novelists," he would rather have been Sandy Koufax. Richler is a master of the comic set piece, such as the filming of the bar mitzvah ceremony in *The Apprenticeship of Duddy Kravitz*; he nearly tops it in *St. Urbain's Horseman* (1971) with a Sunday morning softball game on London's Hampstead Heath. It is a savage version of the pastoral. Nearly all the players are Canadian Jews living abroad, men in their forties who had been radical amidst the Depression and the Spanish Civil War. Now they are deeply immersed in the meretriciousness of popular culture. Typical of the lineup are Gordie Kaufman, "who had once carried a banner that read *No Pasarán* through the streets of Manhattan and now employed a man especially to keep Spaniards off the beach at his villa on Mallorca"; and Moey Hanover, "who had studied at a yeshiva, stood up to the committee, and was now on a sabbatical from Desilu." Observing them from behind home plate are, well, not exactly fans, but their first wives, nicknamed "the Alimony Gallery."[7] The author himself is less interested in the intrinsic complexities of the game itself than in the comic betrayal of the amateurs' effort to revive a vanished innocence.

But the opening and closing episodes to two other novels clinch the case for the pertinence of baseball to the American Jewish imagination. Although neither book was hailed as a classic by the critics, who are the bench jockeys of literature, *The Chosen* and *Good as Gold* both attempted to assess the impact of assimilation, and both Chaim Potok and Joseph Heller did so by depicting a softball game. In the first chapter of Potok's 1967 novel, one team of Orthodox Jewish boys is pitted against another that is even more pious. The narrator, Reuven Malter, can hurl blazing sinkers while yielding to some of the forces of modern secularism. Danny Saunders, the heir to a Hasidic dynasty in Williamsburg, can hit vicious line drives as well as read the Talmud with exemplary facility. His coach is a rabbi who exhorts the team to hustle in Yiddish, and the Hasidim regard with contempt athletic and religious opponents they deem *apikorsim*. Although Heller's 1979 novel is very different from *The Chosen*, the final page also describes a softball game among yeshiva boys wearing skullcaps. Protagonist Bruce Gold is returning from a visit to his mother's grave, although he is unable to mourn her passing and cannot read the Hebrew letters on her marker. But in watching the kids play softball, mixing their American boys' profanity with Yiddish, Gold cannot help wondering how adaptable and enduring this ancient people is.

In his broken English, Cahan's Jake had defined himself as "an American feller, a Yankee;"[8] and Jewish fiction thereafter typically has consisted of parables of assimilation and its discontents. With some hesitation and a few qualifications, most Jews have shared the hunger of other ethnic minorities for acceptance and for full participation in the national consensus. For better or for worse, baseball has helped to forge that consensus and has helped to make a disparate people one. Irwin Shaw captured this process in his tale of Israel Federov, who "had passed through Ellis Island on the long voyage from Kiev by way of Hamburg, and was made into an American in the slums of New York City, in vacant lots along the East River where they played with taped baseballs, homemade bats, and without gloves."[9]

But while talented members of other minorities have gone from coal fields and cotton fields to win fame and wealth on the playing fields, the Jews have left professional competition to the goys of summer. Despite the relative absence of violence in baseball, Jews have been professionally absent from it. Instead a disproportionate number of Jewish novelists have preferred to write about the sport, which has given them the opportunity to explore glory rather than guilt and the possibilities of heroism rather than the certainties of failure. Their books must also be understood not simply as romances or yarns or satires but—even in the second and third generations— as final citizenship papers. Not everyone can follow Saul Bellow and I. B. Singer all the way to Stockholm. But several Jewish writers seem to have found Cooperstown instead.

11

From Publick Occurrences to Pseudo-Events:

Journalists and Their Critics

Two autobiographies almost can be said to mark the rhythm of change within the profession of journalism in this century. The authors' surnames are the same, their lives divergent. In William Allen White's celebrated *Autobiography* (1946), a village doctor's son whose ancestry could be traced to the Revolution graduates from Emporia College, edits his small-town newspaper, registers as a Republican, becomes a spokesman for the Middle Border and wonders what the matter is with his beloved native state of Kansas. Note the contrast with Theodore H. White's recent and equally charming reminiscence, *In Search of History* (1978). Its author is an immigrant's son who grows up in a Boston enclave, graduates from Harvard, becomes a correspondent for the first weekly news magazine, remains a Democrat, interprets the Middle Kingdom and later popularizes the romance of Camelot. In their lives, the arc from parochialism to internationalism, from the village print shop to the mass media can be traced.

It goes without saying that the editor of the Emporia *Gazette* was also a Protestant. It is apt that the *Time* reporter who later rewrote the rules for covering presidential campaigns is a Jew. That particular symbolism is salient, and the aim of this chapter is to measure the impact of Americans of Jewish birth in journalism. That contribution has been twofold, for Jews have exerted a disproportionate influence on the ways that a modern democracy enlightens itself, and they have formulated perhaps the most effective critique of that process of enlightenment. The roles that Jews have played as publishers, editors, and writers cannot be ignored in any full chronicle of the American press. But they have also developed the most intellectually elegant assessment of modern journalism, and of its consequences for the democratic prospect. In both of these roles, Walter Lippmann has been pivotal; this chapter pays special attention to him because his journalistic career has been so exemplary, because his attitude toward his own ethnic background has been representative, and because his analysis of his profession has been so influential. In arguing that the ideal of objectivity is unattainable, Lippmann sought to demonstrate that "in an exact sense the present crisis of Western democracy is a crisis in journalism." He therefore provided theoretical underpinning for one historian's plea that the press be studied not only as a branch of social history, or cultural history, but also "in relation to the workings of democratic government."[1] That the history of the media also exhibits an ethnic dimension, that many Jews are drawn to both the possibilities and dilemmas of public enlightenment, this chapter also seeks to demonstrate.

The first American newspaper was published in Boston in 1690. *Publick Occurrences Both Foreign and Domestick* promised to appear monthly or, "if any Glut of Occurrences happen[,] oftener"; but it was suppressed after one issue.[2] Other newspapers, pamphlets, broadsides, and journals followed, and their impact is an inextricable part of the story of the Revolution, the ratification of the Constitution, the struggle over slavery, and the emergence of an industrialized, mass society. The Jews played a far from negligible role in nineteenth-century journalism, as Jonathan D. Sarna has noted in his recent biography of one of them, Mordecai Manuel Noah. The Jews, Professor Sarna observes, could rise quickly in an expanding profession, which was congenial to a cosmopolitan perspective and to a people already experienced through trade in the distribution and dissemination of information.[3] Joseph Pulitzer was the most creative newspaper executive of the Gilded Age; the format and style of his *St. Louis Post-Dispatch* and *New York World* established standards for layouts, features, and photography that twentieth-century newspapers largely have been content to imitate. Yet while Pulitzer, a Hungarian immigrant, suffered from anti-Semitic jibes, his classification as a Jew is doubtful. His father was part Jewish, his mother was a Catholic, he himself was nominally an Episocopalian, and his children were not raised as Jews.[4]

An authentic "first" came in 1896 when Adolph S. Ochs bought the *New York Times*. Its circulation was then nine thousand (while Pulitzer's *World* was selling 600,000 copies a day), but the publisher soon converted it into a newspaper whose reputation for probity, accuracy, and comprehensiveness was unrivaled. Ochs himself married the daughter of Rabbi Isaac Mayer Wise and shared in his father-in-law's belief in the compatibility of Reform Judaism with dominant American values, such as progress, equality of opportunity, enterprise, and stability. Although the generalization should not be pushed too far, Jews in the twentieth century tended to achieve prominence earlier as publishers than as writers. One exception was Fabian Franklin, a Hungarian immigrant who taught mathematics at Johns Hopkins before rising to the editorship of the *Baltimore News* and the associate editorship of the *New York Evening Post*. He was a conservative and unusually learned newsman.[5] Ochs' competitors have included J. David Stern and later Dorothy Schiff of the *New York Post*; Moses Annenberg and his son Walter of the *Philadelphia Inquirer* and Triangle Publications; and Samuel Newhouse, who now owns the third largest chain of American newspapers. (The *Washington Post*'s Eugene Meyer married a Lutheran and jettisoned his own religious affiliation; and his daughter, Katharine Graham, now the board chairwoman of the *Post*, was not raised as a Jew.)[6] Jews who have founded magazines have included Raoul Fleischmann (the *New Yorker*) and David Smart and William Weintraub (*Esquire*). The suspicions of certain figures from Colonel Charles Lindbergh to General George Brown notwithstanding, Jews own the same percentage of newspapers (3 percent of the 1,748 published) as their proportion of the general population. The circulation of the newspapers that Jews own adds up to 8 percent of the daily press, suggesting that—at least in purely quantitative terms—journalism is not a very prepossessing sign of Jewish entrepreneurship.[7]

More noteworthy has been the prominence of Jews as editors and writers, especially since the Second World War. Newspaper editors have included Lippmann and Herbert Bayard Swope of the *New York World*, Simeon Strunsky and James Wechsler of the *New York Post*, Howard Simons and Meg Greenfield of the *Washington Post*, and Warren Phillips of the *Wall Street Journal*. Magazine editors, especially those working for the most serious publications, have included an even greater proportion of Jewish descent. Two of the three founders of the *New Republic* were Lippmann and Walter Weyl; its current editor is Martin Peretz, who is related to the Yiddish writer I. L. Peretz. The editors of *Seven Arts*, which championed the avant-garde in the World War I era, included James Oppenheim, Waldo Frank, and Paul Rosenfeld. Robert Silvers and Barbara Epstein have from the beginning edited the *New York Review of Books*, which boasts a smaller circulation than, say, the *Oklahoma City Times* but enjoys a greater cachet among literati. *The Public Interest* has been edited by Irving Kristol, Daniel Bell, and Nathan Glazer, *Dissent* primarily by Irving Howe. In this list *Commentary*, published by the American Jewish Committee, doesn't count; but under editors Elliot Cohen and Norman Podhoretz, its distinction has been widely acknowledged. William Shawn has presided over the transformation of the *New Yorker* from a rather precious humor magazine into a formidable locus of social commentary. *I. F. Stone's Weekly* was a unique experiment in personal journalism; and Norman Cousins edited the *Saturday Review*, with which he also was virtually synonymous, for more than thirty years. Among news magazines, David Lawrence long edited *U.S. News and World Report*, and Henry Anatole Grunwald, a Viennese immigrant whose career at *Time* began as a part-time copy boy, became its managing editor in 1968.

Lawrence himself inaugurated the political syndicated column early in the 1920s. His immediate successors included the ubiquitous Lippmann and the arch-conservative George Sokolsky. David Broder is regarded as "the high priest of political journalism, the most powerful and respected man in the trade."[8] His competitors include Joseph Kraft (who coined the phrase "Middle America"), Elizabeth Drew and Jules Witcover. The diacritical history of the *Washington Post* would have been quite different without cartoonist Herbert Block ("Herblock") or local reporter Carl Bernstein. Walter Winchell was perhaps the most influential gossip columnist of his time (but when a Mississippi congressman called him a "little kike," no one in the House of Representatives objected).[9] When Nathanael West imagined *Miss Lonelyhearts* (1931), he hardly could have anticipated the impact of two advisers to the nation, Abigail Van Buren

("Dear Abby") and Ann Landers. The twin daughters of Abraham and Rebecca Friedman of Sioux City, they regularly offer a Middle American version of the Bintel Brief.

Even the shortest survey of Jews in journalism must acknowledge the special case of the *New York Times*. In part because Ochs's descendants have continued to own it, in part because it appears in a city whose Jewish population is about as large as Israel's, the *Times* sometimes strained to disguise its Jewish cast. Not only was its publisher, Arthur Hays Sulzberger, antagonistic to Zionism before 1948, but reporters with given names such as Abraham routinely found the initial A. in their bylines instead. Because Sulzberger did not wish "to put a Jew in the showcase," he refused to permit Arthur Krock to run the editorial page when a vacancy opened in 1937. Krock, the chief of the Washington bureau, protested: since his father was Jewish, mother was part Jewish and upbringing was devoid of religious instruction, and since religious law makes maternal descent the determinant of Jewish identity, he was therefore not a Jew. Unfazed by this demonstration of learning, Sulzberger replied: "Arthur, how do you know all that if you aren't Jewish?"[10] Those who clearly were have included editors John B. Oakes, Theodore Bernstein, Lester Markel, A. M. Rosenthal, and Max Frankel, and columnists and reporters including Meyer Berger, A. H. Raskin, Tad Szulc, Anthony Lewis, Seymour Hersh, and Sydney Schanberg. David Halberstam, a descendant of the famed Rabbi Meir Katzenellenbogen of sixteenth-century Padua, was decisive in altering American attitudes toward the war in Vietnam.

The history of broadcasting has duplicated the pattern that began with entrepreneurship and then extended to editorial and reportorial prominence. The founders of two major networks were Jews (this time of Eastern European rather than German heritage): David Sarnoff of NBC and William Paley of CBS. Leonard Goldenson later headed ABC. Then, still behind the scenes, came the news programmers—from Fred Friendly to Richard Salant at CBS, to Reuven Frank at NBC and to Avram Westin at ABC. Those appearing on camera have included Marvin and Bernard Kalb, Daniel Schorr, David Schoenbrun, Irving R. Levine, Elie Abel, Murray Fromson, and Sander Vanocur. On CBS's *60 Minutes*, often the most watched weekly show on television, two of the four principals are Morley Safer and Mike Wallace. But no newscaster of Jewish background served as network anchor until Barbara Walters broke that particular barrier too. It is therefore unsurprising for the latest revision of Mencken's *American Language* to claim that "the most fruitful sources of Yiddish loans [into English] are the media of mass communications—journalism, radio and television."[11]

The above list is not meant to be exhaustive, or to imply that the prominence of Jews is more than part of the story of modern communications. Jews have remained a minority in the profession of journalism, but their impact has been significant enough to invite speculation and analysis. Stephen D. Isaacs, himself a journalist, has offered the most recent explanations: (1) The intellectual and verbal resourcefulness that the Jews historically have cherished are rewarded in a field such as the mass media; (2) "Journalism, like all forms of mass education, prizes the nonethnicity of universalism" and especially the ideal of objectivity. Those choosing journalism as a career might therefore expect to be judged by their merit, not their origin.[12]

The first explanation is a commonplace—but that, of course, is no reason to dismiss it, since truisms often are inseparable from truths. The argument need no longer be elaborated that many of the Jews emerging from the ghettos and *shtetlach* were endowed with minds easily violated by ideas, and that for them and their descendants verbal and intellectual facility have been sovereign aspects of life. The attraction for Jews of a profession that depends on the verbal transmission and reconstruction of reality is therefore understandable.

Isaacs's second explanation is dubious, however. Whatever the appeal of universalist ideals, journalism itself is more a business than a liberal profession. Editors and reporters are neither self-employed nor accredited through professional examinations nor generally expected to meet educational requirements (Carl Bernstein, for instance, is a college dropout). In the social structure, journalism resembles medicine or science less than it does such cognate fields as public relations, advertising, and polling. Isaacs's explanation cannot account for the presence of innovative Jews in those fields too—Edward L. Bernays, Carl Byoir, and Ben Sonnenberg in public relations; Albert Lasker and William Bernbach in advertising; Ernest Dichter in market research. Beginning with his assessments for John F. Kennedy, Louis Harris became what one authority has called "the world's most successful and influential pollster."[13] Samuel Lubell and Daniel Yankelovich also have excelled in taking the popular pulse, and Gerald Rafshoon, the sculptor of Jimmy Carter's image, soon became an active verb ("to rafshoon"), indicating the continuing insertion of public relations approaches to politics. Although these fields hardly place a premium on objectivity, Jews have not been immune to their appeal. Even Allen Ginsberg did marketing research before fully accepting his vocation as a poet, and Norman Mailer once considered going into advertising (which, in a sense, he did anyway). No wonder then that James Joyce, when he invented a modern Everyman, made Leopold Bloom not only a Jew but an advertising canvasser.

Even within the ambit of journalism itself, the exaltation of objectivity has not been pervasive. Jews have shaped the journals of opinion and were midwives to the birth of the syndicated column. The norm of neutrality is irrelevant to the success of the Newhouse fashion magazines, such as *Vogue*, *Mademoiselle*, and *Glamour*, on which the dominant editorial figure long has been a Russian immigrant, Alexander Liberman. The classic American newspaper play, *The Front Page*, was coauthored by Ben Hecht, whose raffish autobiography recounts his love of Chicago daily journalism because of its seedy excitement, not its impartiality. A Herblock cartoon is regarded, according to its creator, as "a signed piece of work, an example of personal opinion."[14] And beginning in the 1960s, some of the journalists most critical of the ideal of objectivity—and most resistant to it in their own work—have been Jews. One of them, when asked during the Chicago 7 conspiracy trial to give the court the facts, told the judge: "Facts are nothing without their nuance, sir."[15] It is interesting that in the upper reaches of the wire services, which stress the conventions of balanced reporting, Jews are as rare as snail darters.[16]

A wider reference to Jewish history further punctures Isaacs's argument. In the Germany of the Second Empire and the Weimar Republic, many of the leading newspapers were owned by Jews: the *Berliner Morgenpost*, the *Berliner Tageblatt*, the *Vossiche Zeitung* and—perhaps the most prestigious of all—the *Frankfurter Zeitung*. Such newspapers tended to be, according to historian Peter Gay, "liberal in editorial policy, respectable in makeup, and moderate in tone"; but they were not devoted to the Anglo-American norm of neutrality. Arthur Koestler, a correspondent for the formidable Ullstein house during the Weimar period, has recalled that German journalism was based on the writer's *"Weltanschauung,* and the political philosophy of the paper for which he worked. His job was not to report news and facts, but to use facts as pretexts for venting his opinions." Yet under such auspices scribes of Jewish extraction flourished, especially in the literary and intellectual journals.[17] Theodor Herzl, who wrote feuilletons for Vienna's *Neue Freie Presse,* was not unique.

However unconvincing Isaacs's emphasis on the appeal of universalism, certain broad patterns nevertheless can be discerned. Generalizations permit exceptions, so that it can be safely stated that the liberal stance of most journalists of Jewish origin suggests a particular concern for the fate of free institutions. Since emancipation Jews have tended to stake their hopes on the extension of liberalism, on representative government under the rule of law. They have commonly believed that their own destiny was to be intertwined with the dissemination of the ideals of tolerance, equality, and individual dignity. They therefore have often been the foes of privilege, of societies founded on ascription rather than achievement. They have not exalted Dostoevsky's Christian trinity of miracle, mystery, and authority. But the promise that civil society offered came with a price tag, which has been absorption of the dominant social values and acceptance of its codes of conduct. The Jews who achieved the greatest prominence after emancipation therefore tended to be the most distant from the *Judengasse* or from Hester Street; and the regularity of this pattern of acculturation and assimilation must therefore be viewed as more decisive than the vagaries of individual ambition, purpose, and talent.

This estrangement from the compulsions of Judaic tradition does not mean that those who won fame as journalists cannot be understood in terms of modern Jewish history, for no one who escapes from an ethnic or religious past that he may consider burdensome is thereby automatically converted into a human being and nothing else. Such a creature—stripped of the concreteness and particularity of race, sex, class, nationality, culture, historical moment, and milieu—does not exist. Language alone marks an austere limit on universalism, and the various failures to elide that restriction—a Jew even invented Esperanto—point to the recalcitrance of human differences. The effort to transcend one's past in no way demonstrates freedom from its grip, for even the struggle to evade its spell is a revealing datum of identity, unintelligible apart from other clues to that past. What one is, is what one has become; in sociological terms, the hunger for assimilation is no less significant as evidence of origin than comfort with the claims of ethnic allegiance. What the late critic Harold Rosenberg once observed in Jewish art is applicable to the history of journalism as well. For writers as well as painters, their work "has been the closest expression of themselves as they are, including the fact that they are Jews, each in his individual degree."[18]

In this sense the penumbra of American Jewish history is relevant, even though many of the names listed above are not even recognizably Jewish, and even though their bearers rarely have associated themselves with communal causes. Most of the journalists who are Jews propelled themselves rather furiously away from the realm of their parents and grandparents, and have shown only the most marginal interest in Jewish themes.

Perhaps one measure of this estrangement has been indifference to Zionism and even hostility to the state of Israel. Nat Hentoff of the *Village Voice* once wrote that "if there were no United Arab Republic, Ben Gurion would have had to invent one." I. F. Stone has called himself a "Jewish dissident," ostracized for advocating a binational state in the Middle East. Far more typical, however, has been Joseph Kraft, who was "raised without religious training of any kind in a home that observed even holidays only casually." He found himself "indifferent to the faith of my fathers. Neither does the history of the Jews as a people invoke keen interest." Although not unmindful of Jewish resilience and accomplishment, Kraft acknowledged, rather ruefully, that "the community which was my Jewish inheritance cannot be passed on . . . and I myself have strayed from the fold."[19] This set of attitudes resembled that of Jewish journalists more generally in the Diaspora. In this context Theodore White is somewhat unusual in that, even in the seventh decade of his life, "when a Biblical phrase runs through my mind, I am trapped and annoyed unless I can convert it into Hebrew—whereupon the memory retrieves it from its proper place." As a correspondent in China during the Second World War, White found himself at a banquet with the Communists, and was unable to eat pork until

Chou En-lai artfully persuaded him that it was duck.[20] Several re-viewers of White's autobiography took note of this incident; it is also doubtful whether many other reporters of Jewish background would have cared.

This was certainly true of Walter Lippmann. The author of a score of books, almost three hundred articles, more than two thou-sand editorials and four thousand newspaper columns, he almost never mentioned the Jews. When he did so, his tone was dismissive or derogatory, as in his early criticism of their "bad economic habits, their exploiting of simpler people." Although Lippmann described the "thwarted nationality" of the Irish, Poles, Negroes, and Jews before the Great War, although he found poignant their "kind of homelessness on the planet," he himself never championed Zionism. In the late 1930s he still regarded Africa as the most suitable des-tination for refugees from nazism—the very solution a Zionist Con-gress had rejected four decades earlier, and which the Nazis themselves diffidently revived.[21]

Only once did Lippmann really break his public silence on the subject of Jewry. In 1922 he accepted an offer to write something for the *American Hebrew*, and announced himself as "a Jew writing in a Jewish weekly to Jews." Lippmann took the occasion to min-imize the extent of Gentile antagonism, which he dismissed as a matter of "summer hotels and college fraternities," of "childish" ignorance exhibited by the likes of Henry Ford. Anti-Semitism survived because "the Jew is conspicuous," being "fairly distinct" in personal appearance and in the spelling of his name. Difference attracts attention, and Lippmann therefore expressed some anguish that insufficient care was being taken in self-regulation. He con-demned "the rich and vulgar and pretentious Jews of our big Amer-ican cities" as "perhaps the greatest misfortune that has ever befallen the Jewish people. They are the real fountain of anti-Semitism." Even though they are no worse than "other jazzy elements in the population," these particular Jews, Lippmann warned, are "every-where in sight." They therefore "undermine the natural liberalism of the American people," who "ask themselves: If this is what liberty for the oppressed comes to in the end, what is the use of tolerance and the tradition of asylum?"[22]

Lippmann's strategy was transparent. He did not play down the significance of vulgarity among Jews, or define it as defamation of the Jewish people itself, or explain it away as the product of special historical circumstances, or stress its resemblance to the traits of other nouveaux riches. He did not articulate an anatomy of prejudice itself; he did not invoke the fallacy of taking the part for the whole. Nor did he appeal to the tradition of individualism as the test for judging the behavior of others. Instead, appalled by "crude wealth in the hands of shallow people," Lippmann called upon the Jews to uphold "the classic Greek virtue of moderation." He complained that representatives of American Jewry were "hypochondriacs and morbidly defensive about their critics, and indulgent and complacent about what the Jewish people is and does." They should, Lippmann advised, elevate their own standards of taste and propriety. By practicing "the art of moderate, clean and generous living," the Jews would not only honor themselves but deflect and defeat anti-Semitism as well.[23]

The asperity of these remarks burst the boundaries of *ahavath yisroel*, that tradition exemplified by a character in I. B. Singer's novel *Shosha* who proclaims: "I love the Jews even though I can't stand them."[24] Lippmann's shame was unrelieved by the bonds of a shared history; his criticism was not tempered by pride, sentiment, or appreciative feeling. His only public affirmation of his association with Jewry was in effect an act of dissociation. Yet he was well aware of the perils of alienation, for he had argued in an early book that one has to "be at peace with the sources of his life. If he is ashamed of them, if he is at war with them, they will haunt him forever. They will rob him of the basis of assurance, [and] leave him an interloper in the world."[25] Nevertheless no one was more anxious to suppress whatever bound him to ancestral custom and belief. Lippmann's denial was so deep that friendship might be endangered. For a book of tributes on his seventieth birthday, the psychiatrist Carl Binger, who had known Lippmann since childhood, was afraid to mention one topic. According to David Halberstam's account, Binger "could not say that Walter was Jewish. Otherwise Walter would never forgive him, and would never speak to him again." Instead Binger recalled only that his friend had attended Dr. Julius Sachs's School for Boys, which happened to be the private school for the scions of "our crowd."[26]

Binger's fear may have been exaggerated, for Lippmann could hardly have been unaware that others regarded him as a Jew. On that basis he had been excluded from the inner circles of social life at Harvard College, despite an extraordinary academic record. Six years after his graduation, the radical critic Randolph Bourne praised "the younger generation of Jewish intelligents" whose contributions to American culture were "so incomparably greater than that of any other American group of foreign cultural affiliations that one can scarcely get one's perspective." In this group, whose "clarity of expression ... radical philosophy ... [and] masterly fibre of thought can hardly be over-valued," Bourne placed Morris Raphael Cohen, Felix Frankfurter, Horace Kallen—and Walter Lippmann. *Time* later identified him as the "most statesmanly Jewish pundit in the U.S.," and books on Lippmann's career that appeared in his lifetime mentioned his religious background.[27]

Lippmann therefore was accustomed to public identification as a Jew. But he was reluctant to come to terms with "the sources of his life," and preferred to blame the Jews themselves for the discrimination they faced. His tendency to accept as valid the accusations of bigots was, however, hardly unique to him. The very term *anti-Semitism* had been coined in imperial Germany in the 1870s; within a decade Jewish leaders were admonishing their coreligionists to be more "modest," to repudiate the ostentatiousness and presumption that seemed to offend Gentiles. Walter Rathenau's anxieties about Jewish vulgarity strikingly anticipated Lippmann's, and this image of immoderation long outlived its origins. Reviewing *Mein Kampf* in 1933, H. L. Mencken in no way minimized the horror of the new Nazi regime. But he conceded that Hitler's views were "often sensible enough" and, as though echoing Lippmann's article in the *American Hebrew*, observed that "the disadvantage of the Jew is that, to simple men, he often seems a kind of foreigner." Besides, Mencken added, "many of the current Jewish leaders in this country are very loud and brassy fellows."[28]

Lippmann had reinforced this tradition even though the rest of his work cannot easily be reconciled with it. *Public Opinion*, published in the same year as his *American Hebrew* essay, had underscored the discrepancy between "the world outside" and "the pictures inside our heads," between reality and our expectations and desires. Without renouncing the claims of rationalism, Lippmann had emphasized the persistence of subjectivity, the distance between actuality and our habits of perceiving it.[29] Yet he seemed to ignore his own thesis when he thought about the Jews, whose altered conduct was supposed to spike prejudice. The tenacity of the pictures inside the heads of bigots was unrecognized. It was appropriate to criticize Jewish faults in the *American Hebrew*, but Lippmann's mode of analysis was oddly inconsistent with his own general assessment of how fully the unconscious and the irrational permeate individual motivation and social arrangements.

Instead of dissecting the factors that inhibited the intellectual clarity of those who found Jewish misconduct peculiarly repugnant, Lippmann accepted anti-Semitic images without seeking to balance them with more affirmative feelings. Yet his was no pathology of *Selbsthass*. His self-denial was never obsessive or dysfunctional, although his biographer Ronald Steel has with much depth of insight shown how fully Lippmann separated himself from Jewry—and how cautious and withdrawn he may have become as a result.[30] His own religious involvement with Judaism simply lapsed after the bar mitzvah ceremony in New York's Temple Emanu-El, and his lifelong curiosity about religion never flared into piety.[31] Both of Lippmann's marriages were outside the faith, but while he agreed fully with the art critic Bernard Berenson's rejection of parochialism, he did not imitate his close friend's conversion to Roman Catholicism. Finding no solace in organized religion, Lippmann was drawn increasingly to the doctrines of stoicism; and especially in *A Preface to Morals* (1929), he argued that emotions were to be controlled rather than satisfied. Life was to be vindicated by the responsibility it demanded to restrain the passions and to exercise rational sovereignty over one's self.

It is therefore difficult to resist the suspicion that Lippmann's withdrawal from "the sources of his life" and his plea for self-discipline are connected. In urging Jews to practice "the classic Greek virtue of moderation," Lippmann was calculating the price of acceptance within civil society. Those Jews who could not or would not pay that price endangered those who, like Lippmann, were graced with the requisite breeding and gentility to expect to be judged on the basis of ability alone. Those he called "the Jewish would-be smart set" imperiled others in a society that, for all its exaltation of equality of opportunity, was uncomfortable with uncultivated upstarts. It can therefore be surmised that Lippmann embraced the character ideal of gentility to ward off the threat that coarse and profligate Jews posed to his status. Protecting himself from his past, he would become a virtuoso of instinctual renunciation, haunted by the elemental power of the emotions yet determined to restrain them for the sake of respectability. The austerity that he cultivated Lippmann's acquaintances viewed as coldness; the aloofness that he sought ran the risk of pomposity. (Later in his career there were jokes that Lippmann had descended *upon* Olympus.) Certain aspects of his personality therefore make sense as a reaction to what Lippmann feared, which was that too many Jews would be unequal to what one sociologist has termed "the ordeal of civility."[32]

His own renunciation therefore did not exorcise his heritage. As Kafka once shrewdly remarked about Heine, his "conflict with Jewry . . . is exactly what makes him so typically Jewish."[33] Lippmann's virtual silence on the subject of his origins (despite rare sensitivity and catholicity of interest), the anxiety that bubbled to the surface about his fellow Jews, his appeal to reason even as he acknowledged the force of the irrational, the distinctiveness of his temperament and the character ideal to which he aspired—this constellation is not easily divorced from the larger contours of the modern history of the Diaspora, from both the promises and the penalties imposed on talented and ambitious Jews in civil society. The "conflict with Jewry" in Lippmann, as in Kafka and Heine and others, can be seen as a conflict within the self. Its consequences were not only tension and estrangement but intellectual fertility and creativity as well.

For Lippmann is too often categorized merely as a journalist; his success in his profession has made it harder to gauge the full significance of his calling. In a nation whose only fresh contribution to political philosophy—the *Federalist*—consisted of a series of newspaper articles, it should be possible, without discomfort, to regard Lippmann as a representative intellectual. His French counterpart (also a Jew), Raymond Aron, has been easily absorbed into the history of contemporary thought; that too is where Lippmann belongs.[34] Viewed not only as an acute analyst of events at home and abroad, but as a Jewish intellectual, Lippmann ought to be included in the company of those who made of their own marginality a fulcrum to explore the central riddles of society. Unable to enjoy the birthright of automatic acceptance of the status quo, Jewish intellectuals have tended to be more skeptical than their Gentile confreres, and have been more inclined to treat sacred cows as rather ordinary heifers. The result has sometimes been fundamental criticism of existing arrangements and institutions.[35]

This, at any rate, was Freud's explanation for the novelty and audacity of his theories, and of his own inclination to formulate them. On the occasion of *his* seventieth birthday, the founder of psychoanalysis told his fellow members of the B'nai B'rith that his Jewish origins had enabled him to be detached from the rationalizations with which the majority hides from itself its true and subterranean nature.[36] Without this self-scrutiny, Lippmann too developed a theory of politics and of a free press which was, in relation to the assumptions then reigning in America, subversive. He refused to treat the press, despite its First Amendment immunity, as sacrosanct; his mandarin stance should not obscure the fact that no one was more successful than Lippmann in showing how radically the problems of journalism affected the "crisis of Western democracy." Allowing for differences of scale and penetration, one might suggest that Lippmann did for the newsroom what Marx did for the boardroom and Freud for the bedroom. Because of what they wrote, each of those locales has come to appear not only different but also more problematic.

As an undergraduate Lippmann had served as president of the Harvard Socialist Club; his first book, published three years after graduation, applied psychoanalytic ideas to politics so adeptly that Freud wanted to meet him. Lippmann's intellectual facility was so impressive that, in a sense, according to David Halberstam, he belonged "not in journalism but in academe. His role models were not journalists but the great figures of the Harvard Philosophy Department"; and only the shock of the Great War drove him from "the field of abstract philosophy."[37] Yet neither Halberstam nor previous biographers offered any evidence that Lippmann ever seriously considered a career in philosophy. The books he wrote very early and very late in his career are more convincing as explications of the ideas of others than as original contributions to speculative thought. And while he adhered to the Greek virtues rather than ghetto traits, the young Lippmann must have suspected that his own future in Harvard's philosophy department was uncertain. The salaries of the only two Jews allowed to stay on permanently in the two decades after Lippmann's graduation were paid by Jewish philanthropists. New Ph.D.'s were recommended elsewhere in a manner that confirmed prejudices; applicants for academic jobs were described as Jewish—but "by no means offensive," or "with none of the faults which are sometimes expected in such cases." In any event philosophy at Harvard had become so arcane that, already by the 1920s, Lippmann had become an exemplar of the philosophically trained intelligence flourishing outside the academy.[38]

Much of the stature he enjoyed derived from his power to express himself in crystalline prose. His style was a model of concision, elegance, and effectiveness, reflecting the cadence of sustained thought and leading Max Lerner to warn that "even when he is wrong he is dangerously persuasive." Lippmann embodied, in Norman Podhoretz's estimation, "what a writer of the very first rank can do in a field that is largely barren of educated literary talent," for Lippmann's taste was so exact that he frequently managed to "hit upon images of . . . surprising inevitability."[39] From the world of printing, he took a term like *stereotype* and made it a permanent part of the vocabulary of social psychology as well as popular discourse. It was probably Lippmann who coined the phrase *Atlantic community* to represent the center of his geopolitical vision. And though Swope and Bernard Baruch came up with *the Cold War*, it was Lippmann whose dissemination made the phrase an essential ingredient in the idiom of recent diplomacy. Whatever the validity of critic Edmund Wilson's youthful generalization that many Jews, "however clever they may be, seem unable to write a really sound style," Lippmann himself certainly deserves to be exempted.[40]

His thoughtfulness and stoic disinterestedness made him a most unusual journalist. He took no satisfaction in getting scoops or discovering smoking guns, and did not traffic in gossip or sensationalism. The news may be that men bite dogs, but Lippmann was more likely to brood over the epidemiology of rabies. Yet his syndicated columns appeared in 184 newspapers, and other journalists saw in him an adornment of their profession. James Reston, who succeeded Krock as the chief of the *Times*'s Washington bureau, held Lippmann (according to one report) "in respect bordering on awe." And through Reston, in continuously rippling waves, Lippman nicked the working lives of countless other members of the Fourth Estate. His impact on educated readers throughout the world was immense.[41]

It is nevertheless possible to exaggerate Lippmann's influence. He was of course a kibitzer, helping to write the speeches of presidents from Woodrow Wilson to Kennedy. In dealing with American officials, he located the hidden assumptions of open minds and put ideas into empty ones. But Lippmann was commonly disenchanted even with those presidents he helped and, as an independent intellectual, he often tried keeping some distance from the temptations of power.[42] His hostility to the policies of Franklin D. Roosevelt is well known, and apparently did not diminish the overall popularity of the New Deal. Lippmann's support of Al Smith, Alf Landon, and Thomas E. Dewey hardly saved their presidential campaigns from defeat. Indeed Landon himself did not know that Lippmann had endorsed him in 1936 until Arthur Schlesinger, Jr., who was in Kansas in the early 1950s to do research for *The Age of Roosevelt*, so informed him. There are other examples of ineffectuality. Lippmann warned darkly of the "morbid derangement of the true functions of power" while the Eisenhower administration was seeking to apply the doctrine of the withering away of the state.[43] His syndicated columns are credited with helping to make acceptable the European recovery program of the Truman administration, but he was unavailing in his indictment of the containment policy against the Soviet Union. Nor did the prescience of his little book on *The Cold War* (1947) abort the American intervention in Vietnam less than two decades later, and which he continued to condemn. Lippmann in fact often moved upstream, against the rush of events.[44]

His only attempt to influence the federal government from a position within it occurred during and immediately after the First World War. Lippmann served as secretary to The Inquiry in designing peace proposals, and wrote eight of the Fourteen Points. He then became a captain in military intelligence, assigned to the propaganda section. But he left Versailles early and, in collaboration with a future editor of the *Times*, analyzed the failure of that newspaper to provide its readers with an accurate account of the Russian Revolution. His deepening despair over the prospects of democratic enlightenment triggered the reflections set down in the three books that so cogently analyzed the limitations of the media: *Liberty and the News* (1920), *Public Opinion* (1922), and *The Phantom Public* (1925).

Lippmann was hardly the first critic of the American press to emerge from within its precincts. Even Benjamin Franklin, although always proud of his trade as printer, stressed the calumny and defamation that his fellow journalists permitted themselves; the solution he rather uneasily proposed was "the liberty of the cudgel," or tarring and feathering. Henry Adams, the dour great-grandson of one of Franklin's associates, recalled that at age twenty-six he became a journalist: "The enormous mass of misinformation accumulated in ten years of nomad life could always be worked off on a helpless public, in diluted doses, if one could but secure a table in the corner of a newspaper office." Mencken had become a reporter even earlier in life, and in his maturity took delight in blasting "the stupidity, cowardice and Philistinism of working newspaper men," whose heads were full of "trivialities and puerilities" that would "make even a barber beg for mercy."[45] And since the 1920s the performance of the press has been regularly evaluated—in the *New Yorker*, *Time*, later *Esquire*, and in various journalism reviews that were typically born in the 1960s and died thereafter. Some of the best-known monitors of the press have, incidentally, been Jews: A. J. Liebling, Nat Hentoff, Nora Ephron. But Lippmann alone endowed this tradition of journalistic self-examination, which consisted of local perceptions, with the dignity of a compelling theory.

What troubled him was the subjectivity that has with increasing intensity haunted Western thought since Kant. For Lippmann realized that the mind is not a blank slate that simply registers the flux of experience. Far from being mimetic, it organizes experience, within the frame that the social world of symbols and values provides. "In the great blooming, buzzing confusion of the outer world," Lippmann announced, "we pick out what our culture has already defined for us, and we tend to perceive that which we have picked out in the form stereotyped for us by our culture." Stereotypes are thus "the pictures inside our heads," without which we would be entirely at the mercy of "the ebb and flow of sensation." These stereotypes are integral to the representation of reality, but they are also contaminated with emotional preferences and moral feelings. They are fictions, but without them we could not find our way in the world.[46]

That world has become increasingly complicated, intricate, and dense, and in the modern era the democratic citizen is obliged to make judgments about matters he does not directly experience. Political conclusions can no longer be reached, in this interdependent world of nation-states, exclusively within a primary environment in which each citizen might know his own self-interest and might hold certain truths to be self-evident. Inserted into the modern world is therefore what Lippmann called a "pseudo-environment"—a set of mental images or fictions that are aroused in the individual citizen, whose connection to the sources of power and decision-making is remote. A more centralized administration has become commensurate with the complexity of a highly organized economy and society, rendering more fragile the citizen's grasp of political actuality.

The ordinary person therefore has become increasingly dependent on the mass media to convey information from the politically decisive secondary environment. But journalists themselves share stereotypes and therefore cannot penetrate reality either, and, lacking independent and disinterested expertise, news gatherers can only relay what others tell them. The press therefore transmits from the unseen environment signals that are often confused, erratic, weak, or erroneous, and the citizen responds primarily to symbols that can galvanize his own emotions. Lippmann therefore was compelled to assume that the "public is inexpert in its curiosity [and] intermittent, that it discerns only gross distinctions, is slow to be aroused and quickly diverted." Because it cannot under modern conditions be well informed, the public "personalizes whatever it considers, and is interested only when events have been melodramatized as a conflict." Lippmann therefore presented the dilemma of public opinion in dramaturgical terms: "The public will arrive in the middle of the third act and will leave before the last curtain, having stayed just long enough perhaps to decide who is the hero and who the villain of the piece." That decision is necessarily based on the fragmentary information that the press has imparted, while the prevalence of stereotypes further decreases the likelihood that judgment can be rendered on the intrinsic merits of an issue.[47]

No American work struck a more provocative challenge to the premises of popular sovereignty. No other thinker had studied so convincingly the weak link of opinion—which was required to be informed if representative government was to work. The fact that the American political system rolled with the punch and continued to operate as usual is, of course, no test of the merit, importance, or influence of a book like *Public Opinion*. John Dewey called it "a more significant statement of the genuine 'problem of knowledge' than professional epistemological philosophers have managed to give." Justice Holmes was amazed at Lippmann's "intimate perception of the subtleties of the mind and of human relations."[48] Scholars retrospectively have concurred. Political scientist Heinz Eulau considered *Public Opinion* probably the author's "most lasting contribution to the study of human affairs" and the concept of stereotypes Lippmann's "most permanent contribution to political psychology." Arthur Schlesinger, Jr., remarked: "The stupefying mass of writing" that has appeared since 1922 on the subject of popular opinion "has added surprisingly little to Lippmann's analysis; and none of it has had anything like his fertility of insight or elegance of expression." That such praise was not merely a matter of political predilection is suggested by the fact that the dark satanic Mills of radical sociology echoed the liberal Schlesinger's endorsement. "Despite the truly enormous amount of study in the last quarter of a century devoted to the subject of public opinion," C. Wright Mills wrote, "Walter Lippmann's work still remains, in terms of conception and theory, the definitive statement."[49] Other scholars have not revised these judgments.[50]

The actual impact of Lippmann's criticism on journalism is somewhat elusive, however, although Fred Friendly, for example, has mentioned his indebtedness to *Public Opinion*.[51] Elsewhere the effect of Lippmann's work occasionally can be measured. Judge Learned Hand, to whom *The Phantom Public* is dedicated, followed Lippmann's description of the news-gathering process quite closely in his landmark opinion in *United States* v. *Associated Press* (1943), which declared the wire service in violation of the antitrust laws. Sometimes the influence is plain, as in this generalization by Theodore Sorensen, President Kennedy's alter ego: "Public opinion is often erratic, inconsistent, arbitrary, and unreasonable—with 'a compulsion to make mistakes,' as Walter Lippmann put it . . . It is frequently hampered by myths and misinformation, by stereotypes and shibboleths."[52]

His theory probably has exerted more impact on social science than on the practice of journalism. Lippmann's grand theme is hard to miss in Murray Edelman's description of what politics ordinarily means—"a series of pictures in the mind, placed there by television news, newspapers, magazines, and discussions . . . a world the mass public never quite touches." Although *Public Opinion* neglects the subject of collective behavior, its thesis can be detected in the work of sociologists such as Mills and Robert Park, himself a former newsman. Jacques Ellul has also noted the extent to which public opinion, since it is based on symbols, fails to correspond to reality.[53] Most important perhaps has been Lippmann's anticipation of the "sociology of knowledge." Its founder, Karl Mannheim, was familiar with Lippmann's formulations, and he managed in *Ideology and Utopia* and other works to put to systematic use what Lippmann had observed—the bias inherent in all social thinking.[54] Both writers had stressed the unconscious drives and hidden assumptions that tincture comprehension of the world. Mannheim more than Lippman, however, analyzed the function of class, since one's position in the social hierarchy also affects vision and judgment.

The clarity and completeness of "objectivity" are therefore asymptotic; both Lippmann and Mannheim suspected that only intellectuals might manage to transcend the limitations of social and psychological bias. *Public Opinion* had called for a class of experts who might ratify reality for the press as well as for the government. Without explanation *The Phantom Public* abandoned this solution a mere three years later, although its author continued to press for the expansion of the scientific spirit.[55] For the person disciplined by the scientific method "is ready to let things be what they may be, whether or not he wants them to be that way. It means that he has conquered his desire to have the world justify his prejudices." Yet Lippmann was if anything too optimistic about the corrosion of stereotypes. Recent work in the history of science has undermined the faith in science as somehow independent of other mental operations. So seductive has the sociology of knowledge become that historians such as Thomas Kuhn, aware of the intractable character of scientific prejudgments, have wondered whether it is indeed helpful to think about scientific accomplishment in terms of increasing proximity to "some one full, objective, true account of nature."[56] Such views mark a radical extension of the theory of stereotypes.

One immediate measure of Lippmann's legacy was unintentional. One year after the appearance of *Public Opinion*, Edward L. Bernays, a nephew of Freud's, published *Crystallizing Public Opinion* as a manual for his fellow public relations counselors. The mental processes that Lippmann had dissected Bernays accepted as a challenge to manipulate; he would "make news happen" through the concoction of the "created event." Had Lippmann never written *Public Opinion*, Bernays still would have advocated and attempted the management of opinion. Nevertheless the book was not only cited by public relations men but undoubtedly pondered as well; their increasingly sophisticated ministrations, which Lippman himself had warned against, made the "pseudo-environment" even more tenaciously opaque.[57] Names continued to make news—but so, in a different sense, did the public relations counselors themselves.

Lippmann had observed in 1922 that, despite the importance of news gathering to the theory of popular sovereignty, no social scientist had ever seriously examined its operation. Fifteen years later came the first attempt at a remedy, with the publication of a doctoral dissertation, *The Washington Correspondents*. Its author was Leo Rosten, who was to win greater fame for his Hyman Kaplan novels and for his Yiddish lexicon. Defining his portrait of reporters in the nation's capital as "a study in public opinion," Rosten found bias closer to the surface than Lippmann had allowed for. Sixty percent of the correspondents Rosten questioned agreed that "it is almost impossible to be objective. You read your paper, notice its editorials, get praised for some stories and criticized for others. You 'sense policy' and are psychologically driven to slant your stories accordingly." They added that their mandate required objectivity—but they also knew how their editors wanted their stories to be played.[58] The news, Rosten concluded, could be deemed a commodity that publishers seek to sell, editors select, and reporters produce in the light of what their superiors presumably expect. *The Washington Correspondents* thus confirmed Lippmann's distinction between news, which serves "to signalize an event," and truth, which functions "to bring to light the hidden facts, to set them into relation with each other, and make a picture of reality on which men can act." The seat of government magnified this distinction by raising the odds of "journalistic manipulation. For political news is not news of observable fact, as is a fire, a flood, or an accident. It permits elaboration, interpretation, prophecy."[59]

Rosten's book inaugurated an important extension of Lippmann's analysis of the press, for the young sociologist argued that, given the impossibility of objectivity, "the social heritage, the 'professional reflexes,' the individual temperament, and the economic status of reporters assume a fundamental significance." Here was the controlling idea of the sociology of news. Its empirical investigators have included Herbert Gans, Bernard Roshco, Gaye Tuchman, and Edward Jay Epstein—all Jews. They have observed how knowledge is organized and where news people fit in the class structure.[60] They tend to adhere to the position that "the formulation of 'news' might . . . be explicable in terms of what the news organization has to do to stay in business." News gatherers therefore adapt "their own personal values in accordance with the requisites of the organization."[61] What sort of news is transmitted is therefore situationally determined. In 1690 *Publick Occurrences* had promised more frequent publication in case of "a Glut of Occurrences." By contrast the regular arrival of news in the contemporary world requires the efficiency that bureaucracies—with their own imperatives—provide.

This "organizational hypothesis" accounts, for example, for the prevalence of the ideal of objectivity. Were it not for a norm that permits generalists, Gans remarked, reporters and editors would have to be more knowledgeable. They would be expected to "evaluate the data they gather." But since expertise would require "more time to gather and report the news," its cost would rise substantially, which is hardly in the interest of the organization. The economic logic of television news in particular discourages investigative journalism on the regular evening programs. The advertising revenues these shows generate depend on the number of viewers, who tune in because of time slot and format—not because television reporters have expended any effort to dig independently into a story.[62]

To Lippmann's appeal half a century ago for an empirical study of news gathering, Epstein's *News from Nowhere* is the most impressive response to date. Its title, although drawn from the English utopian William Morris, echoes Lippmann: the phantom public has at last found the news medium it desires—or deserves. The book's opening reference notes the prescience of *Public Opinion*. Epstein, a quite versatile and prolific political scientist, thereafter showed how fully the major news networks depend on a repertory of stereotypes to make events intelligible. "The highest power of television journalism," NBC's news chief is quoted as telling his staff, "is not in the transmission of information but in the transmission of experience . . . joy, sorrow, shock, fear." Experience is therefore fit into formulas and told as a story, with the "attributes of fiction." The NBC executive added that such stories "should have structure and conflict, problem and denouement, rising action and falling action, a beginning, a middle and an end." This was also the key to Theodore White's approach to the making of presidents, and thus Lippmann's "medium of fictions" was made vivid.[63]

The protagonists of television news stories are few because, to reduce costs, crews are assigned to a small number of "news makers" considered most likely "to produce usable happenings." And since it is cheaper to anticipate news than to be at the mercy of sudden events, editors tend to assign crews to cover activities that are devised for the sake of being reported (Bernays's "created events"). These are newsworthy, Epstein commented, "if only in a self-fulfilling sense." Moreover, the cost of electronic transmission of film by ground cable or satellite makes shipment by place preferable— which takes longer, enhances editorial control in New York and even affects the definition of news by lengthening the immediacy to events. Epstein noticed, for instance, that California was depicted almost entirely through off-beat stories. Given the expense of sending "hard news" on a specially rented cable, that state's crews were more likely to get their stories on the air in New York if features were provided. And since the program editors liked to conclude each evening's telecast with a light story, the California bureau was encouraged to satisfy common assumptions by forwarding film that highlighted the eccentricities of the Golden State. Far from simply mirroring reality, such programs may be—through techniques of selection and emphasis—affecting our grasp of it.[64]

For in the decades since Lippmann developed his analysis of the importance of the organs of communication to the functioning of mass society, the impact of the media has become immeasurable. Indeed the texture of American life is unimaginable without taking into account what we can now hear, read, and see. Exactly at midcentury sociologist David Riesman had detected a transformation in social character. Within the urban and suburban middle class in particular, not parents, teachers, or ministers but the mass media and peer groups were most effectively tutoring children in taste and giving them cues for conduct. A recent study asked children four to six years old whether they liked television or their fathers better, and 44 percent replied in favor of television. The most popular weekly magazine is *TV Guide*, although other mass magazines have, of course, helped shape the American ambience as well. Comedian Mort Sahl's assertion about *Playboy*—that "an entire generation of American males is growing up in the belief that their wives will have staples in their navels"—was one way of suggesting its influence. What may be banal in "real life" has become validated if reproduced on television, where millions can see it and thereby authorize what might otherwise be a humdrum actuality.[65]

The evasiveness of reality is the theme of Daniel J. Boorstin's *The Image*, perhaps the most extensive meditation on Lippmann's books, which Boorstin called "succinct and prophetic." Born in Atlanta, where his father had been a friend of the martyred Leo Frank, Boorstin coauthored an early study of anti-Semitism (1939) before engaging in turn in legal, intellectual, political, and social history. Although he is generally classified as a conservative, *The Image* is anything but complacent. Lippmann had distinguished between news and truth, but Boorstin was unable to define what reality is, and feared that "the rise of advertising has brought a social redefinition of the very notion of truth." The historian did, however, profess to "know an illusion when I see one," and, he insisted, "what dominates American experience today is not reality."[66] While Lippmann had doubted how the ordinary citizen could fathom the unseen environment, Boorstin countered that the environment was all too visible, threatening to blur the differences between shadow and substance, between the artificial and the authentic. Lippman had described a "pseudo-environment" that made information uncertain and judgment arbitrary. Boorstin by contrast attended the rise of the "pseudo-event," which is designed to be noticed and which, according to Boorstin, therefore makes reality so elusive.

The "pseudo-event," which is devised "for the immediate purpose of being reported or reproduced," has an ambiguous relation to actuality. It is an interview rather than an earthquake, a monkey trial (which was supposed to be civic promotion for Dayton, Tennessee) rather than a train wreck. Numerous examples can be found in the magisterial histories of Erik Barnouw, the Braudel of broadcasting. Television news in the 1950s was often content to confine its international coverage to images of the secretary of state. "World events," Barnouw argued, "were seen to a large extent through the eyes of [John Foster] Dulles.... A filmed press conference excerpt, or a newsman's report 'from a reliable source,' or a filmed statement by Dulles from a lectern at the edge of an airstrip, *became* the news." One result was that "a 90-second report on Southeast Asia by the Secretary of State himself seemed grand and took care of Southeast Asia nicely. That television was beginning to pay a high price for its dependence on pseudo-events was guessed by few." The consequences of ignorance about Indochina can hardly be minimized, although it is possible to inflate the danger that pseudo-events themselves pose. As William Safire, a public relations man turned columnist, pointed out, "A surprising and newsworthy position taken in an interview is not rendered counterfeit by the fact it was arranged for maximum coverage. But the idea and the phrase are helpful in ... watching out for 'pseudo-events' " even if Boorstin's "concept ... overdramatizes the degree of successful manipulation in American commercial and political affairs." The political vernacular has meanwhile altered the term to "media event."[67]

The degree of manipulation is nevertheless high. Lippmann himself, who had denounced publicity agents half a century before, submitted several times in the 1960s to the supreme pseudo-event, the televised interview. CBS's intention was to restore credibility to the medium in the wake of the quiz show scandals. Other evidence of the encroachment of fictions also can be cited. *The Image* had traced the "dissolution of forms," and suggested that the lines separating the genres that shape perception were no longer respected. The two *Washington Post* reporters who unraveled the plot to burglarize Democratic headquarters and then to cover it up sold the film rights to *All the President's Men* before they wrote the book. In writing from their own experience and for the historical record, Carl Bernstein and Bob Woodward accepted the advice of actor Robert Redford to give their account the proper story line.[68] The fidelity of the cinematic re-creation to the historical narrative therefore was assured; it is only a coincidental touch that the film's associate producer was Jon Boorstin, a son of the historian who could no longer discern or define reality in American life.

The Image stretched to the furthest point the line of analysis first drawn in *Public Opinion*. The line itself was somewhat sinuous however. Lippmann had been concerned with what amid the flood of news is true, Boorstin with what in the glut of occurrences is real. Lippmann had worried about inadequate information, Boorstin about ersatz experience. Lippmann had grounded his analysis in psychological theory; Boorstin had none. Lippmann drew political implications from his evidence; *The Image* is apolitical. Lippmann had proposed an "intelligence bureau" to enlighten both press and government; the only solution Boorstin suggested was vigilance. The relationship between journalists and officials is still so cloudy and ambiguous, so fraught with manipulation and news management, that vigilance can only help. As Epstein emphasized in a sequel to *News from Nowhere*, journalists still depend primarily on offical sources for their information; even Woodward and Bernstein drew their disclosures from government agencies. Yet bureaucrats may have reasons of their own, hidden from reporters, for releasing information; organizational imperatives, not merely the dissemination of truth, therefore continue to contaminate the methods of public enlightenment.[69] Epstein's work therefore suggests that Lippmann's proposed "intelligence bureau" would hardly have disentangled news from truth.

A phantom public has become an unseen audience watching news from nowhere. A tube of plenty can multiply experiences, but the bonds of community have become thinner. To restate democratic theory is to recognize how unresolved is the problem that the mass media have posed. For the press, Jefferson believed, should serve as a "formidable censor of the public functionaries.... It is also the best instrument for enlightening the mind of man, and improving him as a rational, moral and social being." This dynamic and inspired view of the role of the press and of public opinion has in the twentieth century been replaced by more sober and even pessimistic expectations for self-improvement and popular sovereignty. An active public is now depicted as a passive audience. The vision of the press as the conscience of the community, arousing citizens to defend their liberties, has yielded to the economic and organizational realities of the box populi, in which ratings determine programs. One network president, asked to define the public interest, gave as an example "a program in which a large part of the audience is interested."[70] In minimizing the responsibility to monitor the public functionaries, the executive was inadvertently demonstrating the failure of the modern press to comply with the demands of classical democratic theory.

In raising questions about the purpose and procedures of journalism, Lippmann and those who later extended his insights formulated the most cogent and persuasive critique to date of the limitations of the press. As a theory its only rival is the view that stresses the partisanship of the media as expressions of capitalism. The superstructure of society is supposed to reflect the power of dominant interests; editors and reporters are therefore little more than puppets for owners and advertisers, and the news accordingly tends to reinforce existing stereotypes. There is some merit to this view. Yet as Lippmann observed (using Upton Sinclair's expose, *The Brass Check*, as target practice), if big business domination produced bias in newspapers, then greater objectivity and accuracy might be expected in the left-wing press. That was patently not so, and therefore the effort to comprehend the problem of journalism would have to go deeper.[71]

American Jews have contributed decisively to that understanding, even as they have found the mass media a hospitable ambience for their own talents and interests. But America itself has given the profession of journalism a special place. For in a political culture in which secrecy and privacy are suspect, a society drenched in what Emerson called "pitiless publicity," the role of the press is not only assured but magnified. To members of a minority that has long favored an open society and that has come to expect the accessibility of public life, that role is unlikely to become less attractive or less problematic.

Part IV

The Jew as Southerner

12

Jews and Other Southerners

In his 1971 collection of essays, *American Counterpoint*, C. Vann Woodward did for Southern whites what W. E. B. Du Bois had done at the turn of the century for American blacks, underscoring their ambivalence toward the rest of the nation. Both minorities have been burdened with a double consciousness, have been Americans with a difference, have adhered to the national consensus even as estrangement has complicated their loyalties. Professor Woodward's book, however, is not unusual among major studies in Southern history in its neglect of Jews, whose cultural characteristics and social situation in the region nevertheless can be approached contrapuntally. Consider the possibilities.

Compared with the rest of America, the region has been characteristically agrarian, and the financier, the banker, the lien merchant have been special targets of rural hatred and resentment. Jews by contrast were rarely granted the right to own land in Europe and have traditionally earned their living in commerce, sometimes not by choice. Even in the South they have preferred to meet a payroll rather than to walk behind a plow. They have rarely been confined to the rank of unskilled workers, which even in Russia's Pale of Settlement was termed "black labor." And even the most publicized of Jewish "farmers," Bernard Baruch of Hobcaw, South Carolina, was a cosmopolitan financier, which did not prevent him from eloquently praising the agrarian life that he so frequently escaped.

The romantic attachment of Southerners to the land must bewilder the rest of the United States, which is the most mobile, the most restless, the most active of nations. Southerners often have been suspicious of Yankee meddlers (and of Jewish peddlers) and have made "carpetbagger" and "outside agitator" terms of opprobrium. Mississippi's Willie Morris has claimed that "Southerners of both races share a rootedness that even in moments of anger and pain we have been unable to repudiate or ignore." Another Mississippian, Eudora Welty, clings to her roots as the very incentive of her fiction: "The place where I am and the place I know, and other places that familiarity with and love for my own make strange and lovely and enlightening to look into, are what set me to writing my stories."[1] American Jewish fiction, by contrast, tends to be introspective or allegorical; when it is attentive to environment, those surroundings are urban, depicted without the warmth of nostalgia or the impulse to sentimentalize poverty and ugliness. Eastern European Jewry was so cut off from its environment that its Yiddish vocabulary contained no indigenous names for wild birds and only two names for flowers (rose, violet). Yet try to imagine the Southern environment and sensibility without the magnolia blossoms and azaleas and honeysuckle and summers of wisteria and Robert Penn Warren's bearded oaks, without "nature writing"!

The sense of place, which in Southern writers is as keen as an animal's, is organically entwined with filiopietism. Apart from race, the distinguishing mark of the Southern mind is embodied in the slogan of the French right-wing propagandist Maurice Barrès: *la terre et les morts*. An echolalic passage in Faulkner's "The Bear" is streaked with such romanticism, in which Ike McCaslin honors "men who could believe that all necessary to conduct a successful war was not acumen nor shrewdness nor politics nor diplomacy nor money nor even integrity and simple arithmetic but just love of land and courage"—to which McCaslin Edmonds adds: "And an unblemished and gallant ancestry and the ability to ride a horse . . . . Don't leave that out."[2] After the inexorable defeat, nearly all the leaders of the rebel government remained in their beloved South— except one. Belle Chasse plantation and Louisiana meant so little to Judah P. Benjamin that after Appomattox he escaped to Great Britain (where he rose to eminence again at the bar, becoming Queen's Counsellor, although not—like Disraeli—her counselor). He died and was buried in France. That Benjamin was also in flight from his Jewish origin and identity does not revoke his membership among the people that Joseph Stalin, in an ominous euphemism, once called "rootless cosmopolitans."

Compared with the rest of America, the South is especially violent, with the highest homicide rates in the nation. With 52 percent of all white Southern families owning guns compared with 27 percent of non-Southerners, with rifle racks boldly displayed on pickup trucks, with manhood defined and achieved not only in the bedroom but in the wilderness, Southerners have created a syndrome of violence that Jews generally have found repugnant. The region has sent disproportionate numbers of its sons to serve and to die in the American armed forces, and military academies dotted its landscape even before the Civil War. It was almost as socially necessary for the academically inclined antebellum Southerner to take his guns with him to college as it was for his cousins to carry theirs while tracking runaways on slave patrols. An important theme of Southwestern humor is the exaggerated violence and cruelty of fistfights, gouging, and wrestling with men and beasts.

Yet the narrator of Isaac Babel's "After the Battle" (1920) is not concerned about how to face death honorably as he rides with the Galician cavalry. Instead he is "imploring fate to grant me the simplest of proficiencies—the ability to kill my fellow men." Militarism has played a paltry role in Judaic tradition, which has fashioned *shalom* not only into a greeting and a farewell but into the core of its aspirations. Jewish humor gets its effects not by exaggerating strength but by underscoring weakness and vulnerability, as in Woody Allen's admission that he was once even beaten up by Quakers. It is true that Baruch took pride in the game that could be shot at Hobcaw; but the Jewish immunity to the charm of killing animals for sport has been more typical because, as Heine once explained, in the Middle Ages, they were the hunted. It is true that some outstanding American gangsters have been Jews, such as Meyer Lansky (who, as a senior citizen residing in Miami Beach, was sort of a Southern Jew as well). But even Lansky's contribution to the Syndicate reportedly consisted more of the application of business methods than of raw violence. Jewish values, by virtually any test that could be devised, either are indifferent or derogatory toward what is fashionably called machismo and are pacific and even antiheroic. The matriculation of Isidor Straus at Georgia Military Academy during the Civil War lasted less than a day, his brother

Oscar recalled, because the other cadets subjected him to hazing: "He had not heard of hazing before, and the incident disgusted him so that he never returned to the academy. He embarked upon his career as a merchant the very next morning."[3]

Compared with the rest of the country, the South has had the lowest rates of literacy and probably the most deeply embedded tradition of anti-intellectualism. Lenny Bruce once said that he could not imagine a nuclear physicist with a Southern accent, a remark delivered before the 1976 candidacy of Jimmy Carter. Perhaps, as W. J. Cash has argued, the Southerner could not help associating the modern mind with the Yankee mind. The fundamentalism, the absolutism, the irrationality and lack of realism, and the discomfort with ambiguity that have been the stigmata of Southern culture might be contrasted with the daily greeting that one future physicist, Isidore Isaac Rabi, got from his mother: "Did you ask any good questions in school today?"[4] Within the religious culture of the *shtetl*, the capacity to ask good questions of the sacred texts was proof of a student's ability—not, as in much of the rural South, a disqualification to teach biology. It is unnecessary to elaborate on the differences between Southern Protestantism—direct, immediate, profoundly emotional—and historical Judaism, with its ratiocination, its codification, its interpretive arabesques, its proclamation that "an ignorant man cannot be pious."

Perhaps the most striking instance of the Jewish distaste for the primitive and the irrational occurred after one phase of the trial of the Scottsboro "boys," when their attorney, Samuel Leibowitz, returned to New York from Alabama in 1933 to describe the jurors as "those creatures, those bigots whose mouths are slits in their faces, whose eyes pop out like a frog's, whose chins drip tobacco juice, bewhiskered and filthy." Travelogues like that undoubtedly have helped to keep the Jewish population of the South at 1 percent. What Leibowitz was promoting in the interview that he granted to a New York newspaper was a stereotype, which is usually not a falsehood but a refraction of reality, a distortion that is tinctured with truth. Even when such testimony is reasonably uncompromised by prior rumors and fears about the region, the Jew tends to see Southerners as though they were part of the supporting cast of *Deliverance*. From the nineteenth century, for example, here is Ludwig Lewisohn's memory of his family's arrival in Queenshaven,

South Carolina, when he was eight years old: "I recall vividly the long, shabby, crowded car and its peculiar reek of peanuts, stale whiskey, and chewing-tobacco. Half of the passengers were burly Negroes who gabbled and laughed weirdly. The white men wore broad-rimmed wool hats, whittled and spat and talked in drawling tones. I very distinctly shared my parents' sense of the wildness, savagery and roughness of the scene, their horrified perception of its contrast to anything they had ever known or seen." And even in the eighteenth century, in a letter Joseph Salvador wrote from South Carolina in 1785, the symbolic overtones of the encounter between Jew and Southerner were already articulated: "I am now in a wild country. . . . The inhabitants are descendants of the wild Irish and their ignorance [is] amazing. . . . They are as poor as rats, proud as dons. . . . They are naked and famished and immensely lazy. They have no religion or morals. . . . Their minds are wholly bent on their horses whom they prize more than their wives and families. They hate society and pass their days in the woods or, loitering about, they drink hard. Rum is their deity; they . . . [are] always happy when they can do any ill-natured thing and molest their neighbors."[5]

The contrast that Salvador, Lewisohn, and Leibowitz evoke is virtually that between civilization and savagery. The coarsened sensibility of the lower-class whites does more than shock these Jews. It seems to excite in them the fear of descent into the primitive, the horror that in the South the membranes of restraint that bind a social order may be broken. The Jew who enters the region thus may be faced, more starkly than elsewhere in America, with the possibility of id overwhelming superego, of the return of the repressed.

The contrapuntal tension is thus between two character ideals. The ghetto and the *shtetl* that encased Diaspora life for almost two millennia required calculation, patience, prudence, cleverness, and, above all, temperance as the conditions of survival, which is why so many Jews prospered when transposed to a country ostensibly grounded in the Protestant ethic. Their equivalent of "bull in a china shop" was "Cossack in a *sukkah*"; and those rambunctious Southerners, those wool hat boys with their incessant drinking and talk of horses, must have seemed like the American equivalent of Cossacks (and therefore to be avoided when aroused). The currently

popular stereotype of the white Protestant of British ancestry—
some overrefined, aloof, inhibited, lifeless quasi aristocrat contem-
plating the bust of William McKinley—should be treated with some
skepticism, for it has very limited applicability to a region so steamy
that it has produced Earl Long, Kissin' Jim Folsom, Pappy O'Daniel, Cyclone Davis, Lester Maddox, Elvis Presley, Janis Joplin,
Zelda Sayre Fitzgerald, Tallulah Bankhead, Burt Reynolds, Jerry
Lee Lewis, Martha Mitchell, Dolly Parton, and Elizabeth Ray,
among other demotic types. The normative male character ideal for
the Jew has been first the scholar, and later the business and professional man, in contrast to the prestige attached to the role described
in *The Mind of the South*: "To stand on his head in a bar, to toss
down a pint of raw whiskey at a gulp, to fiddle and dance all night,
to bite off the nose or gouge out the eye of a favorite enemy, to
fight harder and love harder than the next man, to be known eventually far and wide as a hell of a fellow—such would be . . . [the
Southerner's] focus. To lie on his back for days and weeks, storing
power as the air he breathed stored power under the sun of August,
and then to explode, as that air explodes in a thunderstorm, in a
violent outburst of emotion—in such fashion would he make life
not only tolerable but infinitely sweet."[6] Even the more casual
descendant of this hell of a fellow—the good old boy— is far removed in his romantic exuberance and instinctual ease from the
character ideal of the Jew outside the South. Indeed, the stereo-
typical Southerner has been sufficiently distant from the image of
the WASP that the dangers of exaggeration have set in. It has become
a little too easy, indeed treacherous, to accept Cash's "man at the
center" (the average ex-hillbilly on the make) as exclusively a man
in extremis. As Flannery O'Connor once remarked about regional
writing, "Anything that comes out of the South is going to be called
grotesque by the Northern reader, unless it is grotesque, in which
case it is going to be called realistic."[7]

Nevertheless, for all these differences of value and perception,
the Jews who came to live and die in Dixie generally did not witness
the realization of further nightmares. Although the region was less
sinister than might have been expected, its response to Jews in its
midst was so distinctive that further analysis is warranted.

In the June 13, 1945, entry in his diary, the British politician
and belletrist Harold Nicolson distinguished between mass pathol-

ogy that had resulted in genocide and a personal attitude that governed social relations. He wrote: "Although I loathe anti-Semitism, I do dislike Jews."[8] Nicolson's feelings might be contrasted with those expressed four years earlier in William Alexander Percy's elegiac *Lanterns on the Levee*. Its author was a patrician, or at least what passed for one in a nation that had done so much to corrode claims of status based on blood and birth. Reversing Nicolson's distinction, Percy marveled at individual Jews like the small store owner in Mississippi who asked him, "Do you know Pushkin? Ah, beautiful, better than Shelley or Byron!" Percy's schoolteacher, Caroline Stern, the daughter of another village merchant and a later convert to Episcopalianism, ranked as Percy's "favorite friend," from whom he "learned more . . . of what the good life is and of how it may be lived than almost anyone else." But although this Catholic planter's war record included the fight against the Ku Klux Klan in the 1920s, the Jewish people itself was another matter. Caroline Stern was special, for Jews in general exhibited qualities "which have recurrently irritated or enraged other people since the Babylonian captivity. Touch a hair of a Jewish head and I am ready to fight, but I have experienced moments of exasperation when I could willingly have led a pogrom."[9] In a book published the year that the German government's Final Solution was secretly and systematically organized, Percy expressed neither a loathing of anti-Semitism nor the slightest dislike of individual Jews.

It is this paradox that best illuminates the life of Jews within the history of the South, that most intelligibly locates the peculiarity of their situation. In *The Sound and the Fury*, Jason Compson, after attacking "a bunch of damn eastern jews," comes as close as he can to making a civil rights speech: "I give every man his due regardless of religion or anything else. I have nothing against jews as individuals. . . . It's just the race." The paradox was recognized by perhaps the most influential of Southern rabbis at the turn of the century, David Marx, who told his Atlanta congregation in 1900: "In isolated instances there is no prejudice entertained for the individual Jew, but there exists widespread and deep-seated prejudice against Jews as an entire people."[10] Marx himself probably was unaware of the most striking illustration of his generalization. During the Civil War, a grand jury in Talbotton, Georgia, issued a presentment critical of "the evil and unpatriotic conduct of the representatives of Jewish houses" of finance. There was only one Jewish-owned store in all of Talbot County and only one Jewish family in town, and its patriarch, Lazarus Straus, took the grand jury's presentment as a personal insult and decided to move. His son Isidor should be allowed to complete the story: "Father's action caused such a sensation in the whole county that he was waited upon by every member of the grand jury, also by all the ministers of the different denominations, who assured him that nothing was further from the minds of those who drew the presentment than their action could be [so] construed . . . it never would have been permitted to be so worded."[11] As the Straus family left Georgia to activate Macy's, one can almost hear the citizens of Talbotton uttering the envoi so familiar to all Southerners: "Y'all come back."

Leonard Dinnerstein's "Note on Southern Attitudes Towards Jews" has emphasized the precariousness some Jews have felt in a region so scarred by bigotry and so hostile to outsiders. If anti-Semitism is defined as the unjustified hatred of Jews, examples of it certainly have not been condemned to obscurity. "Beginning in the late 1880's," John Higham has written, "the first serious anti-Semitic demonstrations in American history occurred in parts of the lower South where Jewish supply merchants were common. In several parishes of Louisiana debt-ridden farmers stormed into town, wrecked Jewish stores, and threatened to kill any Jews who remained in the area. During the worst year, 1893, night-riders burned dozens of farmhouses belonging to Jewish landlords in southern Mississippi, and open threats drove a substantial number of Jewish businessmen from Louisiana."[12] Southern political history has, of course, reverberated with the voices of malevolence, such as Tom Watson's; and his vitriol against "the libertine Jew," "the lascivious pervert," "the sodomite murderer" undoubtedly fueled the mob that lynched Leo Frank.[13] The bloodstained record of the Populists' vice presidential candidate was not so offensive to Georgians as to disqualify Watson from representing them thereafter in the United States Senate. Mississippians elected the "Bilbonic plague," Theodore Bilbo, as governor and senator, even though his bigotry was so unsheathed that when the paladin of a Jewish defense agency protested, Bilbo addressed his reply on official Senate stationery with "My dear kike . . . " On the floor of Congress, John Rankin, also from Mississippi, once called Walter Winchell a "little kike,"

and none of his colleagues, Northern or Southern, rose to object.
And of all the justifications for allying with the Soviet Union during
the Second World War, Rankin's list of reasons was the oddest,
beginning with "Stalin is a Gentile and Trotsky was a Jew."[14] Certainly the list of unashamed anti-Semites representing Southern con-
stituencies could be extended.

But what is surprising is how short that list is, how sporadically
anti-Semitism erupted in the Old South and the New. There was
some anti-Semitism in the early phases of Mississippi whitecapping,
for example, when notices appeared in 1892 in a few counties proclaiming: "This Jew place is not for sale or rent, but will be used
hereafter as pasture." Yet William F. Holmes's article on the subject
is striking for the paucity of evidence of anti-Semitism, unlike Ne-
grophobia, that could be uncovered. In 1889 an agrarian mob rode
into Delhi, Louisiana, and, according to one newspaper, "demol-
ished the stores of I. Hirsch, S. Blum & Company, Casper Weil,
and Mr. Rosenfield." But Woodward denies that the incident reflected "widespread anti-Semitism. . . . Jewish supply merchants
were quite common in the region in the period." The target was
economic, not ethnic. Louis Galambos's study of the agricultural
press from 1880 to 1940 has located "only the slightest evidence of
anti-Semitism. . . . Instead of attacking Jews . . . the Southern farmer
made big business the target for his animosities, a choice indicating
that, while he felt oppressed and was often confused about the
source of his discontent, his reactions to a changing environment
were not devoid of reason."[15]

Higham has noted the exclusiveness of clubs in Richmond,
New Orleans, and elsewhere by the early twentieth century, yet he
has also written that "most of the Klan's anti-Semitism was dis-
charged against the shadowy, imaginary Jew who lived far away in
the big cities. Klansmen felt a little guilty and ashamed at picking
on the Jews whom they had known as good neighbors all their
lives." About 1922, Edward Kahn has recalled, a young man inadvertently walked into the office of Atlanta's Federation of Jewish
Charities, where he asked directions to the Klan office, then located
in the same building. The secretary gave him the directions and
went on with her work, when suddenly the young man realized
where he was, walked back up to the receptionist, and apologized:
"No offense intended, ma'am."[16]

Atlanta had not yet become "the city too busy to hate," but more generally Jews were able to serve as senators in the Old South and to hold a variety of offices since the cause was lost. The Southern political climate has been hospitable enough to permit association even with the pyrogenic demagogues whom Jews normally would distrust. One confidant of the fin de siècle Arkansas rabble-rouser Jeff Davis was Charles Jacobson—an assistant attorney general, a state senator, and an identifying Jew at a time of rampant racial bigotry that his mentor fomented. The treasurer of Huey Long's organization was Seymour Weiss, the guardian of the vaunted "deduct box"; another Long sachem was Abe Shushan, who, like Weiss, earned a thirty-month prison sentence amid the wave of convictions for corruption after Long's death. Although the notorious anti-Semite Gerald L. K. Smith was also part of the Kingfish's entourage (and was a Southerner by choice, having been born and raised in Wisconsin), Long himself was remarkably free of religious bigotry and once called it a mistake for Hitler to "mix" religion and politics—which utterly missed the point of nazism, but in a reassuring way. And it is consistent with the central paradox to note that Tennessee's Cordell Hull, while secretary of state, was indifferent to the horrible fate of European Jews during the Holocaust. He did not sufficiently loathe Nazi racism to do much of anything about it, and yet he liked one particular Jew enough to marry her.

Even the worst outburst of anti-Semitism, the lynching of the president of the Atlanta lodge of the B'nai B'rith, can bear placement in a historical and comparative perspective. H. L. Mencken claimed in "The Sahara of the Bozart" that "the Leo Frank affair was no isolated phenomenon"; nevertheless, in a way it was unique.[17] Frank was the only Jew thus to lose his life in the region, although it hardly needs to be said that any victim of religious bigotry is one corpse too many. Some Gentiles fared worse. Shortly after Frank was murdered, two Mormons were lynched, and in the decade between 1891 and 1901, twenty-two Italian immigrants were killed by Southern mobs. It does not diminish Frank's martyrdom to note that, more than a decade earlier, at least forty-seven Jews had been killed in the pogrom in Kishinev. There is scattered autobiographical evidence—for example, from Bernard Baruch in South Carolina and Stanley Marcus in Texas, who encountered greater anti-Semitism when they went North—to lend credence to Herbert Stember's conclusion from attitude sampling that the South is less hostile to Jews than are other regions of the country. Moreover, the psychologist E. L. Hartley apparently discovered the existence of a generically prejudiced mind, in that his tests showed a high correlation between hostility to actual minority groups and hostility to Daniereans, Pireneans, and Wallonians, who are fictional.[18] Some Americans are primed to hate anyone. But given the recalcitrance of some forms of ethnic and racial animosities, the hostility toward Jews in the South generally has been mild, and more latent than blatant.

Southern anti-Semitism mostly has been unencumbered by ideology and has lacked the Nazi compulsion to define Jewry as prepotent evil. Even from a Berlin devastated by Allied bombing, Hitler's last testament proclaimed his enmity to Jews. The Southern equivalent undoubtedly would be the suicide note left by Edmund Ruffin, in the wake of the defeat of the Confederacy, reaffirming "unmitigated hatred to . . . the perfidious, malignant and vile Yankee race."[19] He at least did not blame the victim. Anti-Semitism has instead been one aspect of the xenophobia that has hovered over the white South, a way of expressing anxiety at the shift from gemeinschaft to gesellschaft, a protest against the violation of the self-images of an agrarian order and its gods of the hearth. Thomas Wolfe's agent, for example, reported that the North Carolina novelist "had the villager's dread and dislike of urban Jews." (Nevertheless, "the great love affair of his entire life" was with Aline Bernstein, whom Wolfe called "my Jew.") W. J. Cash, whose *Mind of the South* was published in the same year as Percy's *Lanterns on the Levee*, explained that "the Jew, with his universal refusal to be assimilated, is everywhere the eternal Alien; and in the South, where any difference has always stood out with great vividness, he was especially so."[20]

The Jews have been resented as wanderers and interlopers who often have been forced, like Blanche DuBois, to depend "upon the kindness of strangers"; and in the South many of those strangers intensified their suspicion of outsiders with religious intolerance. When T. S. Eliot, lecturing at the University of Virginia in 1933, argued that the idea of a Christian society necessarily limited the number of "free-thinking Jews" to be included in the corporate body, he was reformulating the opposition voiced earlier by a chairman of the faculty of the University of Virginia, W. W. Thornton, who in 1890 told the editors of the *American Hebrew*: "All intelligent Christians deplore the fact that the historical evidences for Christianity have so little weight with your people." The educator added that anti-Semitism, which he too apparently did not loathe, could be explained (as Cash was later to do) by the "mere fact of difference."[21]

Given the religious origins of much of the historical derogation of Jews, given the importance of Protestantism in Southern society, the absence of violent or systematic hostility needs to be accounted for. Hodding Carter of the Pulitzer Prize-winning *Delta Democrat-Times* has wryly observed that "it takes perseverence to hate Jews and Negroes and Catholics all at the same time." (Carter himself left Hammond, Louisiana, for Greenville, Mississippi, on the advice of Will Percy and David Cohn and has recalled that "at almost every decisive period in my life, some Jew . . . has stood beside me and helped me forward.") Cash believed that hostility toward Catholics has in fact run deeper in the South than anti-Semitism. Demagogues such as Alabama's primitive Tom Heflin, lacking Republican opposition, campaigned against the pope instead; and Watson's weekly *Jeffersonian* conducted a vicious seven-year campaign against Roman Catholicism, once calling the pope a "fat old dago." How widely the antagonism to papal influence suffused the outlook of Southern Protestantism can be gauged from the 1960 presidential campaign, when the Democrats' intercession with the Georgia judge who had sentenced the Reverend Martin Luther King, Jr., to hard labor inspired King's father to switch his support from Nixon to Kennedy. In his pronouncement, the Reverend Martin Luther King, Sr., explained his previous opposition was because of Kennedy's Catholicism, leading the Democratic candidate to remark privately: "Imagine Martin Luther King having a bigot for a father. Well, we all have fathers, don't we?"[22]

But if it makes sense that the Jew has been saved by the deflection of hatred elsewhere, there has been a more obvious target than the Catholic. "In most Southern towns," Jonathan Daniels wrote in 1938, "except where many Jews have recently come in, the direction of racial prejudice at the Negro frees the Jew from prejudice altogether—or nearly altogether." The man whom Daniels's own father served as secretary of the Navy, Woodrow Wilson, is a singular case in point. While the forthright militancy of Monroe

Trotter was so offensive to the president that he refused to permit further audiences with that spokesman of Northern Negroes, the Virginia minister's son spoke glowingly of the "Christian character" of the ardent Zionist Louis D. Brandeis. And when an acquaintance regretted that a man as great as Brandeis should be a Jew, it was then that Wilson gallantly replied that Brandeis would not have been so great a man were he *not* a Jew—the sort of remark that the segregationist Democrat would not conceivably have made about, say, W. E. B. Du Bois. When the president's friend Thomas Dixon, in a burst of emotion, shouted across the screening room that the title of the film version of his novel *The Clansman* should be altered to *The Birth of a Nation*, Dixon meant the Aryan nation, but one in which blacks rather than Jews were to be degraded and excluded.[23]

Dixon himself is an arresting case for those attuned to the complexities and surprises that lurk in the interstices of American cultural and social history. It is true that the modern Ku Klux Klan exploded from the nucleus of the Knights of Mary Phagan, who lynched Leo Frank. It is also probable that the Klan was inspired by the D. W. Griffith film, that celluloid miracle transmuted from the base metal of Dixon's fiction. With the royalties from the novel and film, it is less well known, Dixon was able to purchase a 1,400-acre estate in North Carolina, which he was forced to sell during the Great Depression to a Jew who converted it into a B'nai B'rith Youth Organization "human relations" camp. It is tempting to stress the irony here (the B'nai B'rith's Anti-Defamation League also was formed in the aftermath of the Frank case). Even though Thomas Dixon was undoubtedly the most racist litterateur in American history, he was no enemy of Jews, whom he called "the greatest race of people God has ever created." Warming to his subject, Dixon explained hostility to the Jew "not because of his inferiority, but because of his genius. We are afraid of him; we Gentiles who meet him in the arena of life get licked and then make faces at him. The truth is, the Jew has achieved a noble civilization—had his poets, prophets, and kings when our Germanic ancestors were still in the woods cracking coconuts and hickory nuts with the monkeys."[24] The social Darwinism is quaint, the anthropology bizarre; and the filiopietism has that distinctive Southern accent. Dixon undoubtedly also knew that Jews were harmless. After a wave of synagogue bombings and cemetery desecrations about 1960, a conference was organized in Jacksonville, Florida, for various Southern politicians and law-enforcement officials. A list of violence-prone Southern whites was read aloud but, by a most impolitic oversight, the name of Birmingham's commissioner of public safety, Eugene C. Connor, was intoned. "Bull" Connor, who was in attendance, is reported to have blurted out an expletive and responded to the accusation as follows: "Nigras, maybe, but Jews—why?"

Why indeed. Few in number and unobtrusive in manner, most Southern Jews have seemed to want nothing more than to make a living; their history can perhaps most fully be categorized as a branch of business history. The traveler in the rural South still can observe how commonly the peddlers put down their packs to open stores and become pillars of the local community, still can lose count of the dry-goods stores, hardware stores, jewelry stores, clothing stores, and shoe stores that bear Jewish names. But those names can be misleading, as an Anti-Defamation League representative once discovered after spotting a sign for Cohen's dry-goods store in a Southern hamlet. He stopped by, but met only a man named Johnson, since Cohen had sold the store eight years earlier to move to Jacksonville. Johnson explained that "the sign's still Cohen's 'cause I bought the store with Mr. Cohen's good will."[25] A Gentile preserving a Jew's name "for business reasons" has a certain only-in-America charm about it; it is also another piece in the characteristically Southern puzzle of individual acceptance, combined with general intolerance, of the outsider.

Aside from business success, Southern Jews were rarely conspicuous—preferring to merge into the landscape, which their numbers made feasible. They seemed in fact to partake, generation after generation, of virtually the same values as their neighbors. Although her relatives were Jews, Lillian Hellman does not consider their religious and ethnic background—or her own—worthy of mention or reflection in her reminiscences; it apparently made no difference. And in her famous letter to the House Un-American Activities Committee in 1952, she mentioned her upbringing in "an old-fashioned American tradition," which for her meant "ideals of Christian honor." James K. Feibleman, a Tulane University philosopher, has recalled growing up in a New Orleans "where there was very little religious prejudice. . . . I was Jewish and that was that, but nobody seemed to care very much and nobody so far as I could see was very excited about it." In his memoirs, Kentucky's Arthur Krock, later Washington bureau chief of the *New York Times*, dismissed the subject entirely: "No religious instruction or attendance was ever required of me. . . . I was an early agnostic and have remained that way."[26] The novelist Hortense Calisher, whose father had been born in Richmond in 1861, remembers his "towering pride in his Jewishness *and* his Southernness." Her aunts found comfort "with Gentiles, having had them as close friends and neighbors, but this generation, except for one maverick, would not have married them. Their sons and daughters, including me, will do so entirely." Ludwig Lewisohn was even more adaptable, growing up in South Carolina as "an American, a Southerner, and a Christian." (His first book-length work, published in 1903, was a literary history of South Carolina entitled *Books We Have Made*; the pronoun suggests the intent of the young immigrant to use his study as his final citizenship papers.)[27] These feelings confirmed the impression of the Philadelphia rabbi and tireless publicist Isaac Leeser, who in 1850 came to New Orleans to help dedicate the synagogue building that Judah Touro had purchased. The religious receptivity of the city did not reassure him: "People came thither from all parts of the world to amass a fortune. . . . A degree of freedom in living was indulged in but little promotive of the growth of piety."[28]

Even for those Jews who maintained fidelity to institutional religion, adaptations to the Southern environment were wrought that suggest how eagerly many wanted to resemble their neighbors. In his Atlanta synagogue, at the dawn of the century, the New Orleans-born Rabbi David Marx abolished the wearing of skullcaps, inaugurated Sunday-morning services, minimized Hebrew in the liturgy, changed the age of confirmation to sixteen, and refused to perform the bar mitzvah ceremony even when parents and sons wanted it. Marx's primary responsibility was not, however, to innovate in Jewish ritual and liturgy but to improve and stabilize interfaith relations, which meant making a good impression on the Gentiles.[29] One advertisement at the turn of the century read as follows: "Rabbi wanted by Congregation Temple Emanuel of Beaumont, Texas. He must be a good mixer. . . . Salary $1,500." Good mixing meant not only the assurance of no divided loyalties (and therefore led often to a disparagement of pre-1948 Zionism) but, more importantly, silence, if not explicit support, on the subject of the region's racial mores—the central characteristic, in Ulrich B. Phillips's opinion, of Southern history.[30]

No wonder that the Bull Connors of the region often have been baffled that anti-Jewish feeling could be ascribed to them. No Jews who came to live in the antebellum South were deeply affected by abolitionism, though their ethical anxiety over the peculiar institution can sometimes be demonstrated—but not abundantly. Many Southern Jews supported the Lost Cause with converts' zeal. In the twentieth century, Will Percy's friend David Cohn became an apologist for racial segregation, and it was largely a result of Percy's influence that James Feibleman in adolescence became "a full-fledged professional Southerner. I was prepared to explain that Northerners did not understand the Negro question and ought not to presume to interfere."[31] During the civil rights struggle, the Jew tended to fit the region's folk definition of a moderate as a "white man without sidearms."

Having won the right to be equal (except where snobbery has held sway), many Jews showed far less interest in the right to be different. Perhaps there is more than a half-truth to a Lenny Bruce routine that might be paraphrased as follows: If you live in New York or any other big city, you are Jewish. It doesn't matter that you're Catholic. If you live in Macon, Georgia, you're going to be goyish even if you're Jewish. ... Revisiting the Mississippi Delta, Percy's friend David Cohn realized that the "Jews, by legend both intellectual and shrewd, seem in this soft climate to have lost both these qualities. They are distinguished neither by learning nor by riches."[32] One price paid for the emulation of other Southerners has been the thinness of Jewish institutions, which have had to negotiate an endless series of compromises and to make quite meager demands on many adherents. A considerable proportion of Southern Jews would have had no difficulty meeting the challenge that angered Shammai, who was asked to summarize all of Judaism while standing on one foot. The cultural price that was paid might best be expressed, here as elsewhere, not by measuring but through metaphor. The fact that the Jews who came South disproved a folk belief that they have horns adds further meaning to the poignant scene in *The Glass Menagerie* in which Laura shows the gentleman caller the unicorn in her collection. "Poor little fellow," Jim responds, "he must feel sort of lonesome." "Well," Laura smiles, "if he does he doesn't complain about it. He stays on a shelf with some horses that don't have horns and all of them seem to get along nicely together." But when Laura and Jim waltz, they bump into the table and the piece of glass is shattered. "Now it is just like all the other horses," Laura says. "Now he will feel more at home with the other horses, the ones that don't have horns."[33]

There was indeed an aura of make-believe in the attempts of Jews to be completely assimilated into Southern society. Since even the Jew who sought to become a professional Southerner had to do so through self-conscious effort, such an identity could not be realized fully and convincingly. The Jewish fear that the civil rights movement might disrupt presumably excellent relations with Christian neighbors suggests that those relations may have been less solid than had been acknowledged, that the equilibrium was more precarious than even the most defiantly Southern of Southern Jews would have liked to believe. It may not strain credulity to find an inadvertent symbolic touch in the choice of a Jew to play the role of Ashley Wilkes, the compleat antebellum Southern aristocrat, in *Gone with the Wind*—for Leslie Howard's is the least impressive performance, the least successful impersonation of an archetypal Southerner, in the film. The identity of the Southern Jew thus can be seen as problematic, for in their regrouping from pariahs to parvenus, Jews escaped the wrath of Russia's Black Hundreds without becoming fully accepted at Sutpen's Hundred either, much less at the homes of the gentry Sutpen displaced; and many of them have been completely at home neither in the borscht belt nor in the Bible Belt. A Jew whose family had lived in Savannah for generations once told Harry Golden: "Frankly, Ah don't have many relationships with mah Christian neighbors. Ah'm more comf'table with mah own. Ah puf-fer the Yudim."[34] And while this obviously bad mixer is an extreme case, he suggests the presence, if not the pervasiveness, of a double consciousness—based, however subtly, on the "mere fact of difference."

Nevertheless, Jews have shared something with Southerners that may distinguish both groups from other Americans. That common bond is the sixth sense, the sense of history, the disturbing weight of a collective past. For since that moment when the soldiers were told that they could keep their horses for the spring plowing, the memory of defeat infiltrated the Southern consciousness, causing so many dreams and ambitions to turn rancid, helping to ensure the failure of many of the best Southern whites to break the cycle of poverty and misery and resentment, making of the past a nemesis. Percy's adopted son Walker Percy once explained with ungrammatical exactitude that Southern writing has been so resonant because "we got beat." That surely has deepened insight into the sadness and failure that are so frequently and so inescapably the stuff of human experience, for after the Civil War Southerners no longer could be simply considered the children of pride. The nursing of the Southern obsession with loss has shown that, while remembrance can be redemptive, forgetfulness is not necessarily worse. The obligation to transcend despair perhaps was best understood by Faulkner, probably the only American-born novelist of this century to whom Northrup Frye's statement applies, that his readers have grown up inside his work "without ever being aware of a circumference." The sonorous faith Faulkner expressed in Stockholm that "man will not merely endure, he will prevail" was not grounded in complacency or thoughtlessness or the compulsive optimism that has afflicted the American spirit; it was not merely a ceremonious expression of consolation intended to raise the threshold of pain, or a cosmetic to disguise the scar tissue left by suffering.

But that faith does find partial corroboration in the history of the Jewish people, in which martyrdom and defeats have been commemorated but in which the past also has been rendered usable and borne as an ironic solace. (In the 1973 war, the Israeli army's impenetrable code for the various positions on the front was based on the geography of Poland's Jewish communities that had been destroyed during the Holocaust.) The rather benign response to Jews in the South may be a result of their commitment to family cohesiveness and the loyalty to ancestry that their neighbors could not help noticing. More importantly, Jews posed no genuine threat to the stability of Southern society and traditions, since they were not only white in color but few in number. Even as the cultural contradictions linger, perhaps the paradox can be resolved by acknowledging how peripheral Jews have been, for even the archetype of the alien and the Christ killer could not have had the same weight and urgency as the fear of the power of blackness. The "Dutch man of warre, that sold . . . twenty negars" to John Rolfe and the Virginians in 1619 was certainly more fateful for American and Southern history than was the ship from which twenty-four Jews disembarked in Nieuw Amsterdam in 1654. For Jews, the ubiquity of Gentiles could never be minimized or forgotten; but for Southerners, it has been relations with blacks that have mattered economically, socially, morally. Not casting so long a symbolic shadow, Jews could be recognized (and liked or disliked) as individuals.

But perhaps Southerners also saw in Jews an adaptability, an elasticity, a sense of how to bend in order not to break, that offered wry lessons in survival. Perhaps Southerners detected an indomitable spirit beneath the ingratiation, saw in their "solitary" presence in the region, as McCaslin Edmonds did, "a sort of courage."[35] Such qualities are part of the puzzle of history that stretches back to the first mention of Hebrews that archeologists have been able to uncover from the detritus of the secular past. It is a pharoah's victory column, more than three thousand years old; and it contains the only mention of Israel in ancient Egyptian writing. The inscription announces that "Israel is laid waste" and will never rise again.[36]

13

The Southern Jew as Businessman

The most illuminating student of this country has remained a foreigner, Alexis de Tocqueville; and in *Democracy in America* he noted the extraordinary flair for business that the citizens of the Jacksonian era exhibited. Tocqueville generalized that "in democracies nothing is greater or more brilliant than commerce; it attracts the attention of the public and fills the imagination of the multitude; all energetic passions are directed toward it." The cultivation of mercantile skills, he continued, helps to distinguish a democratic society from an aristocratic order and makes businessmen even out of farmers, who would otherwise be peasants uninterested in raising cash crops.[1]

Tocqueville himself spent only ten months in the United States and very little time in the South, and he apparently met no Jews. And yet the historian cannot help noticing how fully Southern Jews have embodied those traits that the French aristocrat concluded were characteristic of all Americans. For the United States illustrated Max Weber's thesis of the ways in which the Protestant work ethic and capitalist values were historically enmeshed. It is the country where Benjamin Franklin's *The Way to Wealth* has gone through almost 500 editions. (Franklin's character, Poor Richard Saunders, also asserted that "nothing but honey is sweeter than money.") In the United States a leading philosopher, William James, could speak of "the cash-value of truth"; and an eminent jurist, Oliver Wendell Holmes, Jr., could posit a "marketplace of ideas." When we study the Southern Jewish past in particular, we really mean business. And if we take the advice that "Deep Throat" gave to Bob Woodward of the *Washington Post*—"follow the money"—we are also being attentive to one of the primary impulses that define the American experience itself.

Yet the pertinence and fascination of a topic such as Southern Jewish entrepreneurship exceed the scholarly energies that have so far been expended on it. No serious books devoted to this theme are extant; articles are not only scattered but, more regrettably, tend to be narrowly conceived. The few monographs that have been published do not see the *tallit* for the fringes. In extenuation historians can plead certain conceptual impediments that discourage research. Just as the regional—as opposed to national—identity of the Southerner in the United States is a standing invitation to scholarly debate, so too the case for the difference between Jews in Dixie and elsewhere must be argued rather than assumed.[2] It is even more problematic how businessmen of Jewish background differ from their Gentile colleagues, and since Jewish businessmen are more likely to have been affected by larger market forces than by religious tradition, the lines that separate American economic history from the economic study of any ethnic group are inevitably blurred.[3] Such issues can scarcely be tackled or resolved here. Nevertheless a modest attempt to rectify scholarly neglect may suggest how snugly Jewish businessmen in the South have exemplified the vitality of Tocqueville's "commercial passions," and how successfully many of them have been implicated in the economic life not only of the region but also of the nation. Finally, it will be argued that Southern Jewish businessmen, however unintentionally, introduced elements of the modern ethos into the region and thereby wrought changes that are felt still, especially in race relations.

Immigrants to the South elected to reside in a region that was, until well into the twentieth century, overwhelmingly agrarian. It was a Northern Jew who lyrically observed of potatoes and cotton that "dem dat plants 'em is soon forgotten," and Jews influenced the region precisely because they refused to imitate the economic stratification of most of their neighbors. The various European prohibitions against Jewish ownership of land had conspired to endow the immigrants with little memory or inclination for agriculture. Their poverty meant that there was rarely enough capital for them to become capitalists, and to work for manufacturers as part of the labor force dimmed the prospects for advancement. To become engaged in mercantile occupations was therefore the most appealing choice, as Oscar Handlin has succinctly explained. Shopkeeping "involved hard work and, at most levels, insecurity; but it enabled the Jew to adjust gently to his new situation in life. In the store he had the boss's sense of independence; he had the dignity of a man who could take time off to observe the Sabbath; and he had the comfort of preserving the family structure, for in these enterprises the family worked together."[4]

No wonder then that, even before the Constitution was ratified, Daniel Boone was dealing with Richmond merchants whose receipts were in Yiddish. (The store they established, Cohen and Isaacs, selling everything from frying pans to medicines to artificial flowers, was designated simply "The Jews' store.")[5] Most of the immigrant peddlers came from the German-speaking parts of Europe, where the word *Judentum* was virtually synonymous with *Handel* (commerce), an association compounded by General Ulysses S. Grant's Order Number 11, which briefly in 1862 sought to eliminate financial speculation by banning "the Jews, as a class" from the Department of the Tennessee.[6] Many of the peddlers who crisscrossed the region settled down, opening stores in order to supply other peddlers who needed to replenish their supplies. The establishments that were created and the retailing that resulted often made their owners the nuclei of the communities formed in the interstices of the plantations and farms that dominated the Southern economy. The fact that many farmers could come into town for their shopping only on Saturdays might well modify Professor Handlin's generalization about commercial freedom. But the attraction of such an occupation was unmistakable.

No wonder then that anthropologists and sociologists studying the region in the twentieth century have stumbled across Jews. For example, in Indianola, Mississippi, the *mise en scène* of John Dollard's *Caste and Class in a Southern Town*, the seven department stores on the main street were almost entirely owned by Jews. In Natchez, the locale of another classic, *Deep South* by Allison Davis, Burleigh B. Gardner and Mary R. Gardner, "the wholesale merchants . . . who once rivalled the banks as credit agencies for planters were, with one exception, Jews. Most of them were socially of the middle class," the authors added, "but a few had risen into the upper class."[7] No wonder then that, even in the White House, the label on Jimmy Carter's suits read: "Hart Schaffner & Marx, A. Cohen and Sons, Americus, Georgia."[8] For Southern Jewry has been, as Napoleon is supposed to have said of England, "a nation of shopkeepers."

The unsuccessful have left few traces behind them for the historian to discover, and the investigator of their lives realizes that their trail quickly gets cold. The remembrance of their struggles has been perhaps best preserved in folklore and pickled in humor, as in an anedote about the peddler selling paper fans. Asked at a rural household how much the fans were selling for, he replied, "One cent." The woman claimed that that was too much, to which the peddler responded: "Okay, lady. So make me an offer." A memoirist from Bacon County, Georgia, recalls a Jewish peddler who came in 1940, dressed only in black. He relied on bartering, trading his thimbles and threads for cured meat or eggs or corn, and neither in sadness nor in joy; he only spoke business. The author, Harry Crews, cannot "remember anybody saying anything bad about him or anybody treating him badly. But he *was* different from the rest of us"—mysterious and nameless, and now otherwise forgotten.[9]

But other salesmen prospered, some spectacularly; and the affluence of some Southern Jews not only brought them the highest prestige within their communities but also testified to the authority of the rags-to-riches ideal that had earned the allegiance of so many Americans. The buccaneer capitalism that the nineteenth-century railroads represented was most notoriously revealed in William H. Vanderbilt's remark: "The public be damned." Jewish enterprise operated according to a different principle, however. "The public be pleased" might well have been the slogan of such establishments as Garfinckel's in Washington, Thalhimer's in Richmond, Goldsmith's in Memphis, Neiman-Marcus in Dallas, Sakowitz's in Houston, Godschaux's in New Orleans, Cohen Brothers' in Jacksonville and Rich's in Atlanta.

The saga of the very successful was in any event an index of the economic and social opportunities that beckoned as much as it reflected the tenacity and virtuosity of some of the Jews of the region. Here historical generalization requires biographical illustration. Lazarus Straus, for example, came to Talbotton, Georgia, in 1852, with his wife and children joining him two years later. During the Civil War the family moved briefly to Columbus, where they established a wholesale business in crockery, china, and glassware, Fearful of anti-Semitism however, the firm of L. Straus and Sons transferred to New York City and in 1871 leased a basement of the Quaker-founded R. H. Macy store for its crockery display. A decade later, "Macy's was still a profitable concern," business historian Ralph M. Hower has written, "with widespread patronage, policies of tested value, and a well-established reputation for variety and low prices. Its future, however, was endangered by slow stagnation." To avoid this danger, Lazarus and his sons, Nathan and Isidor, became part owners; and Macy's got what Professor Hower, bending over backwards, has called "an injection of fine Jewish blood." The Strauses became complete owners in 1896, and an American institution was born.[10]

There is more to this story, in disclosing the Jewish relationship to the majority culture. A third son, Oscar, became the first cabinet officer of Jewish faith when Theodore Roosevelt named him secretary of commerce and labor in 1906, and Roosevelt's recollection of that appointment reveals much about the myth of undifferentiated Americanism and the reality of ethnic pressures. At a dinner to commemorate the Straus nomination, the president reminisced about how he had sought the most qualified American for the post, regardless of race or color or creed or party. Roosevelt added that Jacob Schiff could confirm this quest for individual merit. But the aged banker, presiding at the banquet, was then rather deaf, missed his cue, and is alleged to have chimed in: "That's right, Mr. President. You came to me and said, 'Jake, who is the best Jew I can appoint Secretary of Commerce?' "[11]

It is curious that the second Jew to serve as secretary of commerce also was a Southerner, Lewis L. Strauss, whose grandfather had settled in Culpepper, Virginia, and had fought for the Confederacy. Although not formally educated past high school, Strauss began his career at the age of sixteen as a "drummer" selling shoes wholesale to Virginia merchants. "As I observed the Sabbath by not working on Saturday," he later recalled, "and since most of my customers did not work on Sunday," he took advantage of two days a week for study; and eventually, after a partnership with the investment banking house of Kuhn, Loeb in New York, Strauss became chairman of the Atomic Energy Commission. He served temporarily in the cabinet in 1959. Then, by a vote of 49 against and 46 for confirmation, the Senate decided that he was not the best American—and perhaps not even the best Jew—that President Eisenhower could appoint secretary of commerce.[12]

Another New York institution that became a national institution, besides Macy's, is the *New York Times*; and it too owes its reputation to a family of Southern Jews. Julius Ochs had been minding the store in Natchez when he met his wife, Bertha Levy, who married him in Nashville. Their son Adolph's career in publishing began at the age of fourteen, sweeping the floors of the *Knoxville Chronicle*. Rising from office boy to printer's apprentice, he saved enough money to buy into part-ownership of a dying newspaper, the *Chattanooga Dispatch*, before buying outright on his own the *Chattanooga Times* for a $250 down payment in 1878. Adolph Ochs's father came down from Knoxville for the ceremony signaling the change of ownership, not only out of pride for his enterprising son but also to sign the legal papers for him, since Adolph was not yet twenty-one years old. The newspaper prospered, and he married Iphigene Wise, the daughter of Rabbi Isaac Mayer Wise, even as his brother became mayor of Chattanooga. It was indicative of the ambiguous circumstances of Southern Jewry that Ochs's mother was buried draped with the Stars and Bars, his father with the Stars and Stripes. In 1896, the same year that the Strauses seized full control of Macy's, Ochs moved to New York to buy the *Times*, a respectable newspaper, which his exceptional rectitude, energy, and canniness helped transform into an adornment of American journalism.[13]

Albert Lasker, who was born in Germany and grew up in Galveston, Texas, also began in journalism. Already at the age of twelve, Lasker was editing and publishing the *The Galveston Free Press*, which earned him a profit of $15 per week. Because his father, the president of three different banks and the owner of a milling business, considered journalism disreputable, Albert was sent to Chicago in 1898 to work for the advertising firm of Lord & Thomas. (It is unclear why the senior Lasker believed journalism to be less respectable than advertising.) Beginning at a salary of $10 a week, Albert Lasker was soon—and for the next half century—making $1 million per year. He made Lord & Thomas the most profitable, the largest, and perhaps the most inventive advertising agency in the world. Lasker himself, however, spent much of his own income on

cancer research, on his art collection, and in the defense of Leo
Frank, the superintendent of an Atlanta pencil factory who had also
been president of his B'nai B'rith lodge. By his own calculation,
Lasker spent $100,000 in legal fees and took away a year from his
own agency to organize support for Frank.[14]

One of the most idiosyncratic of Southern Jewish entrepreneurs
was Joseph Fels, who was born in Halifax Court House, Virginia,
in 1855 and was raised and educated in Yanceyville, North Carolina,
and in Richmond. He began his business career selling soap with
his father, Lazarus, in Baltimore; and with the manufacture of naph-
tha soap, the company burgeoned, centering its operations in Philadelphia and New York. Fels himself lived much of his life in
London, where the Fabian Socialist Beatrice Webb described him
in her diary as "a decidedly vulgar little Jew with much push, little
else on the surface." Yet Fels became a prominent philanthropist,
and was rare among wealthy Jews from the South in the radicalism
of his political sympathies. He generously subsidized the single tax
movement, including its colony at Fair Hope, Alabama. And in one
of the most intriguing episodes in the history of the Russian Social
Democratic Labor Party, Fels loaned the revolutionaries 1,700
pounds without interest, so that their fifth congress could be held
without interruption or disruption in London in 1907. Trotsky
himself thanked Fels for his generosity, although Lenin could not
bring himself to show gratitude to a capitalist. Fels died in 1914,
before the Bolshevik wing of the RSDLP got the power to redeem
the note that 240 delegates had signed; but the Russian trade del-
egation to London fully repaid his widow in 1922. By then Fels's
political interests lay elsewhere, at least according to Mary Fels,
who claimed that from the dead her late husband advised her that
"support for Zionism was the right thing to do."[15]

Undoubtedly the most publicized Southern Jew to exemplify
the capitalist ethic was Bernard Baruch, who was born in Camden,
South Carolina. His great-grandfather had been the cantor of
Charleston's Beth Elohim. His father, Simon Baruch, had been born
in Germany and wrote a couple of medical works of consequence.
Following a duel in which Dr. Baruch was not directly involved,
the family moved to New York City, where his son grew into a
financier of vulpine reputation and the organizer of economic victory in the Great War. After the Second World War, Baruch's

advocacy of the elimination of a nuclear arms race went unheeded, leaving unsolved a problem that still bedevils the planet. He also relished playing Mordecai to whichever King Ahasuerus was in the White House, winning the sobriquet of *shtadlan*, although it was never clear whom he designated himself to represent. Baruch himself joined no Jewish organizations, and always defined his allegiances in patriotic rather than ethnic terms. He married an Episcopalian, the religion in which their children were raised. Baruch considered himself an agnostic, but he faithfully attended Yom Kippur services. The financier "liked to remind people that his name meant 'blessed' in Hebrew," his biographer has written, "which led some to conclude that he attended services only to hear his name mentioned frequently." Jordan Schwarz surely is right in minimizing the influence on Baruch's South Carolina origins. Yet he nevertheless maintained a home in that state and claimed to be "at heart . . . a South Carolinean."[16]

A far less celebrated figure who also ended up in New Orleans was Samuel Zemurray, who was born in Kishinev, Russia. Accompanied by his aunt, young Zemurray came by steerage to Alabama in 1892 and was soon making a dollar a week as an assistant to an old peddler, bartering tinware for pigs. By the age of eighteen, Zemurray had earned enough to bring the rest of his family from Russia to Selma, Alabama; and then his real career began. He bought $150 worth of ripe bananas and, at least according to apocrypha, peddled them from a barrow that was a converted railway car. He thus got to New Orleans with a modest profit. Eventually he was able to buy a couple of tramp steamers and later five thousand acres of banana plantations in Honduras. Speaking Spanish with his Russian accent, Zemurray became chief of operations for United Fruit and was named its president in 1938. After having organized at least one revolution to protect his company's investments, Zemurray retired in 1951. But his interests went beyond bananas. Chaim Weizmann considered his 1923 meeting with Zemurray "one of the highlights of my visit to the States in that year" and found the so-called Banana King generous and sympathetic toward the Zionist cause. In his memoirs Weizmann also recalled Zemurray's "simplicity, his transparent honesty, his lively interest in people and things, and his desire to serve. His chosen studies in leisure hours were mathematics and music." The only study of United Fruit is unscholarly, but if it can be believed, Zemurray helped buy the ship *Exodus* and secure its registration during the struggle to run the British blockade of Palestine. He was an enlightened philanthropist in the context of Central American business practices as well. Zemurray, who kept two residences in Louisiana, died in 1961, after a varied career that deserves—and still needs—fuller treatment.[17]

Currently the most important international investment banking house may be Lazard Frères, which had its distant origins in New Orleans. There Alexandre Lazard came in 1847 from Lorraine, France, to establish a dry-goods business. The next year he and two of his brothers formed a partnership. But in 1849 a fire destroyed the store and a major section of the city as well. The news of the gold strikes in California, however, prompted Alexandre and Simon Lazard to move to San Francisco, where they shifted from dry goods to trading in gold. Another financier to emerge from the ranks of Southern Jewry was Louis Wolfson, who was born in Georgia to immigrant parents, was raised in Jacksonville (where he boxed under the name of "Kid Wolf"), and was educated at the University of Georgia. Wolfson's career began in his father's junk business, and he soon specialized in taking over "sick" companies. In a spectacular proxy fight in 1954–56, he tried unsuccessfully to gain control over Montgomery Ward from the troglodytic S. L. Avery. (Disgruntled employees often made reference to the word that their boss's initials and surname formed.) It was a check from Wolfson's foundation accepted by Justice Abe Fortas that floated the imputation of impropriety, forcing Fortas's resignation from the bench, after which Wolfson himself was imprisoned for violating securities laws.[18]

The blazing careers of such businessmen, while hardly representative, nevertheless suggest the parameters for other ambitious Southern Jews, and demonstrate the openness and opportunity that a region long mired in poverty made available. The leaders of communities with major economic ambitions, such as Atlanta, often welcomed in their midst Jewish immigrants, who projected a reputation for industriousness, energy, and resourcefulness. Yet it is striking that such opportunities often were insufficient, and in the above list all but Wolfson chose to leave the South and to base their corporate operations elsewhere. As though the region could not offer enough stimulus or scope for entrepreneurship, these men refused "to live and die in Dixie"; and thus its capacity to keep pace with the rest of the American economy was not enhanced. The South was unable to attract the industries and factories that could compete with the humming economies of other parts of the United States, despite assurances to investors that their labor force would be as nonunion as its fighting forces had been in 1865.

Wolfson himself had been typical in the involvement of his brothers and other relatives in the businesses he created. There long has been a transparent connection between the expansion of such enterprises and the participation and cohesiveness of families. Such intimate involvements would appear to be a necessary, although not sufficient, condition for the escape from poverty, as though verifying the wisdom of the adage that "success is relative—the more success, the more relatives." Yet probably no Southern Jewish businessman brought as many family members in with him as the movie tycoon Louis B. Mayer, whose company's initials, M-G-M, were said to stand for Mayer's *ganze mishpoche*. The other side of the story has been described by the subtlest chronicler of Southern Jewish life, Eli N. Evans, who has observed that its real drama "revolves around the fathers who built their business for the sons who didn't want them."[19] Evans himself, the son of a Durham, North Carolina, store owner and himself a lawyer, writer, and foundation executive, is a case in point.

At least until recently family businesses have been so pervasive a part of the landscape and have so dominated the Southern Jewish imagination that not even the learned professions attracted many of the sons. Despite the Judaic heritage of scholarship, commercial passions generally exerted an unchallenged influence within the region, so that those with an intellectual vocation tended to seek in Northern oases refuge from the "Sahara of the Bozart." Jacob N. Cardozo was an exception: this self-taught journalist and political economist, born in Savannah, moved with his family to Charleston at the age of ten. There he became, in Joseph Dorfman's estimation, "the only man in pre–Civil War America whose mind operated on that high level of abstraction that characterized the work of [David] Ricardo and his school."[20] But there was not enough encouragement in the Southern atmosphere to sustain the work of the Semiticist and leader of the Conservative movement in Judaism, Cyrus Adler, born in Arkansas; the novelist and literary critic Ludwig Lewisohn, raised in South Carolina; the classicist Moses Hadas, born in Atlanta; the legal philosopher Edmond Cahn, born in New Orleans; the sociologist Edgar Z. Friedenberg, born in Shreveport; the historian Daniel J. Boorstin, also born in Atlanta; the composer Milton Babbitt, raised in Jackson, Mississippi; or the playwright Lillian Hellman, born in New Orleans. Some of those who departed from the region looked back in anger, including Hellman, whose play, *The Little Foxes* (1939), is a most unflattering portrait of the scheming and greedy relatives on her mother's side of the family.[21] It is one of the curiosities of American Jewish history that Elliot Cohen, who was raised in Mobile, became the editor of the *Menorah Journal* (1924–31) and the founder of *Commentary* in 1945. Thus it was a Southerner who, in Elinor Grumet's words, more than anyone else "encouraged and maintained a community of secular Jewish discourse in English from which writers of two generations made their way." But Cohen had to do so in New York City.[22]

Further evidence of the sapping of intellectual vitality comes from an unfriendly source, W. W. Thornton, who was a chairman of the faculty of the University of Virginia in an era when there was no office of the president. Disturbed that Jews continued to repudiate the Savior, Thornton also complained in 1890 that they "certainly care less for what is embraced in the term culture than Christians who are equally well off. They are immersed in business and money-getting." Thornton neglected to consider Jesus' claim that he too had gone about his Father's business, but added that "we have Jewish students at this University every year, and . . . we have never had in my day a really scholarly man among them."[23] Although Gentiles often have considered Jews ill-bred, to lament that they are ill-read is unusual. But even if Thornton's remarks were exaggerated, they at least suggest the impact that the commercial passions registered in the Jewish communities of the South by the end of the nineteenth century.

Yet mercantile values may have helped to provoke important change in the region, particularly in race relations, the most distinctive facet of Southern life. If Oxford University was, in Edward Gibbon's phrase, "steeped in port and prejudice," then Oxford, Mississippi, and similar towns might be said to have been drenched in booze and bigotry. To such hamlets came intruders in the dust— peddlers and merchants who were both temperate and moderate and at the same time immune to the charm of spontaneous and unchecked emotion and violence that was the Southern male ideal.[24] These merchants were also more interested in customers than in customs of racial discrimination, more committed to making sales than to making trouble, more worried about inventory than about integration. Before the Civil War some Jews admittedly had been slaveholders and slave traders, and one wonders whether they skipped the passages in the Passover Haggadah that extol freedom after the torment of Egyptian bondage. But Southern Jews, without directly challenging the racial etiquette of the region, without proclaiming their enmity to Jim Crow, still tended to diverge from other whites in their relations with blacks.

Their willingness to trade with and to associate with blacks, for example, did not escape notice. Frederick Law Olmsted, the most observant of the antebellum travelers to visit the South, wrote in 1856 that "a swarm of Jews, within the last ten years, has settled in nearly every Southern town, many of them of no character, opening cheap clothing and trinket shops; ruining, or driving out of business, many of the old retailers, and engaging in an unlawful trade with simple negroes, which is found very profitable." Olmsted was a Northern liberal who helped found a progressive magazine, *The Nation*, which Zemurray later subsidized. But Olmsted did not fail to notice that, in Richmond, the German Jews were "very dirty." Their shops emitted "their characteristic smells" and were "thickly set in the narrowest and meanest streets, which seem to be otherwise inhabited mainly by negroes."[25] These were not neighborhoods characterized by what Jimmy Carter once termed "ethnic purity"; and given such a mixture, suspicions of exploitation were difficult to suppress. Nor were accusations confined to those "old retailers," whose higher prices or manifest hostility helped push black customers to Jewish tradesmen. Even Fyodor Dostoevsky, whom a much-heralded 1967 volume in black history deemed an unimpeachable authority on Southern Jewish businessmen, caught the drift. Writing in 1877, the novelist mentioned how in the American South the Jews "have already leaped *en masse* upon the millions of liberated Negroes, and have already taken a grip upon them in their, the Jews' own way, by means of their sempiternal 'gold pursuit' and by taking advantage of the inexperience and vices of the exploited tribe." Dostoevsky added that although "the Negroes have now been liberated from the slave owners . . . they will not last because the Jews . . . will jump at this new little victim."²⁶

Whatever the extent of exploitation, contact with Jewish businessmen also brought benefits to blacks. If Indianola, Mississippi, is typical, merchants "let the Negro know that his dollar is as good as anyone else's." Professor John Dollard also reported that "over and over again one hears from Negroes that Southern [Gentile] dry goods merchants have been crowded out of the territory by their hostile, categorical treatment of Negroes." Jewish storekeepers by contrast "treated Negroes with courtesy, or at least without discourtesy, in strictly business relations. They find some way of avoiding the 'Mr.' and 'Mrs.' question, such as by saying 'What can I do for you?' and letting it go at that." Although Dollard concluded that some Jewish merchants took advantage of caste by coercing black customers toward making particular purchases, he also learned from his interviews that Jews "bargain with the Negroes and the Negroes like this. Other merchants are more likely to follow a strict one-price policy. . . . Negro tenants . . . get satisfaction out of the fact that the Jewish merchant appears to allow himself to be beaten."²⁷ Other shopkeepers broke precedent by allowing blacks to try on clothing before deciding whether to purchase it. It is easy to scoff at such gestures; Lillian Hellman has insisted that her family's aim was "to make money, nothing else."²⁸ Nevertheless the expectation was aroused in many blacks that the Jews would act more responsively than other whites to the struggle for racial equality.

There is fragmentary evidence that blacks did indeed perceive Jews as sympathetic to the need for dignity and for relief from oppression. Almost nothing is known about Southern black attitudes toward Jews, and even in recent times polling data is ambiguous. But it may be because of Muhammad Ali's Southern background that he once prophesied that "there's gonna be some whites who'll escape Allah's judgment, who won't be killed when Allah destroys this country—mainly some Jewish people who really mean right and do right." And when anthropologist Elliot Liebow was conducting his research into the lives of street-corner men in Washington, D.C., one black man in a bootleg joint asked Liebow if he were Italian. No, Jewish, the anthropologist replied, to which the black man responded: "That's just as good. I'm glad you're not white."[29] As late as 1961 the dental school at Emory University did not consider Jews whites either, since applicants to it were required to identify themselves as Caucasian, Jew, or Other.[30] Whatever the other differences between Southern Jews and blacks, they shared a certain legacy of discrimination, a certain stigma as outsiders. Two years after the Ku Klux Klan had been formed in Tennessee, a masked mob lynched S. A. Bierfield, the young Jewish owner of a dry-goods store in Franklin, Tennessee, and his black clerk, Lawrence Bowman.[31] When the Klan was reborn in the region, it was not after the lynching of a black American but rather of Leo Frank. And any assessment of the contributions of private philanthropy in improving the conditions of Negro life in the South would have to include the conspicuous role of not only the Rosenwald family of Chicago but also of its New Orleans branch, the Sterns, as well.

In the effort to fulfill the promise of the American Constitution, the impact of Southern Jewish businessmen should not be neglected. The case of *Cohens* v. *Virginia* (1821), in which the Cohen brothers' sale of lottery tickets ran afoul of Norfolk authorities, is familiar to constitutional scholars because of the opportunity it afforded Chief Justice John Marshall to affirm the judicial supremacy of the federal government over "states' rights." Its consequences for civil rights law in the twentieth century have been traced elsewhere.[32] But what should be stressed is the more direct influence that Jewish businessmen exerted on regional mores. Their capitalist values impugned the racial definition that had for so much of Southern history distorted what it means to be human, and the professed philosophy of a store like Neiman-Marcus that anyone alive should be considered a prospect reflected an admirably democratic spirit.[33]

This historical sketch is not the proper place to assess the strengths and weaknesses of capitalism, to investigate its frequent historical correlation with the development of democracy, or to dispel the radical suspicion that Adam Smith's Invisible Hand has long been engaged in picking the pockets of the poor. But just as Karl Marx could discern in British imperialism, for all its considerable faults, an improvement over the Indian feudalism that it crushed, the capitalism that so many Southern Jews embodied was animated by a moral appeal that made it defensible and effective. In a region locked into agrarian habits of mind and conduct, their peddler's packs and sample cases helped cultivate a taste for the products of the modern world. The department store balance sheet thus became the death warrant of the old order, as the process of secularization—what Max Weber called the disenchantment of the world—became accelerated. When a merchant such as Jacob Goldsmith originates the "Spirit of Christmas" parade in Memphis, or when more than a hundred thousand Atlantans regularly attend the lighting of the great Christmas tree at Rich's, something has happened to the piety and exclusivity of this holiday in this, the most thoroughly Protestant area in the Western Hemisphere.[34] In helping to make the South more modern, more like the rest of the United States, Jewish businessmen altered the moral climate that all Southerners breathed.

That role has not been an especially dramatic or publicized one, in part because the most flamboyant Jewish fortunes generally were accumulated outside the region; and even many of the diadems of Southern Jewish wealth, the department stores, have attached themselves to chains such as the ubiquitous Federated Department Stores of the Lazarus brothers of Ohio. The claims for the moral contributions of the entrepreneurs admittedly may seem tame for a people whose ancestors have included Isaiah and Jeremiah. Jewish businessmen in the South nevertheless esablished a record of fostering—in some small measure—the ideals of equality and autonomy. Tocqueville grasped a century and a half ago that these were the axial principles of American society. And that is why, on the agenda of American Jewish historiography, the merchants who would not be undersold need not be undervalued.

14

The Prism of Literature

Consider the career of an American writer who was born in 1923, flew numerous combat missions during the Second World War, and then returned home to attend college and receive a master's degree in literature. After teaching the subject he entered advertising before his writing on the side brought acclaim and success. If this outline of an author's career sounds vaguely familiar, it may be because it has emerged in duplicate. Two writers fit its profile: James Dickey and Joseph Heller. How they differ, however, is both more interesting and more suggestive of the cultural imperatives that distinguish Southern Gentiles from Jewish Americans. Such contrasts may provide important evidence of the recalcitrance and resilience of Jewish identity, highlighted against the most historically intolerant part of American society.

Dickey's poetry exerts its power through its descriptiveness. For him the poet is above all an observer, "someone who notices and is enormously taken by things that somebody else would walk by." Although Dickey himself was born in Atlanta, rather than in the countryside, he believes that the best Southern verse has been inspired not by its people but by its landscape. Therefore, the supreme subject for the contemporary poet, he argues, is "dying nature," because "the animals are going, the trees are going, the flowers are going, everything is going." That is the fear with which he imbues the character of Lewis in *Deliverance* (1970). Dickey's only novel taps a sense of the disappearance of the natural order before the inexorable intrusion of industrial "progress." Of course the tale also certifies the achievement of manhood in the wilderness, which imposes tests of courage that contemporary society ordinarily forsakes. Its setting is nature rather than society, its characters are men without women, and it is streaked with violence. That is why one critic shrewdly observed that Dickey has composed the kind of book Norman Mailer has tried in vain to write—the ultimate WASP novel, the fiction of Esau. It also might be added that, although right-wing political views have been attributed to Dickey, he denies harboring such opinions and insists that he holds no explicit political stance whatsoever.[1]

The contrast with Heller is illuminating. For he admits that he cannot write descriptive passages in his novels, that the detailed observation of the environment is outside his range. Unlike Dickey, Heller writes no poetry and lacks a lyrical gift. Instead his novels are thick with psychological nuance and convolution, which are often endowed with a comic twist lacking in Dickey's work. The milieu of Heller's fiction is urban (he was born in Brooklyn), or bureaucratic, or both. Oddly enough, he claims that he cannot write a novel until an opening sentence occurs to him, which gives added significance to what was initially intended to be the opening of *Something Happened*: "In the office in which I work, there are four people of whom I am afraid. Each of these four people is afraid of five people." That passage became the opening of the second section of the novel, whose final draft began as follows: "I get the willies when I see closed doors." The stance of the novels therefore is one of radical alienation. It is not implausible to believe that Heller had himself in mind when, in *Catch-22* (1961), the psychiatrist, Major Sanderson, tells John Yossarian: "You have a morbid aversion to dying.... And you don't like bigots, bullies, snobs or hypocrites. ... You're antagonistic to the idea of being exploited, degraded, humiliated or deceived."[2] In the original draft of Heller's most celebrated novel, the protagonist was a Jew, but became an Assyrian American in the final version—even as the protagonist of Philip Roth's *The Great American Novel*, "the greatest rookie of all time," is Gil Gamesh, a Babylonian and another exotic outsider. The human virtue that is most problematic in *Catch-22* is not courage but justice, and what matters to its hero is not the capacity to kill but the struggle to avoid being killed. Although *Catch-22* is a war novel, it reveals no interest in bravery.

Here some generalizations may be introduced. Southern whites often have been initiated into manhood through the ritual of the hunt, and from the earliest regional writers through Faulkner, the bear hunt has symbolized the passage into adulthood. (This theme was ludicrously misappropriated in Mailer's last attempt at the WASP novel, *Why are We in Vietnam?* [1967]). By contrast Jews historically have felt an aversion for such sport and have experienced little fondness for hound dogs going into a frenzy. Coursing through the works of many Jewish writers of the twentieth century, from Kafka through Heller, is the persistent sense of being hunted, beleaguered, vulnerable.

The Southerner typically has lived on farms or in small towns and has been deeply attached to the soil and to his roots. His sense of place and locale has seemed almost visceral, and his association with the land has formed bonds that other Americans undoubtedly find eccentric. A "mournful, discommoded, fundamentally displaced tone . . . came to Southerners when they moved even from their own small town to the next," Mailer has noticed. "No one suffered so much as Southerners with uprooting."[3] So aware have Southern writers been of their setting that such knowledge can become intrusive. For instance, in William Styron's *The Confessions of Nat Turner* (1967), lush descriptions of the land and the climate are provided by the narrator, whose historical model—the real Nat Turner—surely would have had much else to worry about.

By contrast the Jews have been primarily an urban people, even in Russia's Pale of Settlement at the end of the nineteenth century. Long prohibited from owning land, they became accustomed to being walkers—and talkers—in the city. Long despised as pariahs, they experienced fully the meaning of displacement. Observation of the natural world, its trees and flowers, animals and birds, has been rarely recorded by Jewish writers. Notice the mistake that even Isaac Bashevis Singer made when, in being introduced to a Poe scholar at the University of Buffalo, he gushingly hailed Poe as "a genius. . . . but the poem about the crow is overrated." As for those small towns from which Southerners hated to be detached, Gertrude Stein for once can be taken as representative of many other Jews when she remarked of such hamlets: "When you go there, there is no there there." Even in the modern South outside of Florida, about two-thirds of all Jews live in cities whose population is greater than 250,000. Ironically enough the Jewish experience of exile and estrangement, their habituation in cities and therefore early confrontation with modernity may today make them less disoriented in the region than natives. John Bickerson "Binx" Bolling, the New Orleans stockbroker of Walker Percy's National Book Award-winning *The Moviegoer*, asserts: "I am more Jewish than the Jews I know. They are more at home than I am. I accept my exile."[4] But for most Jews, at least until recently, the paradigm of their experience has been not brotherhood but "otherhood," often in the South itself.

Both Southerners and Jews have been haunted by the past and burdened by their histories. They have sensed that they were somehow special, different. But the lessons that they have absorbed from the past have been quite different. William Faulkner's resonant reverie bears quotation: "For every Southern boy fourteen years old, not once but whenever he wants it, there is the instant when it's still not two o'clock on that July afternoon in 1863, the brigades are in position behind the rail fence, the guns are laid and ready in the woods, and the furled flags are already loosened to break out and Pickett himself [is] . . . is waiting for Longstreet to give the word and it's all in the balance, it hasn't happened yet."[5] Here then are the contours of a community, sealed in warfare, in defeat, in cussedness, in fantasy. The special moment of the Jews has not been military, but moral. Their history stretches back ever so sinuously and mysteriously, at least as far back as the giving of the law on Mount Sinai, where, according to Midrashic legend, all Jews—past, present, future—were present. Here the destiny of a people was forged that had promised to live according to the yoke of ethical monotheism, chosen to assume special moral responsibilities, to be a kingdom of priests and a holy people. Its demands—and its memories—are therefore quite distinctive, and quite long. "I have been a Jew for four thousand years," Rabbi Stephen S. Wise wrote in 1939. "I have been an American for sixty-four years."[6]

Perhaps even more than other Americans, Southerners regarded positive law as an impediment. The historian Daniel J. Boorstin, born in Atlanta, where his father had been involved in the defense of Leo Frank, has stressed the fidelity of the gentlemen of the Old South to the code duello.[7] For these children of pride, conflicts were to be resolved on the field of honor, not in a court of law. The only equality that many white Southerners have been inclined to affirm was supplied by Colonel Colt, and the character ideal they tried to emulate was emotional rather than rational. That character could become something explosive and dangerous, rich in red-clay craziness. The tradition that emerged was so immoderate that only the violent bear it away. Southerners have long acknowledged their bellicosity, and circulated a story about former Confederate General Robert Toombs, rushing to the telegraph office to hear the news of the great Chicago fire of 1871. Toombs passed on to his fellow Georgians the report that the city was taking all possible protective measures to prevent the spread of the flames and then added: "But the wind is in our favor." When Willie Morris of Yazoo, Mississippi, came to New York to find a job among the city's publishers and editors, expecting to tell them that Willie Boy is here, he was treated with such indifference and condescension by Jason Epstein at Random House that Morris began to get angry: "A slow Mississippi boil was beginning to rise north from my guts, a physical presence that had always warned me . . . to beware of my heritage of violence, bloodshed, and spur-of-the-moment mayhem." But Morris resisted the impulse to hurl "this little man out of a second-story window into a courtyard." Even the journalist Robert Sherrill, born in Frogtown, Georgia (which no longer exists), could doubt, after brilliantly indicting the national cult of guns, whether reform is possible. For even in himself he conceded that "those genes that came over to supply labor for Oglethorpe's debtor colony keep responding the wrong way." During a literary quarrel in the late 1940s, the poet Allen Tate, author of "Ode to the Confederate Dead," challenged an editor of *Partisan Review* to a duel.[8] That is, in part, how Southerners have defined themselves.

Here again the contrast with Jewish values is striking. Whatever the requirements of realpolitik, within which the state of Israel has felt constrained to operate for its survival, the ideal of *shalom*, of peace, has remained the essence of Jewish aspiration. Antagonism to military values, which are part of European Jewish folklore, made the passage to the New World as well. One example is Irving Berlin's "Good Bye Becky Cohen," popular on the old East Side. When Becky's boyfriend goes off to war, she replies: "What, fight for nothing / where's the percentage in that? / No, you better mind your store / let McCarthy go to war."[9] Civilian life has been far preferable; and for the sake of prudence, the Jews generally have avoided heroism. Lionel Trilling observed that "the Rabbis, in speaking of virtue, never mention the virtue of courage, which Aristotle regarded as basic to the heroic character. The indifference of the Rabbis to the idea of courage is the more remarkable in that they knew that many of their number would die for their faith." Perhaps no other ethnic group would tell a joke about itself or find its truth so piercing, as in the tale of the two Jews lined up against the wall to be shot. When one of them demands from the leader of the firing squad a final cigarette, the other Jew whispers to him: "Shhh, don't make trouble." Here is no ideal of unreconstructed ferocity, no cult of violent response to adversity or authority. After slapping and kicking an American soldier in a military hospital in Sicily in 1943, General George S. Patton, a Virginian, announced: "There's no such thing as shell shock. It's an invention of the Jews."[10]

Because the Southern character ideal has been emotional, Ellen Glasgow could write of the protagonist of her novel *Virginia*: "She was capable of dying for an idea, but not of conceiving one." Yet the region had not always been H. L. Mencken's Sahara of the bozart, and most of the political ideas that sparked the American Revolution and the subsequent creation of the republic had been formulated in Glasgow's own state of Virginia. (Indeed President Kennedy once engaged in justifiable hyperbole when, in welcoming America's Nobel Prize winners to the White House, he lauded "the most extraordinary collection of talent, of human knowledge, that has ever gathered together at the White House, with the possible exception of when Thomas Jefferson dined alone.") Nevertheless the intellectual power of the Old South waned quickly enough, and has never been replenished. Henry Adams generalized boldly from his association at Harvard College with the son of Robert E. Lee: "The Southerner had no mind; he had temperament. He was not a scholar: he had no intellectual training, he could not analyze an idea, and he could not even conceive of admitting two."[11] Particularly in our century many very talented writers have resisted the temptation to live and die in Dixie. One of the problems in defining who Southern writers are is their inclination in many cases to leave the region. The anabasis (going North) of Styron, Thomas Wolfe, Tom Wolfe, Stark Young, Joseph Wood Krutch, James Agee, Robert Penn Warren, Carson McCullers, Truman Capote, C. Vann Woodward, and others, including major black writers, has long threatened to lend credence to the American intellectuals' riddle:

What is the difference between the South and yogurt: Answer: Yogurt has an active culture. Even today Robert Penn Warren's home county in Kentucky lacks a public library and bookmobile.[12]

The Jewish character ideal has stressed self-control rather than the expression of instinct; it has promoted self-discipline rather than spontaneity of emotion. Moderation, discretion, continence, and even resignation were supposed to be the way one responded to the bad luck which, as the proverb went, could always find a Jew. And beginning with Spinoza, who invested thought with moral passion and who bore a most ambiguous relationship to his "coreligionists," the contribution of the Jews to Western civilization in the modern era is far out of proportion to their numbers. This phenomenon needs no embroidery here. But as Pasternak's Lara says to Dr. Zhivago, "If you do intellectual work of any kind and live in a town as we do, half of your friends are bound to be Jews." Such circumstances have their equivalents in the United States as well. "There wouldn't be any active American culture now without the Jewish element," Robert Lowell commented in 1964. "They are small in numbers, but they're a leaven that changes the whole intellectual world of America. It's a painful reality that a minority should have such liveliness and vigor. You're sort of at a loss why the rest of the country doesn't equal that."[13] What has been bequeathed to America's Jews is a tradition whose rationalism and skepticism, whose critical intensity and creative dissidence cannot easily be squared with what Southerners find most compelling and most vivid in their own heritage.

Differences in literary expression have escaped the attention of all but a couple of critics. One of the few scholars who has attempted to assess, however briefly, the divergent paths of Southern and Jewish writers is one who is both, Louis D. Rubin. University Distinguished Professor of English at Chapel Hill, Rubin has noted that both Southerners and Jews are "ancestor-conscious." They are "strong on familial ties, and not thoroughly assimilated into the mainstream of modern American life." Yet Rubin added that the central character in the typical American Jewish novel "accepts the practical conditions and values of the dominant culture, which is . . . largely Protestant . . . But at the same time he feels a bit uneasy in it, cannot quite make entire sense of it, and so refuses to be engulfed in and fully defined by it." Rubin's view is echoed by

Irving Howe, the author of a fairly early and enthusiastic study of Faulkner, although better known as the elegiast of the *World of Our Fathers* (1976). The Southerner, Howe argues, has of course been a Christian, and therefore the condition of being an outsider is "a partial and temporary one, by now almost at an end." The Jew, however, cannot escape entirely the sense of distinctiveness, which historical memory has imposed, no matter how decisively religion has gone into eclipse and no matter how fully Western civilization has become secularized. The vestigial claims of the past are too powerful, Howe has insisted, implying that some spirit of estrangement is inevitable for the Jewish writer.[14] The poet Delmore Schwartz tried to rebut the critical claim that he was trying to be a second T. S. Eliot by arguing that Eliot could not have been "motivated by the alienation which only a Jew can suffer, and use, as a cripple uses his weakness in order to beg."[15] Reuben Warshovsky, the character of the New York labor organizer played by Ron Liebman in the film *Norma Rae* (1979), is more gnomic. An intruder in the dust, he is the first Jew that the eponymous Carolina textile worker played by Sally Field has ever seen. As they become friends, she wonders what makes the Jews different, since they don't *seem* to be. Warshovsky, her political and cultural Pygmalion, replies: "History."

That experience is something that, paradoxically, Southern whites and blacks have in common. When Willie Morris settled in New York and was appointed editor of *Harper's*, he discovered less of a bond with New York's predominantly Jewish literati than with certain black writers, such as Ralph Ellison and Albert Murray. Although Morris had been born and raised in a segregated town, they "shared the same easy-going conversation; the casual talk and the telling of stories, in the Southern verbal jam-session way; the sense of family and the past and people out of the past; the congenial social manner and the mischievous laughter." Morris added to this list a common "love of the American language in its accuracy and vividness and simplicity; the obsession with the sensual experience of America in all its extravagance and diversity; the love of animals and sports, of the outdoors and sour mash; the distrust . . . of certain manifestations of Eastern intellectualism." In the extensive writing of American Jews, it is impossible to find any nostalgia for the meal that the Morrises, the Ellisons, and the Murrays enjoyed one New

Year's Day in Harlem: collard greens, ham hocks, black-eyed peas, corn bread and bourbon.[16]

Morris does not mention the Christian origins they shared, but that too should be remarked upon, if only in passing. Gentile attitudes toward Jews historically have been shaped by religious doctrines. It should not be too surprising that Southern Baptists whom sociologists interviewed in California for the Anti-Defamation League in the early 1960s were more likely than members of any other denomination to believe that no salvation outside of Jesus is possible. Only conversion to Christianity therefore could avoid the danger of damnation; and Eli Evans, a Southern Jew who also made the trek north, has recalled how widespread was the Southern Jewish anticipation of meeting proselytizers sincerely anxious to save souls.[17] In the United States today, it is not often realized that about a quarter of all evangelicals are black, although the impact of Protestantism on the black imagination is a staple of historical and sociological discourse.

Yet even though the South is often depicted as a God-intoxicated region, very few traces of religiously inspired anti-Semitism can be found in its literature. Carson McCullers's *Ballad of the Sad Cafe* (1943) is hardly to be read as a tale of realistic exactitude, but it is set in a Southern mill town where "the soul rots with boredom." There the grotesques and freaks who inhabit the village have taken delight in harassing one Morris Finestein, "a quick, skipping little Jew who cried if you called him Christkiller, and ate light bread and canned salmon every day." Finestein had departed after a calamity but ever since, "if a man were prissy in any way, or if a man ever wept, he was known as a Morris Finestein." The author's detestation of such cruelty is clear enough, however, even out of context.[18] When Richard Wright was growing up in Elaine, Arkansas, the first Jew he ever saw was the proprietor of a grocery store, just as the grocery store that the Wingfields patronize in Tennessee Williams's *Glass Menagerie* (1945) is Garfinkel's. But in Wright's autobiography he recorded the hostility that was triggered: "All of us black people who lived in the neighborhood hated Jews, not because they exploited us, but because we had been taught at home and in Sunday School that Jews were 'Christ killers.' " Although Wright believed that such hatred "was bred in us from childhood ... it was part of our cultural heritage," no empirical evidence has yet sustained the view that such anti-Semitism was rampant among Southern blacks—or among whites either.[19]

A comparison with blacks further documents how much more deeply the spirit of alienation has sunk among Jews than among Southerners. Stripped of all but the residue of their African origins, they became native sons. Their resilience, inventiveness, and adaptability have been exhibited within one culture, and blacks have often asked only to be included in a society that would grant them equality and dignity. Names are a giveaway. When Booker T. Washington, having been born in slavery, went to public school for the first time, he did not know that he had a surname. So he bestowed on himself that of the father of his country, even though the first president had been a slaveholder. When historian John Hope Franklin's grandfather, a runaway slave, got north, he assumed the surname of Benjamin Franklin, among the most conservative of the founders.[20] And Ellison was named Ralph Waldo, in honor of the poet who is far better known for his sagacity than for his subversiveness.

The Jews generally have identified more closely with Americans who represented either dissidence or a fuller expression of the democratic experiment. One immigrant family, the Rostows, named their sons after Walt Whitman and Eugene V. Debs (which is why the radio station of the *Jewish Daily Forward* in New York was called WEVD). The eminent explicator of Puritanism and translator of Yiddish literature, Sacvan Bercovitch, was named after Sacco and Vanzetti. When little Alexander Portnoy is asked which Americans in history he most admires, he replies: Thomas Paine and Abraham Lincoln (not Franklin or Washington). The status of the outsider sometimes still clings to the Jew. Even though the New Orleans philanthropist Judah Touro subscribed half of the funds to erect the Bunker Hill monument, even though the Levy family rescued Monticello from ruin a century ago, the sense of Jews as not quite belonging is illustrated in F. Scott Fitzgerald's *Last Tycoon* (1941). Narrated by a movie producer's daughter, Celia Brady, the novel opens in Nashville, which is visited by a Jew who is also in the movie business: "He had come a long way from some ghetto to present himself at that raw shrine. Manny Schwartz and Andrew Jackson—it was hard to say them in the same sentence."[21] A friend of mine, a graduate student from Chicago who was recently en route to do research on antebellum Southern Protestantism, went

into a store in Montreat, North Carolina. He was almost immediately asked: "Are you Jewish?" My friend was a little taken aback,
wondering if he'd indeed run into a coreligionist, and replied: "Yes,
are you?" There was a pause, and then the manager replied: "No,
I'm an American." There, on native grounds, the manager probably
would not have said that to a black, who could not have been
perceived as a stranger in the same way.

Part of the difference may well be, in literary terms, noticeable
through language, as Willie Morris has written. Already at Tuskegee
in the 1930s, with the area aflame with the scandal of the Scottsboro
trial, Ellison was absorbed in Faulkner's prose. It is no secret that
Southerners long have prided themselves on their rhetorical skills,
on their flair for oratory and indeed orotundity. (Visiting New
Orleans in 1960, the New York journalist Adolph Joseph Liebling
attempted to get outside the W. J. Cash nexus by remarking that
the 1941 classic should have been entitled "The Mouth of the South.")
Southern writers often have considered themselves the legatees of
Shakespeare's ripeness and of the stateliness of the King James version. Katherine Anne Porter, who was born in Texas and raised in
Louisiana, once insisted: "We are in the direct, legitimate line, we
are people based in English as our mother tongue, and we do not
abuse it or misuse it, and when we speak a word, we know what
it means. These others," she commented, without naming names,
"have fallen into a curious kind of argot, more or less originating
in New York, a deadly mixture of academic, guttersnipe, gangster,
fake-Yiddish, and dull old wornout dirty words—an appalling
bankruptcy in language, as if they hate English and are trying to
destroy it along with all other living things they touch."[22] Class
dismissed. But she also showed prescience, since *Portnoy's Complaint* was not to be published until four years later. Porter's sensibility, with its stress on historical fidelity and normative elegance,
could not accommodate the kind of writing that has by now quick-
ened the beat of the American idiom, enlarging its possibilities for
paradox and incongruity and irony. Our national tongue is not only
more salty but also more expressive and more resourceful, for that
"fake-Yiddish" has put a spin on our vernacular and sent it hopping
into those realms of fiction where the language renews itself.

That is probably why the success of the Southern literary renascence has yielded, in the opinion of many observers, to Jewish

writing. "The most dramatic change in the American literary situation," Styron remarked in 1971, "has been the efflorescence of
Jewish writers in all fields ... There have been occasions when
upon reading an issue of the *New York Times Book Review* I have
gained the impression that *all* the new and interesting novelists were
Jews." He added that the cause has undoubtedly been in part a
result of "the shift in America from the pastoral, small-town life
style to the urban equivalent with its weird and singular frights and
tensions. They in turn comprise such a setup for the Jewish sensibility: that comic awareness so exquisitely poised between hilarity
and anguish which seems the perfect literary foil for the monstrous-
ness of life in the big cities."[23]

Such observations have become commonplace, but some qualifications are surely in order. One is that "schools" are categories
that include the very talented and the less so, those who demonstrate
their membership in the pantheon of art and those who are simply
gate-crashers. Moreover it is too easy to exaggerate the luster of
earlier Southern fiction and poetry. In the Gutenberg galaxy that
includes American literature in this century, Faulkner is the only
supernova, the only one to light up the sky over Stockholm. As
the sole owner and proprietor of Yoknapatawpha County, he alone
belongs to the world, having managed to leave behind an oeuvre
that does not betray the highest expectations and consolations of
art. If, among the nineteenth-century figures, Poe and Twain are
not included in the classification of Southern writers, then even the
term *renascence* is something of a misnomer, for similar literary
power was not exhibited by those few authors still remembered
today, such as George Washington Cable, a liberal who went into
Northern exile; Kate Chopin, only recently rediscovered because
of one slender but moving tale; and O. Henry, whose name is
preserved—in an increasingly analphabetic age—as a candy bar.
These are not major writers, even though they may be superior to
other regions' literary figures. It is also entirely false to assume that
Southern literature is burned out, although some of its earlier stars—
most notably Thomas Wolfe—now appear much less luminous.

The same warnings apply to any critical judgments of Jewish
writers. They form even less of a cohesive school, and are even
more various, than Southerners. To try to find similarities between
those Saul Bellow has nicknamed the Hart, Schaffner and Marx of

Jewish letters (himself, Bernard Malamud, and Philip Roth) and such disparate writers of Jewish birth as Gertrude Stein, Susan Sontag, Chaim Potok, S. J. Perelman, Tillie Olsen, Paul Goodman, and Alan Friedman—to say nothing of such half-Jews as J. D. Salinger and Dorothy Parker, or of Isaac Bashevis Singer, the only American winner of the Nobel Prize for literature whose books have to be translated *into* English—is to realize that here is no monolithic group, no kosher nostra. No Faulkner has emerged among them as preeminent, as authoritative enough to generate the anxiety of influence.

If they share a primary topic of interest at all, which is doubtful, it may well be the family romance. For many of them have understood that the family has been the secret of cultural transmission, the Jewish double helix that codifies and replicates the historic destiny of an ancient people. At least until the recent phase of the history of American Jews, their English may have been broken, but their homes were not. The family romance, with all the loyalty that it engendered and all the rage that it stirred, has been so pervasive and irresistible a theme that Roth's utterly unpleasant academic poet, Ralph Baumgarten, perversely refuses to write about his family. "Can you actually get worked up over another son and another daughter and another mother and another father driving each other nuts?" he asks David Kepesh, Roth's "professor of desire." "All that loving; all that hating; all those meals. And don't forget the *menschlichkeit*. And the baffled quest for dignity. Oh, and the goodness . . . I understand somebody has just published a whole book on our Jewish literature of goodness"—perhaps an allusion to the dissertation Josephine Z. Knopp published on *The Trial of Judaism in Contemporary Jewish Writing* (1975). Baumgarten continues, ever so slyly: "I expect any day to read . . . an article by some good old boy from Vanderbilt on hospitality in the Southern novel: 'Make Yourself at Home: The Theme of Hospitality in Faulkner's "A Rose for Emily." ' "[24] Few Jewish writers seem to have followed Baumgarten's example, since such themes are virtually the only story most of them know. Yet Irving Howe has identified only one masterpiece so far on the shelves of American Jewish novels: Henry Roth's dissection of an immigrant family, *Call It Sleep* (1934).[25] Such a judgment, while probably erring on the side of severity, nevertheless provides a useful corrective to the praise that has been showered on talents that are assumed to be formidable because they were burnished in Flatbush or in the Delta, where such writers presumably got a contact high from proximity to serious artists.

Why these two literatures became so pertinent has not been examined in any systematic way. Howe has argued that both have emerged when the doom of the cultures they described had already been sealed. Only when the power of a culture has evaporated, he speculates, can it be understood adequately to be transmuted into art. For "such a moment of high self-consciousness offers writers the advantages of an inescapable subject: the judgement, affection and hatred they bring to bear upon the remembered world of their youth, and the costs exacted by their struggle to tear themselves away." Thus the critic and storyteller Isaac Rosenfeld could assert that Faulkner's best work was not written "about the South, but *over* it, over its dead body, in a moment of complete triumph."[26] Such an interpretation would not apply to *The White Rose of Memphis*, written by his great-grandfather, Colonel William Falkner.

Yet this formulation, although it has merit, is not entirely satisfactory. In modern times, it often has been observed, the only constant is change, and yet every age of transition does not produce literature of permanent excellence. The Old South also died, and yet the pebbles thrown on its grave could not be transformed into radiant and enduring literature. Certainly some of the best Southern literati, such as Faulkner, Warren, and Tate, have been endowed with a historical consciousness. Their work has civic spirit, which does not mean that it produced larger voter turnouts but that it made meaningful connections between private experience and communal pressures. Yet others who contributed to the distinction associated with Southern literary life have lacked that sense of a disintegrating culture. These would include not only several women but also Agee and Wolfe, who are not strictly speaking regionalists at all and who may therefore be regarded as lapsed Southerners.

The Jewish authors are likewise so varied that Howe's generalization cannot possibly embrace them all, unless the sense of an ending itself is what defines the Jewish writer. Some of them can scarcely be connected to the Eastern Europe from which most American Jews have stemmed; many have only the faintest inkling of the religious texture of Judaism; many do not write about the

Jewish condition at all. For virtually all modern intellectuals, God is an imaginary character whose absence is occasionally missed. The relationship of its intellectuals to a people historically defined by its ethical monotheism is therefore problematic, and may well instigate the formulation of an artistic response. It is curious, however, that earlier beliefs in the imminent end of the Jewish religion or people did not stimulate the release of comparable literary expressiveness. "There was hardly a generation in the Diaspora period which did not consider itself the final link in Israel's chain," one Judaic scholar has written in an essay ironically entitled "Israel, the Ever-Dying People." For "each generation grieved not only for itself but also for the great past which was going to disappear forever, as well as for the future of unborn generations who would never see the light of day."[27] Yet despite the continual fears that the vital signs of group life were flickering, only since the Second World War have Jewish writers conspicuously emerged to confront what supposedly remained of a once-vibrant culture. Howe's conjecture does not account for the particular moment in which the ambivalence of postreligious Jews shaped itself into literature worthy of attracting national attention.

Moreover the impact of a dying tradition should have encouraged the literature of Southern Jews, in whom the twentieth-century experience of dislocation and disinheritance should have been compounded. The disjunctions and incongruities in being both Southern and Jewish ought to have created many more serious writers than in fact can be identified. The conflicting values and incompatible ideals that could not be logically resolved might at least have been artistically formulated. This has not yet occurred.

Yet out of such dissonance literature is supposed to flourish. Southerners and Jews are supposed to be intoxicated with words, and yet few Southern Jews have quarreled enough within themselves to create imaginative literature of incontrovertible value. They have been largely silent. To be sure the first book of verse published by a Jew in the United States was *Fancy's Sketch Book* (1833), by Penina Moise of Charleston. But she may be more interesting for being first, the Jewish equivalent of Anne Bradstreet or Phyllis Wheatley; and those familiar with her work concede that she was not blessed with poetic gifts.[28] She is omitted from the *Bibliographic Guide to the Study of Southern Literature*, whose only writer of Jewish origin is Lillian Hellman of New Orleans, of whom more later. There has been an occasional undistinguished novel (Ronald Bern's *The Legacy*) and play (Gus Weill's *To Bury a Cousin*), in which good intentions outstrip the capacity to create vibrancy and complexity. There have been historical novels about Southern Jews, such as Judah P. Benjamin (*Gray Fox*) and Leo Frank (*Member of the Tribe*)—but these were not written *by* Southern Jews. There have been minor Jewish novelists raised in the South, such as Ludwig Lewisohn, but his work was mostly apologetic and apodictic. There have been intellectuals born or raised in the South—journalists, historians, sociologists. But with some very recent exceptions— Rubin's *Surfaces of a Diamond*, Roy Hoffman's *Almost Family*, Ellen Monsky's *Midnight Suppers*—they have not composed novels. Like Sebastian Venable in *Suddenly Last Summer*, who every summer went away to compose his summer poem, Southern Jews have not been productive writers.

Such silence merits reflection. Perhaps so many Jews have been busy minding the store that they could not contribute to the mind of the South. The rule that writing is a full-time occupation allows for only a few exceptions; it is too exorbitant in its demands to allow much room for maneuver. Nevertheless what is odd is that the class of businessmen and storekeepers produced so few offspring with creative and intellectual gifts, although this was the class that produced a vibrant Jewish intelligentsia in Europe and often in the North. Nor is demography an absolute impediment, for sometimes a distinctively minority community can blossom with literature of international importance. The Protestant middle class of Dublin, for instance, produced Shaw, Wilde, Yeats, and Beckett; and either by birth or through conversion, Catholicism has attracted Walker Percy, Allen Tate, and Flannery O'Connor, even though few Southerners subscribe to that faith.

It even would be possible to argue that the Jewish community in the South has produced enough fascinating, striking, conspicuous, and even exotic characters to serve as incentives to the imagination. Perhaps none has been as strange as Two-Gun Cohen, who was the bodyguard of Sun Yat-sen. But consider the doctors (for example the surgeon general of the Confederacy; or the father of Bernard Baruch, who rode with the Ku Klux Klan), lawyers (such as Judah P. Benjamin, with his reputation for Levantine guile and his patina of mystery, as well as his proximity to Jefferson Davis), and Indian chiefs (such as Al Rosen, from Spartanburg, South Carolina, the former Cleveland third baseman who became the team's general manager). The first Jew to hold elective office in American history, perhaps even in the modern world, was Francis Salvador, who served in the first and second South Carolina provincial congresses before he was scalped by Indians. The first movie cowboy, the star of *The Great Train Robbery*, and therefore the antecedent of Tom Mix and Hopalong Cassidy and John Wayne, was "Bronco Billy," a pseudonym for Gilbert Anderson, *né* Max Aronson, born and raised in Little Rock, Arkansas. Even stranger was Marx E. Lazarus, a mystic, an abolitionist, a vegetarian, and a utopian who joined the Alcotts' Brook Farm. He was "probably the first Jewish socialist in the history of the United States," according to Lewis Feuer, although Lazarus later served as a Confederate Army private before dying in obscurity. Here surely is the stuff of fiction, although perhaps not realistic fiction (since few readers would believe it). And yet Southern Jews remain in the missing persons bureau of the republic of letters, although they belong to a heritage that provoked Mordecai Richler's father—a scrap dealer—to ask, when the Canadian's first novel was about to be published: "Is it about Jews or about ordinary people?"[29]

But if any important writer of Southern Jewish background has emerged, it is Lillian Hellman. She was born in New Orleans in 1905, where her paternal grandparents had come during the German immigration of the 1840s. Her mother, Julia Newhouse, had been born in Demopolis, Alabama, to a family of bankers and storekeepers. From the age of six until the age of sixteen, she resided and attended public schools in both New York City and New Orleans, where she did not stay. Beginning in the 1930s came a series of theatrical successes, including *The Children's Hour* (1934); *Days to Come* (1936); *The Little Foxes* (1939); *Watch on the Rhine* (1941), which won the Drama Critics' Circle Award; and *Another Part of the Forest* (1946). Hellman is undoubtedly the most distinguished female playwright ever to live in America—although such praise may appear faint, upon reflection.

Although she is also the only literary figure of Jewish birth canonized in the *Encyclopedia of Southern History*, Hellman's career testifies to the elusiveness of such designations. She cannot be categorized convincingly as a regionalist, or as a recorder of Jewish life there or elsewhere. In reviewing the most informative study of Southern Jewry ever written, Eli Evans's *The Provincials* (1973), Hellman doubted whether "there ever was a 'South' even during the artificial confederation of states to fight the Civil War." Similarly she asserted that "Jews are as unalike as most other people, only, as somebody else said, more so."[30] She is not beguiled by the vicissitudes of either Southern or Jewish history, and she does not write directly about Jews.

When asked whether the rapacious Hubbards of *The Little Foxes* and *Another Part of the Forest* were based on anyone she had known, Hellman once cryptically replied: "Lots of people thought it was my mother's family." Later, as her autobiographical volumes were published, the mask was peeled off. When she remembers hocking the ring that her uncle Jake had given her for graduation and then reporting to him what she had done, he replied: "So you've got the spirit after all. Most of the rest of them are made of sugar water." The lines reappear in *The Little Foxes*. Hellman admits to experiencing greater difficulty with writing that play than any of her others, because it "had a distant connection to my mother's family and everything that I had heard or seen or imagined had formed a giant tangled time-jungle in which I could find no space to walk without tripping over old roots." For she herself had remembered the Sunday dinners with her mother's family, "with high-spirited talk and laughter from the older people of who did what to whom, what good nigger had consented to thirty percent interest on his cotton crop and what bad nigger had made a timid protest, what new white partner had been outwitted, what benefits the year had brought from the Southern business interests they had left behind for the Northern profits they had sense enough to move toward." Given such ugliness it is understandable that she underwent conflicts with her mother's family that were not successfully resolved until *The Little Foxes* was written.[31] The Hubbards, although they are given names like Ben and Leo, do not in any way betray an ethnic identity, which must have produced a purr of satisfaction from the defense organizations fighting against bigotry.

Gratifying though such obfuscation may be, Hellman's sensibility allowed little place for speculation upon the mystery or history of the Jews. Members of her family were quite assimilated and unaffected by their ethnic origins, and seem to have exempted themselves from religious observance or belief. Such indifference made them typical of many Southern—and American—Jews. Her immediate social world was Jewish, as was her husband Arthur Kober, who was once admired for his comic Jewish dialect tales. But Hellman herself has lacked explicit interest in the Jewish people, with whose fate she has not directly associated herself. Even after visiting the Maidanek camp after the Red Army had liberated it, Hellman did not bother to mention that the overwhelming majority of the victims were Jews.[32]

She went to some length to evade confrontation with the deeper recesses of Jewish history and destiny. Her appearance before the House Committee on Un-American Activities resonated with her gallant statement that she would refuse to cut her conscience to fit that year's fashions. It has been less noticed that she did not make the customary invocations to the Judeo-Christian tradition, but instead announced that she respected and had tried to abide by the "ideals of Christian honor" alone. These included truthfulness and the refusal to bear false witness (which, if memory serves, were first promulgated on Mount Sinai), the prohibition "not to harm my neighbor" (compare with Lev. 19:18), and loyalty to her country (which, despite all evidence to the contrary, she has not deemed inconsistent with support for Alger Hiss).[33]

Scoundrel Time (1976) more fully reveals how poorly she fits into the category of Southern or even Jewish writer. The region hardly has been, for American radicalism, a burned-over district and only a small fraction of American Jews have been radicals. Yet Hellman, without ever quite boarding the Dixie Special, still purchased a one-way ticket on that train to the Finland Station. For her memoir is far harsher on Americans who opposed communism, often foolishly and crudely and spitefully, than it is on the Stalinist system that consigned nameless millions to their deaths in the Gulag Archipelago. Soviet terror claimed more lives than did the Holocaust. Yet *Scoundrel Time* prefers to criticize those who cooperated with the McCarthyites, such as "the children of timid immigrants," who, for all their admirable industriousness, intelligence and energy, "often . . . make it so good that they are determined to keep it at any cost."[34]

Hellman makes no attempt to demonstrate the validity of such a generalization, which is in fact quite unpersuasive. Eight of the "Unfriendly 10" were from such a background, as were other uncooperative witnesses such as her fellow playwright, Arthur Miller. Among the most cooperative Hollywood witnesses, on the other hand, were Gary Cooper, Ronald Reagan, and Robert Taylor. Nor does Hellman identify herself with the Jewish spirit of dissidence, which she might have praised, averring instead that "whatever is wrong with white Southerners—redneck or better—we were all brought up to believe we had a right to think as we pleased, go our own, possibly strange ways."[35] Such amazing disregard of the conformist pressures in Southern society—on race, the Lost Cause, labor unions, radicalism, and atheism—is downright bizarre, although it does reflect one way of resolving the possible tension between being Southern and being Jewish. Hellman's remarks indicate a certain pride in the region of her birth that she could not, or would not, summon for her Jewishness.

Other writers from the South rarely have treated Jewish life there or elsewhere, and have shown little effort to invent Jewish characters. In the canon of regional letters, there is no Robert Cohn or Meyer Wolfsheim or even Henry Bech, much less any characters conceived as indelibly as Fagin or Daniel Deronda or Leopold Bloom or Shylock or Monsieur Swann or Nathan the Wise. Mark Twain once blamed the Civil War, with its nimbus of romanticism, on Sir Walter Scott, but no Southern novelist followed Scott's example of drawing on Philadelphia's Rebecca Gratz for the model of *Ivanhoe*'s Rebecca. Demography alone cannot be held accountable. Jews have constituted a tiny fraction of the population of western and central Europe. And yet of the major figures in twentieth-century fiction, one (Kafka) was Jewish, and another (Proust) was half Jewish. Three others (Virginia Woolf, Thomas Mann, and Vladimir Nabokov) were married to Jews. Not only does the most important novel of the century (*Ulysses*) make a Jewish character into Everyman, but Thomas Mann also located the Hebrews in modern literature in *Joseph and His Brothers*. Nor are other ethnics entirely absent from Southern literature, even though few Southern whites can trace their ancestry outside the British Isles and few are not Protestant. But figures such as the Irish-born father of Scarlett O'Hara, or Stanley Kowalski, or the deaf-mute Antonapoulos in *The Heart is a Lonely Hunter* are not easily forgotten.

The Jews who are mentioned in the literature of the region tend not to live there. Charleston's William Gilmore Simms set *Pelayo* (1838), a romance in which Jews are prominent, in eighth-century Spain.[36] In the fourth section of "The Bear" (1942), the Jew who has come to Yoknapatawpha is described as "solitary, without even the solidarity of the locusts and in this [there was] a sort of courage since he had come thinking not in terms of simple pillage but in terms of his great-grandchildren, seeking yet some place to establish them to endure even though forever alien." Here the Jew meets the moral standards Faulkner exalts above all others—the capacity to endure through perpetuation of the family and through valor. But no individual Jews are named or identified. In *The Sound and the Fury* Jason Compson is, besides his other faults, a bigot. But his targets are distant and also abstract—Eastern Jews. Individual Jews appear briefly in several of Faulkner's novels, however—in *Soldier's Pay* (1926), *Mosquitoes* (1927), *Sanctuary* (1930), *Pylon* (1935), *A Fable* (1954), and others. Alfred Kutzik, the closest reader of these books investigating the portrayals of such figures, has speculated that the unflattering portraits are a result of Faulkner's willingness to make the Jew "a symbol of the rapacity and inhumanity of modern industrial society. This is why . . . the only bosses and traveling salesmen and shyster lawyers in his writings are Jews."[37] But Jews are hardly prominent in Faulkner's fiction, which is characterized by a low estimate of the human estate itself, from which few are exempt.

The Southern writer who most often had the Jews on his mind was Thomas Wolfe, an author who had difficulty sundering his own attitudes from those of alter egos such as Eugene Gant and George Webber. This point is important because of the reputation for anti-Semitism that continues to hover over Wolfe's work. His agent, Elizabeth Nowell, claimed that he "had the villager's dread and dislike of urban Jews." Louis Rubin has added, rather defensively: "It was because there were Jews in the city, and not because he naturally and primarily hated Jews as such, that Wolfe wrote his so-called 'anti-Semitic' passages."[38] Wolfe's first novel, set in the South, partly bears this out. The Jews in *Look Homeward, Angel*, like the boarder in the Gant home or the owner of the grocery store down the street, are depicted in kindly, or at least not unsympathetic, terms. When Gant moves north, in *Of Time and the River*, the meditations on the Jews become more frequent; and some of the passages become unsavory. Is it because Jews are metropolitan that they are described, among the undergraduates Gant teaches in New York, as "all laughing, shouting, screaming, thick with their hot and swarthy body-smells, their strong female odors of rut and crotch and arm-pit and cheap perfume, and their hard male smells that were rancid, stale and sour"?[39]

Nevertheless such depictions easily can be countered with many others that are favorable and admiring, and whatever his discomfort in the city may have been, the Jewish East Side is made vivid as "the richest, most exciting, the most colorful [part of] New York he had ever seen." Gant becomes a close friend of one of his Jewish students, Abraham Jones, "a wonderfully good, rare, and high person"; and Jewish women are depicted as sexually desirable and enticing. In *The Web and the Rock*, posthumously published, Gant has become Webber, experiencing a tumultuous affair with Esther Jack, described as half German and half Jewish. This relationship is presumably modeled on Wolfe's own affair with the stage and costume designer Aline Bernstein, whom Wolfe referred to as "my Jew." Wolfe and his protagonists were certainly somewhat ambivalent about Jews; the antagonism is always qualified and often undercut by expressions of admiration and attraction. Perhaps the strongest case against Wolfe's anti-Semitic reputation was his response to nazism. Although his novels were very popular in Germany, he made clear before his death in 1938 his sympathies with the Jewish victims of barbarism, which he considered "the spiritual disease which was poisoning unto death a noble and mighty people."[40]

The shadow of German racism extended to the South as well, and some Southern writers acknowledged its moral repugnance. Flannery O'Connor mentions the Holocaust in one of her letters, claiming that she was "always haunted by the boxcars." She added, quite aptly, that "they were actually the least of it."[41] Katherine Anne Porter's only novel, *Ship of Fools* (1962), set on a German liner bound for Mexico in 1931, is not set in the South, but includes a Jewish character, a salesman of Catholic religious objects, who is already segregated from the "Aryan" passengers.

Two novels attempt to render more explicit some connection between the racial injustice that has scarred Southern history and the persecution that culminated in Nazi genocide. In Harper Lee's

Pulitzer Prize-winning *To Kill a Mockingbird* (1960), it is current-events time in the classroom of Miss Gates. She denounces the German government's undemocratic discrimination against the Jews, who "contribute to every society they live in, and most of all, they are a deeply religious people. Hitler's trying to do away with religion, so maybe he doesn't like them for that reason." Miss Gates cannot acknowledge that the Nazi motive might not be antireligious but "racial"; and sensitive Scout Finch realizes, however inarticulately, that Miss Gates, like other respectable whites in the town of Maycomb, Alabama, is a hypocrite. Scout's father Atticus, an attorney and a man of honor, cannot even listen to Hitler on the radio, and dismisses him as "a maniac." Only one set of Jews seems to be living in Maycomb, and the Levy family has been there for five generations. Atticus recalls that, about 1920, the local chapter of the Klan "paraded by Mr. Sam Levy's house one night, but Sam just stood on his porch and told 'em things had come to a pretty pass, he's sold 'em the very sheets on their backs. Sam made 'em so ashamed of themselves they went away." If only sardonic wit and the power to shame with such effectiveness had been employed more often in actual towns like Maycomb! In any event Atticus acknowledged that the Levy family "met all the criteria for being Fine Folks."[42] How vulnerable such families might have been to the canaille had they not met local standards of excellence, had they been "freethinkers," or had they tried to address black residents as social equals—these possibilities were unstated.

Like Eugene Gant, Stingo in William Styron's *Sophie's Choice* (1979) has to go north from Virginia to find Jews and to brood on their qualities. True, his first love had been Miriam Bookbinder, "the daughter of a local ship chandler, who even at the age of six wore in her lovely hooded eyes the vaguely disconsolate, largely inscrutable mystery of her race." Like Gant, Stingo claims to resemble "numerous Southerners of a certain background, learning and sensibility, [who] . . . have from the beginning responded warmly to Jews." (Styron's own wife is Jewish). One of the three central characters, who live in a Brooklyn apartment, is a Polish Catholic survivor of Auschwitz, Sophie Zawistowska. The second is Nathan Landau, supposedly a brilliant but crazed, Harvard-educated scientist. He is a nasty figure upon whom Styron grants the honor of a distinctively drawn and compelling personality. Stingo himself is depicted as haunted by the history of slavery, a topic this budding author will treat in fictional form later by focusing on the Nat Turner rebellion.[43] (Any resemblance to any living persons is surely not coincidental.) Styron himself is nothing if not ambitious and, unlike Katherine Anne Porter, treats the death camp experience itself, rather than the antecedent period. And he does so not allegorically but directly. His victim/survivor is Gentile rather than Jewish, and Styron/Stingo has to get out of the South to confront the anguish of Jewish history. But it is a rare, though not reckless, attempt by a Southern novelist to do so.

Like Stingo, Will Barrett in Walker Percy's recent novel, *The Second Coming* (1980), remembers an early crush. This time its object is Ethel Rosenblum, a cheerleader who beats out Will as the class valedictorian. "She was short, her hair was kinky, her face a bit pocked," he recalls. "But as if to make up for these defects, nature had endowed her with such beauty and grace of body, a dark satinity of skin, a sweet firm curve and compaction of limb as not easily to be believed." As the novel opens, however, Barrett is experiencing a middle-age crisis, requiring the attention of a physician. For among the symptoms is his impression that Jews could no longer be found in that part of North Carolina. "Weren't there Jews here earlier?" he asks Dr. Vance, who replies: "Well, there was Dr. Weiss and Dutch Mandelbaum in high school who played tackle." And the doctor concedes that those two men are no longer around, although the novel itself notes that the ten thousand Jews in North Carolina, with their twenty-five synagogues and their median family income of $21,000, constitute a "small, though flourishing" community. Yet Will Barrett is disturbed because the absence of Jews represents a sign of some sort: "When the Jews pull out, the Gentiles begin to act like the crazy Jutes and Celts and Angles and redneck Saxons they are. They go back to the woods." The non-Jews, he fears, were "growing nuttier by the hour."[44] Here is an unanticipated task assigned to the chosen people—to save the sanity of the goyim (as though obedience to 613 divine injunctions were not burdensome enough). But in its own way, *The Second Coming* is a representative Southern depiction of the role of the Jews, who are noteworthy for their absence.

The South itself rarely has been treated in the fiction of American Jews either. It is as though, like certain other parcels of real estate in the past, this particular territory were restricted, for Gentiles only. Perhaps only one well-known novel by an American Jew, *A Walk on the Wild Side* (1956), is set in the region. But Nelson Algren, *né* Abraham, was only partly *né* Jewish, and his depiction of the underside of New Orleans (called "N'wawlins") hardly counts as local color. It is not animated by an interest in the special characteristics of the city or its environment. Set on Perdido Street, the tale is, according to Algren himself, "really about any street of any big town in the country," as the following passage suggests: "In the cheery old summer of '31, New Orleans offered almost unlimited opportunities to ambitious young men of neat appearance willing to begin at the bottom and work their way up the ladder of success rung by rung. Those with better sense began at the top and worked their way down, that route being faster."[45] Other books might be mentioned. Perhaps the central character of *The Naked and the Dead* (1948) is Sergeant Sam Croft, but he comes from west Texas, and the novel itself is set primarily on a mythical island in the Pacific. Mailer himself has tried to be many things in his life, from white Negro to Aquarius to mayor to president, although the one identity he has tried to elude is "the nice Jewish boy from Brooklyn." But ever since the film version of *All the King's Men*, he writes, he has "wanted to come on in public as a Southern demagogue"—surely one of the most bizarre ambitions to which any novelist ever has admitted. An electronics salesman from the Bronx achieves the White House that eluded both Mailer and Willie Stark in Michael Halberstam's *The Wanting of Levine* (1978). Like our first chief executive, Alfred Levine has made a considerable fortune in his real estate investments. He also displays considerable skill getting along with "crazy backwoods farmers in the South," which is part of his territory, and in bedding compliant, lonely Southern women. The wisdom and compassion that Levine exudes not only make him welcome in the region, despite his cosmopolitan liberalism, but also make Halberstam's *tzaddik* with a sample case a most appealing American president.[46]

The Southern whites in *The Wanting of Levine* are not only libidinous but decent and amiable and fair-minded, but this benign portrait also must be set against the fears of bigotry that the region has tended to inspire. By now such fears can be twisted for humorous purposes, as in *The Great American Novel* (1973), in which

Philip Roth imagines a baseball team owned by a Jewish family named Ellis (after the island). A rookie—a young man from the provinces—is shocked by this discovery, writing home as follows: "Dear Paw we bin trikt. The owner here is a ju. He lives over the skorbord in rite so he can keep his i on the busnez. To look at him cud make you cry like it did me just from lookin. A reel Nu York ju like you heer about down home. It just aint rite Paw."[47] In such passages Roth manages to mock Jewish anxieties about anti-Semitism as well as the benighted prejudices of kids like Slugger. Roth's only rival as a national resource of humor, Woody Allen, had a nightclub routine in which he visits the South and is invited to what he believes is a costume party. The others in the car taking him to the party are all wearing sheets. One of the passengers, who is referred to as a "grand dragon," seems to be their leader, Allen conjectures, because he is wearing contour sheets. Then Allen realizes what is occurring. His own identity is revealed when, instead of donating money to the cause, he makes a pledge. As he is about to be lynched, his whole life passes in front of him: the swimmin' hole, the country sto' where he has gone to fetch some gingham fo'Emmy Lou, the mess o' catfish he'd fried. Then in an ultimate sign of the schlemiel, Allen realizes that "it's not my life" but someone else's, thus deriving laughter from the recognition of the incompatability of being both Southern and Jewish. Incidentally the routine has a happy ending: Allen makes a brief speech in behalf of brotherhood, and the inspired Klansmen give money to Israel Bonds.[48]

Such routines suggest the possibility that the Jew and the Southerner, who have confronted one another so infrequently and so obscurely in the pages of serious fiction, have met with greater resonance in popular culture. There, if anywhere, gospel singers have encountered jazz singers. Roth's imaginary letter points to the possibility of finding Jews in folklore and legend whom Southerners might have preserved in oral traditions. And the contributions of Jews to media-made Dixie also require investigation. Such a study might include Jerome Kern and Oscar Hammerstein's musical *Showboat* (whose interracial theme can be found in other Broadway productions that Jews have written), David O. Selznick's masterpiece of the primal screen *Gone With the Wind* (partly written by Ben Hecht), the Gershwins' *Porgy and Bess* (which Oscar Levant once called "a folk opera—a Jewish folk opera"), and even Al Capp's Dogpatch. Sid Caesar once parodied Southern speech on *Your Show of Shows*, describing his insomnia: "I'm having more trouble sleepin' than a gray-eyed possum fleein' from the hungry, saliva-filled jaws of bayin' hounds in the black swamp on a foggy night in the middle of the month of July." In a Mike Nichols-Elaine May routine, a playwright named Alabama Gross concocts a tale whose heroine has "taken to drink, dope, prostitution—and puttin' on airs." Tom Lehrer satirized the region in "I Wanna Go Back to Dixie" (1954), describing decadence, pellagra, the boll weevil, lynchings, and cornpone. There "ol' times . . . are not forgotten, whuppin' slaves and sellin' cotton."[49]

The influence of such images undoubtedly has been far more extensive—and perhaps more intriguing—than in American Jewish fiction, which has found little space on Mr. Sammler's planet for the region that has so enthralled the imaginations of others. But that is another story.

Conclusion

Much of this book has at least implied that the obstacles that religion would place before its adherents have not encumbered many modern Jews. Their concerns are rarely otherworldly, and they are inescapably affected by the eclipse of religious belief that is one of the obvious signs of contemporary culture. They even may be distrustful of souls on fire, of religion carried to extremes of passion, of faith that is taken too seriously rather than with at least a touch of self-consciousness, self-deprecation, or irony. George Orwell once observed that he knew he was living in a postreligious age when he met Christians who were more afraid of cancer than of hell, and though the specific image of the hereafter has been of lesser significance for historical Judaism, a similar phenomenon has been noticeable.

The reasons for the change cannot be detailed here, but it seems clear that once the acids of skepticism have corroded religious convictions, piety on a grand scale cannot be regained. Once imbued with a genuinely critical spirit, few can know the faith that, in all its acetylene power and purity, seared our ancestors. As a result, the divine will is probably not the pivot of consciousness, and deeds do not seem consistently stamped with a religious dimension. Such a faith inspires more than it inflames; it appeals at least as much to our practical natures as to our emotional lives. To the traditionalist Jew it may not seem authentic enough, to the connoisseur of religious diversity it may not seem exotic enough. However haunting is the Torah description of the binding of Isaac, Jews are unlikely to encounter anyone willing to sacrifice his or her son upon a vocal command.

And yet to be a Jew should mean to honor at least the residue of that faith, to assume the responsibility of commemoration and adaptation, of reinterpretation and reevaluation of the message of patriarchs and prophets. Judaism is never more somber or more forceful than when it promises to sear the spirit, requiring of its believers that they ponder the meaning of their lives, the nature of their existence, the purpose of their creation. It helps frame the most intimidating final exam question of all, which a philosopher has so sparingly expressed in a different context: "Why is there something—and not nothing?"[1] The question is metaphysical, but the partial answer that Judaism, I believe, provides is not metaphysical but ethical, not a matter of being but of doing. That partial answer to the question of existence was best articulated—in characteristically Jewish fashion—by another question, for there is no more cogent an expression of the dilemma of conduct than what Hillel asked: If I am not for myself, who will be for me? If I am only for myself, what am I? The rest is indeed commentary, for our response to the paradox of being for one's self and yet not only for one's self cuts to the center of human experience.

Hillel's question testifies to the persistence of the struggle between self and society. Jews especially are incessantly torn between the personal and the collective, between the particular and the universal, between the singular and the common, between the one and the many. For Jews celebrate the tenacity of their people on such occasions as Hanukkah and Purim, while Rosh Hashanah and Yom Kippur demand the exposure of self before God, in the one-on-One relationship that prayer is designed to elicit. Yet even on the High Holidays, worshippers pray not in solitude but joined in a community, not alone but with other Jews, not stripped of a distinctive culture but voicing a historic idiom of faith that is hallowed with traditional appeals to the God of Israel. It is no modest part of the achievement of Judaism that it has produced Jews, others with whom a faith and a fate are shared.

Here religion can offer not only solace but the possibility of restoring a certain balance to contemporary life. Pitted against the American cult of individualism and the national suspicion of the claims of community, against the culture of narcissism that we are reported to inhabit, and against the existentialist tenet that "hell is other people," Judaism reassures us that "life is with people," that there is common residence in a universe that rarely seems hospitable enough to human aspiration and dignity. Ideologies that have stressed community, whether in the form of cosmopolitanism or as the varieties of socialism, sometimes have produced false messiahs and too often have fostered cruelty in the name of kindness. But Judaism has commanded such allegiance across the centuries because it has contrived with such subtlety to align the general with the particular, to tap the vision of human brotherhood without forsaking a special covenant or neglecting a unique history.

When Morris Bober, the grocer in Bernard Malamud's novel *The Assistant*, claims that being a Jew is simply being a good person, he ceases to impart wisdom because he ignores that specificity of virtue. Norms of moral conduct are best anchored in something less vague and abstract than "goodness" if they are to stick. If the sense of righteousness is to operate, it is less likely to be inculcated in ecumenical settings, or in philosophy courses in ethics, than in the distinctive flavor and texture that an ancient complex of values— binding people across time and space—can inspire. It might be added that proclamations of love for humanity, without showing concern for specific human beings, tend to arouse justifiable suspicions. Yet it is one of the fascinating aspects of Judaism that it can vindicate a feeling for the particular without endorsing the ethics of the parochial, so that fidelity to its spirit can enlarge rather than diminish its claimants.

This plentitude of spirit becomes even more impressive when we consider how statistically insignificant the Jewish people have been, and how thin is the strip of land that has stimulated such formidable loyalties. The love of Zion long has been a challenge to the successful application of Hillel's paradox, and it has long be- deviled those who have sought to live comfortably within Western society without abandoning allegiance to the destiny of the Jewish people. It is a balance that is not easy to strike, for it is only within the last couple of generations that Zionism has exerted its rightful influence on American Jews. It is sometimes necessary to remind the young how stigmatized the struggle to reestablish sovereignty in Palestine once was. But it can be mentioned in passing that, at the dawn of the century, three professors at the Hebrew Union

College were fired because they espoused Zionism. It was also at that time that the influential Rabbi Kaufman Kohler took aside Stephen Wise's bride at their wedding reception, told her what a promising young rabbi she was marrying, but then added: "But he will accomplish much more if you can cure him of his *meshugas*, this lunacy of Zionism."[2] Such incidents testify to the difficulty of resolving Hillel's paradox.

Today most American Jews think they know better, and have become as securely happy in their citizenship as they are implicated in the welfare of a renascent Zion. Most of them, I believe, remain committed to the lovely ideal of the human family—but not a family in which Jews are absent. They still hope, ultimately, for one world—but not one without Israel. They try to be for others as well as for themselves. But in a world still swayed by force, they have come to realize that the desire for peace—no matter how intense—is insufficient for the attainment of peace, that other peoples and their leaders may not share to the same degree a revulsion from warfare. In a world of national rivalries, Israel cannot expect others to be for it. Yet it is much the point of Judaism that efforts to waken the consciences of others should not prevent Jews from reexamining their own.

And in a country like the United States, in which the practice of faith has been unimpeded, the value of such a religion is, if anything, enhanced, precisely because the daily struggle for existence is more muted than elsewhere. The relative ease of living in America, with the resources of its economy and its ideal of an open society, makes it more desirable that ethical burdens be assumed. That is why the hostility to Zionism of a few generations ago, however unfortunate and misguided it now appears, should not be impossible to comprehend. It once occurred rather suddenly to Lord Lionel Rothschild that it must have been difficult to be a Jew in Europe—if one's name were not Rothschild. But to be a Jew in America generally has not been difficult, no matter what one's name. Here Jews largely have been free to seek their political aims without violating their self-respect as a minority, or without fudging their full citizenship as Americans. Here they frequently have been critics of the national experiment without being enemies of its promise. And to have been born in America, especially since midcentury, has meant a certain immunity from the complicity of history, a certain exemption from the sadness and unrewarded toil that, in so many places and centuries, have seemed natural to life. The future historian, looking back to our time, might be almost forgiven for hyperbolically concluding that, for many, pain was tennis elbow, mortality was the ending in *Love Story*, injustice was going off to college and not getting into a *Jewish* fraternity or sorority. If Jewish blood has flowed here, it has sometimes been because plastic surgeons have been asked to alter noses with deviations. It takes little skill in arithmetic for many Jews to be able to count their blessings; it takes more instruction in religion and history to grasp the implications of so benign a condition.

Jews, therefore, have been faced with special and rather unprecedented distractions and opportunities. Free to practice their religion and to perpetuate their ethnic heritage, they are equally free to squander their birthright and to weaken the links that have bound them to their ancestors and to the covenant they established. It is not surprising that the ease of assimilation sometimes has resulted in historical despair, in a pessimistic outlook for the future of this people. Yet they continue to face the challenge that may be unique to Jewish history, which is how to make adherence to a majestic faith and involvement in a common fate compatible with the comfort that affluence has created and with the liberalism that the public culture has sponsored.

Theirs is therefore a peculiar and an ambiguous identity, and the effort to reconcile America and Judaism, place and time, matter and spirit is more complicated than it might sometimes appear. For all their love of Zion, they need not be defensive about the decision to try to apply Hillel's paradox within an American setting, not when the U.S.A. is like a Broadway hit, with tickets sold out for years and still lines at the box office, not when Vietnamese and Cubans recently have risked drowning and death in order to set foot on these shores, not when Soviet symphony orchestras that have come here on concert tours risk returning as string quartets. It is therefore tempting to relax and appreciate good fortune.

That is precisely why the message of Judaism, however muffled, can be so valuable and so compelling. For theirs is a religion and a people that has arranged to renew itself for well over four milennia; and yet, although they are the heirs of an ancient tradition, they are pressed to fulfill ethical injunctions. Judaism still can be charged with urgency and immediacy. Hillel's question "If not now, when?" is as integral to his paradox as the other two questions. Although Judaism is stamped with a sense of the eternal, although it may soar above the finitude of our condition, its teachings italicize the passing of time and admonish its adherents not necessarily to complete the task, only to begin it. From the perspective of the abiding, Judaism asks how adroitly the particular and the general have been balanced. It regularly asks not only to reach out to others, but also to turn within and confront our own fragile selves.

For at its best, modern Judaism is a religion that resembles Robert Frost's woods—"lovely, dark, and deep." The accumulated wisdom of psalmists and prophets, rabbis and *tzaddikim*, is inexhaustible in its power to steel believers against both adversity and affluence, inexhaustible in its capacity to help them absorb the torment and void of existence, inexhaustible in its reminders of the precariousness of life even as it cannot fully assuage the pain of loneliness or the burden of toil, or account for the prevalence of want and cruelty and suffering and troubled sleep, even as it cannot truly illuminate the mystery of death. Despite the accelerated velocity of the historical process that all peoples have experienced, each generation remains equidistant from eternity.

Notes

Introduction

1. Stephen J. Whitfield, *Into the Dark: Hannah Arendt and Totalitarianism* (Philadelphia: Temple University Press, 1980).
2. Steinberg quoted in Robert Hughes, "The World of Steinberg," *Time*, 111 (April 17, 1978), 95.

In the Shadow of Europe

1. American Jewish Intellectuals and Totalitarianism

1. George F. Kennan, "Totalitarianism in the Modern World," in *Totalitarianism*, ed. Carl J. Friedrich (New York: Grosset & Dunlap, 1954), p. 17.
2. Irving Howe, "The New York Intellectuals," in *Decline of the New* (New York: Horizon, 1970), pp. 211–22; Charles Kadushin, "Who Are the Elite Intellectuals?" *Public Interest*, No. 29 (Fall 1972), pp. 115–19; Richard Kostelanetz, *The End of Intelligent Writing: Literary Politics in America* (New York: Sheed & Ward, 1974), pp. 12–15, 25; David A. Hollinger, "Ethnic Diversity, Cosmopolitanism and the Emergence of the American Liberal Intelligentsia," *American Quarterly*, 27 (May 1975), pp. 134–35, 147–50.
3. Leonard Schapiro, *Totalitarianism* (New York: Praeger, 1972), pp. 13–14; Giovanni Gentile, "The Philosophic Basis of Fascism," *Foreign Affairs*, 6 (January 1928), pp. 299, 301; Franz Neumann, *Behemoth: The Structure and Practice of National Socialism, 1933–1944* (New York: Harper & Row, 1944), pp. 47–49; John P. Diggins, *Mussolini and Fascism: The View from America* (Princeton: Princeton University Press, 1972), pp. 202–3, 259–61.
4. Diggins, *Mussolini*, pp. 464–65; Hannah Arendt, *The Origins of*

Totalitarianism (New York: Harcourt, Brace, 1951), pp. 257–58, 308–9; Irving Louis Horowitz, *Genocide: State Power and Mass Murder* (New Brunswick, N.J.: Transaction, 1977), p. 66.

5. Harold Rosenberg, "The Shadow of the Furies," *New York Review of Books*, 23 (Jan. 23, 1977), p. 47; Muste quoted in Nat Hentoff, *Peace Agitator: The Story of A. J. Muste* (New York: Macmillan, 1963), p. 12; Stringfellow quoted in Dorothy Rabinowitz, *New Lives: Survivors of the Holocaust Living in America* (New York: Avon, 1976), p. 191.

6. Mortimer J. Adler, "God and the Professors," *Vital Speeches of the Day*, 7 (Dec. 1, 1940), pp. 100, 102; Pierre Teilhard de Chardin, *The Phenomenon of Man* (New York: Harper & Brothers, 1959), p. 257; Teilhard quoted in Mary and Ellen Lukas, *Teilhard* (Garden City, N.Y.: Doubleday, 1977), pp. 237–38.

7. B. F. Skinner, *Beyond Freedom and Dignity* (New York: Knopf, 1971), p. 174; Noam Chomsky, *For Reasons of State* (New York: Vintage, 1973), p. 344; Harriman quoted in John Lewis Gaddis, *The United States and the Origins of the Cold War* (New York: Columbia University Press, 1972), p. 242.

8. Hans Kohn, "Communist and Fascist Dictatorship: A Comparative Study," in *Dictatorship in the Modern World*, ed. Guy Stanton Ford (Minneapolis: University of Minnesota Press, 1935), p. 151; Sigmund Neumann, *Permanent Revolution: The Total State in a World at War* (New York: Harper & Brothers, 1942), pp. x, 40–41, 42.

9. Erik H. Erikson, "Wholeness and Totality," in Friedrich, *Totalitarianism*, pp. 162, 170; Else Frenkel-Brunswik, "Environmental Controls and the Impoverishment of Thought," in Friedrich, *Totalitarianism*, p. 187; Martin Jay, *The Dialectical Imagination: A History of the Frankfurt School and the Institute of Social Research, 1923–1950* (Boston: Little, Brown, 1973), pp. 234–50; H. Stuart Hughes, *The Sea Change: The Migration of Social Thought, 1930–1965* (New York: Harper & Row, 1975), pp. 70–72, 80–81.

10. Neumann, *Behemoth*, pp. 47, 51, 67, 261; Hughes, *Sea Change*, pp. 102–4, 105–8.

11. Alfred Kazin in "Outstanding Books, 1931–1961," *American Scholar*, 30 (Winter 1961), 612; Howe, *Decline of the New*, pp. 244–45.

12. Lucy S. Dawidowicz, *The War Against the Jews, 1933–1945* (New York: Holt, Rinehart & Winston, 1975), pp. 429n, 436n; Hannah Arendt and Gershom Scholem, "Eichmann in Jerusalem," *Encounter*, 22 (January 1964), 51–53; Jacob Robinson, *And the Crooked Shall Be Made Straight* (New York: Macmillan, 1965); Hughes, *Sea Change*, pp. 123–25; Howe, *Decline of the New*, p. 237.

13. Robert Conquest, *The Great Terror: Stalin's Purge of the Thirties* (New York: Macmillan, 1968), pp. 302, 317; Evgenia S. Ginzburg, *Into the Whirlwind* (London: Penguin, 1967), pp. 109–10; Aleksandr I. Solzhenitsyn, *The Gulag Archipelago, 1918–1956: An Experiment in Literary Investigation* (New York: Harper & Row, 1975), pp. 98–99, 100–102.

14. E. F. Benson, ed., *Henry James: Letters to A. C. Benson and Auguste Monod* (New York: Scribner's, 1930), p. 35.

15. Alfred Kazin, *Starting Out in the Thirties* (Boston: Little, Brown, 1965), p. 153; Bertram D. Wolfe, *Communist Totalitarianism: Keys to the Soviet System* (Boston: Beacon, 1961), pp. 269, 276.

16. Sidney Hook in "Liberal Anti-Communism Revisited: A Symposium," *Commentary*, 44 (September 1967), 45; Lewis S. Feuer, "From Ideology to Philosophy: Sidney Hook's Writings on Marxism," in *Sidney Hook and the Contemporary World: Essays on the Pragmatic Intelligence*, ed. Paul Kurtz (New York: John Day, 1968), pp. 35–36; Robert Allen Skotheim, *Totalitarianism and American Social Thought* (New York: Holt, Rinehart & Winston, 1971), pp. 44–51.

17. Sidney Hook, *Reason, Social Myths and Democracy* (New York: Humanities Press, 1940), p. 76; Sidney Hook, *Political Power and Personal Freedom: Critical Studies in Democracy, Communism and Civil Rights* (New York: Criterion, 1959), pp. 17, 145–46.

18. Skotheim, *Totalitarianism*, pp. 79–81; Milton Friedman, *Capitalism and Freedom* (Chicago: University of Chicago Press, 1962), p. 13.

19. Hans Morgenthau, *The Purpose of American Politics* (New York: Vintage, 1960), p. 249; Franz Neumann, *The Democratic and the Authoritarian State: Essays in Political and Legal Theory* (Glencoe, Ill.: Free Press, 1957), p. 210; Max Lerner, *Ideas for the Ice Age* (New York: Viking, 1941), p. ix; Ernst Cassirer, *The Myth of the State* (New Haven: Yale University Press, 1946), pp. 275–76.

20. Daniel Bell, *The End of Ideology: On the Exhaustion of Political Ideas in the Fifties* (New York: Free Press, 1960), pp. 32–33; Oscar and Mary Handlin, *The Dimensions of Liberty* (New York: Atheneum, 1966), pp. 107–11; Michael Paul Rogin, *The Intellectuals and McCarthy: The Radical Specter* (Cambridge: M.I.T. Press, 1967) pp. 14–26; Edward A. Purcell, *The Crisis of Democratic Theory: Scientific Naturalism and the Problem of Value* (Lexington: University of Kentucky Press, 1973), pp. 254–60.

21. William Kornhauser, *The Politics of Mass Society* (Glencoe, Ill.: Free Press, 1959), p. 15; Clinton Rossiter and James Lare, eds., *The Essential Lippmann: A Political Philosophy for Liberal Democracy* (New York: Vintage, 1965), p. 5; Walter Lippmann, *Essays in the Public Philosophy* (Boston: Little, Brown, 1955), p. 83; Skotheim, *Totalitarianism*, pp. 84–87; Morton White, *Social Thought in America: The Revolt Against Formalism* (Boston: Beacon, 1957), pp. 264–78.

22. Lippmann, *Public Philosophy*, p. 81; Bell, *End of Ideology*, p. 393; Daniel Boorstin, *The Genius of American Politics* (Chicago: University of Chicago Press, 1953), pp. 3–4, 184–86; Daniel Boorstin, *The Americans: The Colonial Experience* (New York: Vintage, 1958), p. 154.

23. Daniel Bell in "Ideology—A Debate," *Commentary*, 38 (October 1964), 73; Seymour Martin Lipset, *Political Man: The Social Bases of Politics* (Garden City, N.Y.: Doubleday Anchor, 1963), pp. xxii–xxiii, 439, 442; Edward A. Shils, *The Torment of Secrecy: The Background and Conse-

quences of American Security Policies (New York: Free Press, 1956), pp. 225–34; Lewis S. Feuer, Ideology and the Ideologists (New York: Harper & Row, 1975); David Riesman et al., The Lonely Crowd: A Study of the Changing American Character (Garden City, N.Y.: Doubleday Anchor, 1953), pp. 246–58; David Riesman, Individualism Reconsidered (Garden City, N.Y.: Doubleday Anchor, 1955), pp. 2, 24–25; Richard Hofstadter, The Age of Reform from Bryan to F.D.R. (New York: Vintage, 1955), pp. 60–130; Marian J. Morton, The Terrors of Ideological Politics: Liberal Historians in a Conservative Mood (Cleveland: Case Western Reserve University Press, 1972), pp. 10–12, 18–21, 129–30.

24. Philip Rahv in "Our Country and Our Culture: A Symposium," Partisan Review, 19 (May–June 1952), 308; James B. Gilbert, Writers and Partisans: A History of Literary Radicalism in America (New York: John Wiley, 1968), pp. 158–60, 241, 281–82.

25. George Charney, A Long Journey (Chicago: Quadrangle, 1968), p. 229; "The Battle over the Tomb," Time, 83 (April 24, 1964), 29; Skotheim, Totalitarianism, pp. 66–67, 124.

26. Norman Mailer, The Presidential Papers (New York: Bantam, 1964), p. 134; Norman Mailer, The Armies of the Night (New York: New American Library, 1968), pp. 136, 199; Norman Mailer, Of a Fire on the Moon (New York: New American Library, 1971), p. 65; Christopher Lasch, The New Radicalism in America,1889–1963: The Intellectual as a Social Type (New York: Knopf, 1965), pp. 334–35, 345.

27. Mailer, Armies of the Night, p. 315; Norman Mailer, The Prisoner of Sex (New York: New American Library, 1971), p. 124; Mailer, Presidential Papers, p. 147.

28. Herbert Marcuse, One-Dimensional Man: Studies in the Ideology of Advanced Industrial Society (Boston: Beacon, 1964), p. 3.

29. Alasdair MacIntyre, Herbert Marcuse: An Exposition and a Polemic (New York: Viking, 1970), pp. 76–78; Richard King, The Party of Eros: Radical Social Thought and the Realm of Freedom (Chapel Hill: University of North Carolina Press, 1972), pp. 150–52, 156; Ronald Aronson, "Dear Herbert," in The Revival of American Socialism, ed. George Fischer (New York: Oxford University Press, 1971), p. 264.

30. Betty Friedan, The Feminine Mystique (New York: W. W. Norton, 1963), pp. 305–8, 309.

31. Alexis de Tocqueville, Democracy in America (New York: Vintage, 1945), II, 336–37.

32. Stanley Elkins, Slavery: A Problem in American Institutional and Intellectual Life (Chicago: University of Chicago Press, 1959), pp. 104, 111–15, 128–32; Stanley Elkins, "Slavery and Ideology," in The Debate over Slavery: Stanley Elkins and His Critics, ed. Ann J. Lane (Urbana: University of Illinois Press, 1971), pp. 349–60; Earl Thorpe, "Chattel Slavery and Concentration Camps," in Lane, Debate over Slavery, pp. 23–42.

33. Marie Jahoda and Stuart W. Cook, "Ideological Compliance as a Social-Psychological Process," in Friedrich, Totalitarianism, pp. 205–6, 213, 219; Milgram quoted in Carol Tavris, "Frozen World of the Familiar

Stranger," *Psychology Today*, 8 (June 1974), 80; Stanley Milgram, *Obedience to Authority: An Experimental View* (New York: Harper & Row, 1974), pp. 5, 33.

34. Milgram, *Obedience to Authority*, pp. xii, xv, 6, 178.

35. Daniel Bell, "Is Eichmann in All of Us?" *New York Times* (May 26, 1974), sec. 2, pp. 1, 13.

36. Herman Wouk, *The Caine Mutiny* (Garden City, N.Y.: Doubleday, 1951), pp. 447–48; William H. Whyte, Jr., *The Organization Man* (Garden City, N.Y.: Doubleday Anchor, 1956), pp. 269–75; Raul Hilberg, *The Destruction of the European Jews* (Chicago: Quadrangle, 1961), pp. 614n, 624.

37. Sidney Hook, *The Paradoxes of Freedom* (Berkeley: University of California Press, 1964), pp. 124, 128–29; Hannah Arendt, *Crises of the Republic* (New York: Harcourt, Brace Jovanovich, 1972), pp. 101–2; Abe Fortas, *Concerning Dissent and Civil Disobedience* (New York: New American Library, 1968), pp. 9, 62–63; Felix Frankfurter in Minersville School District v. Gobitis, 310 U.S. 586 (1940); Felix Frankfurter in West Virginia State Board of Education v. Barnette, 319 U.S. 624 (1943); Abe Fortas in Tinker v. Des Moines School District, 393 U.S. 503 (1969).

38. Irving Howe and Eliezer Greenberg, eds., Introduction to *A Treasury of Yiddish Stories* (New York: Viking, 1954), p. 38; Rosenberg, "Shadow of the Furies," p. 47; Michael Walzer, "World War II: Why Was This War Different?" in *War and Moral Responsibility*, eds. Marshall Cohen et al. (Princeton: Princeton University Press, 1974), pp. 86, 101.

39. Bruno Bettelheim, "Surviving," *New Yorker*, 52 (Aug. 2, 1976), 38; Oscar Handlin, "Jewish Resistance to the Nazis," *Commentary*, 34 (November 1962), 405.

40. Mordecai Richler, *Shovelling Trouble* (London: Quartet, 1973), pp. 90–91; Henry Kissinger, "Reflections on a New Era," *New Leader*, 60 (Jan. 31, 1977), p. 10; *New York Times* (July 18, 1975), p. 4.

41. Riesman, *Individualism Reconsidered*, pp. 419, 424; Bell, *End of Ideology*, pp. 324-325; Robert Jay Lifton, *History and Human Survival* (New York: Vintage, 1971), pp. 19–20; Horowitz, *Genocide*, p. 64; George Steiner, "A Kind of Survivor," in *Language and Silence: Essays on Language, Literature, and the Inhuman* (New York: Atheneum, 1970), pp. 140–41, 148, 153–54.

42. Wiesel quoted in Morton A. Reichek, "Out of the Night," *Present Tense*, 3 (Spring 1976), p. 42; Elie Wiesel in "Jewish Values in the Post-Holocaust Future," *Judaism*, 16 (Summer 1967), 283; Lothar Kahn, *Mirrors of the Jewish Mind* (New York: Thomas Yoseloff, 1968), pp. 176–80, 185–87, 192; Robert Alter, *After the Tradition: Essays on Modern Jewish Writing* (New York: Dutton, 1969), pp. 156–60.

43. Isaac Rosenfeld, "Soviet Labor and Western Horror," in *An Age of Enormity: Life and Writing in the Forties and Fifties* (Cleveland: World, 1962), pp. 200–205; Jerzy G. Gliksman, "Social Prophylaxis as a Form of Soviet Terror," in Friedrich, *Totalitariansim*, pp. 60–74.

44. Rosenfeld, "Terror Beyond Evil," p. 197.

2. The Holocaust in the American Jewish Mind

1. Harold Rosenberg, *Discovering the Present: Three Decades in Art, Culture and Politics* (Chicago: University of Chicago Press, 1973), p. 280; Khrushchev quoted in Abraham Rothberg, *The Heirs of Stalin: Dissidence and the Soviet Regime, 1953–1970* (Ithaca, N.Y.: Cornell University Press, 1972), p. 45.

2. Lionel Trilling, *The Liberal Imagination: Essays on Literature and Society* (New York: Scribner's, 1950), pp. 264–65.

3. Isaac Rosenfeld, *An Age of Enormity: Life and Writing in the Forties and Fifties* (Cleveland: World, 1962), p. 197; Irving Howe, *World of Our Fathers* (New York: Simon and Schuster, 1976), pp. 626–27.

4. Irving Howe, *Decline of the New*, pp. 244–45; Rosenberg, *Discovering the Present*, pp. 259–269; Daniel Bell, "Reflections on Jewish Identity," in *The Ghetto and Beyond: Essays on Jewish Life in America*, ed. Peter I. Rose (New York: Random House, 1969), pp. 465–76.

5. Steven Bauman, "An Interview with Milton Himmelfarb," *Jewish Spectator*, 43 (Spring 1978), 33; Harold Weisberg, "Ideologies of American Jews," in *The American Jew: A Reappraisal*, ed. Oscar I. Janowsky (Philadelphia: Jewish Publication Society, 1964), p. 342.

6. Erik H. Erikson, *Life History and the Historical Moment* (New York: W. W. Norton, 1975), pp. 27–28; Marshall Berman, "Erik Erikson: The Man Who Invented Himself," *New York Times Book Review* (March 30, 1975), pp. 1, 3; Alexis de Tocqueville, *Democracy in America*, II, 105.

7. Erikson, *Life History*, p. 43, and *Childhood and Society* (New York: W. W. Norton, 1963), pp. 353–57.

8. "Under Forty: A Symposium on American Literature and the Younger Generation of American Jews," *Contemporary Jewish Record*, 7 (February 1944), 4, 16, 23, 24.

9. "Jewishness and the Younger Intellectuals," *Commentary*, 31 (April 1961), 308–9, 335, 346, 355.

10. Will Herberg, *Judaism and Modern Man: An Interpretation of Jewish Religion* (New York: Farrar Straus and Young, 1951), p. 3.

11. "The State of Jewish Belief," *Commentary*, 42 (August 1966), 134, 143, 144.

12. Eliezer Berkovitz, *Faith after the Holocaust* (New York: KTAV, 1973); Irving Greenberg, "Cloud of Smoke, Pillar of Fire: Judaism, Christianity, and Modernity after the Holocaust," in *Auschwitz: Beginning of a New Era?*, ed. Eva Fleischner (New York: KTAV, 1977), pp. 7–55; Arthur A. Cohen, "Thinking the Tremendum: Some Theological Implications of the Death-Camps" (New York: Leo Baeck Institute, 1974); Richard L. Rubenstein, *After Auschwitz: Radical Theology and Contemporary Judaism* (Indianapolis: Bobbs-Merrill, 1966), pp. 1–58; Emil L. Fackenheim, "The Human Condition After Auschwitz" (Syracuse, N.Y.: Syracuse University, 1971).

13. Robert Brustein, "History as Drama," in *The Storm over The Deputy*, ed. Eric Bentley (New York: Grove, 1964), p. 24.

14. Lawrence L. Langer, *The Holocaust and the Literary Imagination* (New Haven: Yale University Press, 1975), pp. 3–8; Howe, *World of Our Fathers*, pp. 451, 453–56.

15. George Steiner, *Language and Silence: Essays on Language, Literature and the Inhuman* (New York: Atheneum, 1970), pp. 301–2; Irving Howe, *The Critical Point: On Literature and Culture* (New York: Delta, 1975), pp. 163, 165–66.

16. Arthur Hertzberg, "A Generation Later," *Midstream*, 16 (June–July, 1970), 13.

17. Alfred Kazin in "Under Forty," p. 10; Alfred Kazin, "The Heart of the World," in Fleischner, *Auschwitz*, pp. 65–72; and Alfred Kazin, *New York Jew* (New York: Knopf, 1978), pp. 26, 34.

18. Robert Jay Lifton, *History and Human Survival* (New York: Vintage, 1971), pp. 19–20, 195–207.

19. Michael Wyschogrod, "Some Theological Reflections on the Holocaust," in *Living After the Holocaust: Reflections by the Post-War Generation in America*, eds. Lucy Y. Steinitz and David M. Szonyi (New York: Bloch, 1976), pp. 65–66, 67; Michael Wyschogrod, "Faith and the Holocaust," *Judaism*, 20 (Summer 1971), 286–94; Jacob Neusner, "The Implications of the Holocaust," *Journal of Religion*, 53 (July 1973), 293–308.

20. Norman Mailer, *Advertisements for Myself* (New York: Putnam's, 1959), p. 338.

21. Susan Sontag, *On Photography* (New York: Farrar Straus & Giroux, 1977), pp. 19–20; Hertzberg, "A Generation Later," p. 9.

3. Anti-Semitism and the Problem of Evil: The Case of Hannah Arendt

1. Hannah Arendt, *Eichmann in Jerusalem: A Report on the Banality of Evil* (New York: Viking, 1965), pp. 276, 287; Hannah Arendt, *The Life of the Mind* (New York: Harcourt Brace Jovanovich, 1978), pp. 1, 3–4.

2. Arendt, *Eichmann*, pp. 26, 41–42, 215.

3. Scholem and Arendt, "Eichmann," pp. 53, 56.

4. Scholem and Arendt, "Eichmann," pp. 53, 56.

5. Arendt, *Eichmann*, p. 150.

6. Walter Kaufmann, ed., *The Portable Nietzsche* (New York: Viking, 1954), p. 687.

7. Elie Wiesel, *One Generation After* (New York: Avon, 1972), p. 11.

8. Thomas Merton, *Raids on the Unspeakable* (New York: New Directions, 1966), pp. 45–47.

9. Gideon Hausner, *Justice in Jerusalem* (New York: Harper and Row, 1966), pp. 6, 7.

10. Hausner, *Justice in Jerusalem*, pp. 6, 7; Michael Selzer, "The Murderous Mind," *New York Times Magazine* (Nov. 27, 1977), pp. 35, 112, 117, 121.

11. Thomas Litwack, Letter, *New York Times Magazine* (Dec. 18, 1977), p. 110; Selzer, "The Murderous Mind," p. 120.
12. Truman Capote, *In Cold Blood* (New York: Random House, 1966), pp. 244, 245.
13. Sigmund Freud, *Character and Culture* (New York: Collier, 1963), p. 112.
14. Milgram, *Obedience to Authority*, pp. xv, 5–6, 22–23.
15. Robert Lowell, Letter, *New York Times Book Review* (June 23, 1963), p. 5.

In the Light of America

4. The Challenge of American Jewish History

1. Henry Wadsworth Longfellow, "The Jewish Cemetery at Newport," in *The Works of Henry Wadsworth Longfellow* (Boston: Houghton Mifflin, 1886), III, 33–36.
2. Quoted in Leon Wieseltier, "You Don't Have to be Khazarian," *New York Review of Books*, 23 (Oct. 28, 1976), 33.
3. Steven Hertzberg, *Strangers Within the Gate City: The Jews of Atlanta, 1845–1915* (Philadelphia: Jewish Publication Society, 1978), p. 214.
4. Seymour Martin Lipset and David Riesman, *Education and Politics at Harvard* (New York: McGraw-Hill, 1975), pp. 145–46; Marcia Graham Synnott, *The Half-Opened Door* (Westport, Conn.: Greenwood, 1975), pp. 58–80.
5. Arthur Liebman, *Jews and the Left* (New York: John Wiley & Sons, 1979), p. 267; Eli N. Evans, "Southern-Jewish History: Alive and Unfolding," in *Turn to the South: Essays on Southern Jewry*, eds. Nathan M. Kaganoff and Melvin I. Urofsky (Charlottesville: University Press of Virginia, 1979), pp. 158–67.
6. Carol Kur, "The Hadassah Way," *Moment*, 3 (March 1978), 19.
7. Whittaker Chambers, *Witness* (Chicago: Henry Regnery, 1952), pp. 204–5.
8. David Wyman, *Paper Walls: America and the Refugee Crisis, 1938–1941* (Amherst: University of Massachusetts Press, 1968); Henry L. Feingold, *The Politics of Rescue: The Roosevelt Administration and the Holocaust, 1938–1945* (New Brunswick, N.J.: Rutgers University Press, 1970); Saul S. Friedman, *No Haven for the Oppressed: United States Policy Toward Jewish Refugees, 1938–1945* (Detroit: Wayne State University Press, 1973).
9. Merle Miller, *Plain Speaking: An Oral Biography of Harry S.*

Truman (New York: Putnam, 1974), pp. 104, 128, 184, 217–18; Melvin I. Urofsky, *We are One!: American Jewry and Israel* (Garden City, N.Y.: Doubleday, 1978), pp. 165–66, 186.

10. Neil Larry Shumsky, "Zangwill's *The Melting-Pot*: Ethnic Tensions on Stage," *American Quarterly*, 27 (March 1975), 29–41; Arthur Mann, "The Melting Pot," in *Uprooted Americans: Essays to Honor Oscar Handlin*, eds. Richard L. Bushman et al. (Boston: Little, Brown, 1979), pp. 291–314.

11. Quoted in Marshall Sklare, *America's Jews* (New York: Random House, 1971), p. 18.

12. Jane Kramer, *Allen Ginsberg in America* (New York: Random House, 1969), pp. 23, 43.

13. Ezra Goodman, *The Fifty-Year Decline and Fall of Hollywood* (New York: Simon & Schuster, 1961), pp. 340–41, 377.

14. John Updike, *Bech: A Book* (New York: Knopf, 1970), pp. 5–6.

15. Leslie Fiedler, *To The Gentiles* (New York: Stein & Day, 1972), pp. 136–37.

16. Fiedler, *To the Gentiles*, pp. 68–69; William R. Taylor, "Psyching out the City," in Bushman, *Uprooted Americans*, p. 251.

17. "Ray Charles," *Current Biography, 1965* (New York: H. W. Wilson, 1966), pp. 79–80; Ray Charles and David Ritz, *Brother Ray: Ray Charles' Own Story* (New York: Warner, 1979), pp. 15, 27–29, 34, 106–7.

18. H. Wayne Schuth, *Mike Nichols* (Boston: Twayne, 1978), pp. 19–20; Ruth Link-Salinger Hyman, *Gustav Landauer, Philosopher of Utopia* (Indianapolis: Hackett, 1977), pp. 1–3.

19. Drora Kass and Seymour Martin Lipset, "Jewish Immigration to the United States from 1967 to the Present: Israelis and Others," in *Understanding American Jewry*, ed. Marshall Sklare (New Brunswick, N.J.: Transaction, 1982), pp. 278–89.

5. The Legacy of Radicalism

1. Quoted in J. P. Stern, *Hitler: The Führer and the People* (Berkeley: University of California Press, 1975), p. 206.

2. Moses Hess, *Briefwechsel*, quoted in David McLellan, *Marx Before Marxism* (New York: Harper and Row, 1970), p. 71.

3. John Calvin, *Against the Anabaptists*, quoted in Michael Walzer, *The Revolution of the Saints: A Study in the Origins of Radical Politics* (New York: Atheneum, 1968), p. 47.

4. Lewis S. Feuer, *Ideology and the Ideologists* (New York: Harper and Row, 1975), pp. 3, 168–69.

5. Quoted in J. P. Nettl, *Rosa Luxemburg* (London: Oxford University Press, 1966), p. 860.

6. Simone Weil, "Spiritual Autobiography," in *The Simone Weil Reader*, ed. George A. Panichas (New York: David McKay, 1977), p. 26.

7. Arthur Liebman, *Jews and the Left* (New York: John Wiley and Sons, 1979), p. 93.

8. Quoted in A. J. P. Taylor, *From Napoleon to Lenin: Historical Essays* (New York: Harper and Row, 1966), p. 174.

9. Irving Howe, *Leon Trotsky* (New York: Viking, 1978), pp. 173–77.

10. Hugh Thomas, *Cuba: The Pursuit of Freedom* (New York: Harper and Row, 1971), pp. 577, 1,101; Arthur Koestler, *The Invisible Writing: An Autobiography* (Boston: Beacon, 1955), p. 394.

11. L. Glen Seretan, *Daniel De Leon: The Odyssey of an American Marxist* (Cambridge, Mass.: Harvard University Press, 1979), pp. 3–4, 8–9, 53, 102, 216–17.

12. Abraham Cahan, *The Rise of David Levinsky* (New York: Harper and Brothers, 1917), p. 282.

13. Quoted in Bernard K. Johnpoll, with Lillian Johnpoll, *The Impossible Dream: The Rise and Demise of the American Left* (Westport, Conn.: Greenwood, 1981), p. 291.

14. Theodore Draper, *American Communism and Soviet Russia* (New York: Viking, 1960), p. 191.

15. Liebman, *Jews and the Left*, pp. 540–41.

16. Quoted in Irwin Unger, *The Movement: A History of the American New Left, 1959–1972* (New York: Dodd, Mead, 1974), p. 129.

17. Lewis S. Feuer, *The Conflict of Generations* (New York: Basic, 1969), pp. 423–31, 434.

18. Howard Zinn, *SNCC: The New Abolitionists* (Boston: Beacon, 1965), pp. 18. 173–74.

19. Staff of the *Washington Post, The Fall of a President* (New York: Delacorte, 1974), p. 222; "Another Day in the Oval Office," *New York Times* (Sept. 27, 1981), p. 2E.

20. Lawrence H. Fuchs, *The Political Behavior of American Jews* (Glencoe, Ill.: Free Press, 1956), pp. 173–91.

21. Quoted in Robert Warshow, *The Immediate Experience* (Garden City, N.Y.: Doubleday Anchor, 1964), pp. 40–41.

22. Arthur Waskow, *The Freedom Seder*, quoted in Stephen D. Isaacs, *Jews and American Politics* (Garden City, N.Y.: Doubleday, 1974), pp. 93–94.

23. Clarence Darrow, "Attorney for the Defense," *Esquire*, 80 (October 1973), 227.

24. Peter Clecak, *Radical Paradoxes: Dilemmas of the American Left, 1945–1970* (New York: Harper and Row, 1974), p. 73.

25. Robert Michels, *Political Parties* (New York: Free Press, 1962), pp. 247–48.

26. William Barrett, *The Truants* (Garden City, N.Y.: Doubleday, 1982), p. 190.

27. Quoted in Howe, *World of Our Fathers*, pp. 270, 484.

28. Kenneth Keniston, *Young Radicals: Notes on Committed Youth* (New York: Harcourt, Brace and World, 1968), pp. 14, 111–19; Nathan

Glazer, "The Jewish Role in Student Activism," *Fortune*, 69 (January 1969), 113, 126; Seymour Martin Lipset, *Revolution and Counter-revolution: Change and Persistence in Social Structures* (Garden City, N.Y.: Doubleday Anchor, 1970), p. 393.

29. Martin Jay, *The Dialectical Imagination: A History of the Frankfurt School, 1923–1950* (Boston: Little, Brown, 1973), p. 35; Gershom Scholem, *From Berlin to Jerusalem: Memories of My Youth* (New York: Schocken, 1980), pp. 30–31.

30. Abbie Hoffman, *Soon to be a Major Motion Picture* (New York: G. P. Putnam's, 1980), pp. 3, 13, 15, 24, 26–27, 48.

31. Mark L. Levine et al., eds., *The Tales of Hoffman* (New York: Bantam, 1970), pp. 140–41.

32. Joshua Rubinstein, *Soviet Dissidents: Their Struggle for Human Rights* (Boston: Beacon, 1980), pp. 17, 244.

33. Hoffman, *Major Motion Picture*, p. 13.

34. Morris Raphael Cohen, *Reflections of a Wondering Jew* (Glencoe, Ill.: Free Press, 1950), p. 4; Alan Lelchuk, "Philip Rahv: The Last Years," in *Images and Ideas in American Culture*, ed. Arthur Edelstein (Hanover, N. H.: University Press of New England, 1979), pp. 218–19.

6. The Persistence of Liberalism

1. Shelley v. Kraemer, 334 U.S. 1 (1948).

2. Dixon quoted in Raymond A. Cook, *Thomas Dixon* (New York: Twayne, 1974), p. 63; Eli N. Evans, *The Provincials: A Personal History of Jews in the South* (New York: Atheneum, 1973), p. 189.

3. Washington quoted in Morris U. Schappes, ed., *A Documentary History of Jews in the United States* (New York: Schocken, 1971), p. 80.

4. Nicholas Horthy quoted in Lucy S. Dawidowicz, *The War Against the Jews, 1933–1945* (New York: Bantam, 1976), p. 44n.

5. Robert E. Park, *Race and Culture* (Glencoe, Ill.: Free Press, 1950), pp. 354–55; Seymour Martin Lipset, *Revolution and Counter-revolution*, p. 148.

6. Jacob Riis, *How the Other Half Lives* (New York: Hill and Wang, 1957), pp. 76–99; Michael Harrington, *The Other America: Poverty in the United States* (Baltimore: Penguin, 1963), p. 140.

7. Martin Mayer, *The Lawyers* (New York: Harper & Row, 1967), p. 16; Stephen D. Isaacs, *Jews and American Politics* (Garden City, N.Y.: Doubleday, 1974), p. 23.

8. "Doing and Believing: A Round-Table Discussion," *Moment*, 4 (September 1978), 41.

9. Thomas B. Morgan, "The Vanishing American Jew," *Look*, 28 May 5, 1965), 42–43.

10. Milton Himmelfarb, *The Jews of Modernity* (New York: Basic Books, 1973), p. 359.

11. Howe, *World of Our Fathers*, p. 195.

12. Joseph P. Lash, "A Brahmin of the Law," in *From the Diaries of Felix Frankfurter* (New York: W. W. Norton, 1975), p. 64.

13. Nathan Glazer, *Affirmative Discrimination: Ethnic Inequality and Public Policy* (New York: Basic Books, 1975), p. 157; "Jews in America," *Fortune*, 13 (February 1936), 130.

14. Nora Sayre, *Sixties Going on Seventies* (New York: Arbor House, 1973), p. 147.

15. Isaacs, *Jews and American Politics*, pp. 6–7.

16. Oscar Handlin, *The Uprooted* (Boston: Atlantic-Little, Brown, 1951), p. 3.

17. Erik H. Erikson, *Childhood and Society* (New York: W. W. Norton, 1950), p. 101.

18. Brandeis quoted in Alpheus Thomas Mason, *Brandeis: A Free Man's Life* (New York: Viking, 1946), p. 439.

19. Ralph Ellison, *Shadow and Act* (New York: Signet, 1966), pp. 132–33.

20. Cynthia Ozick, "Hadrian and Hebrew," *Moment*, 1 (September 1975), 77.

21. Henry L. Feingold, "The Jewish Contribution to American Politics," *Judaism*, 25 (Summer 1976), 315.

22. Jefferson to James Madison, Sept. 6, 1789, in *The Portable Thomas Jefferson*, ed. Merrill D. Peterson (New York: Viking, 1975), p. 449.

23. Gideon Hausner, *Justice in Jerusalem* (New York: Harper & Row, 1966), p. 27.

24. Hardwick quoted in A. Alvarez, *Under Pressure: The Writer in Society* (Baltimore: Penguin, 1965), p. 176.

25. Isaacs, *Jews and American Politics*, p. 149.

26. Gerhard Lenski, *The Religious Factor: A Sociological Study of Religion's Impact on Politics, Economics and Family Life* (Garden City, N.Y.: Doubleday Anchor, 1963), pp. 152–53, 157.

27. Alan Fisher, "Continuity and Erosion of Jewish Liberalism," *American Jewish Historical Quarterly*, 66 (December 1976), 334, 348.

28. Fuchs, *Political Behavior*, pp. 176, 180–82, and Introduction, *American Jewish Quarterly*, 66 (December 1976), 182, 186.

29. Lipset, *Revolution and Counter-revolution*, p. 153.

30. Himmelfarb, *Jews of Modernity*, p. 69.

31. Isaacs, *Jews and American Politics*, p. 119.

32. Benjamin C. Bradlee, *Conversations with Kennedy* (New York: Pocket Books, 1976), p. 193.

33. Will Maslow, "Jewish Political Power: An Assessment," *American Jewish Historical Quarterly*, 66 (December 1976), 353.

34. Benjamin Disraeli, *Lord George Bentinck: A Political Biography* (London: Longmans, Green, 1881), pp. 356–57, 358.

35. Fuchs, *Political Behavior*, pp. 182–84, 190–91; Fisher, "Continuity and Erosion," p. 335.

36. Seymour Martin Lipset and Earl Rabb, *The Politics of Unreason: Right-Wing Extremism in America, 1790–1970* (New York: Harper & Row,

1970), pp. 229, 231, 244; Lucy S. Dawidowicz and Leon J. Goldstein, *Politics in a Pluralist Democracy: Studies of Voting in the 1960 Election* (New York: Institute of Human Relations Press, 1963), pp. 88–89.

37. Anthony Lukas, "The A.C.L.U. Against Itself," *New York Times Magazine* (July 9, 1978), p. 10.

38. Lenski, *The Religious Factor*, pp. 152–69, 209–10.

39. Werner Cohn, "The Politics of American Jews," in *The Jews: Social Patterns of an American Group*, ed. Marshall Sklare (New York: Free Press, 1958), pp. 615–19, 621, 624–25.

40. Robert Conquest, *The Great Terror: Stalin's Purge of the Thirties* (New York: MacMillan, 1968), p. 445; Hugh Thomas, *Cuba: The Pursuit of Freedom* (New York: Harper & Row, 1971), pp. 577, 1,101.

41. Ned Polsky in "Jewishness and the Younger Intellectuals," *Commentary*, 31 (April 1961), 345; Louis Ruchames, "Jewish Radicalism in the United States," in Rose, *Ghetto and Beyond*, pp. 232, 251.

42. Gompers quoted in Morton Keller, *Affairs of State* (Cambridge: Harvard University Press, 1977), p. 397.

43. De Cleyre quoted in Paul Avrich, *An American Anarchist: The Life of Voltairine de Cleyre* (Princeton: Princeton University Press, 1978), pp. 77, 78.

44. Lenski, *The Religious Factor*, p. 139; Dawidowicz and Goldstein *Politics in a Pluralist Democracy*, p. 76.

45. Jonah J. Goldstein quoted in Dawidowicz and Goldstein, *Politics in a Pluralist Democracy*, p. 87.

46. Himmelfarb, *Jews of Modernity*, pp. 66, 91.

47. Fisher, "Continuity and Erosion," p. 326; Isaacs, *Jews and American Politics*, p. 196.

48. Lev Kopelev, *To Be Preserved Forever* (Philadelphia: J. B. Lippincott, 1977), p. 102.

The Jew in Mass Culture

7. The Enchantment of Comedy

1. Norman Mailer, *Marilyn* (New York: Warner, 1975), p. 216.

2. George Burns quoted in Larry Wilde, *The Great Comedians* (Seacaucus, N.J.: Citadel, 1973), p. 150.

3. Ruth R. Wisse, *The Schlemiel as Modern Hero* (Chicago: University of Chicago Press, 1971); Robert Alter, *Defenses of the Imagination: Jewish Writers and Modern Historical Crisis* (Philadelphia: Jewish Publication Society of America, 1977), pp. 155–67; Sarah Blacher Cohen, ed., *Comic Relief: Humor in Contemporary American Literature* (Urbana: Uni-

versity of Illinois Press, 1978), pp. 127–86; Allen Guttmann, "Jewish Humor," in *The Comic Imagination in American Literature*, ed. Louis D. Rubin (New Brunswick, N.J.: Rutgers University Press, 1973), pp. 329–38.

4. Israel Shenker, *Words and Their Masters* (Garden City, N.Y.: Doubleday, 1974), p. 52; Diller quoted in Wilder, *Great Comedians*, p. 227.

5. Alfred Kazin, "Richard Hofstadter, 1916–1970," *American Scholar*, 40 (Summer 1971), 397.

6. "The Mad Mad Mel Brooks," *Newsweek*, 85 (Feb. 17, 1975), 57; Albert Goldman, *Freakshow* (New York: Atheneum, 1971), pp. 236–38; Philip Roth, *Reading Myself and Others* (New York: Farrar, Straus and Giroux, 1975), pp. 20–21.

7. Neil Simon, *The Sunshine Boys* (New York: Random House, 1973), p. 107.

8. Mark Zborowski and Elizabeth Herzog, *Life is With People: The Culture of the Shtetl* (New York: Schocken, 1962), pp. 279–80.

9. Roth, *Reading Myself*, p. 20.

10. Quoted in William Novak and Moshe Waldoks, eds., *The Big Book of Jewish Humor* (New York: Harper & Row, 1981), p. 60.

11. Alfred Kazin, *A Walker in the City* (New York: Grove, 1951), p. 8.

12. Alter, *Defenses of the Imagination*, pp. 156–57, 167.

13. Joseph Heller, *Catch-22* (New York: Dell, 1962), p. 30; James Nagel, "Two Brief Manuscript Sketches: Heller's *Catch-22*," *Modern Fiction Studies*, 20 (Summer 1974), 222–24; Brooks quoted in "Mad Mad Mel Brooks," *Newsweek*, p. 54; Dorothy Parker, *The Portable Dorothy Parker* (New York: Penguin, 1976), p. 99.

14. Albert Camus, *The Myth of Sisyphus and Other Essays* (New York: Vintage, 1955), p. 96.

15. "S. J. Perelman," in *Writers at Work: Second Series*, ed. George Plimpton (New York: Penguin, 1977), p. 250; Wallace Markfield, "The Yiddishization of American Humor," *Esquire*, 64 (October 1965), 114.

16. "Blazing Brooks," *Time*, 105 (Jan. 13, 1975), 56.

17. Kenneth S. Lynn, *Mark Twain and Southwestern Humor* (Boston: Little, Brown, 1960), p. 30; Brendan Gill, *Here at The New Yorker* (New York: Berkley, 1976), pp. 188, 294, 307, 312.

18. Nathanael West, *The Day of the Locust* (New York: Bantam, 1959), p. 3; Theodor Reik, *Jewish Wit* (New York: Gamut, 1962), pp. 111–12.

19. Quoted in Goldman, *Freakshow*, p. 174.

20. Albert Goldman, *Ladies and Gentlemen, Lenny Bruce!!* (New York: Ballantine, 1974), p. 147.

21. Neil Simon, *The Prisoner of Second Avenue* (New York: Random House, 1972), passim.

22. Fred Allen quoted in "Master of Silence," *Time*, 105 (Jan. 6, 1975), 83; S. J. Perelman, *The Most of S. J. Perelman* (New York: Simon and

Schuster, 1958), p. 618; Woody Allen, *The Nightclub Years, 1964–1968* (United Artists).

23. Roth, *Reading Myself*, p. 244.

24. Wallace Markfield, *You Could Live If They Let You* (New York: Knopf, 1974), pp. 75–76.

25. John Murray Cuddihy, *The Ordeal of Civility: Freud, Marx, Lévi-Strauss, and the Jewish Struggle with Modernity* (New York: Basic Books, 1974), p. 233.

26. Shenker, *Words and Their Masters*, p. 364; Pauline Kael, "Raising Kane," in Pauline Kael, Herman Mankiewicz, and Orson Welles, *The Citizen Kane Book* (Boston: Little Brown, 1971), p. 33.

27. Axel Madsen, *Billy Wilder* (Bloomington: Indiana University Press, 1969), p. 17.

28. *Portable Dorothy Parker*, p. 96.

29. Mordecai Richler, *Cocksure* (New York: Bantam, 1969), p. 30.

30. Tom Lehrer, *Too Many Songs by Tom Lehrer* (New York: Pantheon, 1981), pp. 124–25.

31. Goldman, *Lenny Bruce*, p. 152; Gregory quoted in Wilde, *Great Comedians*, p. 259.

32. Markfield, "Yiddishization," p. 114.

33. Irving Kristol, "Is Jewish Humor Dead?: The Rise and Fall of the Jewish Joke," *Commentary*, 12 (November 1951), 434–35.

34. Allen, *Nightclub Years*.

35. Leonard W. Levy, *Against the Law: The Nixon Court and Criminal Justice* (New York: Harper and Row, 1974), pp. xi–xii.

36. "Playboy Interview: Joseph Heller," *Playboy*, 20 (June 1975), 73; Heller, *Catch-22*, p. 312.

37. Allen in Wilde, *Great Comedians*, pp. 30–31.

38. Roth, *Reading Myself*, p. 21; Stephen J. Whitfield, "Comic Echoes of Kafka," *American Humor*, 9 (Spring 1982), 1–5.

39. Franz Kafka, "The Hunger Artist," in *The Complete Stories*, ed. Nahum N. Glatzer (New York: Schocken, 1971), p. 277.

8. The Comedy of Disenchantment: The Case of Jules Feiffer

1. John Culhane, "The Cartoon Killers Thrive Again," *New York Times Magazine* (Nov. 9, 1975), p. 38.

2. John Lahr, *Up Against the Fourth Wall: Essays on Modern Theater* (New York: Grove, 1970), p. 94; Robert Hatch, "Little Murders," *Nation*, 208 (Jan. 20, 1969), 95.

3. James Thurber, *The Years with Ross* (1959; rpt. New York: Ballantine, 1972), p. 56.

4. Feiffer quoted in Martin Garbus, *Ready for the Defense* (New York: Farrar, Straus and Giroux, 1971), pp. 112–13; Robert Brustein, *Seasons of Discontent: Dramatic Opinions, 1959–1965* (New York: Simon

and Schuster, 1965), p. 112, and *The Culture Watch: Essays on Theatre and Society, 1969–1974* (New York: Knopf, 1975), p. 36; Arthur M. Schlesinger, Jr., *A Thousand Days: John F. Kennedy in the White House* (1965; rpt. New York: Fawcett, 1967), pp. 667–68.

 5. Glatstein quoted in Howe, *World of Our Fathers*, p. 452.

 6. Nathanael West, "Some Notes on Miss L," *Contempo*, 3, No. 9 (May 15, 1933), 1–2.

 7. Roth, *Reading Myself*, pp. 80–82; Richard Kostelanetz, *Master Minds* (New York: Macmillan, 1969), p. 216; Edward Rothstein, "Fanfares for Aaron Copland at 80," *New York Times* (Nov. 9, 1980), p. 21; Mordecai Richler, *St. Urbain's Horseman* (New York: Knopf, 1971), pp. 87–88; Wallace Markfield, *To an Early Grave* (New York: Simon and Schuster, 1964), pp. 110–13, 183–86.

 8. Feiffer quoted in Robin Brantley, "Knock, Knock: Who's There? Feiffer," *New York Times Magazine* (May 16, 1976), p. 48, and in Julius Novick, "Jules Feiffer and the Almost-In-Group," *Harper's*, 223 (September 1961), 60; Kevin Michael McAuliffe, *The Great American Newspaper: The Rise and Fall of The Village Voice* (New York: Scribner's, 1978), pp. 83–91; Jules Feiffer, ed., *The Great Comic Book Heroes* (New York: Dial, 1965), pp. 17, 34–36, 49–52; Stephen Becker, *Comic Art in America* (New York: Simon and Schuster, 1959), p. 378.

 9. Leslie A. Fiedler, *Waiting for the End: The American Literary Scene from Hemingway to Baldwin* (1964; rpt. London: Penguin, 1967), p. 74; Flannery O'Connor, *The Habit of Being: Letters*, ed. Sally Fitzgerald (New York: Farrar, Straus and Giroux, 1979), pp. 349, 371; Kenneth Tynan, Introduction to Jules Feiffer, *Sick Sick Sick* (London: Collins, 1959), n. pag.

 10. Elizabeth Frank, "Jules Feiffer: Articulate Rage," *Art News*, 73 (February 1974), 80.

 11. Steinberg quoted in Hilton Kramer, "Getting a Line on Steinberg," *New York Times Magazine* (April 16, 1978), p. 40; David Segal, "Feiffer, Steinberg and Others," *Commentary*, 32 (November 1961), 433–34.

 12. Novick, "Jules Feiffer," p. 59; Feiffer, "Superman," in *Feiffer's Album* (New York: Random House, 1963), pp. 66–69.

 13. Tynan, *Sick Sick Sick*, n. pag.; Novick, "Jules Feiffer," p. 59; Segal, "Feiffer, Steinberg," p. 432; Nabokov quoted in Alfred Appel, Jr., *Nabokov's Dark Cinema* (New York: Oxford University Press, 1974), p. 83.

 14. Vladimir Nabokov, *Lolita* (New York: Putnam's, 1955), p. 285.

 15. Brantley, "Knock, Knock," p. 50; Feiffer, Introduction to *LBJ Lampooned: Cartoon Criticism of Lyndon B. Johnson*, eds. Sig Rosenblum and Charles Antin (New York: Cobble Hill Press, 1968), p. 10.

 16. Feiffer quoted in Brantley, "Knock, Knock," p. 60.

 17. Mort Sahl, *Heartland* (New York: Harcourt Brace Jovanovich,

1976), p. 54: Pauline Kael, *Deeper into Movies* (Boston: Atlantic-Little, Brown, 1973), p. 284.

18. Feiffer, "Crawling Arnold," in *Feiffer's Album*, pp. 108–10.

19. *Feiffer's Album*, pp. 119–20, and Feiffer, *Comic Book Heroes*, pp. 50–53.

20. James Q. Wilson, *Thinking About Crime* (1975, rpt. New York: Vintage, 1977), p. 19; Robert Sherrill, *The Saturday Night Special* (New York: Charterhouse, 1973), pp. 126–27.

21. Feiffer quoted in Lahr, *Up Against the Fourth Wall*, p. 83; Feiffer, *Little Murders* (New York: Random House, 1968), pp. 23, 83, 88, 102–4, 106.

22. Feiffer, *Little Murders*, pp. 52–55, 63.

23. Feiffer, *Little Murders* pp. 64–67, 97–98.

24. Jules Feiffer, *The White House Murder Case* (New York: Grove, 1970), pp. 46–48, 106–7.

25. Feiffer, *White House Murder*, p. 48.

26. Henry Adams, *History of the United States of America* (New York: Scribner's, 1921), VII, 35.

27. Brustein, *Culture Watch*, p. 32; Feiffer, Introduction to *LBJ Lampooned*, p. 14; Feiffer quoted in Brantley, "Knock, Knock," p. 50.

28. Hamlin Hill, "Black Humor: Its Cause and Cure," *Colorado Quarterly*, 17 (Summer 1968), 63.

29. Jenkins v. Georgia, 418 U.S. 153, 160–61 (1974); Clarence Petersen, *The Bantam Story* (New York: Bantam, 1970), p. 126.

30. Ernest Becker, *The Denial of Death* (New York: Free Press, 1973), p. 169; Joan Mellen, *Women and Their Sexuality in the New Film* (New York: Dell, 1973), pp. 63, 68–70; Molly Haskell, *From Reverence to Rape: The Treatment of Women in the Movies* (New York: Holt, Rinehart and Winston, 1974), pp. 360–61.

31. Feiffer quoted in Brantley, "Knock, Knock," p. 50, and in Tom Buckley, "Feiffer Fills Play with Food and Thought," *New York Times* (Feb. 10, 1976), p. 42.

32. Feiffer, *Knock Knock* (New York: Hill and Wang, 1976), pp. 29, 116–17.

33. *New York Times* (Nov. 21, 1967), p. 54.

34. T. E. Kalem, "Kooky Miracle," *Time*, 107 (Feb. 2 1976), 55.

35. Charles Garret Vannest and Henry Lester Smith quoted in Frances FitzGerald, "Rewriting American History: II," *New Yorker*, 55 (March 5, 1979), 42; William Goldman, *The Season: A Candid Look at Broadway* (New York: Harcourt, Brace and World, 1969), pp. 148–51.

36. Nixon quoted in *Washington Post, Fall of a President*, p. 222; J. Anthony Lukas, *The Barnyard Epithet and Other Obscenities: Notes on the Chicago Conspiracy Trial* (New York: Harper Perennial, 1970), p. 103.

37. Levine quoted in Thomas S. Buechner, Foreword to *The Arts of David Levine* (New York: Knopf, 1978), p. x.

38. Feiffer, *Ackroyd* (1977; rpt. New York: Avon, 1978), p. 308.

9. All That Jazz

1. Samson Raphaelson, "The Day of Atonement," rpt. in Moses Rischin, ed., *Immigration and the American Tradition* (Indianapolis: Bobbs-Merrill, 1976), pp. 306–30.
2. Robert L. Carringer, Introduction to *The Jazz Singer* (Madison: University of Wisconsin Press, 1979), pp. 11–20; Lester D. Friedman, *Hollywood's Image of the Jew* (New York: Ungar, 1982), pp. 48–50.
3. Richard Corliss, *Talking Pictures: Screenwriters in the American Cinema* (New York: Penguin, 1975), pp. 165–65, 173; *New York Times* (Jan. 2, 1981), p. C8; Thomas Weyr, *Reaching for Paradise: The Playboy Vision of America* (New York: Times Books, 1978), p. 18.
4. Carringer, *Jazz Singer*, pp. 28–31.
5. Carringer, *Jazz Singer*, pp. 31–32.
6. Michael Freedland, *Jolson* (New York: Stein & Day, 1972), pp. 18, 25–27, 45, 76.
7. H. Junker, "Kid from Brooklyn," *Newsweek*, 72 (Feb. 5, 1968), 82; William Bender, "Tin Pan Tailor," *Time*, 97 (Jan. 11, 1971), 46–47; Edwin Miller, "High-flying Balladeer," *Seventeen*, 32 (July 1973), 100, 130; Robert Windeler, "Song," *People*, 11 (Jan. 22, 1979), 52–55; Jay Cocks, "Bandmaster of the Mainstream," *Time*, 117 (Jan. 26, 1981), 71.
8. E. L. Doctorow, *Ragtime* (New York: Bantam, 1976), p. 39.
9. J. Hoberman, "Is 'The Jazz Singer' Good for the Jews?", *Village Voice* (Jan. 7–13, 1981), pp. 1, 31–33.
10. Thomas Cripps, "The Movie Jew as an Image of Assimilationism, 1903–1927," *Journal of Popular Film*, 4 (1975), 190–91, 202–3; Friedman, *Hollywood's Image*, pp. 50–51, 52.

10. In the Big Inning

1. Abraham Cahan, *Yekl and the Imported Bridegroom and Other Stories of the New York Ghetto* (New York: Dover, 1970), pp. 5–6.
2. Bernard Malamud, *The Natural* (New York: Farrar, Straus & Giroux, 1952), p. 237.
3. Roth, *Reading Myself*, pp. 180–82; Philip Roth, *Portnoy's Complaint* (New York: Bantam, 1970), pp. 8–10, 78–80.
4. Mark Harris, *The Southpaw* (Indianapolis: Bobbs-Merrill, 1953), p. 348.
5. Louis Kaufman, Barbara Fitzgerald, and Tom Sewell, *Moe Berg: Athlete, Scholar, Spy* (Boston: Little, Brown, 1974), pp. 29–44, 65, 264.
6. Quoted in James Atlas, *Delmore Schwartz: The Life of an American Poet* (New York: Farrar, Straus & Giroux, 1977), p. 281.
7. Mordecai Richler, *Hunting Tigers Under Glass* (London: Panther, 1971), pp. 62–77; and *St. Urbain's Horseman* (New York: Knopf, 1971), pp. 236–48.
8. Cahan, *Yekl*, p. 70.

9. Irwin Shaw, *Voices of a Summer's Day* (New York: Delacorte, 1965), p. 142; Irving S. Saposnik, "Homage to Clyde Kluttz, or The Education of a Jewish Baseball Fan," *Journal of American Culture*, 4 (Fall 1981), 58–65.

11. From Publick Occurrences to Pseudo-Events: Journalists and Their Critics

1. Walter Lippmann, *Liberty and the News* (New York: Harcourt, Brace and Howe, 1920), p. 5; Allan Nevins, "American Journalism and Its Historical Treatment," in *Allan Nevins on History*, ed. Ray Allen Billington (New York: Scribner's, 1975), p. 82.
2. Bernard A. Weisberger, *The American Newspaperman* (Chicago: University of Chicago Press, 1961), pp. 1–2.
3. Jonathan D. Sarna, *Jacksonian Jew: The Two Worlds of Mordecai Noah* (New York: Holmes & Meier, 1981), pp. 5–6.
4. George Juergens, *Joseph Pulitzer and the New York World* (Princeton: Princeton University Press, 1966), pp. x–xii, 366, 368; Michael Schudson, *Discovering the News: A Social History of American Newspapers* (New York: Basic, 1978), pp. 95–105; W. A. Swanberg, *Pulitzer* (New York: Scribner's, 1967), pp. 8, 38–39, 42, 136.
5. Allan Nevins, "Fabian Franklin," *Dictionary of American Biography*, Supplement Two (New York: Scribner's, 1958), pp. xxii, 206–7; Rose Zeitlin, *Henrietta Szold: Record of a Life* (New York: Dial, 1952), p. 9.
6. Chalmers M. Roberts, *The Washington Post: The First Hundred Years* (Boston: Houghton Mifflin, 1977), pp. 196, 197.
7. Isaacs, *Jews and American Politics*, p. 49.
8. Edwin Emery and Henry Ladd Smith, *The Press and America* (New York: Prentice-Hall, 1954), p. 567; John Luskin, *Lippmann, Liberty, and the Press* (University, Ala.: University of Alabama Press, 1972), p. 93; Timothy Crouse, *The Boys on the Bus* (New York: Ballantine, 1974), pp. 90–91, 104–5; Bernard Roshco, *Newsmaking* (Chicago: University of Chicago Press, 1975), p. 144n.
9. John Rankin quoted in James MacGregor Burns, *Roosevelt: The Soldier of Freedom, 1940–1945* (New York: Harcourt Brace Jovanovich, 1970), p. 431.
10. Gay Talese, *The Kingdom and the Power* (Cleveland: World, 1969), pp. 59, 60, 91–93, 168; David Halberstam, *The Powers That Be* (New York: Knopf, 1979), pp. 216–17; Arthur Krock, *Memoirs: Sixty Years on the Firing Line* (New York: Funk and Wagnalls, 1968), pp. xii, 8.
11. H. L. Mencken, *The American Language*, eds. Raven L. McDavid and David W. Maurer (New York: Knopf, 1963), pp. 253–56, 260–64.
12. Isaacs, *Jews and American Politics*, pp. 43–45.
13. Richard S. Tedlow, *Keeping the Corporate Image: Public Relations*

and Business, 1900–1950 (Greenwich, Conn.: J. A. I. Press, 1979), pp. 39–45, 91–97; Michael Wheeler, *Lies, Damn Lies, and Statistics: The Manipulation of Public Opinion in America* (New York: Liveright, 1976), p. 38.

14. Marie Winn, "Lieberman: Staying in Vogue," *New York Times Magazine* (May 13, 1979), pp. 50, 52; Ben Hecht, *A Child of the Century* (New York: Signet, 1955), p. 114; Herbert Block quoted in Stefan Kanfer, "Editorial Cartoons: Capturing the Essence," *Time*, 105 (Feb. 3, 1975), p. 63.

15. Norman Mailer in *The Tales of Hoffman*, eds. Mark L. Levine, George C. McNamee and Daniel Greenberg (New York: Bantam, 1970), p. 206; Jack Newfield, *Bread and Roses Too* (New York: Dutton, 1971), pp. 267–80.

16. Isaacs, *Jews and American Politics*, p. 49.

17. Peter Gay, *Freud, Jews and Other Germans: Masters and Victims in Modernist Culture* (New York: Oxford University Press, 1978), pp. 154–55, 156–57, 172–73; Karl A. Schleunes, *The Twisted Road to Auschwitz: Nazi Policy Toward German Jews, 1933–1939* (Urbana: University of Illinois Press, 1970), pp. 42–43; Fritz Stern, "The Burden of Success: Reflections on German Jewry," in *Art, Politics, and Will: Essays in Honor of Lionel Trilling*, eds. Quentin Anderson et al. (New York: Basic, 1977), pp. 132, 134; Arthur Koestler, *Arrow in the Blue: An Autobiography* (New York: Macmillan, 1952), pp. 180–81, 189–90.

18. Harold Rosenberg, *Discovering the Present: Three Decades in Art, Culture, and Politics* (Chicago: University of Chicago Press, 1973), p. 230.

19. I. F. Stone, *Underground to Palestine* (New York: Pantheon, 1978), pp. 229–31; Nat Hentoff and Joseph Kraft in "Jewishness and the Younger Intellectuals: A Symposium," *Commentary*, 31 (April 1961), 330, 336.

20. Theodore H. White, *In Search of History: A Personal Adventure* (New York: Harper and Row, 1978), pp. 22, 119–20.

21. Walter Lippmann, *The Stakes of Diplomacy* (New York: Henry Holt, 1915), pp. 62, 63, 66; Hari N. Dam, *The Intellectual Odyssey of Walter Lippmann: A Study of His Protean Thought, 1910–1960* (New York: Gordon, 1973), p. 159; "We are Wanderers," *Time*, 32 (Dec. 5, 1938), 18.

22. Walter Lippmann, "Public Opinion and the American Jew," *American Hebrew*, 110 (April 14, 1922), 575.

23. Lippmann, "Public Opinion," p. 575.

24. Isaac Bashevis Singer, *Shosha* (New York: Farrar, Straus and Giroux, 1978), p. 18.

25. Lippmann, *Diplomacy*, p. 62.

26. Halberstam, *Powers*, p. 370; Isaacs, *Jews and American Politics*, pp. 44–45; Heinz Eulau, "From Public Opinion to Public Philosophy: Walter Lippmann's Classic Reexamined," *American Journal of Economics and Sociology*, 15 (July 1956), 443–44; Stephen Birmingham, "*Our Crowd*": *The Great Jewish Families of New York* (New York: Dell, 1968), pp. 160–61, 288.

27. Randolph Bourne, "The Jew in Trans-National America," in *War and the Intellectuals: Collected Essays, 1915–1919*, ed. Carl Resek (New York: Harper and Row, 1964), p. 132; "Wanderers," *Time*, p. 18;

David Elliott Weingast, *Walter Lippmann: A Study in Personal Journalism* (New Brunswick, N.J.: Rutgers University Press, 1949), pp. 3–5, 6–7.

28. Ronald Steel, *Walter Lippmann and the American Century* (New York: Vintage, 1981), pp. 186–96.

29. Stern, "Burden of Success," pp. 134–35, 137–38; Cuddihy, *Ordeal of Civility*, pp. 227–28; Mencken quoted in Carl Bode, *Mencken* (Carbondale: Southern Illinois University Press, 1969), pp. 228–29.

30. Walter Lippmann, *Public Opinion* (New York: Macmillan, 1922; rpt. 1965), pp. 10, 16, 49, 63–65, 74–75.

31. Charles Forcey, *The Crossroads of Liberalism: Croly, Weyl, Lippmann and the Progressive Era, 1900–1925* (New York: Oxford University Press, 1961), pp. 91–93; Richard H. Rovere, *Arrivals and Departures: A Journalist's Memoir* (New York: Macmillan, 1976), p. 126.

32. Cuddihy, *Ordeal of Civility*, pp. 4–8, 142–44.

33. Kafka quoted in Gustav Janouch, *Gespräche mit Kafka* (Frankfurt: S. Fisher, 1968), p. 135.

34. Clinton Rossiter and James Lare, eds., Introduction to *The Essential Lippmann: A Political Philosophy for Liberal Democracy* (New York: Vintage, 1965), pp. xi–xii, xv–xx.

35. Thorstein Veblen, "The Intellectual Pre-eminence of Jews in Modern Europe," in *The Portable Veblen*, ed. Max Lerner (New York: Viking, 1950), pp. 469, 472, 473–77; Isaac Deutscher, *The Non-Jewish Jew and Other Essays* (New York: Hill and Wang, 1968), pp. 27, 33, 36, 41; Howard Morley Sachar, *The Course of Modern Jewish History* (New York: Delta, 1963), pp. 394–98, 401–3.

36. Marthe Robert, *From Oedipus to Moses: Freud's Jewish Identity* (Garden City, N.Y.: Doubleday, 1976), pp. 3–5.

37. Halberstam, *Powers*, pp. 368–69; Harlan B. Phillips, ed., *Felix Frankfurter Reminisces* (New York: Reynal, 1960), p. 160.

38. Bruce Kuklick, *The Rise of American Philosophy: Cambridge, Massachusetts, 1860–1930* (New Haven: Yale University Press, 1977), pp. 455–58, 568–69.

39. Max Lerner, *Actions and Passions: Notes on the Multiple Revolution of Our Time* (New York: Simon and Schuster, 1949), p. 302; Norman Podhoretz, *Doings and Undoings: The Fifties and After in American Writing* (New York: Farrar, Straus, 1964), pp. 321–22.

40. Edward L. Schapsmeier and Frederick H. Schapsmeier, *Walter Lippmann: Philosopher-Journalist* (Washington, D.C.: Public Affairs Press, 1969), p. 110; William Safire, *The New Language of Politics: An Anecdotal Dictionary of Catchwords, Slogans, and Political Usage* (New York: Random House, 1968), pp. 21, 83–84; Edmund Wilson, *Letters on Literature and Politics, 1912–1972* (New York: Farrar, Straus and Giroux, 1977), p. 26.

41. Halberstam, *Powers*, pp. 223, 318, 368, 372, 523; James Reston, "Conclusion: The Mockingbird and the Taxicab," in *Walter Lippmann and His Times*, eds. Marquis Childs and James Reston (New York: Harcourt, Brace, 1959), pp. 233, 234, 237–38; J. Anthony Lukas, "Say it Ain't So, Scotty," in *Stop the Presses, I Want to Get Off!* ed. Richard Pollak (New York: Delta, 1975), p. 149.

42. Arthur M. Schlesinger, Jr., "Walter Lippmann: The Intellectual

v. Politics," in Childs and Reston, *Lippmann*, pp. 197–98, 204, 223–25; Rovere, *Arrivals*, pp. 130–31; Steel, *Lippmann*, passim.

43. Schapsmeier and Schapsmeier, *Lippmann*, p. 80; Walter Lippmann, *Essays in the Public Philosophy* (New York: Mentor, 1956), p. 19.

44. Joseph Marion Jones, *The Fifteen Weeks (February 21–June 5, 1947)* (New York: Viking, 1955), pp. 226–29, 230–32; Scott Jackson, "Prologue to the Marshall Plan: The Origin of the American Commitment for a European Recovery Program," *Journal of American History*, 65 (March 1979), 1,051.

45. Benjamin Franklin, "An Account of the Supreme Court of Judicature of the State of Pennsylvania," in *Freedom of the Press from Zenger to Jefferson*, ed. Leonard W. Levy (Indianapolis: Bobbs-Merrill, 1966), pp. 154–58; Henry Adams, *The Education of Henry Adams: An Autobiography* (Boston: Houghton Mifflin, 1918, rpt. 1961), p. 211; H. L. Mencken, "Journalism in America," in *Prejudices: A Selection*, ed. James T. Farrell (New York: Vintage, 1958), p. 217.

46. Lippmann, *Public Opinion*, pp. 10–18, 54–60, 63–65.

47. Lippmann, *Public Opinion*, pp. 161–74; *A Preface to Morals* (New York: Macmillan, 1929), p. 245; and *The Phantom Public* (New York: Harcourt, Brace, 1925), pp. 63–65.

48. John Dewey, "Public Opinion," *New Republic*, 30 (May 3, 1922), 286; Mark De Wolfe Howe, ed., *Holmes-Laski Letters* (Cambridge: Harvard University Press, 1953), pp. 1, 417; Steel, *Lippmann*, pp. 180–84.

49. Eulau, "Public Opinion," pp. 439, 447; Schlesinger, "Intellectual v. Politics," p. 202; C. Wright Mills, ed., Introduction to *Images of Man: The Classic Tradition in Sociological Thinking* (New York: George Braziller, 1960), p. 11.

50. Dam, *Lippmann*, p. 25; Edward A. Purcell, Jr., *The Crisis of Democratic Theory: Scientific Naturalism and the Problem of Value* (Lexington: University Press of Kentucky, 1973), pp. 104–7; Rossiter and Lare, *Essential Lippmann*, p. xviii; Roderick Nash, *The Nervous Generation: American Thought, 1917–1930* (Chicago: Rand McNally, 1970), pp. 57–58.

51. Fred W. Friendly, *The Good Guys, the Bad Guys and the First Amendment: Free Speech vs. Fairness in Broadcasting* (New York: Random House, 1976), p. 257; Roshco, *Newsmaking*, p. 112; Luskin, *Liberty*, p. 52.

52. U.S. v. Associated Press, 52 F. Supp. 362 (1943); Theodore C. Sorensen, *Decision-Making in the White House: The Olive Branch or the Arrows* (New York: Columbia University Press, 1963), p. 45.

53. Bernard C. Cohen, "The Press, the Public and Foreign Policy," in *Reader in Public Opinion and Communication*, eds. Bernard Berelson and Morris Janowitz (New York: Free Press, 1966), p. 134; Murray Edelman, *The Symbolic Uses of Politics* (Urbana: University of Illinois Press, 1967), p. 5; C. Wright Mills, *The Power Elite* (New York: Oxford University Press, 1956), pp. 305, 312–13; Robert E. Park, "News as a Form of Knowledge," in *On Social Control and Collective Behavior: Selected*

Papers, ed. Ralph H. Turner (Chicago: University of Chicago Press, 1967), pp. 39–41, 42; Herbert J. Gans, *Deciding What's News: A Study of CBS Evening News, NBC Nightly News, Newsweek and Time* (New York: Pantheon, 1979), pp. 201–2; Jacques Ellul, *Propaganda: The Formation of Men's Attitudes* (New York: Knopf, 1965), p. 101.

54. Karl Mannheim, *Ideology and Utopia: An Introduction to the Sociology of Knowledge* (New York: Harcourt, Brace and World, 1955), pp. xxii–xxiii, 330, 331; Gans, *Deciding What's News*, p. 310.

55. Walter Lippmann, "Two Revolutions in the American Press," in Rossiter and Lare, *Essential Lippmann*, pp. 405-6; Lippmann, *Public Opinion*, pp. 19, 233-52.

56. Walter Lippmann, *American Inquisitors* (New York: Macmillan, 1928), p. 46; David A. Hollinger, "Science and Anarchy: Walter Lippmann's *Drift and Mastery*," *American Quarterly*, 29 (Winter 1977), 467–69; Thomas S. Kuhn, *The Structure of Scientific Revolutions* (Chicago: University of Chicago Press, 1970), pp. 170–73; Donald Worster, *Nature's Economy: The Roots of Ecology* (Garden City, N.Y.: Doubleday, 1979), pp. xi, 167, 169, 345–46.

57. Edward L. Bernays, *Crystallizing Public Opinion* (New York: Liveright, 1923), pp. 75, 98–100, 107–8, 116–117, 156–57, 194–95, 197; Edward L. Bernays, *Propaganda* (New York: Liveright, 1928), pp. 25, 47, 93; Edward L. Bernays, *Biography of an Idea: Memoirs of Public Relations Counsel Edward L. Bernays* (New York: Simon and Schuster, 1965), pp. 290–91; Ivy Lee, *Publicity* (New York: Industries Publishing, 1925), p. 21.

58. Lippmann, *Public Opinion*, p. 203; Nevins, "American Journalism," p. 90; Roshco, *Newsgathering*, p. 47; Leo C. Rosten, *The Washington Correspondents* (New York: Harcourt, Brace, 1937), pp. xv, 351–52.

59. Lippmann, *Public Opinion*, p. 226; Rosten, *Washington Correspondents*, pp. 232–35, 236, 268, 278–90.

60. Rosten, *Washington Correspondents*, pp. 149-150; Schudson, *Discovering the News*, p. 218n; Roshco, *Newsgathering*, pp. 5–6; Gaye Tuchman, *Making News: A Study in the Construction of Reality* (New York: Macmillan, 1978), pp. 1–2, 4–5; Gans, *Deciding What's News*, pp. 310–11.

61. Edward Jay Epstein, *News from Nowhere: Television and the News* (New York: Vintage, 1974), pp. xiv, xviii, 34, 43, 256–57; *Between Fact and Fiction: The Problem of Journalism* (New York: Vintage, 1975), pp. 201–2, 209.

62. Herbert J. Gans, "The Famine in American Mass-Communications Research," *American Journal of Sociology*, 77 (January 1972), 703; Epstein, *News from Nowhere*, pp. 34–37, 260.

63. Reuven Frank quoted in Epstein, *News from Nowhere*, pp. 4–5, 39; Epstein, *Fact and Fiction*, p. 203; Robert E. Park, "The Natural History of the Newspaper," in Turner, *Social Control*, p. 107; White, *In Search of History*, pp. 451, 453–55; Schudson, *Discovering the News*, p. 89.

64. Epstein, *News from Nowhere*, pp. 15–16, 18–19, 42, 104, 134, 144–46, 244–46, 260–61.

65. David Riesman et al., *The Lonely Crowd: A Study in the Changing American Character* (Garden City, N.Y.: Doubleday, 1953), pp. 37–38, 106, 120–28, 131–32; Lance Morrow, "The Politics of the Box Populi," *Time*, 113 (June 11, 1979), 95; Daniel J. Boorstin, *The Americans: The Democratic Experience* (New York: Random House, 1973), p. 396.

66. Daniel J. Boorstin, *The Image: A Guide to Pseudo-Events in America* (New York: Harper and Row, 1964), pp. iii, iv, 37–38, 233–34, 269, 289.

67. Boorstin, *The Image*, pp. 9–12, 17; Erik Barnouw, *The Image Empire* (New York: Oxford University Press, 1970), p. 96; Safire, *New Language*, p. 363; and *Safire's Political Dictionary* (New York: Random House, 1978), pp. 409, 410, 577.

68. Fred W. Friendly, *Due to Circumstances Beyond Our Control . . .* (New York: Vintage, 1968), pp. 116–18; James Spada, *The Films of Robert Redford* (Secaucus, N.J.: Citadel, 1977), p. 229.

69. Epstein, *Fact and Fiction*, pp. 5–17, 19–32; Schudson, *Discovering the News*, pp. 175–76.

70. Boorstin, *Democratic Experience*, pp. 392, 393, 396; Jefferson to Adamantios Coray (1823), in Levy, *Freedom of the Press*, p. 376; Frank Stanton quoted in Friendly, *Due to Circumstances*, p. 291.

71. Lippmann, *Public Opinion*, pp. 212–13; Alex Inkeles, *Public Opinion in Soviet Russia: A Study in Mass Persuasion* (Cambridge: Harvard University Press, 1950), p. 138; C. Wright Mills, *Power, Politics and People* (New York: Oxford University Press, 1963), pp. 37, 38, 226, 358–59, 361–63.

The Jew as Southerner

12. Jews and Other Southerners

1. Willie Morris, *Yazoo: Integration in a Deep-Southern Town* (New York: Ballantine, 1971), p. 148: Welty quoted in C. Vann Woodward, *The Burden of Southern History* (New York: Vintage, 1961), pp. 23–24.

2. William Faulkner, "The Bear," in *Three Famous Short Novels* (New York: Vintage, 1961), p. 277.

3. Isaac Babel, *Collected Stories* (London: Penguin, 1961), p. 163; Mark Zborowski and Elizabeth Herzog, *Life is with People: The Culture of the Shtetl* (New York: Schocken, 1962), pp. 55, 301, 307; "Oscar Solomon Strauss: A German Immigrant in Georgia," in *Memoirs of American*

Jews, 1775–1865, ed. Jacob Rader Marcus (Philadelphia: Jewish Publication Society, 1955), II, 298.

4. Francis Bello, "The Physicists," in Editors of *Fortune, Great American Scientists* (Englewood Cliffs, N.J.: Prentice-Hall, 1961), pp. 7–8.

5. *New York Herald Tribune*, April 11, 1933, quoted in Dan T. Carter, *Scottsboro: A Tragedy of the American South* (New York: Oxford University Press, 1969), p. 244; Ludwig Lewisohn, *Up Stream* (New York: Boni & Liveright, 1922), pp. 36–37: Joseph Salvador to Emanuel Mendes da Costa, Jan. 22, 1785, quoted in Cecil Roth, "A Description of America, 1785," *American Jewish Archives*, 17 (April 1965), 29, 30.

6. Wilbur J. Cash, *The Mind of the South* (New York: Knopf, 1941), p. 50.

7. O'Connor quoted in Robert Coles, *Farewell to the South* (Boston: Little, Brown, 1972), p. 136.

8. Harold Nicolson, *Diaries and Letters: The War Years, 1939–1945* (New York: Atheneum, 1967), II, 469.

9. William Alexander Percy, *Lanterns on the Levee: Recollections of a Planter's Son* (New York: Knopf, 1941), pp. 17, 138–39.

10. William Faulkner, *The Sound and the Fury* (New York: Vintage, 1956), p. 209; *Jewish Sentiment*, Oct. 5, 1900, p. 3, quoted in Steven Hertzberg, "The Jewish Community of Atlanta from the End of the Civil War until the Eve of the Frank Case," *American Jewish Historical Quarterly*, 62 (March 1973), 285.

11. "Isidor Straus: A Young Confederate Businessman," in Marcus, *Memoirs*, II, 304.

12. Leonard Dinnerstein, "A Note on Southern Attitudes toward Jews," *Jewish Social Studies*, 32 (1970), 49: John Higham, *Strangers in the Land: Patterns of American Nativism, 1860–1925* (New York: Atheneum, 1965), p. 92.

13. Watson quoted in C. Vann Woodward, *Tom Watson: Agrarian Rebel* (New York: Macmillan, 1938), pp. 438, 445.

14. Burns, *Roosevelt*, p. 431; Rankin quoted in John P. Roche, *The Quest for the Dream* (Chicago: Quadrangle, 1963), p. 217.

15. William F. Holmes, "Whitecapping: Anti-Semitism in the Populist Era," *American Jewish Historical Quarterly*, 63 (March 1974), 249; C. Vann Woodward, *Origins of the New South, 1877–1913* (Baton Rouge: Louisiana State University Press, 1951), p. 188; Louis Galambos, *The Public Image of Big Business in America, 1880–1940* (Baltimore: Johns Hopkins University Press, 1975), pp. 63–64.

16. John Higham, "Social Discrimination against Jews in America, 1830–1930," *American Jewish Historical Quarterly*, 47 (September 1957), 30–31; Arnold Shankman, "Atlanta Jewry, 1900–1930," *American Jewish Archives*, 25 (November 1973), 152.

17. H. L. Mencken, *Prejudices: A Selection* (New York: Vintage, 1958), p. 73.

18. Bernard Baruch, *My Own Story* (New York: Little, Brown, 1957),

pp. 48, 49; Stanley Marcus, *Minding the Store: A Memoir* (Boston: Little, Brown, 1974), pp. 27, 32–33; Charles Herbert Stember, "The Recent History of Public Attitudes," in Stember et al., *Jews in the Mind of America* (New York: Basic, 1966), p. 224; Hartley quoted in Richard Hofstadter, *Anti-Intellectualism in American Life* (New York: Knopf, 1963), p. 133.

19. Ruffin quoted in William R. Taylor, *Cavalier and Yankee: The Old South and the American National Character* (New York: Harper & Row, 1961), p. 339.

20. Elizabeth Nowell, *Thomas Wolfe: A Biography* (Garden City, N.Y.: Doubleday, 1960), pp. 86–98; Cash, *Mind of the South*, pp. 333–34.

21. Russell Kirk, *Eliot and His Age* (New York: Random House, 1971), pp. 209–10; W. W. Thornton, *American Hebrew*, 42 (April 4, 1890), 191, quoted in Leonard Dinnerstein, Introduction to Dinnerstein and Mary Dale Palsson, eds., *Jews in the South* (Baton Rouge: Louisiana State University Press, 1973), pp. 17–18.

22. Hodding Carter, *Where Main Street Meets the River* (New York: Rinehart, 1953), pp. 185, 186; Cash, *Mind of the South*, p. 334; Woodward, *Tom Watson*, p. 433; Arthur M. Schlesinger, Jr., *A Thousand Days: John F. Kennedy in the White House* (Boston: Hougton Mifflin, 1965), p. 74.

23. Jonathan Daniels, *A Southerner Discovers the South* (New York: Macmillan, 1938), pp. 258–59; Wilson quoted in A. L. Todd, *Justice on Trial: The Case of Louis D. Brandeis* (New York: McGraw-Hill, 1964), p. 138; Lawrence J. Friedman, *The White Savage: Racial Fantasies in the Postbellum South* (Englewood Cliffs, N.J.: Prentice-Hall, 1970), pp. 164–65.

24. Eli N. Evans, *The Provincials: A Personal History of Jews in the South* (New York: Atheneum, 1973), p. 189; Dixon quoted in Raymond A. Cook, *Thomas Dixon* (New York: Twayne, 1974), p. 63.

25. Nathan Perlmutter, *A Bias of Reflections: Confessions of an Incipient Old Jew* (New Rochelle, N.Y.: Arlington, 1972), p. 66.

26. Hellman quoted in *Thirty Years of Treason*, ed. Eric Bentley (New York: Viking, 1971), p. 537; James K. Feibleman, *The Way of a Man: An Autobiography* (New York: Horizon, 1969), p. 67; Arthur Krock, *Memoirs: Sixty Years on the Firing Line* (New York: Funk & Wagnalls, 1968), pp. xii, 8.

27. Hortense Calisher, *Herself* (New York: Arbor House, 1972), p. 59; Ludwig Lewisohn, *Up Stream*, pp. 77, 101; Stanley F. Chyet, "Ludwig Lewisohn in Charleston, 1892–1902," *American Jewish Historical Quarterly*, 54 (March 1965), 312.

28. "Isaac Leeser: American Jewish Missionary," in Marcus, *Memoirs*, II, 68.

29. Evans, *The Provincials*, p. 276; Alfred O. Hero, Jr., "Southern Jews," in Dinnerstein and Palsson, *Jews in the South*, p. 247.

30. Samuel Rosinger, "Deep in the Heart of Texas," in Stanley F. Chyet, ed., *Lives and Voices: A Collection of American Jewish Memoirs* (Philadelphia: Jewish Publication Society, 1972), p. 134; Malcolm Stern,

"Uncles, Goats, and Family Trees," *Reform Judaism*, 11 (Fall 1982), 19; Ulrich B. Phillips, "The Central Theme of Southern History," *American Historical Review*, 34 (October 1928), 30–43.

31. Feibleman, *Way of a Man*, p. 49; Bertram Wallace Korn, "Jews and Negro Slavery in the Old South, 1789-1865," in Dinnerstein and Palsson, *Jews in the South*, pp. 123–25, 130.

32. David L. Cohn, *Where I was Born and Raised* (Boston: Houghton Mifflin, 1948), pp. 20–21.

33. Tennessee Williams, *Penguin Plays* (London: Penguin, 1962), pp. 301, 302, 303.

34. David Byck quoted in Harry Golden, *Travels through Jewish America* (Garden City, N.Y.: Doubleday, 1973), p. 180.

35. Faulkner, "The Bear," p. 279.

36. James B. Pritchard, *Ancient Near Eastern Texts* (Princeton, N.J.: Princeton University Press, 1955), pp. 376, 378.

13. The Southern Jew as Businessman

1. Tocqueville, *Democracy in America*, II, 46, 164–66.

2. C. Vann Woodward, *The Burden of Southern History* (Baton Rouge: Louisiana State University Press, 1960), pp. 3–25, 167–91; C. Vann Woodward, *American Counterpoint: Slavery and Racism in the North-South Dialogue* (Boston: Little, Brown, 1971), pp. 3–11; Abraham D. Lavender, "Shalom—With a Southern Accent: An Examination of Jews in the South," in *A Coat of Many Colors: Jewish Subcommunities in the United States*, ed. Lavender (Westport, Conn.: Greenwood, 1977), pp. 81–96; Abraham Lavender, "Jewish Values in the Southern Milieu," in *Turn to the South: Essays on Southern Jewry*, eds. Nathan M. Kaganoff and Melvin I. Urofsky (Charlottesville: University Press of Virginia, 1979), pp. 124–34.

3. Salo Wittmayer Baron, "American Jewish History: Problems and Methods," in *Steeled in Adversity: Essays and Addresses on American Jewish Life* (Philadelphia: Jewish Publication Society, 1971), p. 47.

4. Oscar Handlin, *Adventure in Freedom: Three Hundred Years of Jewish Life in America* (New York: McGraw-Hill, 1954), pp. 51–56, 90.

5. Myron Berman, *Richmond's Jewry, 1769–1976: Shabbat in Shockoe* (Charlottesville: University Press of Virginia, 1979), pp. 7–8.

6. David McLellan, *Marx Before Marxism* (New York: Harper and Row, 1970), pp. 141, 42; Morris U. Schappes, ed., *A Documentary History of Jews in the United States, 1654–1875* (New York: Schocken, 1971), p. 472.

7. John Dollard, *Caste and Class in a Southern Town* (Garden City, N.Y.: Doubleday, 1957), p. 4; Allison Davis, Burleigh B. Gardner, and Mary R. Gardner, *Deep South: A Social Anthropological Study of Caste and Class* (Chicago: University of Chicago Press, 1941), p. 264.

8. High Sidey, "Impressions of Power and Poetry," *Time*, 109 (June 20, 1977), 31.

9. Harry Crews, *A Childhood: The Biography of a Place* (New York: Harper & Row, 1978), pp. 73–76.

10. Ralph M. Hower, *History of Macy's of New York, 1859–1919: Chapters in the Evolution of the Department Store* (Cambridge: Harvard University Press, 1946), pp. 122, 190, 211, 218, 226.

11. John Morton Blum, *The Republican Roosevelt* (New York: Atheneum, 1965), p. 37.

12. Lewis L. Strauss, *Men and Decisions* (Garden City, N.Y.: Doubleday, 1962), pp. 1, 3, 374.

13. Meyer Berger, *The Story of the New York Times, 1851–1951* (New York: Simon and Schuster, 1951), pp. 73–86; Gay Talese, *The Kingdom and the Power* (New York: World, 1969), pp. 83–86.

14. John Gunther, *Taken at the Flood: The Story of Albert D. Lasker* (New York: Harper and Row, 1960), pp. 4–5, 17, 28, 36, 88.

15. Arthur P. Dudden, *Joseph Fels and the Single-Tax Movement* (Philadelphia: Temple University Press, 1971), pp. 65, 260; Dudden and Theodore H. Von Laue, "The Russian Social Democratic Labor Party and Joseph Fels," *American Historical Review*, 61 (October 1955), 29, 38, 43, 47.

16. Bernard Baruch, *My Own Story* (New York: Henry Holt, 1957), pp. 4–5, 12, 31–32; Jordan A. Schwarz, *The Speculator: Bernard M. Baruch in Washington, 1917–1965* (Chapel Hill: University of North Carolina Press, 1981), pp. 8–13, 559–66.

17. Chaim Weizmann, *Trial and Error* (New York: Schocken, 1966), pp. 312–13; *New York Times* (Dec. 2, 1961), p. 23; Thomas P. McCann, *An American Company: The Tragedy of United Fruit* (New York: Crown, 1976), pp. 18–27; Julian B. Feibelman, *The Making of a Rabbi* (New York: Vantage Press, 1980), pp. 328–29.

18. T. A. Wise, "Lazard: In Trinity There is Strength," *Fortune*, 78 (August 1968), 158; Robert Shogun, *A Question of Judgment: The Fortas Case and the Struggle for the Supreme Court* (New York: Bobbs-Merrill, 1972), pp. 186–87.

19. Eli N. Evans, "Southern-Jewish History: Alive and Unfolding," in Kaganoff and Urofsky, *Turn to the South*, p. 159.

20. Joseph Dorfman, *The Economic Mind in American Civilization* (New York: Viking, 1946), II, 551–66; Paul K. Conkin, *Prophets of Prosperity* (Bloomington: Indiana University Press, 1980), pp. 135–41.

21. Lillian Hellman, *Pentimento: A Book of Portraits* (Boston: Little Brown, 1973), pp. 171–72.

22. Elinor Grumet, "Elliot Cohen: The Vocation of a Jewish Literary Mentor," in *Studies in the American Jewish Experience*, eds. Jacob R. Marcus and Abraham J. Peck (Cincinnati, Ohio: American Jewish Archives, 1981), I, 8–21.

23. Philip Cowen, ed., *Prejudice Against the Jew: Its Nature, Its Causes and Remedies* (New York: Philip Cowen, 1928), pp. 100–102.

24. Wilbur J. Cash, *The Mind of the South* (New York: Knopf, 1941), p. 50.

25. Frederick Law Olmsted, *The Cotton Kingdom* (New York: Modern Library, 1969), pp. 38, 196.

26. Fyodor Dostoevsky, *The Diary of a Writer* (New York: George Braziller, 1954), pp. 642–43; Harold Cruse, *The Crisis of the Negro Intellectual: From Its Origins to the Present* (New York: William Morrow, 1967), pp. 476–77.

27. Dollard, *Caste and Class*, pp. 128–29; Evans, *Provincials*, pp. 29, 304, 309; Thomas D. Clark, "The Post-Civil War Economy in the South," in Dinnerstein and Palsson, *Jews in the South*, p. 166.

28. Lillian Hellman, rev. of *Provincials*, by Eli N. Evans, *New York Times Book Review* (Nov. 11, 1973), p. 5.

29. Arnold Shankman, "Friend or Foe?: Southern Blacks View the Jew, 1880–1935," in *Turn to the South*, pp. 105–33; "Playboy Interview: Muhammed Ali," *Playboy*, 22 (November 1975), 71; Elliot Liebow, *Tally's Corner: A Study of Negro Streetcorner Men* (Boston: Little, Brown, 1967), p. 252.

30. Benjamin R. Epstein and Arnold Forster, "*Some of My Best Friends* . . ." (New York: Farrar, Straus and Cudahy, 1962), p. 172.

31. Schappes, *Documentary History*, pp. 515–17.

32. Cohens v. Virginia, 6 Wheaton 264; Willard R. Luce, "Cohens v. Virginia (1821): The Supreme Court and State Rights," Diss., University of Virginia 1978.

33. Stanley Marcus, *Minding the Store* (Boston: Little, Brown, 1974), p. 186.

34. Leon Harris, *Merchant Princes: An Intimate History of the Jewish Families Who Built Great Department Stores* (New York: Harper and Row, 1979), pp. 132, 153.

14. The Prism of Literature

1. "James Dickey," in George Plimpton, ed., *Writers at Work*, 5th Series (New York: Penguin, 1981), pp. 199, 201, 209, 211–12, 219, 228.

2. "Joseph Heller," in Plimpton, *Writers at Work*, pp. 231, 234–35, 237; Heller, *Catch-22*, p. 312.

3. Mailer, *Armies of the Night*, p. 191.

4. Walker Percy, *The Moviegoer* (New York: Noonday, 1967), pp. 88–89.

5. William Faulkner, *Intruder in the Dust* (New York: Modern Library [College Edition], 1948), pp. 194–95.

6. Stephen S. Wise to A. B. Horwitz, January 19, 1939, in *Stephen S. Wise: Servant of the People*, ed. Carl Hermann Voss (Philadelphia: Jewish Publication Society, 1970), pp. 231–32.

7. Daniel J. Boorstin, *The Americans: The National Experience* (New York: Vintage, 1965), pp. 206–12.

8. Louis D. Rubin, Jr., *The Curious Death of the Novel: Essays in American Literature* (Baton Rouge: Louisiana State University Press, 1967),

p. 131; Willie Morris, *North Toward Home* (Boston: Houghton Mifflin, 1967), pp. 324–27; Robert Sherrill, *The Saturday Night Special* (New York: Charterhouse, 1973), p. 324; Norman Podhoretz, *Breaking Ranks: A Political Memoir* (New York: Harper & Row, 1979), p. 147.

9. Howe, *World of Our Fathers*, p. 562.

10. Lionel Trilling, *Sincerity and Authenticity* (Cambridge: Harvard University Press, 1972), p. 85; Phillip Knightley, *The First Casualty* (New York: Harcourt Brace Jovanovich, 1975), p. 320.

11. Glasgow quoted in Alfred Kazin, *On Native Grounds* (Garden City, N.Y.: Doubleday Anchor, 1956). p. 194; Schlesinger, *A Thousand Days*, p. 733; Henry Adams, *The Education of Henry Adams* (Boston: Houghton Mifflin, 1961), pp. 57–58.

12. Floyd C. Watkins, "The Hound Under the Wagon: Faulkner and the Southern Literati," in *Faulkner and the Southern Renaissance*, eds. Doreen Fowler and Ann J. Abadie (Jackson: University Press of Mississippi, 1982), p. 113.

13. Boris Pasternak, *Dr. Zhivago* (New York: Pantheon, 1958), p. 300; A. Alvarez, *Under Pressure: The Writer in Society* (Baltimore: Penguin, 1965), p. 173.

14. Rubin, *Curious Death*, pp. v, 268–69, 270, 275, 276–77, 279; Irving Howe, ed., *Jewish-American Stories* (New York: Mentor, 1977), pp. 4–6.

15. Delmore Schwartz to Dwight Macdonald, July 25, 1943, in Box 45, Folder 1116, Dwight Macdonald Papers, Yale University.

16. Morris, *North Toward Home*, pp. 384–85, 387.

17. Charles Y. Glock and Rodney Stark, *Christian Beliefs and Anti-Semitism* (New York: Harper and Row, 1966), p. 23; Evans, *Provincials*, pp. 124–39.

18. Carson McCullers, *The Ballad of the Sad Cafe* (Boston: Houghton Mifflin, 1951), pp. 8, 65; Virginia Spencer Carr, *The Lonely Hunter: A Biography of Carson McCullers* (Garden City, N.Y.: Doubleday, 1975), pp. 236–38.

19. Richard Wright, *Black Boy: A Record of Childhood and Youth* (New York: Harper & Row, 1966), pp. 70–71.

20. Booker T. Washington, *Up from Slavery* (New York: Bantam, 1963), pp. 23–24; F. Holton, "John Hope Franklin, Scholar," *University of Chicago Magazine*, 73 (September 1980), 14.

21. F. Scott Fitzgerald, *The Last Tycoon* (New York: Scribner's, 1970), p. 13.

22. Katherine Anne Porter, "A Country and Some People I Love," *Harper's*, 231 (September 1965), 68.

23. "The Editor Interviews William Styron," *Modern Occasions*, 1 (Fall 1971), 501–2, 510.

24. Philip Roth, *The Professor of Desire* (New York: Bantam, 1978), pp. 129–30.

25. Howe, *Jewish-American Literature*, pp. 14–15, and *World of Our Fathers*, pp. 588–90.

26. Howe, *Jewish-American Literature*, p. 3; Isaac Rosenfeld, *An Age of Enormity: Life and Writing in the Forties and Fifties* (Cleveland: World, 1962), p. 272.

27. Simon Rawidowicz, "Israel: The Ever-Dying People," in *Studies in Jewish Thought* (Philadelphia: Jewish Publication Society of America, 1974), p. 211.

28. Louis Harap, *The Image of the Jew in American Literature: From Early Republic to Mass Immigration* (Philadelphia: Jewish Publication Society, 1974), p. 261; Joseph Blau and Salo W. Baron, eds., *Jews of the United States, 1790–1840: A Documentary History* (New York: Columbia University Press, 1963), II, 417.

29. Ezra Goodman, *The Fifty-Year Decline and Fall of Hollywood* (New York: Simon & Schuster, 1961), pp. 340–43; Lewis S. Feuer, "Spinoza's Thought and Modern Perplexities: Its American Career," in *Spinoza: A Tercentenary Perspective*, ed. Barry S. Kogan (Cincinnati: Hebrew Union College, 1979), p. 58; Richler, *Shovelling Trouble*, p. 6.

30. Hellman, rev. *Provincials*, p. 5.

31. "Lillian Hellman," in *Writers at Work*, ed. George Plimpton, 3rd Series (New York: Viking, 1967), p. 121; Hellman, *Pentimento*, pp. 171–72, 180; Katherine Lederer, *Lillian Hellman* (Boston: Twayne, 1979), p. 39.

32. Lillian Hellman, *An Unfinished Woman: A Memoir* (New York: Bantam, 1970), pp. 2–3, 6, 7, 132–34.

33. Eric F. Bentley, ed., *Thirty Years of Treason: Excerpts from Hearings before the House Committee on Un-American Activities, 1938–1968* (New York: Viking, 1971), pp. 533, 537.

34. Lillian Hellman, *Scoundrel Time* (New York: Bantam, 1977), pp. 38–39.

35. Hellman, *Scoundrel Time*, pp. 39, 43.

36. Harap, *Image of the Jew*, p. 192.

37. Faulkner, "The Bear," p. 279; Alfred J. Kutzik, "Faulkner and the Jews," in *YIVO Annual of Jewish Social Science*, 13 (New York: YIVO Institute for Jewish Research, 1965), 213–26.

38. Elizabeth Nowell, *Thomas Wolfe: A Biography* (Garden City, N.Y.: Doubleday, 1960), p. 86; Louis D. Rubin, Jr., *Thomas Wolfe: The Weather of His Youth* (Baton Rouge: Louisiana State University Press, 1955), pp. 106-7.

39. Leo Gurko, *Thomas Wolfe: Beyond the Romantic Ego* (New York: Thomas Y. Crowell, 1975), pp. 25, 41, 96–97, 118; B. R. McElderry, Jr., *Thomas Wolfe* (New York: Twayne, 1964), p. 151.

40. Richard S. Kennedy, *The Window of Memory: The Literary Career of Thomas Wolfe* (Chapel Hill: University of North Carolina Press, 1962), pp. 88, 329; Nowell, *Thomas Wolfe*, p. 98.

41. Flannery O'Connor, *The Habit of Being: Letters* (New York: Farrar, Straus & Giroux, 1979), p. 539.

42. Harper Lee, *To Kill a Mockingbird* (New York: Popular Library, 1962), pp. 149, 246–50.

43. William Styron, *Sophie's Choice* (New York: Bantam, 1980), pp. 45–46, 196–99.

44. Walker Percy, *The Second Coming* (New York: Farrar, Straus, Giroux, 1980), pp. 7–9, 11–12, 15, 19.

45. Nelson Algren, *A Walk on the Wild Side* (New York: Penguin, 1977), pp. 81,117.

46. Mailer, *Armies of the Night*, pp. 65, 153; Michael Halberstam, *The Wanting of Levine* (New York: Berkley, 1979), pp. 171–77, 220.

47. Philip Roth, *The Great American Novel* (New York: Holt, Rinehart & Winston, 1973), p. 267.

48. Allen, *Nightclub Years*.

49. Jack Temple Kirby, *Media-Made Dixie* (Baton Rouge: Louisiana State University Press, 1978), passim; Eli N. Evans, "Movies Alter the Image of the South," *New York Times* (May 24, 1981), pp. 17, 22; Ted Sennett, *Your Show of Shows* (New York: Collier, 1977), pp. 54–55; Nichols quoted in *This Fabulous Century, 1950–1960* (New York: Time-Life Books, 1970), p. 227; Lehrer, *Too Many Songs* pp. 24–27.

Conclusion

1. George Steiner, *Martin Heidegger* (New York: Penguin, 1980), pp. 34–35.

2. Melvin I. Urofsky, *A Voice that Spoke for Justice: The Life and Times of Stephen S. Wise* (Albany: State University of New York Press, 1982), p. 33.

Glossary

Ahavath yisroel (Heb.).	Love of the Jewish people.
Aliyah (Heb.).	"Going up"; immigration to Israel.
Alrightnik (Yid.)	Someone who boasts of his own success.
Apikorsim (Heb.).	Freethinkers.
Badkhen (Heb.).	Jester at weddings.
B'reshit (Heb.).	"In the beginning" (Gen. 1:1)
B'nai B'rith (Heb.).	Oldest and largest Jewish fraternal and service organization ("sons of the covenant").
Bintel Brief (Yid.).	Advice column of *Jewish Daily Forward* ("bundle of letters").
Chazzan (Heb.).	Cantor.
Chutzpah (Heb.).	Excessive impudence.
Dayenu (Heb.).	"It would have been quite enough for us," sung at Passover.
Dreck (Yid.).	Trash.
Dybbuk (Heb.).	A condemned soul that seizes a living person and acts or speaks through him or her.
Fresser (Yid.).	Big eater.
Goy (Heb.).	"People"; Gentile.
Ganze mishpoche (Yid.).	All the family.
Haggadah (Heb.).	Historical recitals, prayers, and songs uttered on Passover.
Haroset (Heb.).	Condiment eaten with bitter herbs at Seder.
Hasid (Heb.).	Member of religious sect originating in Poland in eighteenth century.
Judengasse (Ger.).	Alley or lane to which Jews were confined.
Judenrein (Ger.).	Free or "cleansed" of Jews.
Kaddish (Heb.).	Mourners' prayer in Aramaic.
Kibbutzim (Heb.).	Collective agricultural settlements in Israel.
Kol Nidre (Heb.).	Opening prayer, in Aramaic, on evening of Day of Atonement ("all the vows").
Malekh-hamoves (Yid.).	The angel of death.

Menschlichkeit (Yid.).	Nobility and decency of character.
Meshugas (Heb.).	Craziness.
Midrash (Heb.).	Interpretation of the biblical text; "study."
Mishpoche (Yid.).	Family.
Moror (Heb.).	Bitter herbs eaten at Seder.
Pilpul (Heb.).	Complicated scholarly interpretation of religious text.
Rebbe (Yid.).	Hasidic leader.
Rebbetzin (Yid.).	Wife of a rabbi.
Sabra (Heb.).	Native-born Israeli.
Seder (Heb.).	Home ritual on first two nights of Passover.
Selbsthass (Ger.).	Self-hatred.
Shabbat (Heb.).	Sabbath.
Shalom (Heb.).	Peace.
Sheyneh layt (Yid.).	The elite ("beautiful people").
Shiksa (Yid.).	Non-Jewish woman.
Shin (Heb.).	Twenty-first letter of the Hebrew alphabet.
Shlemiel (Yid.).	A fool.
Shlepp (Yid.).	To drag or move slowly.
Shmuck (Yid.).	Penis; a dope.
Shmutz (Yid.).	Dirt.
Shpritz (Yid.).	Humorous monologue.
Shtadlan (Heb.).	Figure of influence, wire-puller.
Shtetl (Yid.).	Small town, especially the typical Jewish community of Eastern Europe until the Holocaust.
Shul (Yid.).	Synagogue.
Sukkah (Heb.).	Booth used during Feast of Tabernacles (*Sukkot*).
Tallit (Heb.).	Prayer shawl.
Tikun olam (Heb.).	"Repair of the world"; reform.
Tsuris (Yid.).	Worry; suffering.
Tummeler (Yid.).	Noisemaker or fun maker.
Tzaddik (Heb.).	Righteous person.
Yarmulke (Yid.).	Skullcap.
Yeshiva (Heb.).	Rabbinic academy.
Yichus (Heb.).	Family status or prestige.
Yiddishkeit (Yid.).	Jewish religious life and culture.
Yor'dim (Heb.).	"Those who go down"; emigrants from Israel.
Zemirot (Heb.).	Liturgical hymns chanted during Sabbath meals.
Zeyda (Yid.).	Grandfather.
Zohar (Heb.).	Jewish mystical "Book of Splendor."

Index of Names